The Cambridge
CAE
Course

Mary Spratt & Lynda B. Taylor

Self-Study Student's Book

PUBLISHED BY THE PRESS SYNDICATE OF THE UNIVERSITY OF CAMBRIDGE
The Pitt Building, Trumpington Street, Cambridge CB2 1RP, United Kingdom

CAMBRIDGE UNIVERSITY PRESS
The Edinburgh Building, Cambridge CB2 2RU, United Kingdom
40 West 20th Street, New York, NY 1001–4211, USA.
10 Stamford Road, Oakleigh, Melbourne 3166, Australia.

© Cambridge University Press 1997

First published 1997

Printed in the United Kingdom at the University Press, Cambridge

A catalogue record for this book is available from the British Library

ISBN 0 521 44709 7 Student's Book
ISBN 0 521 44711 9 Teacher's Book
ISBN 0 521 44710 0 Self-study Student's Book
ISBN 0 521 44712 7 Set of 3 cassettes

Contents

Introduction

To the Self-Study Student

The *Cambridge CAE Course* was designed with two kinds of students in mind – firstly, those studying for the CAE exam, and secondly, any advanced students of general English who wish to improve their overall command of the language and their communication skills in English.

The CAE examination is often taken one or two years after the First Certificate in English examination or by students who are new to the Cambridge exam. This course is suitable for either group of students. It is possible to use the Self-Study Student's Book either by working through it or by approaching it selectively according to your needs. You will benefit most from using this course if you are at a good upper intermediate level and beginning to achieve a certain proficiency in the language.

What are the aims of this course?

This course has five main aims:
1   to improve your all-round command and level of English
2   to familiarise you with the content and format of the CAE exam
3   to give you adequate practice in carrying out CAE exam tasks
4   to increase your confidence in your ability to learn and master English
5   to increase your awareness of how to improve your own language and make the most of your own learning style

What are the contents of the Self-Study Student's book?

The Self-Study Student's Book contains seven main parts:
1   Map of the Book
2   Starter Unit
3   Units 1–15
4   Revision Exam Practice (after Units 5, 10 and 15)
5   Exam Tips
6   Unit-by-unit Self-Study Guide (incl. tapescripts, answer keys and notes)
7   CAE answer sheets

All the listening recordings are contained in three accompanying cassettes.

The **Map of the Book** is designed to help you plan a learning syllabus and design a route through the materials in accordance with your particular needs.

The **Starter Unit** is unlike the other units in that its focus is the content of the course as a whole (ways of learning, communication and the CAE exam). It serves as an introduction to each of the strands of the course.

The three blocks of **units (1–5, 6–10, 11–15)** develop particular features of the language, particular communication skills, approaches to different parts of the exam, and an awareness of ways of learning. Each unit is designed around a topic of general interest that could well be covered in the CAE exam.

Revision Exam Practice units occur after each block of five units, and contain additional practice of the exam formats presented in the preceding five units. They are also based on the topics of these units. In this way they provide you with opportunities for revision, checking and consolidation.

There is also a brief supplementary section at the end of the book called **Exam Tips** which summarises the recommendations of the CAE Examination Reports produced by the University of Cambridge Local Examinations Syndicate (UCLES).

The **Unit-by-unit Self-Study Guide** contains tapescripts for the listening activities, answer keys, and additional notes to help you understand exercises and keys as appropriate. These sometimes include background information on exam tasks or other features of the exam, language skills, grammar, cultural information, etc.

How are the units in the Self-Study Student's Book organised?

Each of the units 1–5 contains three sections (Section A, Section B and Section C). Sections A and B contain a similar structure and focus. Each develops a different aspect of the topic of the unit, and contains a focus on reading, listening, speaking and/or writing, grammar and vocabulary. Activities on pronunciation, style, register and functions may also occur in these sections. Section B usually ends with a Vocabulary Summary, which gives you opportunities to review the unit's key vocabulary items.

Section C focuses on the CAE exam. Each Section C looks at one or two different exam tasks by introducing their content and aims, giving practical advice on how to approach the task(s), and providing extensive practice.

The subskills practised in any unit (e.g. reading for a gist, listening for specific information, fluency practice, practice of word stress etc.) will vary. They reappear in more than one unit in order to ensure consolidated attention and practice. The skills and subskills related to reading and listening are focused on by the study of a wealth of authentic texts. The reading texts are taken from a wide range of sources and normally reflect the text types used in the exam. The listening extracts also vary widely in type, and reflect the range covered in the exam. One special feature of the listening extracts is their emphasis on authentic speech. This has been achieved by recording unscripted text where this is appropriate to the text type.

Grammar is treated in two ways: through Grammar reminder and Grammar analysis slots. Grammar reminders cover structures of grammatical items which you have probably learnt many times before yet may continue to make mistakes with. These mistakes happen not so much because you don't know or understand the rules (either consciously or unconsciously), but more because you fail to apply them. Grammar reminders are intended to act as memory jogs to help you overcome these recurring mistakes. The Grammar analysis activities are more exploratory in nature. They require you to think about the use of particular structures or grammatical points and work out rules of use. They focus on grammatical items whose meanings and use you may not yet have encountered or fully explored, and aim to increase your knowledge of the meanings and use of these items as well as to provide practice in them. The grammar selected for coverage in the course is central to the requirements of the CAE exam.

The Ways of learning slot in each unit will be related to a learning theme of the unit, and often to an aspect of the exam task focused on in Section C. The aim of these slots is to increase your awareness of what makes up communication (e.g. interactive language, appropriate language) and the different approaches to learning (e.g. how to read for different purposes, strategies for dealing with listening in an exam context). The course encourages you to reflect on these and to evaluate your own behaviour with a view to modifying it if necessary.

How does the Self-Study Student's Book focus on the exam?

The Self-Study Student's Book focuses constantly on the CAE exam, though not always in an explicit way. Sections A and B aim particularly to develop your general level of language and communication. In doing this, they focus on the exam in an implicit way by aiming to bring your general language proficiency up to the required level. However the book does also focus on the exam in a number of explicit ways:

1. All Sections A and B contain at least one exam practice activity. In the Self-Study Student's Book they are marked by the symbol ✳. The number of such tasks in the sections increases as the book progresses.
2. Section C of each unit focuses on one or two different exam tasks, so that the book as a whole contains a detailed

breakdown of all components of each of the papers.
3. The Revision Exam Practice units consist only of exam tasks. These are presented in the same format as in the exam.

How should the Self-Study Student's Book be used?

This book has not been designed with one fixed approach in mind. It would be possible to use it in several ways. You could, for instance:

- work through the book from beginning to end
- select units in accordance with your own particular needs and interests
- select sections in accordance with your own particular needs and interests

The Map of the Book will help you find your own route through the book. You will find some cross-referencing to other units where this is appropriate. You will also find that there is an increasingly explicit focus on the exam as the book progresses.

The symbols used in the course are as follows:

✳ Exam Practice   📼 Listening

If you intend to follow this course without a teacher or partly on your own, you will find these items useful:

- a piece of card, the same size as this book, to cover the answer keys while you read the self-study notes
- an exercise book to write down your answers to the activities and writing tasks
- a smaller notebook to keep a record of new vocabulary and expressions
- highlighter pens for marking useful vocabulary and expressions
- a cassette recorder for listening to the cassettes and recording your own voice
- a good English–English dictionary
- a good reference grammar book

Is there any other useful CAE-related material I can refer to?

From the University of Cambridge Local Examinations Syndicate (UCLES), you can obtain copies of old exam papers for each exam session, e.g. the version of the CAE administered in winter 1995. You can also obtain copies of the once-yearly CAE Examination Report. This contains an analysis of candidate performance in the exam as a whole, as well as in individual papers. It also contains recommendations for candidate preparation. These publications as well as a publications order form can be obtained from:
UCLES (Marketing Division)
1 Hills Road
Cambridge CB1 2EU
UK
Tel: 01223 553311 Fax: 01223 460278

The authors hope that you enjoy working with this course, that you find it clear, comprehensive and motivating, and that it provides you with the support you need.

Map of the book

Unit and topic	Reading Listening	Writing	Speaking	Grammar
Starter Unit	**A Ways of learning** Reading: advertisements for methods of learning Listening: conversation about learning languages **B What does 'communicating' mean?** Reading: text about communication			
1 Introductions	**A The way we live** Reading: newspaper article about who does what in the house Listening: four excerpts from a radio programme about the way people used to live **B The way we are** Reading: a magazine article about someone's idyllic childhood Listening: various people describe what they were like as children	Letter: describing the way we live	Yourselves	**Reminder:** prepositions **Analysis:** the simple past and present perfect tenses
2 Travelling the world	**A Voyages of discovery** Reading: magazine article about Christopher Columbus Listening: discussion on why people go exploring **B Holiday travel** Reading: four short texts (postcard, holiday brochure, guidebook, novel) about holidays Listening: three short monologues on favourite types of holiday	Magazine article: views on why people go exploring today	Travel/exploration, holidays	**Reminder:** *so* and *such* **Analysis:** the present simple and continuous tenses
3 Living with other people	**A Family matters** Reading: newspaper article about sibling rivalry Listening: conversation about family relationships **B Habits and customs** Reading: four letters to a magazine about 'good manners' Listening: three short monologues describing surprising habits/customs	Personal letter: offering advice on appropriate behaviour at a wedding in *another* culture	Family relationships, different ways of behaving	**Analysis:** stative verbs **Reminder:** *-ing* or infinitive?

Vocabulary	Functions	Phonology	Style and register	Ways of learning	Focus of Section C
Word fields: • means of communication					The CAE Exam: general information
Prefixes and suffixes Word fields: • domestic chores • personality • physical description • childhood	Asking for personal information	Word stress		Approaches to reading	Paper I (Reading): multiple-choice
Word fields: • travel/exploration • holidays Positive adjectives	Discussing opinions Describing a situation	Stress and intonation in phrases	Choosing an appropriate written style	Choosing and using a grammar book	Paper 2 (Writing): Section A
Collocation Word fields: • family relationships • forms of behaviour Grammatical terms	Offering advice	Stress and intonation in phrases	Using appropriate words for a given context	Talking about grammar and vocabulary	Paper 3 (English in Use): Section A multiple-choice cloze and open cloze

Unit and topic	Reading/Listening	Writing	Speaking	Grammar
4 Good and bad health	**A Health on holiday** Reading: magazine article about how to beat holiday stress Listening: questions about illness on holiday **B Health around the world** Reading: article about exercise and health in the UK Listening: discussion about health in Algeria and the UK	Leaflet: instructions for avoiding holiday stress	Illness on holiday, general health issues	**Reminder:** modal verbs expressing obligation and permission **Analysis:** the definite article
5 Body language	**A Animal communication** Reading: extract from textbook about teaching animals to talk Listening: extract from radio discussion on animal communication **B Reading the signals** Reading: extract from book on communication skills Listening: extract from lecture on communication skills	Review of a lecture: on the subject of communication skills	Communication skills	**Reminder:** prepositions of position/direction/time/manner/purpose **Analysis:** substitution
Revision Exam Practice 1				
6 Everyday objects	**A Inventions** Reading: two magazine articles on new telephone inventions Listening: telephone conversation about an inventor **B The art of persuasion** Reading: extract from textbook on advertising Listening: two short conversations about making adverts	Article: discussing new telephone inventions	Important inventions, advertising	**Reminder:** order of adjectives **Analysis:** cleft sentences
7 Jobs	**A What about getting a job?** Reading: book extract about some unusual domestic help Listening: two young people talking about their jobs **B Will I get a job?** Reading: article about success Listening: three people talking about unemployment	Letter of reference: suitability for employment	Jobs and employment	**Reminder:** words for linking sentences/clauses **Reminder:** more words for linking sentences/clauses
8 Crime and punishment	**A Crime and society** Reading: newspaper report on a criminal court case Listening: short radio reports of crimes **B Crime and the writer** Reading: magazine article about writing/televising a crime novel Listening: short story	Review: of a book or film	Crime in society and in fiction	**Reminder:** reporting orders/requests/advice **Analysis:** relative clauses
9 Feelings	**A Recognising feelings** Reading: a report on an experimental study of feelings Listening: a family row **B Expressing your feelings** Reading: magazine article about the differences between men and women Listening: short story	Letter to a newspaper: personal response to a newspaper article	Feelings	**Analysis:** phrasal and prepositional verbs **Reminder:** *as* and *like*

Vocabulary	Functions	Phonology	Style and register	Ways of learning	Focus of Section C
Word fields: • good/poor health • expressions with numbers Collocation	Agreeing and disagreeing	Word and sentence stress		Dealing with listening in exams	Paper 4 (Listening): Sections A and B
Word fields: • communication skills Word-building Collocation	Introducing oneself/ someone else	Stress and intonation patterns		Being aware of body language	Paper 5 (Speaking): Phase A
Compound nouns and adjectives Connotation	Structuring information: ways of marking emphasis	Stress in compound words	Vocabulary of persuasion: using sentence structure for stylistic effect	Deducing word meaning from context	Paper 1 (Reading): multiple matching
Word fields: • jobs and employment Collocation	Ways of comparing	Word pronunciation and stress	Formality and informality in written English	Self-evaluation	Paper 2 (Writing): Section A
Word fields: • crime and punishment Word-building	Reporting orders/ requests/advice		Lexical cohesion Formality/ informality in text		Paper 3 (English in Use): Section B proofreading and text editing skills
Word fields: • feelings Word-building	Speculating	Expressing feelings through intonation	Elements of formality/informality in vocabulary	Different ways of listening	Paper 4 (Listening): Section C

Unit and topic	Reading/Listening	Writing	Speaking	Grammar
10 Assertiveness	**A What is assertiveness?** Reading: a leaflet extract about assertiveness Listening: part of lecture on how to be assertive **B Being assertive** Reading: an extract about the use of language Listening: conversational extracts discussing different degrees of assertiveness	Formal letter: complaint	Talking assertively	**Analysis:** modal verbs for speculation and deduction **Reminder:** adjectives + prepositions
Revision Exam Practice 2				
11 Learning	**A Learning at school** Reading: two articles about unusual kinds of schooling Listening: two teenagers talking about work experience schemes **B What makes us learn?** Reading: article about genes and intelligence Listening: radio documentary about a young genius	Personal letter: describing feelings and experiences	School and other learning experiences	**Reminder:** indirect questions **Analysis:** the present perfect and present perfect continuous tenses
12 Leisure activities	**A Time off** Reading: magazine article about leisure advisers Listening: short monologues about a favourite time of day **B Moving images** Reading: magazine quiz on television viewing habits Listening: discussion about film and video censorship	Formal letter: complaining about violence on TV	Leisure activities, film/TV censorship	**Reminder:** *would* and *used to* **Analysis:** time clauses
13 The world around us	**A It's a weird world** Reading: book extract about miracles Listening: extract from Sherlock Holmes story **B It's a damaged world** Reading: a book extract about environmental problems Listening: extract from a fable about the countryside	Report: account of an unusual incident	Unusual phenomena and environmental issues	**Reminder:** cohesion through substitution **Analysis:** the future
14 Relationships	**A Personal relationships** Reading: magazine article on the state of marriage in Britain Listening: two monologues about influential people **B Working relationships** Reading: extract from a book about relationships at work Listening: radio discussion about team-work	Leaflet: rules for relationships in class	Personal relationships at home and work	**Analysis:** 'empty' *it* **Reminder:** conditional sentences
15 People watching	**A Let's peoplewatch!!** Reading: book extract about *Mona Lisa* Listening: several people talking about peoplewatching **B Reasons for peoplewatching** Reading: a book extract about the role of clothes	1 Personal description 2 Letter: stating opinions	What people look like and clothes	**Analysis:** verbs taking two objects **Reminder:** indirect statement
Revision Exam Practice 3				

Vocabulary	Functions	Phonology	Style and register	Ways of learning	Focus of Section C
Word fields: • behaviour • approval and disapproval Opposites Adjectives and prepositions	Making your point	Word stress Expressing attitude through intonation	Selecting and maintaining the right style and approach for a situation	Situations in which we use different styles of language	Paper 5 (Speaking): Phase B
Word fields: • school • learning Word-building Opposites				Different reasons for reading	Paper 1 (Reading): gapped paragraphs
Word fields: • leisure Contrastive conjunctions Phrasal verbs	Making comparisons Hesitating	Word stress Hesitation techniques	Selecting appropriate layout features	Checking back over written work Understanding the instructions for a task	Paper 2 (Writing): Section B
Word fields: • unusual phenomena • environment • personal reactions	Illustrating your point	Word pronunciation and stress	Style	Remembering vocabulary	Paper 3 (English in Use): Section C gap-filling and notes expansion
Word fields: • personal relationships at home and work Connotation Collocation	Identifying topic, speaker, attitude and opinion in listening	Expressions with numbers		Focusing attention in a listening test task	Paper 4 (Listening): Section D
Word fields: • appearance • personality characteristics Connotation	Making generalisations and exceptions Interacting with other speakers Reporting decisions			Interactional language	Paper 5 (Speaking): Phases C and D

Starter

A

Ways of learning

Starter activities

1 How do you like to learn languages? Look at these extracts from advertisements for methods of learning languages. Tick the methods you would like. Explain and discuss your answers.

> • Superb mini-documentaries on video not only build your command of the language, but also give you a real taste of the country, its people and its culture.

> • *In addition to learning what to say in a situation, you develop a real understanding of **why** you should say it that way – how sentences are structured and how the language works.*

The Unique Physical Learning Video. You watch the action, follow it yourself and repeat the words. Your brain links the word to the action, just as you learned to speak as a child.

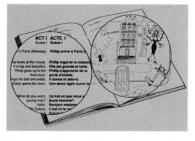

Memory Maps build up vivid mental pictures. When the images are recalled, so are the words. Having the French and English text side by side means that you absorb the words naturally.

The easiest and most natural way to improve or LEARN ENGLISH?

… STAY WITH A FRIENDLY HOST-FAMILY WHERE ENGLISH IS SPOKEN ALL THE TIME.

INDIVIDUAL PAYING-GUEST VISITS FOR STUDENTS OR TEACHERS ARRANGED BY THE EN FAMILLE AGENCY (Established 1945).

We specialise in 'matching' age group, interests and background. Hundreds of families throughout Britain available at all times of the year. Careful attention given to every application by experienced staff.

We also arrange:
• Private formal language tuition • Language courses
• Airport/seaport escort collection service
• Group visits • Sports holidays

Speaking
Many people find speaking their new language the hardest part, but Linguaphone's proven method enables you to start speaking from the very first lesson. You imitate what you hear and immediately after the teacher repeats the sentences so that you can check your progress. What's more, with Linguaphone you'll find you're speaking with the correct accent and pronunciation.

Armchair Theatre. A series of entertaining radio plays. As you get absorbed in the story, you absorb the words and pronunciation without thinking about it.

2 People learn languages in different ways. Here are some descriptions and explanations of different kinds of language learners. Match the descriptions (**1–6**) to the explanations (**A–F**).

1 a risk taker
2 a translator
3 a systems person
4 a reader
5 a child-like unconscious learner
6 a teacher depender

A Someone who likes to study grammar, work with vocabulary lists and generally understand the systems (grammar, vocabulary, pronunciation) of language.
B Someone who needs to read language before they feel they've really grasped it.
C Someone who will try hard to use all the language at their disposal and communicate regardless of how many mistakes they may be making.
D Someone who just absorbs and picks up language without really being aware of it or trying to analyse it.
E Someone who feels they need to translate everything into their own language before they fully understand what something means or how it works.
F Someone who feels they need the approval, guidance and support of someone knowledgeable before or while using the language.

Which of these best describes you?

3 You will hear two people talking about learning languages. Listen to find out (a) what kind of lessons they are discussing and (b) if they enjoy learning.

4 The table below lists the ways of learning referred to on the cassette. Listen again and fill in the columns with a tick (✓) if the speaker likes the way of learning, a cross (✗) if the speaker doesn't like the way of learning and a question mark (?) if you don't know.

Way of learning	Woman	Man	You
Learning in the country where the language is spoken	✗	✓	
Learning the language before you go to the country		✓	
Making mistakes in public	✓	✗	
Being challenged	✓		
Using a dictionary			
Learning with others in a class			
Doing homework			
Lessons involving real-world activities (e.g. ordering food in a real restaurant)			
Repeating grammar		✓	

Which of the descriptions in activity **2** best describes each speaker?

Now complete the third column about 'you' and discuss your answers with another student.

Your thoughts

- **Is it better to be one kind of learner than another?**
- **Are there any advantages or disadvantages in being a particular kind of learner?**
- **Do you think people can change from being one kind of learner to another?**
- **Do you think your own learning style is effective? Why / why not?**

Ways of learning and this book

In each unit of this book, there is a section on different ways of learning. The aim of these sections is to help you become more aware of and build on your own language learning style and strategies. Look at the Map of the book on pages 6–11 to see which of these sections interest(s) you most. Why? Discuss your answers with a partner.

Speaking fluently and confidently.

Sending and receiving the right messages at the right time.

Using your hands, body, voice and face to send messages.

Being able to write, read, speak and listen perfectly.

Being able to chatter in any situation.

B

What does 'communicating' mean?

1 These seven people were asked the question 'What does 'communicating' mean?' Look at their answers. Tick the ones you agree with. Discuss your answers with a partner.

2 Look at the photos below. In what different ways are the people communicating?

Understanding and being understood.

Getting your message across.

1

2

3

4

5

3 Read this text through quickly to complete this sentence:

According to the author, communication involves three main things:
(1) ...., (2) interpretation and (3) ....

Communication

Communicating – or getting our message across – is the concern of us all in our daily lives in whatever language we happen to use. Learning to be better communicators is important to all of us in both our private and public lives. Better communication means better understanding of ourselves and others; less isolation from those around us and more productive, happy lives.

We begin at birth by interacting with those
10 around us to keep warm, dry and fed. We learn very soon that the success of a particular communication strategy depends on the willingness of others to understand and on the interpretation they give to our meaning. Whereas a baby's cry will be enough to bring a mother running with a clean nappy and warm milk in one instance, it may produce no response at all in another. We learn then that meaning is never one-sided. Rather, it is *negotiated*, between the
20 persons involved.

As we grow up our needs grow increasingly complex, and along with them, our communication efforts. Different words, we discover, are appropriate in different settings. The expressions we hear in the playground or through the bedroom door may or may not be suitable at the supper table. We may decide to use them anyway to attract attention. Along with words, we learn to use intonation, gestures, facial expression, and many
30 other features of communication to convey our meaning to persons around us. Most of our communication strategies develop unconsciously, through imitation of persons we admire and would like to resemble to some extent - and the success we experience in our interactions.

Formal training in the classroom affords us an opportunity to gain systematic practice in an even greater range of communicative activities. Group discussions, moderated by the teacher, give young
40 learners important practice in taking turns, getting the attention of the group, stating one's views and perhaps disagreeing with others in a setting other than the informal family or playground situations with which they are familiar. Classrooms also provide practice in written communications of many kinds. Birthday cards are an early writing task for many children. Reports, essays, poems, business letters, and job application forms are routinely included in many
50 school curricula and provide older learners with practical writing experience.

A concern for communication extends beyond school years and into adult life. Assertiveness training, the development of strategies for conquering stage fright, and an awareness of *body language* - the subtle messages conveyed by posture, hand movement, eyes, smile - are among the many avenues to improved communication as adults. The widespread popularity of guides to
60 improving communication within couples and between parents and children illustrates our ever present concern with learning to communicate more effectively in our most intimate relationships, to understand and be understood by those closest to us.

Training of an even more specialized nature is available to those whose professional responsibilities or aspirations require it. Advice on how to dress and appear 'businesslike',
70 including a recommendation for the deliberate use of technical jargon to establish authority, is available to professional women who want to be taken seriously in what has historically been considered a man's world. Specialized courses in interviewing techniques are useful for employers and others who interview people frequently in their professional lives.

One of the important lessons to be learnt here, as in other communicative contexts, is
80 that what matters is not the intent but the interpretation of the communicative act. Conveyance of meaning in unfamiliar contexts requires practice in the use of the appropriate *register* or *style* of speech. If a woman wants to sound like a business executive, she has to talk the way business executives talk while they are on the job. The same register would of course be inappropriate when talking of personal matters with a spouse or intimate friend. Similarly,
90 executives who must cope with an investigative reporter may be helped to develop an appropriate style. They need to learn how to convey a sense of calm and self-assurance. Effective communication in this particular context may require the use of language to avoid a direct answer or to hide one's intent while appearing to be open and forthright. In both instances an understanding of what is *really* happening, as opposed to what one would *like* to see happening is the first step towards
100 improved communication.

Communication, then, is a continuous process of *expression, interpretation* and *negotiation*.

(Communicative Competence: Theory and Classroom Practice)

4 Look back at the photos in activity **2**. Can you relate each of these photos to different parts of the text?

According to the author which of these elements of communication are associated with the types of communication in the photos?

writing
understanding
   facial expression
learning to get
   attention
awareness of body
   language

appropriate use
   of language
negotiation
dress
learning
intonation
technical jargon

learning to take
   turns in talking
assertiveness
   training
stating views

Your thoughts

- Are the elements of communication that the author mentions all equally important?
- Are you equally good at all these elements of communication in English?
- 'Communication involves expression, interpretation and negotiation.' Do you agree?

5 Communicating in the classroom. Here is a progress report written by a teacher for an EFL student. How would you rate the student's performance in each area? Write 1, 2 or 3 for each area. (1 = very good, 3 = weak)

How would you rate your own English in each of these areas? Give yourself scores of 1, 2 or 3. What comments would you put for these areas in a progress report about you? Discuss your answers with a partner then write a report about yourself.

Progress Report

Student: Cristina Sauz   Class: L4

Language Area	Comments
Grammar	Your grammar is really excellent. Congratulations!
Vocabulary	Your use of everyday words is very accurate. Try to extend your knowledge of more formal and technical words.
Pronunciation	Your pronunciation is very clear and couldn't be misunderstood. Listen hard though to English intonation — it's not the same as in your language.
Writing	The language in your written work is accurate and wide-ranging. Sometimes your work could benefit from being better planned and organised.
Appropriate use of language	In speaking you choose your language well. For your written work you need to extend your knowledge and use of formal language.
Negotiation in speaking	This really is your forte! You seem to know exactly how and just when to — hold your own — take the floor — stop talking — invite others to participate — interrupt etc. etc. Well done!
	Teacher: Lucy Hayworth Date: June 10th 1996 Signature: *Lucy Hayworth*

Elements of communication and this book

This book aims to give opportunities to learn about and practise various elements of communication. Look at the Map of the book on pages **6–11** for examples of these. Which of these elements are you most interested in? Discuss your interests with a partner.

C

The CAE Exam

What is CAE?

1 This book aims both to help you improve your general English and pass the CAE exam. You will hear two teachers talking about the CAE exam. Listen and answer these questions.

1 What does CAE stand for?
2 What level is it?
3 Who is it aimed at?
4 What kind of language does it test?
5 How many papers is it made up of?
6 Can you give any details about each paper?

Compare your answers with a partner's.

2 Now listen again and note down your responses to the following questions:

- What might you find difficult in the exam?
- What might you find enjoyable in the exam?
- What might you dislike about the exam?
- What might you find easy in the exam?

With a partner compare and discuss your answers.

Exam practice

Write a letter to a friend of yours (real or imaginary) explaining:

- that you've just started a new English course
- about the CAE exam and why you're going to take it
- what you are good and not so good at in English
- how you intend to organise your studying this year so as to improve different areas of your English and help yourself pass the CAE exam.

Exchange your letter with a partner's, then read and discuss each other's letters.

Exam study and this book

Look at the Map of the book on pages **6–11**. The Section C column tells you which part of the book focuses on which part of the exam. Which aspects of the exam do *you* need to concentrate on most?

One

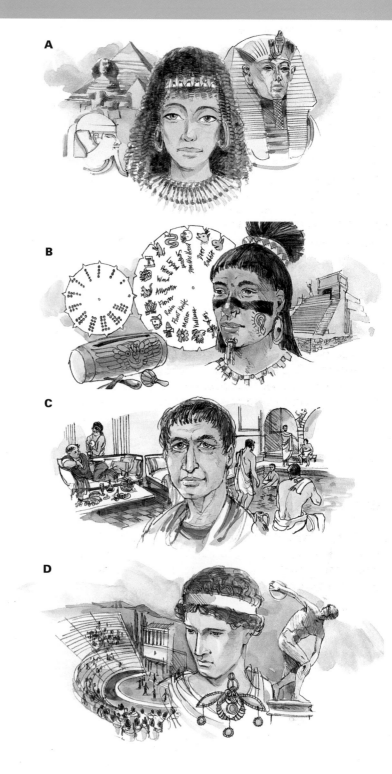

A

The way we live

Starter activities

1 Look at the four pictures. They represent people from four different periods of history surrounded by things that were important in their lives. Can you identify what each of these pictures shows?

Discuss your answers with a partner.

2 From these four people, tick the one whom you would have preferred to be. Why? Discuss your answers with a partner.

3 Briefly note down what you know about each of these people's way of life. Compare your answers.

Listening

1 You will hear four extracts from a series of radio programmes about the way people used to live in different periods of history. Match each extract to one of the cultures opposite.

2 Listen again and take notes on the four lifestyles described in the extracts.

3 What is your opinion of the different aspects of these lifestyles? Write **G** for good or **B** for bad against each aspect you noted down. Compare and discuss your answers with a partner.

Your thoughts

- **How is our way of life different to those described?**
- **Are our values different / better / the same / worse?**

Reading

1 You are going to read an article comparing how much European men from various European countries help in the house. Before you read it, say who in your household is or would be willing to do the following?

Write **M** (man), **W** (woman), **M/W** (either) or **N** (neither) against each of the following items.

shop	**wash-up**
drive the children around	**iron**
cook	**dress the children**
clean	**tidy up**

Compare your answers.

2 Read the article through quickly to decide which country you most admire and why.

Women beware, British man about the house

by David Utting

Percentage of men who will NOT take responsibility for chores

Country	They say	Partners say
Belgium	60.8	61.0
Denmark	51.1	47.5
Former W. Ger.	60.7	71.1
Former E. Ger.	42.7	62.7
Greece	47.2	49.8
Spain	76.6	79.7
France	58.4	60.7
Ireland	84.0	31.9
Italy	55.6	60.2
L'bourg	58.9	64.9
N'lands	45.7	46.2
Portugal	69.3	71.9
UK	74.2	70.6
EU average	61.6	65.4

Europe's legion of working women who long for a caring 'new man' to share their duvet and the household chores would be ill-advised to start searching in the United Kingdom.

Researchers dispatched by Brussels to far corners of the European Union have found that few husbands are quite so disinclined to lift a finger round the house as the British. Even the stereotyped chauvinists of France and Italy emerge as better disposed to visit the supermarket or escort children to playschool.

Challenged with a list of six common domestic tasks, three out of four fathers in Britain claimed not to be in charge of any of them – a proportion larger than for the European Community as a whole. They left it to women to take the lead in shopping, washing-up, cooking, cleaning, transporting children or helping them to dress.

Ex-Communist Eastern Germany, the Netherlands and Greece emerge as the only places where a majority of fathers, interviewed about the years before their children went to school, agreed they were responsible for at least one of the items. In the case of Greek men it emerged that their burst of domesticity was overwhelmingly confined to visiting shops.

Spanish husbands, meanwhile, topped the league for all-round household hopelessness, with almost 8 out of 10 admitting to no responsibilities at all – an assessment which was more than confirmed by the views of Spanish wives and partners who took part in the survey. The strangest results were from Ireland, where 84 per cent of men stoutly maintain that they take no responsibility whatsoever for shopping, cleaning, cooking, washing-up, and dressing the children or driving them to school.

Yet the Irishmen's view of themselves as devil-may-care, unliberated, macho sort of fellows appears to be sheer fantasy. According to their wives and partners, nearly 70 per cent of their menfolk take responsibility for at least one household task, putting them among the most domesticated men in Europe.

The 'Family and Work' survey, one of a series commissioned by the European Commission's Employment and Social Affairs Directorate, was based on almost 17,000 interviews in the 12 member states. The results are due for publication in Britain this summer.

Looking at the domestic tasks where European men – albeit the minority – are prepared to take a lead, the survey identifies a North-South divide. Men in Portugal and the Mediterranean countries appear more concerned with the "public" duties of shopping or dressing and driving their children; further north it is the "private" chores such as dish-washing, cooking and cleaning which are treated with above-average enthusiasm.

Those British husbands who do anything are at their best when clutching a dishcloth or tea towel at the kitchen sink, although their willingness to act as family chef is greater even than Frenchmen's.

The survey authors, Marianne Kempeneers of Montreal University and Eva Lelièvre of the London School of Economics, found that British women were unusual in Europe because of the extensive availability of part-time jobs. Their working lives were marked by interruptions to care for children and they were more prone to feel that promotion had been sacrificed as a consequence.

Former West German, Dutch and Irish women were more likely to mark motherhood with a prolonged or permanent exit from the labour force. But women living in Denmark and southern Europe found less difficulty reconciling work with their family responsibilities – possibly because childcare was easier to obtain.

3   Read the article again, this time in detail, to decide whether the following statements are accurate. Mark them **T** (true), **F** (false) or **?** (don't know).

1   75% of British men take no responsibility for the six common domestic tasks.
2   Greek, former East German and Dutch men take on about the same amount of responsibilities as one another.
3   Spanish women think their men are hopeless round the house.
4   Irish men spend little time helping at home.
5   Each country presents very distinctive trends.
6   Frenchmen cook more than British men.
7   British women tend to sacrifice their careers once they have children.
8   Southern European women give up work once they have children.

4   Look at the two lists of words below. List A contains words and phrases taken from the text. In list B, there are synonyms for each of these words. Look at how the words in A are used in the text and then match them to an appropriate synonym in B, for example *chores = boring domestic work*. (N.B. List B contains more words than you need.)

A	B
chores	limited
disinclined	harmonise
lift a finger	come first
emerge	be revealed
take the lead	general
overwhelmingly	join
confined	strongly
top the league	unwilling
all-round	fat
stoutly	help/work
maintain	take on responsibility
fellows	above all
prone	lazy
	men
	boring domestic work
	willing
	strongly affirm
	inclined

Your thoughts

*   **Which country seems most similar to your own?**
*   **In which country is it best to be a woman? a man? a mother? a father?**

Writing

Your college is going to bury a trunk containing objects and letters typical of our times. If other beings find and open the trunk some time in the future it might give them an idea of how we lived our lives. Write a letter, of approximately 250 words, to future beings describing the organisation of domestic tasks in your household and your general lifestyle.

Grammar reminder: prepositions

As you know, prepositions have many uses in English and it is not always easy to decide or remember what prepositions to use, when and where. The use of many prepositions depends on the language context in which they occur, e.g. *The conclusions are based **on** a long study and her work is based **in** São Paolo.*

In this book we will look at prepositions in four other grammar sections. However, from now on try to be aware of when prepositions are used, which prepositions are used and in what circumstances. You could make a note of these as you meet them.

1   Look at the text 'Women beware, British man about the house' on page 20. The prepositions in the text are used in various ways. Go through the text again and find two examples of each of the following:

Prepositions used in/as:

*   fixed expressions
*   adjective + preposition combinations
*   verb + preposition combinations
*   noun + preposition combinations
*   passive constructions
*   prepositions of place

Compare your answers.

2   How many of these prepositions must always be used with the words they are combined with in the text? Why?

3   What do you think is the best way of learning the use of prepositions? Discuss your answers.

Vocabulary

Work with a partner. Make as many words as you can by adding prefixes (e.g. un/in/dis) or suffixes (e.g. -ible, -able, -ment, -ism, -ly) to the words below, e.g. care: careful, carefully, careless, carelessly. You have one minute only. The winner is the person with the most correct words.

responsible	incline	liberate
likely	concern	affect
overwhelm	willing	

Now play the game again with this set of words:

domestic	usual	enthusiasm
common	public	available
hope	agree	

1

2

B

The way we are

Starter activities

1 Look at these five photos of children. Describe them and what you think they are doing?

2 How have you changed in appearance since you were a child? Write down three specific points. Then discuss your answers.

Listening

1 Listen to the people in the photos talking about themselves. Decide which speaker is talking about which photo(s).

2 Listen again and note down all the phrases or adjectives the speakers use to describe their appearance or their character. Check your answers by listening again.

3 Go through the list of phrases and adjectives and tick those which could apply / have applied to you. Explain your answers to a partner.

3

4

5

Reading

In the magazine article below, a well-known Irish author, Maeve Binchy, recalls her 'idyllic childhood'.

1 What is your idea of an 'idyllic childhood'? List some ideas or words, then compare them with other students.

2 Read the article quickly to see if you think Maeve Binchy's childhood was idyllic.

3 Read the article in more detail this time and make notes on why Maeve Binchy thought her childhood was idyllic.

4 Read the article a final time to find information to complete this description.

Name: *Maeve Binchy*
Occupation:
Country of origin:
Father's occupation:
Mother's occupation:
Religion:
Type of school attended:
Physical description:
Personality (as a child):

When I was a child

Writer Maeve Binchy recalls her idyllic childhood in Ireland

'**M**y parents brought me up to think I was the centre of the universe. They showered me with love and attention and gave me terrific self-confidence. I was the eldest of four. There were three girls and then finally the longed-for boy arrived. We were all indulged, all special. I don't think any one of us was the favourite.

10 My father was a barrister and my mother had been a nurse before she married. She was a big, jolly woman, as big as I am, with a great smile that went right round her face. We never had a lot of money but we had great comfort and lived in a big, shabby old house with nearly an acre of garden looking out over the sea in Dalkey, near Dublin. We each had our own bedroom and we had a maid, Agnes, who is still a friend.

20 We all went to school on the train from Dalkey to Killiney to the Convent of the Holy Child. It was just three miles down the line and now I see it as the most beautiful place, but we never noticed the view when we were children.

I was a terrible goody-goody. At school I was the girl who was always approached if somebody had to write a thank-you letter to a visiting speaker or make the speech of 30 thanks. I was an extrovert. I don't remember any time until I was 16 or 17 that I ever felt self-conscious. I thought I was marvellous because my parents made me feel that way. When I was little they would take me out of bed and bring me down to entertain their friends – to whom I now apologise.

I was a very devout little girl. I was going to be a saint, not just a nun. I intended to be the first Saint Maeve. At home we kept hens 40 and when they died of old age we buried them and held a Requiem Mass. I was the priest, of course, and prayed for their souls and put flowers on their graves. We had an honorary grave for the tortoise once because we thought he was dead, though we couldn't find the body. He turned up again – he had only gone away for the winter.

I was a placid child, very content. I never rebelled. It sounds terribly smug, but all I 50 wanted in life came to me. There is a lot of me in the character, Benny, in my book, *Circle of Friends* (Coronet, £4.99). I remember lovely birthday parties as a girl – jellies and cakes with hundreds-and-thousands on them and people singing *Happy Birthday*, and giving me little bars of soap all wrapped up. And like Benny, despite my size, I longed to be dressed in silly frocks in crushed velvet. I was so innocent. My 60 mother told me the facts of life when I was about 12 and I didn't believe her. I told my father I thought Mother must be having delusions!

> ' I was going to be a saint, not just a nun '

I was a big, bold, strapping schoolgirl but, in fact, I had nothing to be self-confident about. I wasn't very academic; I was quick-minded, but I was very lazy. My reports weren't good, which distressed my parents. In Ireland in those days you had to pay for 70 education after the age of 14 and I remember my father saying that a good education was all he could afford to give me. Homework was considered very important and every evening the breakfast room would be set up with dictionaries and pens and paper and a big fire going. Daddy would often work with us. I always finished as quickly as possible so I could go off and read my *Girl* or *School Friend* comics.

80 Without any doubt, my favourite teacher at the convent was Sister St Dominic. She was a wonderful woman who made a tremendous impression on me. She saw something in every child and thought we were all great. She managed to put some sense into teaching because she always enjoyed herself so much.

Because of her I became a teacher.

At school I lived a fantasy life. I had a book 90 called the *ABC Shipping Guide* and dreamed of travelling the world. My teachers always said of my essays, 'Try to stick to the facts, Maeve,' because I embroidered and exaggerated so much.

The nuns warned us a lot about lust and sex and I was a bit disappointed during my last two years at school to find there wasn't as much lust and sex going on as we'd been told. By then my friends had boyfriends and I 100 became very self-conscious. Because I was told at home that I was lovely, I thought I was. When I went out to dances and didn't fare so well, I was bitterly disappointed. I then realised that I was big and fat and not so lovely. Nowadays I can't believe how quickly time passes, but when I was a child, the summer holidays seemed to last for ever. They were idyllic, and I put a lot of that into my books. Everything about my childhood 110 has been useful material. '

(Woman's Weekly)

5 Here are some adjectives and nouns used to describe Maeve Binchy. Tick (✓) the adjectives if they describe you as a child. Otherwise write an appropriate related word for yourself above it. (Use a dictionary to help you with this exercise if necessary.) Then with a partner, compare and explain your answers.

devout	content	placid
a goody-goody	bold	innocent
a dreamer	an extrovert	strapping
self-conscious	quick-minded	

6 Where is the stress on each of the words in activity 5? Mark it with a • above the stressed syllable. Check your answers in a dictionary. Here are some examples of how stress is marked in dictionaries.

> **extrovert** /ˈekstrəvɜːrt/, **extroverts**. Someone who is **extrovert** is very active, lively, and sociable; used mainly in British English. The usual American word is **extroverted**. *His footballing skills and extrovert personality won the hearts of the public.* ▶ Also a noun. *He was a showman, an extrovert who revelled in controversy.*
>
> ◆◇◇◇ ADJ-Graded = outgoing ≠ introvert
>
> N-COUNT ≠ introvert

> **extrovert** /ˈekstrəˌvɜːt/ *n. & adj.* –*n.* **1** *Psychol.* a person predominantly concerned with external things or objective considerations. **2** an outgoing or sociable person. –*adj.* typical or characteristic of an extrovert. ☐☐ **extroversion** /-ˈvɜːʃ(ə)n/ *n.* **extroverted** *adj.* [*extro-* = EXTRA- (after *intro-*) + L *vertere* turn]

Now say the words paying particular attention to stress.

Grammar analysis: the simple past and present perfect tenses

1 Complete these two sentences with the name of the correct tense:

The .... tense links the past and the present.

The .... tense describes states and actions that are completely finished.

2 Look at these pairs of sentences about Maeve Binchy. Decide

• which sentences are *grammatically* correct. Can you say why or why not?
• which of the correct sentences are factually true about Maeve?

1 a Maeve has always been plump.
   b Maeve was always plump.

2 a Maeve wanted to be a nun before she left school.
   b Maeve has wanted to be a nun before she left school.

3 a Maeve has lived in Ireland since she was born.
   b Maeve lived in Ireland since she was born.

4 a Maeve's childhood has been very important to her.
   b Maeve's childhood was very important to her.

5 a Maeve has always spent her summer holidays in Ireland.
   b As a child Maeve always spent her summer holidays in Ireland.

6 a Maeve wanted to be a writer from when she was a child.
   b Maeve has wanted to be a writer from when she was a child.

7 a Maeve's parents spoilt her.
   b Maeve's parents have spoilt her.

8 a Maeve's childhood provided her with ideas for her writing.
   b Maeve's childhood has provided her with ideas for her writing.

3 Read and complete the following rules on some of the uses of the past and present perfect tenses in English, then add in an extra example of your own about Maeve Binchy for each use mentioned.

> **The past simple tense is generally used in English:**
> a for repeated or single (1) .... that are accompanied by an explicit past time reference, e.g.
>   *I went to South America last year.*
> b for states or actions without an explicit (2) .... reference but that the speaker regards as totally finished and unconnected to the present, e.g.
>   *I didn't see anyone I knew at the party.*
>
> **The present perfect tense is used in English:**
> a for states or actions that have (3) .... finished or for recent 'hot' news, e.g.
>   *I've (just) finished my homework.*
> b for present states stretching back into the (4) ...., e.g.
>   *I've worked here for ages.*
> c for past states or actions that happened at an unspecified time in the (5) ...., e.g.
>   *I've often dreamt of doing that.*
> d for past states or actions whose result (in the speaker's mind) still has an (6) .... on the present, e.g.
>   *He's been spoilt by his parents* (therefore he's a difficult child now).
>   *I've had a bath* (therefore I'm clean now).

4 Write a sentence about yourself for each use of the two tenses mentioned above. Compare your sentences with a partner's.

Speaking: asking for personal information

Although you have been in the same class as your classmates for some time now, you may not in fact know much about them. Here is your opportunity!

1 Complete this description box with details about yourself.

Name:
Occupation:
Father's occupation: *(passport photo)*
Mother's occupation:
Religion:
Physical description:
Country of origin:
Type of school
attended:
Personality:

2 In pairs work out what questions you could ask someone to obtain the information in the box above.

3 Find out more about people in your group using the kind of information you gave in activity **1** and the questions you worked out in activity **2**. Then tell other students about one another.

Vocabulary summary

Go through Sections A and B of this unit to find at least four words to put in each of the categories on the branches of this tree. Compare your answers first in pairs and then in groups.

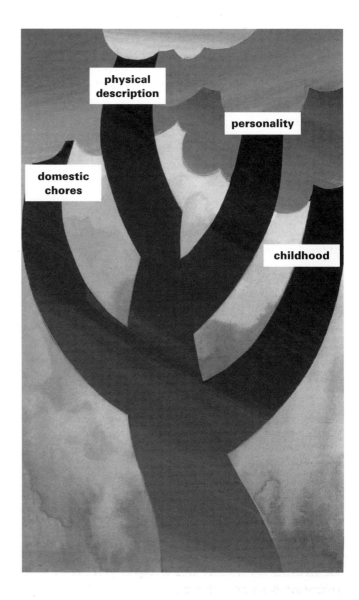

physical description

personality

domestic chores

childhood

C

Paper 1 (Reading): Multiple-choice

Introduction

CAE Paper 1 contains four texts and three types of task. In this unit we focus on one of these tasks: multiple-choice questions. Advice on the other task types can be found in Units 6 and 11.

One of the texts in Paper 1 is always accompanied by multiple-choice questions. These are questions to which several answers are proposed and only one of the answers is correct.

This text is accompanied by multiple-choice questions. Read the text and then answer the questions. As you answer, think about how you decide which is the right answer.

WHEN Christopher Columbus set foot on the shores of the New World on 12 October 1492, the Lacandones, descendants of the Mayans, Mexico's most romanticised Indians, lived in harmony around the great cities and temples their ancestors had built in south-eastern Mexico. Not long afterwards, the forces of colonisation and exploitation forced them to flee into the depths of what is now the largest surviving rain forest in North America.

For centuries they were secure in their jungle isolation. Until the late 1940s – apart from a handful of mahogany loggers, crocodile hunters and gum gatherers – they and the more than 13,000 sq km (5,020 sq miles) of lowland tropical forest, the Selva Lacandona, were largely left alone.

But today, on the eve of the 500th anniversary of Spain's arrival in the Americas, the Lacandones are on the verge of cultural extinction. And just as their way of life has been overwhelmed, so has their environment. Only 30 per cent of the Selva Lacandona remains, and much of that is damaged. The rest has been cleared by thousands of immigrant slash-and-burn farmers, lumber companies, commercial cattle ranchers and the state-owned oil company, whose budget for the area increases yearly.

Even the Montes Azules Biosphere Reserve, a 1,278 sq km (493 sq mile) area set aside by a Mexican presidential decree in 1977, has seen large swathes of its pristine forest cut down. The final round of destruction of the jungle – a massive dam project that would have flooded more than 500 square miles of forest and dozens of archaeological sites – was postponed last April by the president, Carlos Salinas de Gortari. But ecologists know that there is nothing to stop the next president from reviving the project once more.

Throughout the degradation of North America's last great tropical forest, which extends into Guatemala, the Lacandones have been used by the government as a symbol of Mexico's surviving indigenous communities. In the 1970s, in a burst of generosity, President Luis Echeverria gave them thousands of acres, only to snatch back much of the land after advisers convinced him of its value. What the government didn't simply take back, it retrieved by sending agents into the jungle with gifts and ready cash in exchange for thumb-prints on land contracts the Lacandones couldn't understand.

These efforts to incorporate the jungle into the Mexican economy have all but destroyed the traditional values and religion of the Lacandones. Most still dress in the traditional white cotton *shikur*, and keep their long black hair unshorn, but it's no longer clear how many do this out of choice. Western haircuts and T-shirts are not uncommon.

At the archaeological site of Palenque, the dozen or so Lacandones who surround the entrance, selling bows and arrows to tourists, duck into the forest at the end of the day to change into their jeans and trainers. The accumulated knowledge of the past few centuries now resides in the memories of only a few elders, and ceremonies that were once a regular part of life are performed only every few years, often for visiting anthropologists.

The cosmogony of their ancestors and the ceremonial centres built during the Mayan era still hold a sacred importance. But the complex Mayan calendar has been reduced to a wet and a dry season, and apart from a few of the more stalwart northern Lacandones of Naja settlement, most have been converted by fundamentalist Christian missionaries in recent years. Polygamy, once common, is now considered taboo.

Even at the best of times, the Lacandones were never very numerous. Most estimates put their number at around 5,000 before Columbus set sail for the New World: today there are maybe 300 left, a number considered so insignificant that some people believe the point of genetic no-return has been reached. What is certain is that if the current rate of destruction continues, we will witness not only the extinction of the Lacandon Maya, but that of the largest rain forest in the Americas north of the Amazon.

Choose the answer **A**, **B**, **C** or **D** which best answers the question or completes the sentence.

1 Where do the Lacandones live?

  A In South Eastern Mexico
  B In cities
  C In tropical rain forests
  D On mountains

2 The greatest threat to the survival of the Lacandones has been

  A Christopher Columbus.
  B the forces of colonisation.
  C crocodile hunters.
  D destruction of the rain forest.

3 What hasn't damaged the rain forest?

  A Clearance
  B Dams
  C The government
  D Immigrants

4 Lacandon traditions

  A live on in the way the Lacondones dress.
  B are only maintained for the sake of anthropologists.
  C have died with the advent of Christianity.
  D have barely survived.

5 The future of the Lacandones

  A is in severe doubt.
  B depends on that of the rain forest.
  C will definitely be extinction.
  D lies in integration.

Compare and check your answers.

How to approach multiple-choice questions

1   Read the following statements which suggest possible ways of answering multiple-choice reading questions. Add in any further suggestions of your own at (10), then write an **A** against the statements if you agree with them, a **D** if you disagree or **?** if you don't know.

1   One of the four proposed multiple-choice answers is always very obviously wrong.

2   You don't always need to read the passage to answer multiple-choice questions.

3   Finding the correct answer to the multiple-choice question often depends on a very detailed and careful reading of the whole text.

4   It's best to read the multiple-choice questions first, before you read the text.

5   The four proposed answers to a multiple-choice question are always based on the same part of the text.

6   It's best to eliminate the wrong answers first.

7   It's a good idea to underline the part of the text that you think contains the right answer.

8   Reading the text quickly is the best way to find the answers to multiple-choice questions.

9   Multiple-choice questions require you always to read the text in the same way.

10   Other …

Discuss your answers.

2   In pairs write a leaflet entitled **Some advice on answering multiple-choice questions.** Then compare your leaflets and write up the best advice on a poster to display on the classroom wall.

Exam practice

Read this magazine article. The text is followed by a number of questions or unfinished statements about the text. You must choose the answer **A**, **B**, **C** or **D** which you think fits best. Give one answer only to each question.

After so many years of war?

The fighting season has given way to the snows and sub-zero temperatures of winter, and now there is less gun and rocket-fire in the mountains which surround the capital. But at the best hotel in town the wedding season is in full swing.

In the cold and dimly lit lobby, a little brass ensemble in khaki uniform strikes up something lively. Racks of unused room keys rattle behind the bare reception counter. Then the bride and groom, young and flushed, lead a dance into the function room, where dull plates of rice and sweet watered-down juice are laid out for the wedding feast.

'This is nothing like the day we had when I was married,' the groom's father says. 'It's shameful really, but what can you do after so many years of war? I suppose we are lucky our son is still alive to have a wedding.'

More than a million have died – one-fifteenth of the population – since troops invaded the country. A vast exodus of five million refugees has trailed out to neighbouring countries. The numbers of the dead and displaced keep multiplying.

In the capital, vendors squat in the street offering carefully arranged piles of eggs. Meat is available. So is flour and cooking oil. In the lamplit shops on Chicken Street – a compulsory stop on the old hippy trail – embroidered sheepskin waistcoats may not be selling well, but Heinz beans, Pears soap and After Eight mints tempt diplomatic staff.

'We have French wines coming in from Abu Dhabi tomorrow,' the salesman says. 'How many bottles would you like? Do you prefer Côtes de Rhône or Bordeaux?'

Elsewhere, in one of the many queues for heating fuel, two little girls in dresses which are too thin clutch empty oil cans. The mood gets ugly when a veiled woman pushes forward, shouting that she is a war widow. A young conscript uses his rifle butt to shove her to the back of the line again.

Shanty towns have mushroomed around the edge of the capital as its population has trebled from 700,000 to more than two million. Their hearts are not here, though. In a platformed tea house, a group of white-bearded elders sit sipping tea poured from brightly painted enamel pots, and they put it quite simply: 'We have a miserable life here,' Abdul Rashid says. 'There is nothing for us. But what can we do? There's hardly a wall left standing in our village. Perhaps one day our children might return to the countryside, but I cannot see how. There are so many mines – they would be blown to pieces.'

Such a life, such prospects, might have been expected to breed a determination to stop the war at any cost. But most people in the city seem to express no more than a forlorn wish for peace. Those who are more committed take themselves out of the city and into the towns and villages that the troops command – an area amounting to 70 per cent of the country.

Across the city, a boy of nine or ten adroitly swivels a drum of precious kerosene across a drainage ditch and heaves it neatly on to a handcart. It takes a moment to notice that the boy's left leg is a wooden stump, the result of stepping on a mine. He has only ever known a country at war.

1 The article shows how people in this country

   A hate war.
   B have adapted to war.
   C believe in the war.
   D are exploiting the war.

2 The impression given of the capital city is that it is

   A lively.
   B dangerous.
   C starving.
   D in difficulties.

3 The groom's father is

   A penniless.
   B ashamed of his son.
   C ashamed of the wedding feast.
   D unhappy.

4 The people of this country

   A are still being killed.
   B have abandoned the countryside.
   C are mainly country people.
   D are controlled by the military.

5 Daily cooking requirements

   A are generally available.
   B are extremely hard to find.
   C are only available to diplomats.
   D are controlled by the military.

6 The author mentions the young boy because

   A he pities him.
   B the boy is brave.
   C the boy symbolises resilience.
   D the boy has only ever known war.

Can you add now any other guidance to your poster of advice on answering multiple-choice questions?

Ways of learning: approaches to reading

There are several different ways of reading because you don't always read texts in the same way. Compare, for example, how you might read a telephone directory with how you might read a story you were really enjoying. How you read something depends mainly on what the text is about and why you are reading it – your purpose for reading. The CAE exam expects you to read texts with a specific purpose or reason in mind.

It has been suggested that there are four main approaches to reading a text:

- Quickly and superficially – to get a general idea (the gist) of what the text is about.
- Quickly and selectively – to look for particular information.
- More slowly and maybe selectively and in greater detail – to get at the detailed message of the text or parts of the text.
- Slowly, possibly selectively, and with different levels of attention to read for pleasure, as when you read a good story.

1 Go back over each text in this unit and write down which of the four approaches to reading would seem to be the best for each of the tasks on the texts. What is the purpose for reading in each case?

Compare and discuss your answers.

2 Which approach to reading do you find most difficult? Why? Write down some suggestions for overcoming these difficulties, then find someone in your class with the same difficulties as you and discuss the best ways to deal with this kind of reading.

TWO

A

Voyages of discovery

Starter activities

1 Look at these pictures. What do they have in common?

2 Can you think of the name of at least one famous explorer from history? What were they famous for? Is anyone from your own country famous for a voyage of discovery?

Reading

1 Write down anything you know about Christopher Columbus. Compare your answers with a partner.

✳ **2** Read the text 'Island Explorer' on page 30 quickly and select the correct answer. For each question, match the correct option(s) from those listed.

1 Which of the places in the list did Columbus visit for the first time on

  A his first voyage?
  B his second voyage?
  C his third voyage?

Trinidad	Guanahani	Cuba
Mainland America	Haiti	Jamaica
Puerto Rico		

2 Which of the names in the list below did Columbus give to the island of

  A Jamaica?
  B Guanahani?
  C Caira?
  D Puerto Rico?
  E Haiti?

San Salvador	Santiago	Trinidad
Hispaniola	San Juan Baptista	San Martin
Antigua	Montserrat	Guadeloupe
St Christopher		

3 Which five items did Columbus take back with him to Europe?

  A ....
  B ....
  C ....
  D ....
  E ....

bananas	pineapple	birds	silver
coconuts	slaves	gold	spices
pearls	tobacco		

Island Explorer

NUMEROUS EVENTS were held in 1992 to mark the discovery of America by Christopher Columbus. But the intrepid explorer never set foot on the American mainland during that historic voyage in 1492. Indeed, he wasn't even looking for it. He hoped to find the gilded cities of Cathay. Instead he became the first European tourist to visit the isles of the Caribbees. He must have been very puzzled when he saw the little island known to the Lubayans, who had discovered it long before him, as Guanahani. It showed no sign of the oriental splendour he had expected. The natives who greeted him were "naked as their mothers bore them". They watched in what we may assume was equal amazement as the finely-dressed, white-skinned and hairy-faced strangers came ashore. It was here, on a Bahamian coral beach, that history was made.

Like many tourists since, he was fascinated by the crystal clear water of the shallow sea and the multitude of colourful fish. "There are here fish," he wrote, "so unlike ours that it is a marvel: of the finest colours in the world, blue, yellow, red and all of the colours, painted in a thousand ways, and the colours are so fine that no man would not wonder at them or be anything but delighted to see them."

He changed the island's name to San Salvador – a practice he followed throughout his voyage. Many well-known islands owe their now familiar names to him. Caira (land of the Hummingbird) became Trinidad and he also came up with Antigua, Anguilla, Guadeloupe, Montserrat, San Martin and St Vincent.

Not all of his labels have stuck. Las Tortugas, for example, later became the Cayman Islands and Conception became Grenada. Only one was named after himself – St Christopher – but that too was changed. The English anglicised it to St Kitts.

On that first trip, he explored several other Bahamian islands and then went on to Cuba. The extent and natural grandeur of that island led him to think that he had at last reached Japan or even China. But, alas, with the most diligent probing he could find no magnificent cities, no wealthy potentates, and no gold. He therefore abandoned the Cuban search and crossed the Windward Passage to Haiti – the most important island he was ever to find. He honoured the nation that had promised him work by calling it Hispaniola, another name that hasn't survived. He judged it larger than Spain and wrote glowingly to the monarchs of the virtues of its climate and the peacefulness of its people.

On Christmas Day the Santa Maria drifted on a reef and was wrecked. This made it necessary to leave some of his men behind in Haiti when he sailed for home in March.

His haul, on that first voyage, was modest. He had collected samples of gold, exotic plants, spices, strange birds, and feathered 'Indians' to show off at court. He had discovered the pineapple and tobacco – "some leaves which must be highly esteemed among the Indians", though he did not know what it was for.

The court was sufficiently impressed by these souvenirs to give him all the titles he had been promised upon the successful completion of his enterprise, including Admiral of the Ocean Sea.

He also managed to get royal backing for another expedition, this time as commander of a fleet of 17 ships. He discovered a new chain of islands, including Puerto Rico (or San Juan Baptista, as he named it), but when he reached Hispaniola he found that the small outpost he had set up on his first voyage had been burned to the ground and that the 39 Spaniards who had remained behind were all dead. He chose another site, established the first township in the new world, Isabella, and set sail again. It was on his second voyage that Columbus discovered Jamaica, which he thought "the fairest island that eyes have beheld … all full of valleys and fields and plains". He called it "St Iago" or "Santiago" after his country's patron saint. Columbus made two more trips to the Caribbean. On the third he found Trinidad and also made it to the mainland of the new world. On August 14, 1498, he wrote in his log: "I believe this is a very large continent which until now has remained unknown".

On his last journey he was stranded in Jamaica and had to spend a year as a castaway on the island, the longest period that he stayed anywhere in the New World. He returned to Spain in 1504, a sick man. He was in his fifties and the harshness of his life had made him old before his time. He died in obscurity two years later.

Sitting in a modern jet, which can cross the Atlantic in a matter of hours, it's easy to underrate the problems which Columbus faced when he embarked on his great enterprise. In his day, many people still refused to accept that the world was round. The few maps he could find were inadequate and misleading. Navigational aids were primitive. The anniversary of his first landfall was commemorated in more than 30 countries – with festivals, books, TV series, movies, an opera and a musical.

Not everyone approved: it has become fashionable to deride his achievements. He has been described as the archetypical European imperialist who un- leashed the forces of genocide, slavery, and destruction on a harmonious natural world.

The claim that he "discovered" America is widely disputed. The Vikings and even some cod fishermen from Bristol are said to have been there before him.

It is an undisputed fact that millions of native people already lived in the New World when he arrived. But it hardly matters. For me, as for many others, Columbus is a symbol of courage and risk-taking. He was self-educated, ambitious, imaginative, persistent. He had his faults, but one should not view the fifteenth century with twentieth century values and perceptions, and it is clearly absurd to blame him for everything that followed. He was a true explorer whose voyages changed the course of history.

(High Life Magazine)

Your thoughts

- **Did Columbus really 'discover' America?**
- **What do you think were the positive results of his voyages of discovery?**
- **What might the negative effects of his voyages have been?**
- **What is your view of Columbus?**

[handwritten notes at top: such + noun or group noun | such a lot of | so + adjective | so much/many few little]

Grammar reminder: *so* and *such*

> **Remember:**
>
> *So* is used in front of an adjective or an adverb which stands alone, e.g.
> *Columbus' exploits are **so** famous that they were celebrated in many different countries.*
> *The tropical fish were **so** colourful that Columbus was amazed at them.*
>
> *So* can also be placed in front of *many, few, much* and *little*.
>
> *Such* is used in front of a noun or noun group (i.e. a noun preceded by one or more adjectives or a defining clause), e.g.
> *Jamaica was **such** a beautiful place he decided to stay on for a few months.*
> *He showed **such** courage that he was rewarded by the Spanish court.*
>
> *Such* can also be placed in front of *a lot (of)*.
>
> **Usage note:** Both *so* and *such* may be followed by a *that* clause of result. However, in colloquial speech the *that* is often dropped, e.g. *Jamaica was **such** a beautiful place (that) he decided to stay on for a few months.*

Complete the following clauses using **so** or **such**, and then match each clause with the correct sentence completion **a–h**.

1 Columbus' life of exploration was .... hard that
2 Crossing the Atlantic is .... an easy journey today that
3 .... little was known about the world that
4 There were .... few maps that
5 Columbus has achieved .... world recognition that
6 Today there are .... few places in the world
7 We have learned .... a lot about the world in which we live
8 Nowadays exploration is .... an expensive activity

a his achievements were commemorated in more than thirty countries.
b many people still believed it to be flat.
c for men and women to discover.
d we often underrate the problems Columbus faced.
e it made him old before his time.
f it requires business sponsorship to fund it.
g it was difficult to navigate accurately.
h as a result of the travels of men and women over the past five hundred years.

Listening

1 What do you think attracts people to a life of travel and exploration nowadays? With a partner, list the possible attractions.

2 Listen to a group of friends discussing the reasons why people nowadays are attracted to a life of travel and exploration. Tick the reasons on your list which they mention, and note down any additional reasons they suggest.

✳ 3 Listen to the conversation once again and fill in the missing information below.

Modern explorers face two particular problems:	
1	2

Examples of modern explorers:		
	1 Michael Palin	2 Brian Blessed
Job		
Project		
Purpose		

Speaking: discussing opinions

1 Listen to some of the phrases the speakers used when discussing their opinions. Write each one down.

2 Listen to each phrase again and mark in the stress and intonation as shown below:

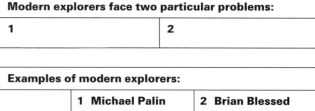

It must be difficult being ...

3 Listen once more and repeat each phrase to practise the stress and intonation.

Your thoughts

- **Do you think twentieth-century explorers spoil the places they visit? (In your discussion, try to use some of the phrases you practised in Speaking activity 3.)**
- **Where might you want to travel and explore? How and why?**

✳ Writing

Write a short article entitled 'Why do they do it?' for a student magazine, giving your views on the reasons why some people are still attracted to a life of travel and exploration in the late twentieth century, the difficulties they face, and the contribution they make to the modern world. Write approximately 250 words.

B

Holiday travel

Starter activities

1 Look at these pictures. Which one would be *your* preferred holiday destination? Explain your choice to a partner.

2 Listen to three people talking about the type of holiday they like to go on. Write down what type of holiday each speaker likes best and the reasons why.

	Type of holiday	Reasons
Speaker 1		
Speaker 2		
Speaker 3		

Which of the speakers do you identify with most/least?

Reading

1 Here are four extracts from 'holiday' texts. Look at the text descriptions below, then match the extracts with an appropriate description.

modern novel	newspaper report
travel guidebook	diary entry
business report	advertising brochure
holiday postcard	

Extract A ....   Extract C ....
Extract B ....   Extract D ....

2 Read extracts **A–D** more carefully to find which text:

1 describes the main airport in Hawaii.
2 suggests where to get brochures, maps, etc. of Hawaii.
3 mentions attending a Hawaiian barbecue.
4 describes the experience of arriving in Hawaii.
5 explains the differences between resorts in Hawaii.
6 describes the scenery of the Hawaiian islands.

3 Read the four extracts again and make a list of all the positive adjectives used to describe features of Hawaii, for example, *interesting, lovely.*

Best source for information is your own travel agent. There's also the *Hawaii Visitors Bureau*, with information available in Honolulu at 2270 Kalakaua Ave., Honolulu, HI 96815 (808–923–1811), and at regional offices in Chicago, New York, Los Angeles, San Francisco, and Tokyo. Once you are in Honolulu, go to the HVB office, 8th floor, to pick up reading material and ask questions. There are also a number of small free brochures packed in kiosks along Kalakaua Ave. in Waikiki. These same brochures are available in hotels and other locations all over the state. They contain maps, event information, restaurant listings, retail ideas, and coupons for savings on excursions such as boat trips. The Honolulu newspapers carry daily schedules of events and provide meeting schedules for service clubs ranging from Rotary and Toastmasters to gay rap and the Brooklyn Club of Hawaii.

A   *Travel guidebook*

Having a good time in Hawaii. We've been to a luau, that's a kind of Hawaiian barbecue, and on a Sunset Cruise, and visited the Polynesian Cultural Center (v. interesting) and Waimea Falls Park (lovely trees and birds) and Pearl Harbor (v. sad). Your father is using up lots of videotape, as you can imagine. I hope you are remembering to lock up every night – and remember, no parties.

B   *Holiday postcard*

The night air at Honolulu airport was like nothing Bernard had experienced before, warm and velvety, almost palpable. To feel it on your face was like being licked by a large friendly dog, whose breath smelled of frangipani with a hint of petrol, and you felt it almost instantly on arrival, because the walkways – stuffy glazed corridors in most airports, mere extensions of the claustrophobic aircraft cabin – were here open at their sides to the air. He and his father were soon sweating again in their thick English clothes, but a light breeze fanned their cheeks and rustled in the floodlit palm trees. A kind of tropical garden had been laid out next to the terminal building, with artificial ponds and streams, and naked torches burning amid the foliage. It was this spectacle which seemed to convince Mr Walsh that they had finally arrived at their destination. He stopped and gawped. "Look at that," he said. "Jungle."

As they waited beside a carousel in the Arrivals Hall, a beautiful brown-skinned young woman in the Travelwise livery came up to them, smiled brilliantly and said, "*Aloha!* Welcome to Hawaii! My name's Linda and I'm your airport facilitator."

C

*T*his beautiful group of islands lying almost in the centre of the Pacific Ocean is more than just another holiday destination. It is another state of mind where peace and contentment can slowly overtake the visitor weaving a spell of irresistible charm, known to many as the spirit of Aloha. Exotic yet familiar, luxurious but unpretentious – Hawaii awaits you. Truly if ever a spot was created solely for holiday it is Hawaii.

But Hawaii is not just one place. It is a myriad of places with an enormous array of resorts and diversions and each island has something different to offer the visitor. For many people the mention of Hawaii brings Waikiki Beach to mind, but all the islands have a multitude of beautiful palm-fringed beaches and to visit Hawaii without seeing something of what the rest of the islands have to offer would be to miss an exciting experience. The lush vegetation and scenic splendour of Kauai contrast sharply with the barren volcanic wilderness and fields of orchids on Hawaii, whilst Maui with its outdoor lifestyle and superb resorts could not be more opposite to the tranquil calm of undeveloped Lanai or Molokai. Ohau, the main island, offers so much more than the bright lights of non-stop Waikiki. Lush pineapple fields, beautiful scenery and world class surfing on its north shore. Wherever you choose to visit, you'll find a delightful mix of east and west mingled with Polynesia plus that special something – the spirit of Aloha.

D

Your thoughts

- **Which text most attracts you to Hawaii? Why?**
- **Would you go to Hawaii on holiday?**

Grammar analysis: the present simple and continuous tenses

1 This extract is from the same novel as one of the texts you have just read. As you read through the extract, underline the verbs in the present simple and present continuous tenses.

'Tourism is wearing out the planet.' Sheldrake delved into his silvery attache case again and brought out a sheaf of press-cuttings marked with yellow highlighter. He flipped through them. 'The footpaths in the Lake District have become trenches. The frescoes in the Sistine Chapel are being damaged by the breath and body heat of spectators. A hundred and eight people enter Notre Dame every minute: their feet are eroding the floor and the buses that bring them there are rotting the stonework with exhaust fumes. Pollution from cars queuing to get to Alpine ski resorts is killing the trees and causing avalanches and landslides. The Mediterranean is like a toilet without a chain: you have a one in six chance of getting an infection if you swim in it. In 1987 they had to close Venice one day because it was full. In 1963 forty-four people went down the Colorado river on a raft, now there are a thousand trips a day. In 1939 a million people travelled abroad; last year it was four hundred million. By the year two thousand there could be six hundred and fifty million international travellers, and five times as many people travelling in their own countries. The mere consumption of energy entailed is stupendous.'
'My goodness,' said Bernard. 'The only way to put a stop to it, short of legislation, is to demonstrate to people that they aren't enjoying themselves when they go on holiday, but are engaging in a superstitious ritual. It's no coincidence that tourism arose just as religion went into decline. It's the new opium of the people, and must be exposed as such.'

2 Look at the examples of the present simple and continuous tenses in the extract and then correctly match the sentence halves below to complete the general rules about using the present simple and present continuous tenses.

The present simple tense is generally concerned with ...	**... present instances rather than general characteristics.**
The present continuous tense is generally concerned with ...	**... the characteristic or permanent nature of things.**

3 Now look at a more detailed analysis of the uses for the present simple and present continuous tenses.

The present simple tense is normally used when you are:

a talking about something that happens regularly or habitually
e.g. *A hundred and eight people enter Notre Dame every minute.*

b saying that something is always or generally true
e.g. *If you swim in the Mediterranean you have a one in six chance ...*

c talking about a current established state of affairs
e.g. *Nowadays over 400 million people travel abroad on business or on holiday.*

d talking about your thoughts, feelings or reactions at the present moment
e.g. *I believe that tourism is the new opium of the people.*

The present continuous tense is normally used when you are:

a talking about something that is happening at the moment of speaking
e.g. *I'm flying to Hawaii to give a series of lectures on the nature of tourism.*

b emphasising the present moment or indicating that a situation is temporary
e.g. *People aren't really enjoying themselves when they go on holiday.*

c talking about a habitual action which is new or temporary
e.g. *People today are travelling far more than they ever used to.*

d talking about changes, trends, development, or progress
e.g. *Tourism is gradually wearing out the planet.*

4 Match each of these eight sentences with a use for the present simple and present continuous tenses described in activity **3**.

1 They're spending the weekend with her parents and they won't be back till tomorrow.

2 You're working far too hard you know – you really should take things easy.

3 I feel awful today – I think I must've caught something.

4 He works for an international bank in Hong Kong so he travels quite a lot.

5 Can't you see what I'm doing? I'm trying to get the lid off this jar.

6 Children often pick up a foreign language far more easily than adults.

7 He's improving slowly but it'll be a long time before he's fit enough to go back to work.

8 I normally try and do my homework as soon as I get home – that leaves the rest of the evening free for other things.

5 Now write your own set of eight example sentences. Exchange your set with a partner's and decide which use of the present simple or present continuous is reflected in each of your partner's eight sentences. Discuss your answers.

Speaking: describing a situation

Look at the photos below. With a partner, discuss the following questions:

a   What do you think these places were like before the days of modern tourism?
b   What are they like now?
c   Do you agree that tourism is 'wearing out the planet'?
d   Can you think of any solutions to the problems tourism causes?

Ways of learning: choosing and using a grammar book

1   What is most important when you choose a grammar book? Put in order of priority the following ten points:

*   **It mustn't cost too much.**
*   **It must be clearly organised.**
*   **It must be hard-wearing.**
*   **It must be easy to carry around.**
*   **The language it uses must be easy to understand.**
*   **It must include practice exercises.**
*   **It must contain an explanation of grammatical terms.**
*   **It must give guidance on pronunciation.**
*   **It must use examples from real-life English.**
*   **It must explain how to use formal/informal English.**

Compare your order with your partner's.

> Whatever grammar book you choose, get to know your way around it so that it can become a useful and effective resource in your learning programme.
> Read the introduction to see the principles on which the grammar has been developed and the type of approach it is taking.
> Try to become familiar with the overall organisation of the main text and the numbering or section heading system. Make sure you can recognise any abbreviations or symbols used.
> When you read an explanation of a grammatical point, look carefully at any examples given and try to add one or two of your own.
> By referring to a grammar book regularly, you will learn a great deal about how to use English.

2   Choose two different grammar books and look up the sections on the present simple and present continuous tenses. How does each grammar book explain or describe the use of these tenses? Which of the explanations do you find most helpful? Note down any information you feel is useful, together with helpful examples.

Vocabulary summary

1   Look back through the unit and make a list of at least twenty words and phrases to do with travelling and exploration.

2   From your list choose the twelve words you think are most useful. Write them on the sails of the ship.

C

Paper 2 (Writing): Section A

Introduction

CAE Paper 2 contains two sections – Section A and Section B. Here the focus is on Section A. (Further advice and practice for Section A can be found in Unit 7, and details of Section B are in Unit 12.)

1 Read this description of Section A of CAE Paper 2. Think about what it means in simple terms and underline the information that it's important for a candidate to remember.

Candidates will be asked to produce one or more pieces of writing (approximately 250 words in all) in response to a *practical* reading input. Satisfactory processing of this input will be required to complete the task(s) successfully. Presentation, register and style should be appropriate to the task. All tasks will be set within a context, and purpose and intended audience will be made clear.

2 Cover the text above and explain to a partner what CAE Paper 2 Section A is like.

How do I begin?

There are a number of steps involved in producing a piece of writing for Paper 2 Section A and it's important to think about each one carefully. What would be the best order for these steps?

- identify the audience you're writing for/to
- choose an appropriate style and tone
- organise the information in an appropriate way
- read the input to identify the relevant information
- decide on the reason for writing
- produce the final piece of writing

Discuss your answers.

What information is relevant?

1 Read this letter from a problem page in a magazine. What is the writer anxious about?

My son and daughter-in-law recently invited me to stay with them for a period of 3 months. They emigrated to Australia five years ago and it will be my first opportunity to visit their new home and to meet my 2 grandchildren whom I only know from their photographs. My only worry is that I have never flown before and I understand that the flight to Australia is rather long. Can you give me any tips that will calm my fears and help me make the flight as comfortable as possible. I do so want to enjoy the experience. *P.H., Bournemouth.*

2 Now read the following short text from an airline magazine and underline any points in it which you think could be included in a reply to the letter from *P.H., Bournemouth.*

Smoking on board

You will have been asked at check-in whether or not you wish to smoke. Should you discover that you are sitting in the wrong section of the aircraft, wait until you have been airborne for about ten minutes and then ask the crew if you may move to another seat, if any is available in an equivalent non-smoking section.

During the flight

Bar service is available. In both First Class and Club cabins, you will find a selection of magazines and newspapers. Slipperettes and eye-shades are provided on inter-continental flights, which also carry children's games, babies' requisites, stationery, blankets and toiletries.

Comfort hints

Because flying has a dehydrating effect, it's wise to drink reasonable quantities of non-alcoholic liquids. On 747s, DC10s and Tri-Stars, you'll find water fountains. During climb and descent, you can relieve any discomfort in your ears by yawning or swallowing. Because feet tend to swell on longer flights it is often a good idea not to remove tight-fitting shoes. Should you need any common pharmaceutical requisites, please ask the cabin crew.

What is my reason for writing?

What could be your reason for writing a reply to *P.H., Bournemouth*? Tick the appropriate box(es).

☐ to dissuade   ☐ to refuse
☐ to reassure   ☐ to criticise
☐ to apologise   ☐ to give advice

Who am I writing for?

From your reading of the problem page letter, what sort of person do you imagine *P.H., Bournemouth* to be? Fill in the details below:

Sex: ....
Age: ....

Occupation: ....
Other information: ....

Your answers will help you decide on an appropriate style and tone for the written reply.

How should I organise the information?

1 Using all of the information you have gathered so far, make a list of all the points you want to include in your reply.

2 Look at your list of points again. Do they fall into some sort of logical sequence or is the order unimportant? Are there some points you could group together?

What style and tone should I use for the reply letter?

Select an appropriate style and tone by ticking the relevant boxes below:

Style

☐ formal
☐ neutral
☐ colloquial

Tone

☐ critical
☐ enthusiastic
☐ reassuring

Writing the reply

Using the information you have gathered and the planning you have done, write an appropriate reply to the letter from *P.H., Bournemouth* on page 36. When you have finished, remember to check back carefully over your grammar, spelling and punctuation.

Exam practice

Here is a Section A writing task. Read the instructions and complete the task. Remember to follow the steps you have already practised in this section of the unit. Use the checklist opposite to help you and tick each step as you complete it.

1 Read the input and identify relevant information
2 Decide on the reason for writing
3 Identify the audience
4 Organise the information for inclusion in the response
5 Choose an appropriate style and tone
6 Produce the final piece of writing

You are busy organising a conference in Amsterdam and you have just received a letter from an overseas colleague who is due to attend the conference. Her letter ends as follows:

> ... I'm really looking forward to seeing you in Amsterdam next month. Don't worry about meeting me at the airport – I'm sure you'll be too busy organising the conference and it can't be that difficult for me to get from the airport to your office in town.
>
> Perhaps you could give me some idea of the best way to get into Amsterdam city centre. I don't know how regular the trains/buses are, especially if the plane is delayed and we don't land until late in the evening. I know you fly in and out of Schipol Airport all the time, so any hints would be greatly appreciated.
>
> Best wishes and see you soon.
>
> Gerda

Read the text about Amsterdam Airport and look at the airport plan. Use the information to write a letter of reply to your colleague making helpful suggestions on how to reach the city centre from the airport. Write approximately 250 words.

AMSTERDAM AIRPORT SCHIPHOL

Trouble-free arrival

To get to the main airport building from your arrival pier follow the yellow EXIT signs. You'll pass through the passport control on your way to baggage claim and customs.

If you need to change any currency you'll find two bank offices in the baggage claim area.

After you've claimed your baggage and cleared customs you enter the public section of the Arrival Hall. There you'll find KLM's Hotel Reservation desk, the Car Rental desks, the Airport Information desk, and the Check-in for NLM-CityHoppers domestic flights. In front of the Arrival Hall is everything you need to continue your journey. For those travelling locally, there's a taxi rank and a shuttle bus service to nearby airport hotels.

The railway station is also in front of the Arrival Hall, and is best reached by an underpass from the hall itself. From there you can go direct to Amsterdam Central Station, Leiden and The Hague (trains leave every 15 minutes) and Rotterdam (every 30 minutes); there are also connections to most major cities in the Netherlands. In addition, there are hourly services to Antwerp and Brussels in Belgium, and to Rheine, Osnabruck and Hannover in Germany. Please check the timetables which are in the Arrival Hall or the station for exact information.

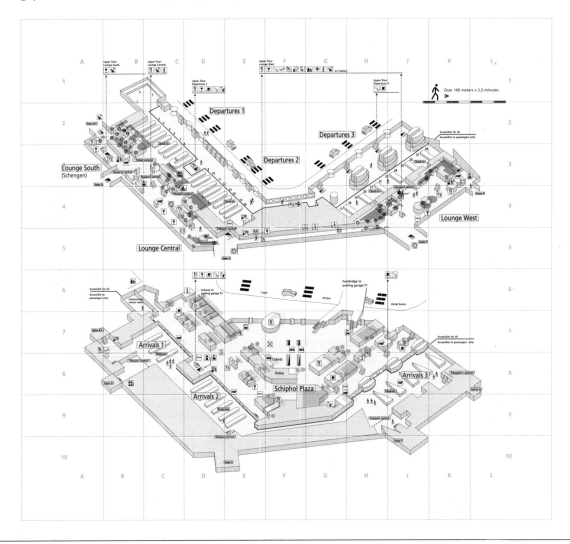

Three

A

Family matters

Starter activities

1 Look at these photographs. With a partner discuss who the people might be and what story these pictures might be telling.

2 Do you remember times when you argued with other children in your family? What sort of things did you squabble about? How were these arguments resolved?

Listening

1 Listen to two friends discussing their relationships with brothers and sisters during childhood and later life. As you listen, complete the sentences below with an appropriate word or short phrase. The first example has been done for you.

Dave has (1) *one sister* who is about four years (2) .... than him. When they were children, Dave felt that he often ended up getting (3) .... because of her. The biggest problems in their relationship occurred when they were (4) .... Dave thought his sister was rather (5) .... and he took the side of his (6) .... Eventually, Dave decided to (7) .... Today Dave and his sister see (8) .... of each other and they get on (9) ....

Celia has two sisters and she is the (10) .... of the three. As a child, she remembers feeling (11) .... towards her (12) .... , perhaps because they were so close in age. She was particularly (13) .... to her other sister who was five years (14) .... Nowadays, they all enjoy a very close relationship.

2 Listen again to the conversation and note down any short phrases the speakers use to:

- **express agreement**
- **check the listener's understanding**
- **express surprise/shock**
- **confirm their own understanding**
- **seek further information/explanation**

3 Listen a third time and mark in stress and intonation for the phrases you noted in activity **2**. Practise saying them aloud to a partner.

4 With a partner discuss how your own relationships with other children (e.g. brothers, sisters, cousins, close friends) changed as you grew older. Try to use the phrases from activities **2** and **3** as you talk.

Reading

1 Look at the first paragraph from the article on page 41 about arguments between children in the same family. What is the technical term for such arguments?

2 Read the rest of the article in detail and note down the methods which are recommended for:

- **avoiding the build-up of tension which leads to conflict.**
- **dealing with conflicts already in progress.**
- **punishing bad behaviour.**

3 Match each item on the left with an item on the right to make a commonly-used phrase in English, e.g. end ... in tears

fight	**at each other's throats**
retain	**face**
break	**in tears**
ease	**like cat and dog**
lose	**your sanity**
be	**the rules**
end	**in turns**
come up with	**tension**
take it	**a solution**
tell someone	**your side of the story**

Check your answers by finding these or similar phrases in the text on 'sibling rivalry'. Use clues from the text or from your own knowledge to help you with the meaning.

When two or more words frequently occur together we say they collocate, e.g.

end ... in tears / violence / disappointment / disaster
gross ... misdemeanours / neglect / inequalities
a mood of ... desperation / despair / optimism

Your thoughts

- **What positive effects can sibling rivalry have?**
- **How do you think sibling rivalry differs between boys and girls?**
- **What do you consider to be acceptable/unacceptable methods for punishing quarrelling children?**
- **Do/should children have 'rights'?**

Sibling Rivalry

Nine-year-old Tom and five-year-old Camilla can fight like cat and dog. Never mind that their father is an eminent child psychologist. "Sibling rivalry" – as the professionals smoothly term these quarrels – is as old as the Bible and affects most families.

During half term, Britain will resound with maternal cries of "stop fighting" and childish rejoinders of "he hit me first".
Now that the quick smack is increasingly out of fashion, especially since the recent Scottish Law Commission's recommendations that hitting
10 a child violently should be made illegal, how should a parent retain their sanity?

'Break the rules,' says Charlie Lewis (lecturer in psychology at Lancaster University and father of Tom and Camilla). 'Bribery is not only acceptable, but essential. Offer them chocolate or a trip
20 to the park if they stop quarrelling.'

Sending a child to a grandparent's or friend's house can also help, says Dr Lewis, who battled with his four brothers in an 18-year-long fight. 'If you can't do this, avoid pressure building up during the day
30 by organising an outing during the later afternoon or early evening. A walk can ease tension and calm you down for the forthcoming bath and bed battles.'

If warfare has already broken out, Dr Lewis will threaten the aggressor with 'severe trouble' if the fighting
40 escalates. If that does not work, punishments range from sending children to separate rooms and (for gross misdemeanours) a withdrawal of treats. In the heat of the moment, it is easy to be rash. Dr Lewis recently forbade Tom from playing in a long-awaited football game
50 but relented without losing face by making him tidy up his room as an alternative correction.

Sarcasm, adds Dr Lewis, is a handy retort for the common childish accusation that 'you love her better because you never tell *her* off'. If he replies 'yes, that's
60 right,' in a joking way, it takes the power away from Tom's statement because his son can see his father is not taking him seriously. Ask yourself too if there's a grain of truth in the complaint, says Tim Kahn, father of two and co-ordinator of Parent Network, an advisory
70 organisation. 'Pay some attention to the aggressor and find out *why* he's behaving badly.'

This is precisely the stage when one feels like smacking. So what does the organisation End Physical Punishment of Children advise? The best method is
80 diversion, says Peter Newell, the organisation's co-ordinator and father of Finn, aged two, Joe, five, and Matthew, six. 'If the two-year-old has the five-year-old's construction bricks, I produce something which the younger one is equally interested in.'

'And how about multi-age
90 activities like cooking? That's something you can get all the children involved in. Introduce laughter – arguments often start because a parent is tired. It's easy for that mood of desperation to affect them. When I come home at night, I stand on the doorstep for a few moments to ask myself
100 what kind of mood I am in and to jolly myself up.'

Analysing your own reactions is wise according to Dr Penny Munn, a psychologist at Strathclyde University, who (with Dr Judy Dunn) studied 43 toddlers and their siblings at play. 'Mothers who
110 reprimanded children by talking about feelings ('He didn't *mean* to hurt you') had more effect than those who simply said 'Don't do that',' Dr Munn says. She confesses to being 'speechless with admiration' at other techniques displayed by mothers who would 'nip
120 in with drinks or other diversions when the atmosphere got tricky'.

Persuading your children to sort out their own fracas is a technique learned by Jan and Peter Breed through a counselling course run by Parent Network. 'If they're arguing over a toy, get them
130 to tell you their side of the story,' advises Mrs Breed, whose offspring (Rhiannon, aged seven, Cerys, five and Joel, two) are constantly at each other's throats. (The baby – 12 week old Sadie – is as yet too young to join in.) "Then say: 'This is the situation. You want it and he
140 wants it so what are you going to do about it? They usually come up with a solution such as taking it in turns."

If all else fails, tell yourself that sibling arguments can be positive. So says Dr Lynn Beardsall, a psychologist at Sunderland University who
150 sat in on 20 six-year-olds with their older brothers or sisters aged between seven and 12 when writing her thesis on conflicts between siblings. 'Younger children who had had physical fights with older brothers or sisters were best at identifying how people *feel*. We tested them by
160 playing audio tapes of adults discussing their own problems. These children were more sensitive at identifying with the dilemma than others.' The study also revealed that out of the younger children, those who were most often the victim were better peace keepers
170 partly because they had learnt sharing and negotiation strategies.

Gender, too, made a difference. Boys tended to be more physically aggressive, whereas girls favoured the sneaky pinch. There was also proof that some fighters are best left alone. 'One third of
180 the children reached a mutually acceptable solution over an argument without parental interference,' Dr Beardsall says. 'I watched some very nasty punch-ups which mothers ignored before the children sorted it out themselves.'

(The Times)

Grammar analysis: stative verbs

1 Read this short paragraph and underline the verbs.

Although I was a year ahead of my brother at school he was always very bright and had glowing reports, while I belonged to the could-do-better group. I don't think I was as bright as him.

Do these verbs normally appear in a simple or continuous form?

2 Look at these sentences. Decide which ones are incorrect and then make the necessary changes.

1 She is believing that her parents love her baby brother more than her.
2 Parents sometimes reach a stage when they feel like smacking their children.
3 Psychologists are agreeing that sibling rivalry is quite normal.
4 Most parents are loving their children equally.
5 Children don't understand the wisdom of taking turns.

Verbs which describe a state of affairs rather than a dynamic action are often called 'stative verbs' and are not normally used in a continuous form.

He always *had* glowing reports.
I *belonged* to the could-do-better group.
I *don't think* I *was* as bright as him.

The most common stative verbs are probably 'be' and 'have', together with 'seem', 'appear', and 'belong'. Here is a list of some other common verbs mostly found in the simple form:

want	**like**	**forget**	**remember**	**know**
need	**wish**	**confess**	**understand**	**love**
mean	**hope**	**think**	**say**	**agree**
see	**hear**	**imagine**	**sound**	**feel**
advise	**deny**	**smell**	**doubt**	**taste**

3 Sort the above verbs into the following three categories:

• **verbs associated with the physical senses, e.g. *look***
• **verbs associated with mental or emotional states, e.g. *believe***
• **verbs which usually introduce statements or declarations, e.g. *admit***

Occasionally stative verbs *do* appear in the continuous form. The continuous form can be used with a stative verb to indicate a specific event in the future:

He is seeing the child's parents tomorrow to discuss their problems.

It can also be used to indicate that a state is tentative, temporary or incomplete:

She's feeling a bit lost now that all the children have left home, but she'll get over it before too long.

4 Now use a verb from the list in activity **2** to complete the following sentences:

1 'You .... her better because you never tell her off!' retorted the child angrily.
2 'He didn't .... to hurt you - it was an accident,' explained the father.
3 Psychologist Dr Munn .... to being speechless with admiration at the techniques parents adopt.
4 Child expert Peter Newell .... the best method for avoiding conflict is diversion.
5 He .... parents to listen to both sides of the story.

5 Complete these sentences to talk about your own childhood or your family relationships today.

1	I remember ...	4	I hope ...
2	I doubt ...	5	It looks ...
3	I admit ...	6	It feels ...

B

Habits and customs

Starter activities

1 Which of the following would be considered acceptable behaviour in public in your country?

- **riding a bicycle along a pedestrian path**
- **leaving a tip in a restaurant**
- **cleaning your plate with a piece of bread**
- **two men kissing each other in greeting**
- **wearing a hat/shoes in a religious building**
- **arriving 20 minutes late for a dinner party**
- **picking your teeth after a meal**
- **keeping your overcoat on in a public building**
- **removing your shoes when you enter someone's home**
- **taking someone's photograph without their permission**
- **giving up your bus/train seat to an older person**

✳ 2 Discuss your answers with a partner and agree on what you consider to be the most unacceptable behaviour. Report your decision to another pair.

🔊 Listening
✳

Listen to three visitors to various countries talking about habits or customs which surprised or shocked them. Fill in the table with the countries they visited and the habits or customs they talk about.

	Country visited	Habit/custom
Speaker 1		
Speaker 2		
Speaker 3		

Reading

1 The four letters (**1–4**) below were all sent to a magazine asking for advice on the subject of 'good manners'. Read each letter quickly and match it to a topic from the list **a–e**.

a behaviour at a wedding reception
b behaviour at a party
c behaviour on greeting someone
d behaviour in a restaurant
e behaviour in a religious building

2 Read the magazine's replies (**A–D**) and match the correct reply to the original letter.

3 Choose an appropriate title for each letter and its reply from the list **a–d** below.

a Get Away!
b Well Met!
c Fancy Fish
d Wedding Nerves

Your thoughts

- **Do you agree with the advice given to each letter-writer?**
- **In what way might the customs on these occasions be different in your country?**

1

My friend has invited us to her son's wedding. Apparently, it will be rather grand and, as it's years since we attended a big function and we will be among many strangers, I am a little apprehensive. Two things worry me. Firstly, what do we say to the bride and groom on arrival at the reception? And, secondly, is it right to thank the bride's parents for inviting us?

2

I love seafood but never choose it at a restaurant because I'm not sure of the right way to eat it. The one time I did order prawns I was alarmed when they arrived with their shells still on. I didn't know how to peel them or what to do with the trimmings. Can you help, please?

3

Suitably demonstrating my feelings when saying 'hello' and 'goodbye' always leaves me confused. I don't know whether to shake hands, peck a cheek or just smile and express my feelings in words. I've even been known to clash noses on trying to kiss a friend on the cheek! Is there a right and wrong way?

4

At a recent party, I got 'stuck' with someone I had only just met and with whom I didn't have much in common. She was on her own and not a good mixer, so I felt I couldn't abandon her … I didn't have a very enjoyable time. If a similar situation happens again, how should I handle it?

A

Poor you. It's so easy to miss out by ordering a second choice to avoid looking embarrassed. To peel a prawn, snap off the head first, then open out the underside of the body shell (it unwraps easily). Pull the fleshy body out, discard the tail and eat with your fingers. Don't feel awkward if it gets a little messy – a good restaurant should provide a side plate for the trimmings and a finger-bowl with a napkin for cleaning up afterwards.

Mussels can present a challenge, too. But just pick up the half-shells with your fingers and either scoop out the mussel with a fork or, if you favour the French way, eat it straight from the shell. Any sauce can be spooned up – or scooped up with a shell.

B

I do understand how you felt. It's not too bad if you get stuck in a group of people, because you can always slip away to the bar or join other friends. And no one will be hurt or insulted if you don't return.

But leaving a lone guest on her own could be difficult. One solution would be to take her with you in search of refreshment; and if, on the way, you meet someone you know or someone you'd like to know, you could get into conversation and introduce her. Or you could both launch yourselves into a group. The majority of people like to make others feel at ease. So, if you are honest and say something like: 'Hello, we are both on our own and don't know many people here, do you mind if we join you?' then I'm sure they will welcome you and include both of you in the conversation.

C

Reception lines have to be kept moving briskly and you won't have long for conversation. But as the wedding will be a large affair and many of the guests – like you and your husband – won't be known to both the bride and groom, do, in introducing yourselves, say briefly what connection you have with the couple.

Say to the bride, for example: 'I am Alice James and this is my husband, Bill. We've lived near Tom's (the bridegroom's) mother and father for years.' If it is very grand, though, don't be surprised to be asked your name on arrival, for it to be announced aloud. In that case, say: 'Mr and Mrs William (or Bill if you prefer) James.'

On leaving, wish the couple well and perhaps comment on something special you remembered about the ceremony. You should also thank the bride's parents personally, if possible; and send them an informal 'thank you' letter the next day.

D

It really depends who you are greeting. Unless it's a relative or close friend, I think a friendly smile and genuinely warm greeting are best. By all means shake hands firmly and sincerely if you wish. But it is far better not to do anything at all, than to cause people embarrassment with an over-demonstrative approach.

When welcoming a member of the family or a dear friend, go ahead and give them a hug or a kiss, or whatever you are both used to. Again, if in doubt, let them take the lead: if they put an arm around you, respond in a similar fashion and if a cheek is proffered, peck it … but try to aim for their right cheek first to avoid any more embarrassing clashes.

Grammar reminder: -ing or infinitive?

> **Remember:**
> Some verbs can be followed by either the *-ing* form or the infinitive verb form, but with a change in meaning.
>
> *like, love, hate, can't bear, prefer*
> *   **I know he's busy and I don't like to disturb him so I'll come back later.**
> *   **I know he's busy and I don't like disturbing him but I must – it's very urgent.**
>
> **The infinitive expresses the feeling *beforehand* about what may happen. The *-ing* form expresses the feeling which *accompanies or follows* what happens or what we know will happen.**
>
> *remember/forget*
> *   **You must remember to renew your passport in time for our holiday.**
> *   **I can't think where my passport's gone – I definitely remember packing it.**
>
> **The infinitive focuses on the activity of remembering/forgetting *before* something happens, while the *-ing* form focuses on the activity of remembering/forgetting *after* something has happened.**
>
> *try*
> *   **I've tried to give up smoking on a number of occasions but it's no good.**
> *   **Why don't you try seeing an acupuncturist – they're supposed to get good *results*.**
>
> **The infinitive expresses an effort/attempt to do something, while the *-ing* form expresses an experiment/trial with something.**

1 Complete these sentences by matching each one with an appropriate clause from **a–h**.

1   She didn't like taking the old man's picture
2   They hate travelling abroad
3   He didn't actually remember sending her a postcard
4   She didn't like to take the old man's picture
5   Try to speak to your father before you go
6   He didn't remember to send her a postcard
7   Why not try speaking to your father about it
8   They'd hate to go abroad for a holiday

a   even though he'd promised he would.
b   but she desperately needed one more for her collection so she went ahead.
c   he may be able to lend you the money you need, even if I can't.
d   so he was surprised to see it taking pride of place on her desk.
e   so she changed her mind and put the camera away.
f   strange language, strange food, etc. – they're always glad to get home.
g   it would mean they couldn't take the dog with them.
h   he'll be so upset if you leave without saying goodbye.

2 Make similar pairs of sentences of your own.

Writing

1 Look at these different ways of giving advice to someone.

You ought to ...	If I were you I'd ...
It's best to ...	You could always ...
It might be a good idea to ...	You must ...
You'd better ...	Why don't you ...?
What about ...?	

Discuss with a colleague which phrases you would use to offer a strong recommendation and which you would use to offer more tentative advice.

2 Add to the list two or three more phrases of your own, e.g. What about ...? You might as well ...

✳ 3 Imagine that a British friend has received an invitation to a traditional wedding in your country and has written to you for advice.

> Dear Bet,
>
> How are you? Guess what? Do you remember the girl I worked with when I was last visiting you? Well she's getting married at the end of the month and was kind enough to send me an invitation. Apparently her family is really traditional and it's going to be a big affair. I don't want to make a fool of myself so I thought I'd ask you to fill me in on what a traditional wedding in your part of the world is like. I'll be coming over on about the 26th or so ...

Write a suitable reply to your friend's letter. Reassure your friend by briefly describing what normally happens at a traditional wedding and by offering appropriate advice on what to wear, what sort of present to give, and generally how to behave. Write approximately 250 words.

Ways of learning: talking about grammar and vocabulary

1   In learning a language it is useful to know the common terms used in dictionaries and grammar reference books. Look at this list.

article	conjunction
noun	pronoun
adjective	modal verb
preposition	verbal auxiliary
adverb	infinitive
participle	verb

Match each term above to a definition below:

1 a word that describes a noun or pronoun
2 a word that describes the manner of a verb
3 a word or phrase that joins together other words or word groups
4 a word such as 'a', 'an' or 'the'
5 a word that is the basic form of a verb
6 a group of verbs which express degrees of possibility and necessity
7 a word used to refer to a person, thing or abstract idea
8 a form of a verb used in compound tenses or as an adjective
9 a word such as 'on', 'to' or 'by'
10 a word used to replace a noun or noun-group already mentioned
11 a word that indicates an action or a state
12 a word used before a main verb to show tense, etc.

2   Read the text below and underline an example of each of the parts of speech listed in activity **1**.

Good manners, in the broad sense of courteous, thoughtful behaviour, aren't something to be wheeled out on special occasions and put aside the rest of the time. A little consideration for others goes a long way towards improving the quality of life and lowering stress in numerous situations, every day of the week. Families co-exist more calmly with a polite approach on all sides, and courtesy can help smooth the path in all those ordinary transactions that take place in shops, restaurants, on public transport, in the office or on the telephone. And, after all, it costs nothing to be polite!

Vocabulary summary

Work in teams. Each team must list fifteen different words to do with **Family matters** and **Habits and customs** and against each add the part of speech (e.g. nouns, adjectives, adverbs, verbs, participle, infinitive). Each team then takes it in turns to read out a word from their list while the other teams try to guess the correct part of speech for each word. The first team with the correct answer wins the point. The team scoring the most points is the overall winner.

C

Paper 3 (English in Use): Section A

Introduction

CAE Paper 3 contains three sections – A, B and C. In this unit the focus is on Section A. (Details of Sections B and C can be found in Units 8 and 13.)

Read this paragraph.

In the first section of Paper 3 there are two blank-filling tasks, each based on an authentic text. The first is a gap-filling exercise which focuses on vocabulary, with multiple-choice items; the second is a gap-filling exercise which focuses on structural words. Each passage will have 15 blanks and will be approximately 250 words in length.

Now cover the paragraph and describe to a partner what Section A of CAE Paper 3 is like.

Choosing the best words to complete a text

1 The first of the gap-filling exercises in Paper 3 focuses on vocabulary, or 'lexical' items. These are the words which carry much of the meaning of a text – nouns, verbs, adjectives, etc. For each gap, four different options are offered to you.

Look at this example:

In this week's issue, our resident film critic discusses the etiquette of cinema going, and the (0) .... who prefer chewing hot-dogs, slurping drinks, gossiping and rustling crisp packets to actually watching the film. Fair complaint, or just cinema snobbery?

A spectators **B** observers **C** witnesses **D** audiences

What do the four options **A–D** have in common?

2 Fill in these sentences to explain the meaning of each of the four words.

'Spectators' are people who ....

'Observers' are people who ....

'Witnesses' are people who ....

'Audiences' are people who ....

3 Decide on the best answer to complete the gap in the text in activity **1**. Remember to think about:

- which word fits best in terms of meaning within the sentence

- which word fits best in terms of collocation

- which word fits best in terms of meaning across the whole text

Explain your choice.

48

Exam practice 1

1 For questions **1–10**, read the text and then decide which word below it best fits each space. The exercise begins with the example (**0**).

> In this week's issue, our resident film critic discusses the etiquette of cinema going, and the (**0**) ...audiences... who prefer chewing hot-dogs, slurping drinks, gossiping and rustling crisp packets to actually watching the film. Fair complaint, or just cinema snobbery?
>
> It's the munchers and talkers, not those who complain about them, who are (**1**) .... other people's (**2**) .... pleasures and the (**3**) .... seem to me to be self-evident. Junk (**4**) .... and even popcorn and choc ices, when eaten in a (**5**) .... and possibly crowded space, are inclined to demand living space. They spread themselves about – usually onto other people's (**6**) .... Crisps, peanuts and boiled sweets make a lot of noise, first when being (**7**) .... then when being crunched or sucked. These are definite (**8**) .... , especially if you yourself – having merely come to see and hear the film – are not eating and not therefore generously (**9**) .... your fried onions, mustard and ketchup with the trousers of the stranger in the (**10**) .... seat.

0	**A** spectators	**B** observers	**C** witnesses	**D** audiences
1	**A** damaging	**B** spoiling	**C** hurting	**D** injuring
2	**A** simple	**B** natural	**C** primary	**D** elementary
3	**A** excuses	**B** accusations	**C** reasons	**D** complaints
4	**A** diets	**B** meals	**C** dishes	**D** foods
5	**A** confined	**B** closed	**C** reduced	**D** narrow
6	**A** dress	**B** costume	**C** outfit	**D** clothing
7	**A** unpacked	**B** untied	**C** unwrapped	**D** unfolded
8	**A** inconveniences	**B** amusements	**C** anxieties	**D** irritations
9	**A** exchanging	**B** dividing	**C** splitting	**D** sharing
10	**A** next	**B** nearest	**C** previous	**D** closest

2 Look over your answers and compare them with a partner's. If you made mistakes, try to identify the reasons why.

Finding the missing words in a text

1 The second gap-filling exercise in Section A of Paper 3 focuses on structural items. These are usually words such as prepositions, conjunctions, pronouns and verbal auxiliaries which are used to link other words and phrases together. In this exercise there are no options for you to choose from; you must think of a suitable word yourself.

In the following passage there are several words missing. Can you replace them?

> Etiquette will never go out of fashion as long (1) .... people get married and buried, meet each other, visit friends, throw parties, go to work or eat out. Knowing how to behave (2) .... any situation makes you feel more confident and puts people around you at ease. And that's why etiquette exists: to oil the wheels of social exchange and make life pleasanter and (3) .... relaxed for everyone.

2 The statements below describe what different people did when they tried to fill the gaps. Tick the approaches you used and add any extra ones.

'I looked at where the word is located in the sentence.' ☒

'I tried to decide what part of speech it was.' ☑

'I looked at the word before it and the word after it.' ☑

'I thought about the topic of the text.' ☒

'I used my common sense.' ☒

'I looked to see if it was part of a common phrase.' ☑

'I used what I know about the world.' ☒

'I tried to see if it might be similar to other phrases in the text.' ☑

'I looked at the text before and after the gap.' ☑

Should you use all these approaches for each gap?

Exam practice 2

1 Continue reading the text on the etiquette of cinema-going and decide on a suitable word to fill each of the gaps **1–10**. The exercise begins with the example (**0**).

> And yet the worst nuisance is not the eating (**0**) ...but.... the talking. People converse in the cinema exactly (**1**) .... they do at home while watching the telly. Those (**2**) .... have seen the film before tell their companions – and (**3**) .... else within earshot – what is going to happen next. And those who have not seen the film before wonder, just as audibly, (**4**) .... might conceivably be about to happen next. Anyone who asks (**5**) .... to keep their voices down will be told to shut up or can even be offered violence. Now let's be clear about (**6**) .... : films are best seen in cinemas, of course they are. And really (**7**) .... I'm saying is, that (**8**) .... everyone showed a little consideration, going to the pictures could again be a pleasure for us all and not just for those who regard the cinema as a place to hold picnics (**9**) .... catch up with the latest gossip. Come on, now – is that too (**10**) .... to ask?

2 Look over your answers and think about the following questions. Does the word you have chosen to fill each gap

- **fit the grammatical slot?**
- **fit with the word(s) immediately before and after it?**
- **fit with the meaning of the sentence?**
- **fit with the meaning of the text as a whole?**

Work with a partner and compare your answers. If you made mistakes, try to identify the reasons why.

Ways of learning: strategies for completing gaps in a text

1 Draw up a list of five pieces of advice you would give another student to help them with either the first gap-filling exercise in this section or the second gap-filling exercise in this section.

2 In a group, agree on ten 'helpful hints' which are relevant to this section of CAE Paper 3 and design a poster to display these on your classroom wall.

Four

A

Health on holiday

Starter activities

1 How could holidays in these places make you ill?

2 Look at the words below. Tick the ones you associate with holidays.

stress	suntan	improved muscle tone
vitality	tiredness	relaxation
insomnia	depression	high blood pressure
exhaustion	bites	

Compare your answers.

3 Here are some of the illnesses associated with holidays. What can cause them?

upset stomach	sprained joints	headaches
sore feet	cuts	hangovers
broken limbs	sunburn	bites

And here are some remedies. Why might you take them on holiday with you?

seasickness pills	bandages	elastoplast
aspirin	antiseptic cream	sun cream
insect repellent	brandy	

How do you pronounce these illnesses and remedies? Check your pronunciation by saying them to one another.

4 Have you ever suffered from any of the above illnesses on holiday? Tell your partner(s) what happened.

Listening

1 You will hear twelve questions about illness on holiday. Listen to each one and then give your answer immediately.

2 Listen to these words and repeat them, paying particular attention to the stress.

accident	bandage	mosquito	aspirin
chemist	sunburn	insurance	elastoplast
poisoning	injection	medicine	pregnant

Now say them to yourself or to a partner.

3 You'll hear seven sentences twice. Write down the stressed word(s) in each sentence, e.g. Number 1: elastoplast, chemist, supermarket.

4 Now listen to the sentences again and repeat them, paying particular attention to word and sentence stress.

5 Look at the stressed words you wrote down. What kind of words (e.g. adjectives, prepositions, nouns, etc.) are they? Why do you think these kinds of words are often stressed in English?

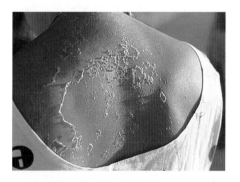

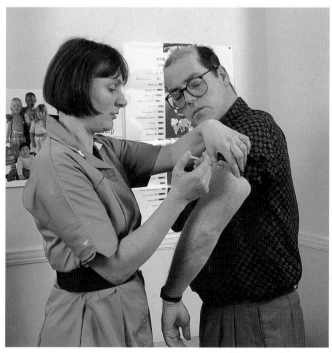

Grammar reminder: modal verbs expressing obligation and permission

The meaning of certain modal verbs is sometimes a little unclear to learners of English. Below are some of the modal verbs and their meanings that can cause problems.

Imposing obligation:	You must wash all this fruit very carefully. You shouldn't eat unwashed vegetables. You really ought to get some injections.
Granting exemption:	They needn't have a check-up at this stage. I don't have to take those pills any more.
Imposing prohibition:	You mustn't go out till you're fully recovered. You can't go unless you take out a health insurance. You can't swim now – you've only just eaten.
Asking about obligation/ exemption:	Do I need to put this mosquito cream on? Do I have to take more pills? Must I really go to the doctor? Don't I have to eat before taking this medicine?
Giving permission:	You can travel there – there's no risk at all. You may eat whatever you want now – you're completely recovered.
Asking for permission:	Can I smoke in here? May I leave now?

Write a sentence for each of the meanings, then compare your sentences with a partner's.

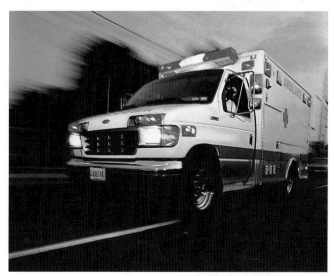

Reading

1 The article on page 53 is about holiday stress. Before you read it make a list of reasons why you think holidays might be stressful, e.g.
It gets crowded everywhere.

Compare your answers with a partner's.

2 Now read through the article to see if it mentions any of the reasons you listed. Tick them and make a note of any other reasons it mentions.

3 Which of the following words from the article collocate with one another? Match them across the groups as in the example, e.g.
foreign currency

high	**fitness**
family	**circle**
vicious	**currency**
crowded	**relationships**
foreign	**blood pressure**
delayed	**airports**
physical	**flights**
deeply	**your batteries**
recharge	**disappointed**
tackle	**problems**
high	**hopes**

4 Look at the article again and find at least three words you can associate with:

a illnesses
b domestic arrangements
c stress

Your thoughts

- **Can holidays really be as stressful as this article suggests?**
- **Have you ever been on any stressful holidays?**

Writing

Read through the article again and for each stress problem it mentions, note down a suggestion of your own for a way of avoiding or preventing that problem. Then use your notes to complete the instructions for the advice leaflet below.

How to avoid the holiday blues

- If everyone wants to do something different, don't be a martyr; include your plans too.
- Arrange health and holiday insurance for your peace of mind.
-
-
-

How to beat holiday stress

Sunshine and Sangria may sound like the ideal cure for all your ills. But holidays can also be a source of stress – and that can affect your health. So if you want to really relax while you're away, follow these simple rules. By Shirley Davenport

Stress is now a major health issue of the Nineties. One survey put the annual cost to British business at £1.3 billion in absenteeism, with around 100 million workdays lost each year.

If left unchecked, stress can lead to illnesses which affect physical fitness, such as heart disease, high blood pressure and severe aches and pains, particularly
10 neck- and backache.

Yet although work is frequently cited as the main cause, holiday stress can be even more damaging. The traditional summer break, regarded by most people as the highlight of their year, can actually undermine health and put pressure on family relationships.

Instead of tackling the problems before they go away, a lot of people believe a
20 holiday will work magic for them. But holidays are spent in strange places where it may be difficult for tense people to relax.

They may feel even more disturbed if they get the idea that others are having a more wonderful time than they are. It becomes a complex vicious circle, with people coming home more stressed than before they went away.

30 Holiday preparations involve a series of mini-stresses, like tying up loose ends at work, remembering to cancel the milk and newspapers, boarding the family pet, arranging foreign currency, last-minute shopping, working out how much spending money to take and worrying about securing the home against burglars.

40 Crowded airports, delayed flights and packed hotels are also major stress factors for most holidaymakers.

Stress experts say we should take two or three short holidays a year instead of a long mid-summer one.

Professor Cary Cooper, psychologist at the University of Manchester Institute of Science and Technology, says: "If your one holiday a year turns out to be a disaster you have nothing to look forward
50 to for another year."

"A big mistake is to take your holidays according to the month, instead of when your body tells you it is time to unwind. July and August can be the two most disastrous months for holidays because there are always crowds, queues and delays. Some people like crowds, but holidays are a time for peace, quiet and personal space."

60 "Another strain is not being able to do what you want on holiday, so you end up compromising, and no-one has a really good time. If the holiday is self-catering, a wife is going to feel stressed at having to cook, look after the children and do all the other chores she handles at home, while her husband goes off to play golf."

"Disappointment is very stressful. If you have high hopes of your holiday and it
70 lets you down, you won't be refreshed, and may feel in need of another holiday. It's not going to kill you, but it won't help you to recharge your batteries."

"Some people become over-anxious when they are going on holiday," says Professor Ben Fletcher, head of psychology at Hertfordshire University, "and worry about what happens if they are taken ill. So, for them, their chosen
80 holiday spot is not a secure place."

"Many couples and families are simply not used to spending a long time with each other, and some people cannot cope with that. Others may try to establish who is boss on holiday, while a lot of people just find it difficult to relax."

(Foresight Magazine)

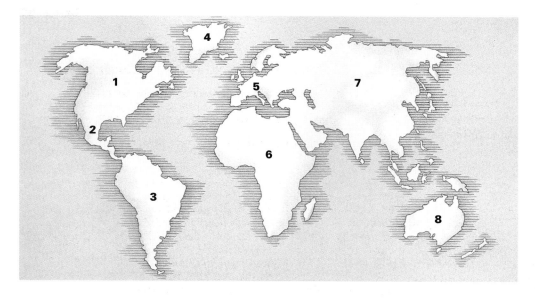

B

Health around the world

Starter activities

1 Can you identify the areas of the world on the map? Are there any serious illnesses you particularly associate with any of them? Compare your answers with a partner.

2 Match the words below to the areas of the world where you think they're most common.

cancer	**respiratory diseases**
infectious diseases	**strokes**
circulatory diseases	**car accidents**
heart diseases	

Listening

1 You are going to hear two people talking about health in Algeria and the UK. What do you think they might say about:

a the kinds of illnesses that occur in Algeria and the UK?
b the reasons for differences in the kinds of illnesses occurring in each country?
c the different ways of treating illnesses in the two countries?

2 List twelve words you think might occur in the conversation. Compare your answers.

3 Listen to check your answers to activities **1** and **2**.

4 Listen again and note down any relevant answers you didn't include at **1**.

Compare your answers.

Your thoughts

- **Why are there differences in the diseases that occur in different places?**
- **Are some parts of the world less healthy than others?**
- **How does your own country compare with Algeria and the UK?**

Reading

1 This is an article giving the results of a survey of exercise and health in Britain. Read quickly through it to decide which of the headlines on the right best fits the article.

a WE ALL NEED TO BE MORE ACTIVE – BRITISH OVERWEIGHT

b MEN FITTER THAN WOMEN CONCLUDES SURVEY

c MOST ADULTS TOO UNFIT FOR A HEALTHY LIFE

d BRITISH EATING HABITS MUST CHANGE

Chris Mihill
Medical Correspondent

SEVEN out of 10 men and eight out of 10 women in England do not take enough exercise to keep themselves healthy, according to the largest ever survey into activity levels.

The survey, published yesterday by the Health Education Authority and the Sports Council interviewed 4,316 adults over the age of 16 about daily activity including sports and recreation pastimes, with two-thirds of the group being given laboratory assessments of fitness levels.

One third of men and two-thirds of women were unable to continue walking at three miles an hour up a one in 20 slope without becoming breathless and having to stop. Half of women over 55 could not sustain a walking pace on level ground for several minutes. Among 16–24 year olds, 60 per cent of men and 91 per cent of women were below activity levels

necessary for a fit and healthy life. Thirty per cent of men and 50 per cent of women aged 65–74 had insufficient strength in their thigh muscles, making tasks such as rising from a chair without using their arms difficult.

The survey found the fittest 10 per cent of men aged 65–74 having a higher aerobic capacity than the least fit 10 per cent of those aged 25–34.

Dr Jacky Chambers, director of public health for the Health Education Authority, said the survey had found 48 per cent of men and 40 per cent of women were overweight, compared with 39 per cent

and 32 per cent in 1980. If the trend continued, most of the population would be overweight by the year 2000.

Professor Peter Fenton, head of physiology at Nottingham University, who acted as scientific adviser to the survey, said although the levels of unfitness came as no surprise, they had to be scientifically quantified if policies were to be formulated to improve activity levels.

There was growing evidence that even moderate physical activity could confer protection against heart disease and strokes as well as improving general well-being and the quality of life.

Sir Donald Maitland, chairman of the authority, said: "Almost everyone in the country can benefit from being a little more active. Just making small changes like using the stairs instead of the lift or walking and cycling instead of taking the car can help people to begin to feel the benefits of living a more active, healthier and enjoyable life."

The survey divided activity levels into five categories, with level five being people who exercised vigorously at least 12 times for 20 minutes or more a session in the previous four weeks, and level zero those who took no exercise.

	Men(%)	Women(%)
Level 5	14	4
Level 4	12	10
Level 3	23	27
Level 2	18	25
Level 1	16	18
Level 0	??	??

(The Guardian)

2 Read the article again just to find the following information:

1 Who take more exercise, men or women?
2 Who are more overweight, men or women?
3 What percentage of the population doesn't take enough exercise?
4 What does the article generally recommend?
5 What does the article recommend in particular?

3 The following expressions with numbers are all taken from the article. How do you say them?

$\frac{1}{3}$	10%	$\frac{2}{3}$
91%	7/10 men	$\frac{1}{2}$
4316	men aged 65–74	48%
39%	40%	32%
8/10 women	the year 1980	the year 2000

Check your answers. Listen and repeat the expressions.

4 Write down at least ten fractions, numbers or percentages, then ask your partner how to say them in English.

Your thoughts

- **Where would you put yourself in the table in the article?**
- **List the sporting and non-sporting activities you could do to be fitter. What stops you doing them?**

Speaking: agreeing and disagreeing

1 Look at the four discussion points below. Do you agree with them? Mark them **A** (agree) or **D** (disagree).

- **People in my country are generally healthy.**
- **Nations are usually healthy if they are rich.**
- **The British are generally healthy.**
- **Medical research should concentrate on preventing rather than curing diseases.**
- **Rich nations should give much more aid to solve the health problems of poorer nations.**

2 List the expressions of agreement and disagreement that you know, then compare your list with a partner's and decide what degree of agreement or disagreement the expressions express, e.g. strong, mild, etc.

Here are some examples to start you off.

agreement: *I agree, that's right.*
disagreement: *I really can't agree, definitely not.*

3 In pairs or small groups, discuss your answers to activity 1 using as many expressions from activity 2 as appropriate.

Grammar analysis: the definite article

1 In the text below most of the lines are correct but some are incorrect because they contain an unnecessary word. In each space, tick the correct lines and write in the incorrect word for the incorrect line.

The survey, published yesterday by the Health Education	1 ....
Authority and the Sports Council, interviewed 4,316 adults	2 ....
over the age of 16 about daily activity including sports and	3 ....
recreation pastimes, with two-thirds of the group being	4 ....
given laboratory assessments of the fitness levels.	5 ....
Dr Jacky Chambers, director of public health for the Health	6 ....
Education Authority, said the survey had found 48 per cent	7 ....
of men and 40 per cent of women were overweight, compared	8 ....
with 39 per cent and 32 per cent in 1980. If the trend continued,	9 ....
most of the population would be overweight by the year 2000.	10 ....
Professor Peter Fenton, head of physiology at the Nottingham	11 ....
University, who acted as scientific adviser to the survey, said	12 ....
although the levels of unfitness came as no surprise,	13 ....
they had to be scientifically quantified if policies were to	14 ....
be formulated to improve the activity levels.	15 ....
There was growing evidence that even moderate physical	16 ....
activity could confer the protection against heart disease	17 ....
and strokes as well as improving general well-being and	18 ....
the quality of life.	19 ....

Now check your answers by reading the article on page 55.

2 Use your work in activity **1** to complete the following rules.

Rules for the use of the definite article in English
In English the definite article is used to refer to something specific and that has usually been talked about (a) .... in the conversation or piece of writing. For this reason we use 'the' in the first of the following sentences but not in the second.

- The people who read the article might listen to the advice it gave.
- People don't usually listen to advice.

In the first sentence the article and the advice have both been (b) .... previously and are therefore (c) .... rather than general. In the second sentence, however, people and advice are referred to (d) ....

N.B. Sometimes it is the speaker's attitude towards something that decides whether it is considered specific or not.

There are exceptions to the above rule.
The definite article (e) .... be used before:

- plural (f) .... , e.g. the Netherlands, the United States
- rivers, e.g. (g) .... (h) ....
- mountain (i) .... , e.g. the Andes, the Alps
- things that are considered unique, e.g. The earth revolves around (j) .... sun; Many people take the train to work.

3 Complete the following sentences with 'the' where necessary. You may find that in certain sentences it is possible either to use or not use 'the'. Why is this?

a 7 out of 10 of .... men surveyed did not take enough exercise.

b .... meat eaten these days doesn't contain as much fat as some years ago.

c You should avoid using .... lift when possible.

d .... work can be good for your mental health.

e .... exercise I did as a child made me love keeping fit.

f Many people don't realise that .... walking is valuable exercise.

g To travel to .... moon you would need to be pretty fit.

h People's genes may affect their health more than .... way they live.

i .... older people in the survey were generally unfit.

j We should try to walk up .... stairs whenever we can.

Vocabulary summary

You are going to hear some questions checking whether you remember some of the vocabulary in the first two sections of this unit. Divide into three or more teams and listen to the questions. The first member of any team to answer the question correctly gets a point for the team. The team with the most points at the end is the winner.

You might want to read through Sections A and B to revise before doing this quiz.

C

Paper 4 (Listening): Sections A and B

Introduction

CAE Paper 4 contains four sections. In this unit we focus on Sections A and B. Advice on Sections C and D can be found in Units 9 and 14.

1 You will hear on cassette details of the aims and content of Sections A and B of CAE Paper 4, as well as general instructions for the paper. Listen and complete the exam information table below.

Now check your answers with a partner and, if necessary, by listening to the cassette again.

2 Read through the exam information below then complete this table about your reactions to Sections A and B of CAE Paper 4.

	Section A	Section B
Which section seems easier? **Why?** **Which section seems more interesting?** **Why?** **Suggest ways in which you could help yourself prepare for these sections.**		

Compare and discuss your answers.

Exam information: the contents of Section A and Section B of CAE 4

Section A
Number of voices:
Section A is a monologue so you only hear one (1) ....
Number of times the extract is played:
You hear the monologue (2) ....
Length of the extract:
Approximately (3) .... minutes.
Possible text types:
You may hear an announcement or a radio (4) .... , a recorded telephone message, a talk or a (5) ....
Type of comprehension tested:
Understanding (6) .... of the text and the text as a (7) ....
Possible types of exam exercises:
Note-taking, box (8) .... , multiple-choice, etc.

Section B
Number of voices:
Section B is essentially a monologue too, though it may also contain short contributions or (9) .... from a (10) .... speaker.
Number of times the extract is played:
You hear this section (11) .... only.
Length of the extract:
It lasts (12) .... 2 minutes.
Possible text types:
These are the same as in Section A, except that they can also include (13) ....
Possible types of exam exercise:
The same as in Section A.

General information
Timing:
You are given time (14) .... each section to read it through, and there is also a (15) .... after each section. At the end of the paper you are given (16) .... minutes to transfer your answers to an (17) ....
Writing your answers:
You can write your answers in pencil or pen. While you are listening you write your answers on your (18) .... , then after all the sections of the listening are finished, you (19) .... your answers from the question paper to the answer sheet. You are given 10 minutes transfer time for the (20) .... paper.

Exam practice

Here is an example of a Section A and a Section B
listening exercise. Do the tasks as instructed.

Section A

You will hear the boy in the photo below talking about his illness. As you listen, complete in a few words the information for
questions **1–7**. When you have finished you will hear the piece again.

SCHOOL MEDICAL RECORD CARD

Name: John Hall
Age: 13
Illness: Haemophilia

1 Symptoms: ....

2 Medicine: ....

3 How medicine is taken: ....

4 Frequency of illness: ....

5 Activities not allowed: ....

6 Activities he does / has done : ....

7 Attitude to illness: *(Tick the appropriate adjective)*
    depressed ☐   worried ☐   indifferent ☐   positive ☐

Section B

Now look at Section B. You will hear an extract from a radio programme about the voice problems suffered by some famous
singers. Listen to the recording and then complete the information for questions **8–14**. Listen carefully as you will hear this piece
once only.

The radio programme mentions various factors which affect a singer's voice. Tick the correct column, according to whether the
programme indicates that each factor is good or bad for the voice.

	Good	Bad			Good	Bad
8 chatting with fans	☐	☐	**12**	low humidity	☐	☐
9 taking aspirin	☐	☐	**13**	long tours	☐	☐
10 regularly taking steroids	☐	☐	**14**	warming your voice down	☐	☐
11 air conditioning	☐	☐				

What do I need to remember?

UCLES (the Cambridge University Local Examinations Syndicate) brings out annual CAE Examination Reports. They are published each year and available from UCLES. Here is an extract from the report on Paper 4. Read it and underline in it those points which you think are relevant to you. Compare and discuss your answers.

> Teachers should encourage their students to limit the length of their answers in questions where the rubric clearly states 'using a number or a few words'. Nothing is gained by the candidate who writes more than is relevant and in any case the length of the box allowed for the answer in transfer to the OMR sheet is designed to cater for an approximate maximum of 3 words. Moreover, the candidate who writes unnecessarily long answers increases the likelihood of making a slip when transferring an answer. Training candidates to focus on the key word(s) of an answer and to reproduce exactly that in their answers to gap-fill questions will enable them to make more effective use of the time available.
>
> It is important to train students to be as accurate and as concise as possible and to carefully check spelling in the time available.
>
> Although Section B is heard ONCE only, it is clear from the statistical evidence that it is not always this section of the Test which candidates find significantly more difficult.

(Adapted by permission of the University of Cambridge Local Examinations Syndicate)

Ways of learning: dealing with listening in exams

1 Here are some aspects of listening exams that often cause problems. Tick the ones *you* find most difficult.

fast speed of delivery	☐	accent	☐
number of voices	☐	intonation	☐
word stress	☐	the meaning of grammar	☐
sentence stress	☐	the meaning of words	☐
length of the text	☐	other ...	☐

Now complete this table with your own problems and solutions

To improve my...	I could...
ability to cope with fast speed of delivery	• only listen for the information requested by the task • watch TV programmes in English
	• • •

Discuss your ideas with a partner.

2 Imagine you are writing the Cambridge CAE Examination Report. Write out five pieces of advice to students on how to perform best on Sections A and B.

Compare your answers, then design a poster giving advice on how to approach CAE 4 Sections A and B.

Five

A

Animal communication

Starter activities

1 Look at the photos of these different animals. How do they communicate with other members of the same species?

Can you think of any other ways animals communicate?

2 What are the different reasons why animals need to communicate?

Reading

1 Look at the text 'Teaching animals to talk' on page 61. Read it quickly to find out which animal has been used most successfully in experiments to teach animals to 'talk'.

✳ **2** Read the text in more detail and choose from **A–H** the type(s) of treatment each of these three animals received.

1	Gua	**A**	fed with a spoon
2	Viki	**B**	dressed like a baby
3	Washoe	**C**	forced to brush her teeth
		D	exposed to human speech
		E	brought up alongside a human child
		F	kept in a caravan
		G	taught sign language
		H	given intensive training schedules

3 Which words did Washoe use the following four signs to mean?

1 putting her finger on top of her wagging tongue
2 putting the tip of her finger on her nose and snorting
3 holding her fingertips together and touching her nostrils
4 rubbing her index finger against her teeth

Teaching animals to talk

In discussing attempts to teach language to animals it is important to distinguish mimicry from 'true' language. Parrots and mynah birds can imitate humans with uncanny accuracy. But it is unlikely that they ever understand what people are saying. There are reports of a grey parrot which could say 'Good morning' and 'Good evening' at the right times, and 'Good-bye' when guests left. But most talking birds are merely 'parrotting' back what they hear. For example, a budgerigar I knew heard a puppy being trained with words such as 'Sit!' 'Naughty boy!' and used to shriek 'Sit!' 'Naughty boy!' whenever anyone went near its cage, whether or not the dog was present.

Although psychologists have spent considerable time experimenting with mynah birds, it is perhaps not surprising that the results have been disappointing. Apes seem more promising candidates. Over the past fifty or so years several attempts have been made to teach human language to chimpanzees.

The first experiment was a failure. An animal named Gua was acquired by Professor and Mrs Kellogg in 1931, when she was seven months old. She was brought up as if she was a human baby, and was fed with a spoon, bathed, pinned up in nappies, and continuously exposed to speech. Although she eventually managed to understand the meaning of over seventy single words, she never spoke. Gua showed clearly that it was *not* just lack of opportunity which prevents a chimp from learning language. The Kelloggs' son Donald, who was brought up alongside Gua, and was approximately the same age, grew up speaking normally.

A second chimp acquired by Keith and Cathy Hayes in 1947 also proved disappointing. Viki was given intensive coaching in English. She eventually learnt four words: PAPA, MAMA, CUP, UP. But these were very unclearly articulated, and remained the sum total of Viki's utterances after three years of hard training.

It is now clear why these attempts failed. Chimps are not physiologically capable of uttering human sounds. More recent experiments have avoided this trap and used sign language, the manipulation of tokens, or button pressing. Let us consider some of this later research.

Over the past twenty years, teaching language to apes has become a popular pastime among American psychologists. There was a minor population explosion of 'talking chimps' in the 1970s. Washoe was one of the first chimps to acquire a significant amount of language.

Washoe's exact age is unknown. She is a female chimp acquired by Professor and Mrs Gardner in 1966, when she was thought to be approximately a year old. She has been taught to use modified American sign language (ASL). In this system signs stand for words. For example, Washoe's word for 'sweet' is made by putting her finger on the top of her tongue, while wagging the tongue. Her word for 'funny' is signalled by pressing the tip of her finger on to her nose, and uttering a snort.

Washoe acquired her language in a fairly 'natural' way. The Gardners kept her continuously surrounded by humans who communicated with her and each other by signs. They hoped that some of this would 'rub off' on her. Sometimes they asked her to imitate them, or tried to correct her. But there were no rigorous training schedules.

Even so, teaching a wild chimpanzee can be quite a problem: 'Washoe can become completely diverted from her original object, she may ask for something entirely different, run away, go into a tantrum, or even bite her tutor.' But her progress was impressive and, at least in the early stages, her language development was not unlike that of a human child.

First, she acquired a number of single words, for example, COME, GIMME, HURRY, SWEET, TICKLE – which amounted to thirty-four after twenty-one months, but later crept up to well over one hundred. The number is accurate because a rota of students and researchers made sure that Washoe, who lived in a caravan in the Gardners' garden, was never alone when she was awake. And a sign was assumed to be acquired only after Washoe had used it spontaneously and appropriately on consecutive days.

Washoe's speech clearly had meaning. She had no difficulty in understanding that a sign 'means' a certain object or action, as was shown by her acquisition of the word for 'toothbrush' (index finger rubbed against teeth). She was forced, at first against her will, to have her teeth brushed after every meal. Consequently, she had seen the sign for 'toothbrush' on numerous occasions, though she had never used it herself. One day, when she was visiting the Gardners' home she found a mug of toothbrushes in the bathroom. Spontaneously, she made the sign for 'toothbrush'. She was not asking for a toothbrush, as they were within reach. Nor was she asking to have her teeth brushed, a procedure she hated. She appeared simply to be 'naming' the object. Similarly, Washoe made the sign for 'flower' (holding the fingertips of one hand together and touching the nostrils with them) when she was walking towards a flower garden, and another time when she was shown a picture of flowers.

Washoe could also generalize from one situation to another, as was clear from her use of the sign meaning 'more'. Like all chimps, she loved being tickled, and she would pester any companion to continue tickling her by using the 'more' sign. At first the sign was specific to the tickling situation. Later, she used it to request continuation of another favourite activity – being pushed across the floor in a laundry basket. Eventually, she extended the 'more' sign to feeding and other activities. Similarly the word for 'key' referred originally only to the key used to unlock the doors and cupboards in Washoe's caravan. Later, she used the sign spontaneously to refer to a wide variety of keys, including car ignition keys. Her 'speech' also incorporated a limited amount of displacement, since she could ask for absent objects and people.

(The Articulate Mammal)

4 Find as many verbs and adjectives as you can from the text to collocate with 'language', e.g. to mimic language, true language.
The words in the table all come from the text. Complete the table, e.g. *construct , construction, constructive*

Verb	Noun	Adjective
construct	construction	constructive
acquire		
understand		
speak		
	meaning	
	communication	

Your thoughts

- **What do you think about these experiments on animals?**
- **Why do you think people are so interested in trying to communicate with animals?**

Listening

1 You will hear an extract from a radio programme about an experiment to teach dolphins to 'talk'. Listen to find out:

a whether the experiment was successful.

b whether the speaker on the programme accepts the research findings.

2 Listen again and this time fill in the missing details of the experiment below using only one or two words.

STAGE 1

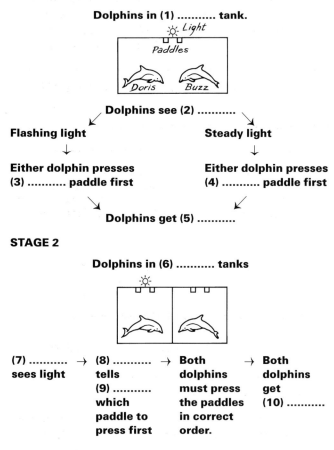

Dolphins in (1) .... tank.

Dolphins see (2) ....

Flashing light → Either dolphin presses (3) .... paddle first

Steady light → Either dolphin presses (4) .... paddle first

Dolphins get (5) ....

STAGE 2

Dolphins in (6) .... tanks

(7) .... sees light → (8) .... tells (9) .... which paddle to press first → Both dolphins must press the paddles in correct order → Both dolphins get (10) ....

Speaking

1 Work with a partner and decide who will be Student A and who will be Student B. Student A should describe the picture on page 212 while Student B looks at the set of pictures on page 217 and tries to decide which picture is being described. At the end you can both compare your pictures.

2 Change roles and carry out the same tasks with different pictures. Student B should describe the picture on page 217 while Student A looks at the set of pictures on page 212 and tries to decide which picture is being described.

Grammar reminder: prepositions of position/direction/time/manner/purpose

> **Remember: Prepositions can be used to express different concepts in English, e.g.**
> **position, direction, manner, reason/purpose, time**

Look at these sentences. Which of the five concepts above is being expressed by the prepositions in *italics*?

a Human sounds are produced by means of vocal chords located *in* the throat.

b Animal talk consists of a few relatively basic signals that are necessary *for* survival.

c Snakes and reptiles can detect vibrations passing *through* the ground.

d Crabs and lobsters warn or threaten others *by* vibrating a claw until it rattles.

e Certain researchers feel that man may be able to communicate with animals *within* the next few decades.

Now complete sentences **1–10** using the prepositions below. You may not need to use all the prepositions and there may be more than one possible answer.

Position	Direction	Period of Time	Manner	Reason/ Purpose
between	through	for	by	for
in	to	within	with	as
within	along	in	in	
on	towards	until		
over	across	after		
above		above		

1 Parrots and mynah birds can imitate humans ..... surprising accuracy.

2 Viki the chimp had only learnt four words ..... three years of hard training.

3 The senses of smell and taste are highly developed ..... snakes and lizards.

4 ..... the past twenty years, teaching language ..... chimps has become very common.

5 Lobsters and crabs have taste buds ..... the bottom of their feet.

6 Washoe acquired her language ..... a fairly 'natural' way.

7 There was a minor population explosion of 'talking chimps' ..... the 1970s.

8 Washoe loved being pushed ..... the floor in a laundry basket.

9 The sounds made by frogs are used ..... threats and warnings, and ..... territorial defence.

10 When they discover a food source, bees return ..... the hive and inform the others of its location and distance ..... doing a specialised dance ..... the surface of the hive.

B

Reading the signals

Starter activities

1 Look at the illustrations above. Write two adjectives which you think describe the attitude or feelings of each person illustrated, e.g. disgruntled, bored

2 Work with a partner and compare your adjectives. Discuss how the people in the illustrations are showing their attitudes and feelings. Agree together on three adjectives for each illustration.

3 Look at this cartoon. What do you think is the answer to the question the two people are asking themselves?

How come no-one talks to me?

Listening

1 Some people would say that the two people in the cartoon have a problem with their 'body language'. Discuss with a partner what the phrase 'body language' means and then complete the following sentence:

'Body language' is ....

Why do you think body language is important? Write down your reason(s).

Body language is important because ....

....

2 Listen to a short extract from a talk on communication skills. As you listen, fill in the relevant information in the notes below using one or two words only. Listen carefully as you will hear this piece only once.

Communication Skills
Body language = one of most important conversational skills.
Research indicates (1) .... of communication is non-verbal.
Body language can communicate our (2) .... and (3) ....
Examples of *receptive* body language: open posture, (4) ....,
(5) ....
Examples of *non-receptive* body language: (6) ...., little eye contact, (7) ....
Non-receptive body language often leads to (8) .... conversations.
First impressions need to be (9) .... and (10) ....

3 Compare the definition and effects of body language given in the talk with the sentences you wrote down in activity **1**.

4 With a partner decide on two pieces of advice you would give to the people in the cartoon which might help them and then report your recommendations to the rest of the class.

1 A pleasant smile is a strong indication of a friendly and open attitude and a willingness to communicate. It is a positive, nonverbal signal sent with the hope that the other person will smile back. When you smile, you demonstrate that you have noticed the person in a positive manner. The other person considers it a compliment and will usually feel good. The result? The other person will usually smile back.

Smiling does not mean that you have to put on a phony face or pretend that you are happy all of the time. But when you see someone you know, or would like to make contact with, do smile. By smiling, you are demonstrating an open attitude to conversation.

2 You might not realize that closed posture is the cause of many conversational problems. Typical closed posture is sitting with your arms and legs crossed and your hand covering your mouth or chin. This is often called the "thinking pose," but just ask yourself this question: Are you going to interrupt someone who appears to be deep in thought? Not only does this posture give off "stay away" signals to others, but it also prevents your main "signal sender" (your mouth) from being seen by others looking for receptive conversational signals. Without these receptive signals, another person will most likely avoid you and look for someone who appears to be more available for contact.

To overcome this habitual way of standing or sitting, start by keeping your hands away from your mouth, and keep your arms uncrossed. Crossed arms tend to indicate a defensive frame of mind, and thus one not particularly favorable to outside contact. They can also indicate impatience, displeasure, or judgment – any of which would discourage people from opening up.

Open posture is most effective when you place yourself within communicating distance of the other person – that is, within about five feet. Take care, however, not to violate someone's "personal space" by getting too close, too soon.

3 Leaning forward slightly while a person is talking to you indicates interest on your part, and shows you are listening to what the person is saying. This is usually taken as a compliment by the other person, and will encourage him to continue talking.

Often people will lean back with their hands over their mouth, chin, or behind their head in the "thinking" pose. This posture gives off signals of judgment, skepticism, and boredom from the listener. Since most people do not feel comfortable when they think they are being judged, this leaning-back posture tends to inhibit the speaker from continuing.

It's far better to lean forward slightly in a casual and natural way. By doing this, you are saying: 'I hear what you're saying, and I'm interested – keep talking!' This usually lets the other person feel that what he is saying is interesting, and encourages him to continue speaking.

4 In many cultures the most acceptable form of first contact between two people who are just meeting is a warm handshake. This is true when meeting members of the same or opposite sex – and not just in business, but in social situations, too. In nearly every situation, a warm and firm handshake is a safe and positive way of showing an open and friendly attitude toward the people you meet.

Be the first to extend your hand in greeting. Couple this with a friendly 'Hello', a nice smile, and your name, and you have made the first step to open the channels of communication between you and the other person.

5 The strongest of the nonverbal gestures are sent through the eyes. Direct eye contact indicates that you are listening to the other person, and that you want to know about her.

Eye contact should be natural and not forced or overdone. It is perfectly okay to have brief periods of eye contact while you observe other parts of the person's face – particularly the mouth. When the person smiles, be sure to smile back. But always make an effort to return your gaze to the person's eyes as she speaks. It is common to look up, down, and all around when speaking to others, and it's acceptable not to have eye contact at all times.

Too much eye contact, especially if it is forced, can be counterproductive. If you stare at a person, or leer in a suspicious manner, the other person may feel uncomfortable and even suspicious about your intentions. A fixed stare can appear as aggressive behavior if it takes the form of a challenge as to who will look away first.

Reading

1 Look at the text about body language on page 64. Read it quickly and match the most appropriate illustration **A–E** to each of the sections **1–5**.

2 Now match one of the headings **a–f** to each of the five sections.

a Eye contact
b Forward lean
c Smile

d Stand close
e Open posture
f Touch

3 Read the text again more carefully and note down any practical suggestions on positive body language.

4 Use the information in the text to complete the grid showing the messages which different postures send out. The first example has been done for you.

Posture/gesture	Message
smile	'I am keen to communicate'
arms/legs crossed	
open posture	
leaning forward	
leaning back	
warm handshake	
nod of the head / eye contact	

5 In the text find as many noun phrases (adjective + noun) as possible which describe different types of body language, e.g. pleasant/nice smile, phony face.

6 Collocate an adjective from list A with a noun from list B to produce as many phrases as possible. You can use the same noun with more than one adjective.

A
strong
friendly
open
positive
non-verbal
conversational
receptive
defensive
personal
brief
social
outside
first

B
indication
space
attitude
situations
problems
periods
signals
step
frame of mind
contact

How many different adjectives can you find in the text which can collocate with the words 'way' and 'manner'?

Your thoughts

- To what extent do you agree with the advice given in the text?
- How far would you personally wish to adopt the advice given?

Ways of learning: awareness of body language

The body language of individuals may vary in two important ways:

- cultural background
- personality

Variation according to cultural background

1 Make a list of any gestures or postures which you know can have different meanings in different cultures, e.g. nodding your head. Compare and discuss your lists.

2 Look at the following short extract from a business handbook which was written to give practical advice to English speaking visitors to Turkey.

> *Greeting – It is usual to greet people with a loose handshake. It is not considered polite to grasp hands firmly. It is normal to shake hands on meeting everyone in a group and again upon leaving. Kissing by touching both cheeks is a common form of greeting and leavetaking among close friends.*

Write a paragraph which would offer similar advice to visitors to your own country. Compare your advice with a partner's and then discuss any issues which arise.

Variation according to personality

Think about your own body language. How comfortable do you feel when doing the following:

very comfortable → very uncomfortable

smiling at people you don't know?
shaking hands firmly?
looking someone straight in the eye?
sitting with your leg touching someone else's leg?
making expressive gestures with your hands?

Discuss your views with a partner.

Grammar analysis: substitution

1 Look at these sentences and answer the questions which accompany them.

1 **A pleasant smile is a strong indication of a friendly and open attitude and a willingness to communicate. (It) is a positive, nonverbal signal.**

Does the circled word refer back to

- **a** a pleasant smile?
- **b** a strong indication?
- **c** a friendly and open attitude?
- **d** a willingness to communicate?

2 **Typical closed posture is sitting with your arms and legs crossed, and your hand covering your mouth or chin. (This) is often called the 'thinking pose'.**

Does the circled word refer back to

- **a** closed posture?
- **b** your arms and legs crossed?
- **c** your mouth and chin?
- **d** sitting with your arms and legs crossed, and your hand covering your mouth or chin?

3 **Often people will lean back with their hands over their mouth, chin, or behind their head in the thinking pose. (Such a posture) gives off signals of judgment, skepticism, and boredom from the listener.**

Does the circled phrase refer back to

- **a** leaning back with hands over their mouth, chin or behind their head?
- **b** hands over their mouth?
- **c** hands over their chin?
- **d** hands behind their head?

Think about the function of the circled item in each sentence.

2 When we speak or write, we make connections in language between the things we say. There are various ways of doing this and they provide links in our use of language. One way is to replace a word or phrase with another (i.e. substitution). When doing this, we refer back to something which has already been mentioned and establish a clear connection between different parts of a text.

3 There are several different types of word which are used to refer backwards in a text and establish connections. They include

a personal pronouns, e.g. The President warmly welcomed the new ambassador and together they posed for photographs.

b possessive pronouns, e.g. Although the lecturer spoke well on the whole, the audience found some of his mannerisms annoying.

c demonstrative pronouns, e.g. It's not a matter of what you say but of how you say it. That's what's really important.

d other referring words, e.g. There are many ways of showing an open and friendly attitude. One is a warm handshake; another is a pleasant smile.

Underline the referring word(s) in each of the four examples above.

4 The words below often refer backwards in a text. Sort them into the four types **a–d** illustrated in activity **3**.

the	they	its	many
that	their	those	then
this	he	such	there
him	she	these	theirs
her	it	another	
his	hers	so	
one	them	some	

5 In these sentences substitute the underlined phrases using suitable words from activity **4**.

1 **Leaning forward slightly while a person is talking to you indicates interest on your part and shows you are listening to what the person is saying. Leaning forward slightly usually lets the other person feel that what the other person is saying is interesting, and will encourage the other person to continue talking.**

2 **Crossed arms tend to indicate a defensive frame of mind and thus a frame of mind not particularly favorable to outside contact. Crossed arms can also indicate impatience, displeasure or judgment – any of which would discourage people from opening up.**

6 Now look once again at the paragraph in activity **2**. Put a circle round each linking word and then underline the phrase to which it refers.

Writing

Imagine that you recently attended a public lecture on the subject of 'Body language' by a famous personality. Write a short review of the lecture for publication in your local newspaper. Try to describe not only some of the content of the speaker's talk, but also your impressions of the speaker's own conversational skills. You should write approximately 250 words.

Vocabulary summary

1 Read the following short text and then decide which word, **A**, **B**, **C** or **D**, best fits each space.

Face-to-face conversation is a two-way process: you speak to me, I reply to you and so on. Two-way (1) ... depends on having a coding system that is understood by both (2) ... and receiver, and an agreed convention about (3) ... the beginning and end of the (4) ... . In speech, the coding system is a language like English or Spanish; the convention that one person speaks at a time may seem too obvious to (5) ... . In fact, the (6) ... that people use in conversations and meetings are often non-verbal. For example, lowering the pitch of the voice may mean the end of a sentence; a sharp intake of breath may signal the desire to (7) ..., catching the chairman's (8) ... may indicate the desire to speak in a formal setting like a (9) ..., a clenched fist may indicate anger. When these (10) ... signals are not possible, more formal signals may be needed.

1 **A** exchange **B** correspondence **C** interchange **D** communication
2 **A** transmitter **B** messenger **C** sender **D** announcer
3 **A** signalling **B** symbolising **C** signing **D** showing
4 **A** idea **B** theme **C** topic **D** message
5 **A** notice **B** mention **C** recognise **D** judge
6 **A** signs **B** signals **C** symptoms **D** symbols
7 **A** interfere **B** interchange **C** interrupt **D** intercept
8 **A** elbow **B** shoulder **C** hand **D** eye
9 **A** debate **B** chat **C** lecture **D** broadcast
10 **A** auditory **B** visual **C** verbal **D** sensory

2 Work in teams. Each team must write down a list of five words and then think of a way of communicating each of their five words to the other teams using sign language. The first team to guess the other team's words correctly scores a point. The winning team is the one with the most points at the end.

C

Paper 5 (Speaking): Phase A

Introduction

In this unit the focus is on Phase A of Paper 5. (Details and practice for Phase B can be found in Unit 10; Phases C and D are dealt with in Unit 15.)

1 First look at the general information below about the CAE Paper 5 (Speaking):

CERTIFICATE IN ADVANCED ENGLISH – PAPER 5 (SPEAKING)

Number of candidates: 2   Length: 15 minutes
Number of examiners: 2   Number of phases: 4

---

2 Now read this description of Phase A.

In Phase A the examiners will first of all introduce themselves to you and to your fellow candidate. Then it will be your turn to introduce yourself or perhaps to introduce your partner if you know each other already. After this, you may be asked some questions to find out more about you – your work or study, your interests or hobbies, how long you've been learning English and what your future plans are. You may also have to ask your partner questions on the same subjects. This phase of the Speaking Paper is designed to test your English conversation skills in a social context.

---

3 Now cover the text above and describe Phase A to a partner.

Introducing yourself or someone else

1 Listen to three examples of introductions between people. As you listen, tick the appropriate box to show whether the speakers are introducing themselves or someone else.

	1	2	3
Introducing themselves			
Introducing someone else			

2 Tick any of the following phrases which you remember being used in the extracts:

This is ☐   Can I introduce you to ☐

Hello, I'm ☐   My name's ☐

How do you do ☐   Pleased to meet you ☐

Nice to meet you ☐   I'd like you to meet ☐

Here's somebody you
should meet ☐

Listen to the three extracts again to check your answers.

3 Listen to some of these phrases and repeat each one, paying particular attention to the stress and intonation.

4 Listen to how the three extracts continue after the initial introduction. Tick the topics which the speakers talk about.

	1	2	3
Family			
Friends			
Background			
Work			

5 Listen to both parts of the three extracts again and note down any short phrases the speakers use to:

a show interest in what another speaker is saying
b agree with what another speaker is saying
c show understanding of what another speaker is saying
d contradict what another speaker is saying
e show they haven't heard or understood something another speaker is saying

Compare your notes with a partner's.

What should my body language be on meeting someone for the first time?

1 Think back to the ideas discussed in Section B of this unit. What practical advice on body language would you give to candidates preparing for the CAE Speaking Paper? For example:

Do:
smile on meeting the examiners / other candidate

Don't:
lean back in an uninterested manner

Compare your answers.

2 Work in pairs. Imagine that you are meeting your partner for the first time. Introduce yourself to him/her making use of what you have learned from the previous exercises in this section.

3 Work in groups of three. Practise introducing one member of the group to the third member, using the information you already know about him/her. Then change groups.

What are the important features of speaking ability?

In each phase of the CAE Speaking Paper, the examiners assess a candidate's spoken ability according to the features 1–5. Match each of the five features with its explanation A–E.

1 fluency
2 accuracy and range
3 pronunciation
4 task management
5 interactive communication

A the quality of individual sounds and features of intonation
B the speed and rhythm of speaking
C the organisation and use of language
D the variety and correctness of grammar and vocabulary
E the ability to be sensitive to other speakers

Order the five features above according to how easy or difficult you find them.

How can I improve my speaking ability?

1 Look at the suggestions in the right-hand column of following table. Try to add some more of your own.

To improve my...	I could...
speed and rhythm of speaking	spend more time listening to English on the radio.
variety and correctness of of the grammar and vocabulary hobbies/interests/work.	extend my knowledge vocabulary related to my
quality of individual sound and features of intonation	practise the stress patterns in long words.
ability to organise and use language appropriately for a given purpose	listen carefully to the for instructions for any task
ability to show sensitivity to other speakers	be a more active and cooperative listener.

2 Discuss your ideas with a partner.

3 Read the comments on candidate performance in the CAE Speaking Paper taken from a CAE Examination Report. As you read, underline three things which you find encouraging about the CAE Speaking Paper, and three things which you should remember in your preparation. Discuss your answers.

> Candidates were generally thought to have worked well together and to have found the experience less stressful than the traditional one-to-one interview.

> ... the social interaction phase worked well and seemed to put the candidates at their ease. The strongest candidates were those who were able to go beyond small talk to make interesting and original comments on topics raised during the interaction.

> Candidates should not feel that they will be advantaged by rehearsing Phase A with their partner. Candidates should be aware that genuine interaction will score better than memorised dialogue.

> Candidates should not be afraid to ask for repetition or clarification if they have not heard or understood what has been said.

Revision Exam Practice 1

Paper 1 (Reading): Multiple-choice

Read this magazine article. The text is followed by a number of questions or unfinished statements about the text. You must choose the answer **A**, **B**, **C** or **D** which you think fits best. Indicate your answers **on the separate answer sheet**.

1 In Beverley Hills, Depardieu
    A dressed smartly.
    B behaved badly.
    C starred in a film.
    D received an award.

2 Depardieu believes
    A success comes with work.
    B work is depressing.
    C his size has affected his career.
    D his films have been unsuccessful.

3 Depardieu started acting
    A as part of his education.
    B while working on boats.
    C after attending classes.
    D while travelling round Europe.

4 According to Depardieu
    A acting makes you sincere.
    B French actors think themselves wonderful.
    C success went to his head.
    D actors deserve praise.

5 In the next few years, Depardieu
    A will give up the theatre.
    B will become a winemaker.
    C will make more films.
    D may do something different.

Remember to put your answers on a separate answer sheet.

GÉRARD DEPARDIEU

IT'S BEVERLY HILLS: The Golden Globe Awards. Part of the Hollywood season, when film's finest – bejewelled and tuxedoed, make-up flawless and stomachs tucked firmly in – come to see and be seen. Everyone is here.

Around the tables shambles a bear-like figure, shoulders stooped above his paunch, strands of greasy hair falling over his broken nose, bow-tie undone and a glass of wine in hand, occasionally stumbling onto the stage to accept one or another award in mumbling, heavily-accented English. The eyes of every woman in the room are glued to this unlikeliest object of lust in barely-concealed adoration.

This is Gérard Depardieu, star of *Cyrano De Bergerac, Green Card* and over 80 other French films.

Sitting in a Beverly Hills restaurant the day after the awards, he seems to fill not only his chair, but the entire table. He likes rich French food and would not consider accompanying it with anything but wine. "I'm always too fat," he shrugs, cheerfully. It does not seem to have held him back.

"I'm more of an artisan than a star," he has said. "If I dreamed of being a star, I'd be depressed all day. I've made over 80 films. At least 60 of them were boring. About 10 were very, very good. When it comes down to it, 10 out of 80 isn't bad. So there's been a lot of failures – but there have been some interesting films, too. I like to work – I can't stand boredom. And I don't believe in undiscovered genius."

EARLY DAYS
Depardieu was born poor in the provincial town of Châteauroux, the third of six children, in a family in which, he says, "people didn't speak much and drank a lot". He left home when he was 12. "I wanted to see the sea. I felt better on the road ... I wanted to be locked up in a Catholic boarding school. But they didn't want me, they shooed me away. I really would have liked a formal education."

Instead, he took to the open road. "I went to see the Atlantic, at Arcachon. I worked there on boats, cleaning up after people, or I'd sell soap for the blind, or sell brushes, door-to-door."

While hitch-hiking all over Europe, one day a lorry driver asked him what he did, and for no particular reason, "I lied," he says. "When you get into a stranger's car, you've really got to pour it on." So Depardieu told him he studied theatre. The more he thought about it, the better he liked the idea.

At the age of 16, he enrolled for drama classes at the Théâtre Nationale Populaire in Paris. It was there, he says freely, that his life was turned around. Movies made him a giant but theatre remains his first love. "The theatre brings out a certain sort of discipline and humility. You can be an egomaniac one night and can screw up the next."

FIRST BREAK
But it was on film that he had his first big break. In 1974, director Bertrand Blier cast him and friend Patrick Dewaere in *Going Places*, a type of French *Easy Rider*, which became a smash hit. Much to his surprise, he had become a star.

A star he has stayed for two decades.

In 1492, Depardieu sails the ocean blue...

He remains supremely unimpressed by his own, or anyone else's success; and in a profession not noted for its sincerity, his bluntness comes as a breath of fresh air. "French actors are stuck on themselves. They have a sort of egomania; they get big heads from all the media attention. But everyone's a pain in the ass at one moment or another. I went through that, too. Now, when I have a big head, it's because I drank too much wine, not because I earned too much bread!"

Helping him to keep his feet firmly on the ground is his wife, actress

Elisabeth Guignot, 50, a former fellow student at the Théâtre Nationale. "I was born a second time", he has said of their first meeting, and they have been together since that moment.

Every movie director in Hollywood is knocking at his door but his old love, the theatre, beckons ... and yet he might just throw everything up and go and concentrate on his vineyard – he recently decided to change the occupation stated on his passport from "actor" to "winemaker".

"I'm at a delicate age," he says. "I'm volatile, as they say of wine when it's in danger of turning to vinegar. I'm capable of anything."

Whatever he does, we can be certain it will be worth watching.

Paper 2 (Writing): Section A

You and a friend have recently returned from a rather expensive holiday in Hawaii. Sadly, your 'holiday of a lifetime' did not turn out as well as you had both hoped. Read the holiday brochure extract with the handwritten comments, and also the letter received from your friend. Using the information given, write a letter of complaint to the travel company explaining why you and your friend were disappointed and what sort of compensation you think would be appropriate. Your letter should be approximately 250 words long.

not in our opinion!

half an hour up a steep hill!

broke down twice!

couldn't see it at all from ours!

Pacific Beach Hotel ＊＊＊＊

Although the Pacific Beach Hotel is quite large, it gives the impression of a smaller, select hotel offering its guests the highest standards of personal care and attention. Situated on a rocky headland, the hotel enjoys superb views of the setting sun and the twinkling lights of the town which, with a big choice of restaurants, shops and entertainments, is just a short stroll away.

The 445 guest rooms are comfortably furnished and feature private bathrooms, air conditioning, cable TV, mini-bar and private balconies with beautiful full or partial sea views.

The swimming pool is complemented by a unique salt water lagoon and the world's best sport fishing is just nearby. For the active there is a floodlit tennis complex, and just a short drive away, five 18 hole golf courses.

Dear Chris,

Thanks for offering to draft a letter to the travel company complaining about our Hawaiian holiday.

I agree with you – we should certainly complain that we couldn't actually hire a car until the 3rd day even though car hire was included in the total price. In the end, it meant we didn't get to do as much sport as we had planned nor did we get to see some of the famous sights on the island.

More importantly, I think you should mention the hotel's attitude when you were ill. They really should've been able to get hold of a doctor more quickly and he should've come to the hotel to see you – it was a four-star hotel! They can't just expect hotel guests to turn up at the local clinic. That insect bite could have been really serious!

No doubt you'll include all the other complaints about the room, etc. Let me know when you've written the letter and I'll sign it with you.

So much for the 'holiday of a lifetime' – I suppose the best we can hope for in the way of compensation is a partial refund.

Love, Jamie

Paper 3 (English in Use): Section A

1 For questions **1–15**, read the text below and then decide which word best fits each space. Put the letter you choose for each question in the correct box on the answer sheet. The exercise begins with an example (**0**).

Sibling memories

My brother and I used to fight a great deal as children. We did a (**0**) .... of things together, not always in complete (**1**) .... In (**2**) ...., he actually (**3**) .... my arms on one occasion. It meant that I missed the school exams for that year, so I suppose that really he did me a (**4**) .... Tony was a year older than me, so he was always first at doing things that I wanted to do – to (**5**) .... in public, for example, at school. I was full of (**6**) .... when, at fourteen, he got to play solo in a schools concerts at the City Hall. I had to (**7**) .... fifteen years before I could do the same as a professional musician. He definitely blazed a (**8**) .... for me. It was obvious that Tony was always going to be successful in his choice of career. When he had just left school and had (**9**) .... a job as a designer in Glasgow, he was soon in demand from other companies wanting to (**10**) .... him part of their team. For him, music was just something that you (**11**) .... at school. And his (**12**) .... were always in the visual arts – that was his main area of interest and obviously the (**13**) .... thing for him. When our mother was running an Art Gallery for a (**14**) .... Tony, still in his teens, used to organise all the publicity for her – he was incredibly (**15**) ....

0	**A** lot	**B** deal	**C** collection	**D** quantity
1	**A** concert	**B** unison	**C** harmony	**D** unity
2	**A** essence	**B** fact	**C** general	**D** reality
3	**A** ripped	**B** smashed	**C** snapped	**D** broke
4	**A** courtesy	**B** privilege	**C** favour	**D** benefit
5	**A** perform	**B** present	**C** produce	**D** practise
6	**A** anxiety	**B** envy	**C** guilt	**D** contempt
7	**A** postpone	**B** delay	**C** suspend	**D** wait
8	**A** path	**B** road	**C** trail	**D** way
9	**A** taken	**B** changed	**C** resigned	**D** abandoned
10	**A** have	**B** keep	**C** make	**D** get
11	**A** did	**B** made	**C** played	**D** carried
12	**A** feelings	**B** insights	**C** senses	**D** instincts
13	**A** precise	**B** right	**C** straight	**D** proper
14	**A** turn	**B** time	**C** tour	**D** stage
15	**A** practical	**B** workable	**C** realistic	**D** useful

Do not forget to put your answers on the answer sheet

Example: | 0 | A |

2 For questions **16–30**, complete the following article by writing each missing word on the answer sheet. Use only one word for each space. The exercise begins with an example (**0**).

Today the move away from rigid rules makes it much easier to judge the right way to behave because (**0**) .there. are fewer out and out 'wrongs'. Of course there are still a (**16**) .... situations where inflexible rules apply, although (**17**) .... are mainly concerned with official functions. But nine times out of ten, (**18**) .... way you choose to behave is up to you, with one very important proviso: that you keep firmly (**19**) .... mind the basis on which etiquette (**20**) .... grown up; in other words, the need always to consider (**21**) .... people's feelings first.

Some people, (**22**) .... instance, are very informal and outgoing by nature, (**23**) .... others prefer to be more reserved and formal. Younger people tend to be less formal than (**24**) .... parents. Habits can vary in different parts of the country. Behaviour (**25**) .... may be commonplace in the capital – like arriving later than the stated time – can often be unconventional elsewhere. Just remember the basic rule of consideration for others, and (**26**) .... in doubt, follow the example of those around you.

Etiquette is a skill that is easily learned and it brings the benefits of other people's appreciation whenever you put (**27**) .... into practice. It's a pleasure to spend time with people (**28**) .... are reliably courteous and considerate; it's also pleasant to feel that you will always know (**29**) .... to do or say in any circumstances, mundane (**30**) .... extraordinary.

Do not forget to put your answers on the answer sheet.

Paper 4 (Listening): Sections A and B

Section A

For questions **1–9** you will hear an exercise instructor giving information and advice to her class. Listen to the instructor and circle the correct answer **A**, **B**, **C** or **D**, according to what she says. You will hear the recording twice.

1 The instructor is working with
   A an advanced class.   **B** beginners.   **C** an intermediate level class.   **D** all levels.

2 The training involves
   A just working out on equipment.   **B** breathing deeply.   **C** no equipment.   **D** a mixture of exercises.

3 There are
   A three lessons in all.   **B** three rounds of individual exercise.   **C** only joint exercise.   **D** 20 exercises.

4 The exercises are all designed to develop
   A your biceps and stomach muscles.   **B** your heart rate.   **C** all your muscles.   **D** your muscle tone and breathing.

5 The instructor will
   A guide everybody.   **B** check everybody.   **C** explain everything to each person.   **D** warn everybody.

6 The instructor wants to check that everyone
   A is fit and healthy in general.   **B** has a good clean medical record.   **C** is young.   **D** is fit enough to do the activities.

7 The instructor is concerned about
   A insurance claims.   **B** particular health problems.   **C** broken bones especially.   **D** any health problem.

8 By 'vigorous exercise' the instructor means
   A steady exercise.   **B** energetic exercise.   **C** long exercise.   **D** squash.

9 The instructor seems
   A anxious.   **B** helpful.   **C** arrogant.   **D** bored.

Section B

Now look at Section B. You will hear an extract from a radio health programme in which a doctor answers listeners' queries. As you listen, complete in a few words only the information for questions **10–19**. Listen very carefully as you will hear this piece once only.

Brian
Brian's symptoms: low and **10** _____ ; no energy; **11** _____
Brian hasn't been to the doctor because **12** _____
Brian's usual state of health: **13** _____

The doctor's reply

Queries
The doctor asks about possible changes in diet and **14** _____ and house and **15** _____

Advice
• People should **16** _____ to emotional problems and **17** _____ with friends or other people.
• Brian should go to the doctor for **18** _____
• Brian could also **19** _____ to discuss things further.

Now transfer your answers for questions 1–19 to the answer sheet.

Paper 5 (Speaking): Phase A

Work in groups of three. Take it in turns for one person to play the part of a CAE examiner and the other two to play the part of the two CAE candidates. Decide who will be Candidate A and who will be Candidate B.

Choose either Task 1 or Task 2 below. The 'examiner' should follow the script and the 'candidates' should respond appropriately.

Task 1	
Examiner:	Good morning (afternoon/evening). My name is ..... And your names are ...?
Candidates:	Good morning (afternoon/evening). *(Tell the examiner your names.)*
Examiner:	First of all, I'd like to find out a little more about you both. Do you know each other?
Candidates:	Yes, we do.
Examiner:	In that case, perhaps *(name of Candidate A)* would like to tell me about *(name of Candidate B)* – where he/she is from, what his/her hobbies and interests are, what he/she does in terms of work and study, and so on. Candidate A: *(Imagine that you already know Candidate B well. Introduce him/her to the examiner.)*
Examiner:	*(name of Candidate B)*, would you like to tell us about *(name of Candidate A)* now please? Candidate B: *(Imagine that you already know Candidate A well. Introduce him/her to the examiner.)*
Examiner:	Now can you ask each other why you're learning English and talk about your plans for the future?
If you are taking the CAE exam IN BRITAIN, the 'examiner' might go on to ask some of the following questions:	
Examiner:	How long have you been in Britain? What do you think are the biggest differences between Britain and your own country? Is there anything you especially like or dislike about life in Britain? How long are you intending to stay?
If you are taking the CAE exam IN YOUR OWN COUNTRY, the 'examiner' might go on to ask some of the following questions:	
Examiner:	What would you say are the best things about life in your country? Are there any disadvantages? Where do you do your English studies? How do you usually travel to school/college?

Task 2	
Examiner:	Good morning (afternoon/evening). My name is ..... And your names are ...?
Candidates:	Good morning (afternoon/evening). *(Tell the examiner your names.)*
Examiner:	First of all, I'd like to know a little more about you both. Do you know each other?
Candidates:	No, we don't.
Examiner:	In that case, could you please find out about each other? Talk about where you're from, your families, what you do in terms of work or study, what you're interested in, how you like to spend your time, and so on.
Candidates:	*(Imagine that you are meeting each other for the first time. Ask each other questions to find out about one another.)*
Examiner:	Now can you ask each other why you're learning English and talk about your plans for the future?

Continue as for Task 1.

Six

A

Inventions

Starter activities

1 The objects listed in the grid below all play an important role in our life today. Fill in as many details as you can about who invented them, when and where.

invention	name of inventor?	where?	which century?
telephone			
parachute			
printing press			
jet engine			
microscope			
pendulum clock			

✳ Which of the six objects do you think have proved the most useful? Discuss your answers.

2 List all the 20th-century inventions you can think of. Compare your list with a partner's and then agree on the five *most* important inventions since 1900. Report your conclusions to another pair.

Listening

✳ Listen to two students discussing the history of the telephone. As you listen to their conversation, complete the notes using a few words only. Listen carefully as you will hear this piece only once.

History of the telephone

Inventor: Alexander Graham Bell: 1847 – (1) ....

- born in (2) ....

- eventually settled in (3) ....

- worked as a (4) .... by day

- pursued interest in (5) .... at night

- developed plans for new type of (6) ....

- made friends with (7) ....

- together they officially invented the first version of a telephone in (8) ....

- opened first telephone line in 1915, between New York and (9) ....

Reading

1 Two recently invented phones are described in the texts which follow. Read the opening sections of each text to find out what sort of phones they are.

2 Read the rest of the texts and make notes on the advantages and disadvantages given in the texts for each type of phone. Compare your notes with a partner's.

You'll never believe who's on the line

A NEW TYPE of telephone has arrived in Britain. It looks innocent enough, just like a normal household appliance, in fact, but there's one very big difference. The "truth phone" tells the user when the person on the other end of the line is lying.

Manufactured by an American company specialising in a range of surveillance and counter-surveillance equipment, the truth
10 phone contains a "voice-stress analyser", otherwise known as a lie-detector. The company claims that it monitors uncontrollable, sub-audible tremors which exist in the human voice when the subject is under stress.

"Voice-stress analysis [VSA] has long been recognised as a proven method of lie detection," says Joanne O'Neill, manager of the shop in London which acts as the retail
20 outlet in Britain. "What we've done is to combine the technology of VSA with the telephone, where so many of the most important conversations in life take place."

During a conversation, a digital read-out is constantly displayed on the telephone console, reflecting the sub-audible tremors in the subject's voice. An answer to a simple, stress-free question such as "Is today Saturday?" produces a reading
30 somewhere between 10 and 40. A more searching question such as "Are you having an affair?" might produce a reading of 80 or 90.

According to the manufacturer, however, it's not just a case of the higher the reading, the bigger the whopper. Correct use of the truth phone requires a series of carefully structured questions in the context of a formal interrogation and a

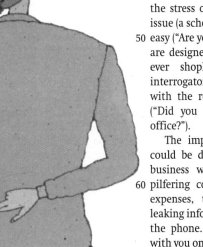

Lying was easier on the telephone, but not any more. Jon Stock dials the truth phone

40 detailed analysis of the readings. (In America, where VSA is admissible as court evidence in certain states, there is a certificate of qualification for voice stress analysers. VSA is not admissible in a British court.)

"Control questions" help to distinguish between the anxiety of interrogation and the stress of lying. Unrelated to the main issue (a school theft, say), some of them are
50 easy ("Are you wearing a tie?"), while others are designed to produce stress ("Have you ever shoplifted?"). These provide the interrogator with bench-marks to compare with the response to the main question ("Did you steal £200 from the bursar's office?").

The implications of the truth phone could be devastating, particularly in the business world. Employees suspected of
60 pilfering company money, fiddling their expenses, talking to the opposition or leaking information could be summoned to the phone. ("It's the boss. Wants a word with you on the truth phone.")

At £2,499, the phone is not cheap. According to the manufacturer, the first people to spot its potential in Britain have been insurance firms wanting to check the validity of their clients' claims.

70 But Liberty, a civil rights organisation, expresses some concern about the equipment. "I think it's an issue of privacy as much as anything," says John Wadham, Liberty's legal officer. "People could be measuring your emotional response without you knowing. The information could also be very inaccurate if it's taken out of context."

(The Times Magazine)

Look who's calling ?

DAVID TAYLOR answers the videophone

"ANSWER THE PHONE, could you darling? I look an absolute mess."

"Oh, let it ring. I don't much like the look of him, whoever he is."

Telephones may never be the same again. The long-awaited "videophone" will be with us within a year or so, according to telephone engineers.

They are working on a wide-screen model for use in offices, and a more compact version for the home. Both, they promise, will offer pin-sharp pictures. You can see who's calling you – and they can see you answer.

Cordless phones, phones in cars, phones in your pocket – and now this. Naturally, the telephone companies take it as read that such wonders of technology will be instant best-sellers. Who is going to want just to listen on the telephone, when they could be face-to-face on camera exchanging knowing glances, tell-tale gestures, loving smiles? Videophones will be so much more informative, more personal, they say. Revealing, in fact.

They have had them for years, of course, aboard space-ships in science fiction. But whether the real-life, down-to-earth thing will seem like such a good idea is another matter. There are times – a lot of times when you pause to consider – when the phone's "voice-only" limitations are its greatest asset.

"Darling, hi! Stuck late at the office again, I'm afraid. The meeting dragged on and on."

"*What's that red smudge on your collar?*"

"Sorry I'm running a little late, sir. The traffic is just terrible."

"*Is that a new sofa you have in your car?*"

"We're just fine, mother."

"*You look thinner to me. Are those bags under your eyes?*"

Videophones are going to change all the games that telephone-users play.

Take the insistent ring – or warbling chirrup, as it is on most phones now. It is an insistent, even hectoring call. As with a baby's cry, it's a sound that you cannot ignore. When a call comes, you feel you have no choice but to answer it.

It will be a different matter if you know you're about to be seen. You'll not want to pick up the phone without at least straightening your tie, running a comb through your hair, or powdering your nose. And extensions in the bathroom will presumably have to go.

Or supposing it's a long-distance call?

'Hank, what time is it your end? My God, Hank, are you ill?'

What is clearly going to be needed as a matter of urgency is a videophone equivalent of the answering machine.

"I'm sorry, we're not able to take your call just at the moment, but if you'd like to leave a message, please speak after the tone; the holiday pictures you are about to see are of us all looking bronzed and fit in the South of France."

Anyone who has an answering machine on the home phone knows it has another sneaky use, besides answering calls when you're out. You can use it for "sampling" calls when actually you're in all the time.

"Oh, darling, it's you. I forgot to turn the silly machine off." Or if the call turns out to be an unwelcome one, you can "forget to turn it off" again.

Will videophones feature a sort of preview button, doing much the same job as a peephole in your front door? A must, you might think.

The well-known office secretary's routines will have to be reconsidered as well. "Just a moment. I think he may be in a meeting. I'll see if I can locate him for you." Every caller knows that is code for "He is sitting right beside me, but he may not want to talk to you. Let me find out what sort of mood the old buzzard is in." But what happens if would-be callers happen to see the old buzzard sprinting for the door? Office videophones may well need curtains or some sort of pull-down modesty blind.

Or perhaps we'll have to get used to turning the lights off whenever the boss phones unexpectedly.

"I think there must be a fault at your end, sir. I can see you loud and clear."

Picture quality: that's another thing. Definition will be sharp, promise the phone engineers – but they would say that, wouldn't they? What if you get a bad line or, worse still, a crossed line?

"Darling, you look just wonderful in black. Oh, I'm terribly sorry, madam, I must have a wrong number."

The much-vaunted business "conference calls" could turn out to be tricky things to handle on videophones, besides: rather like television hook-ups where people sit in the studio looking dazed, embarrassedly fiddling with their ear-pieces, as the satellite links vainly struggle to establish a connection.

"Just wave if you can hear me, would you, New York? Hong Kong is going to give us a close-up of the bottom line ... hello, hello? Look, it's no use just grinning at us, Moscow. Put the thing down and we'll try to call you back. I said *Put the thing down!* Oh, to hell with it, let's just send them a fax."

Perhaps videophones will be every bit as wonderful as they say. But if not, don't call us, we'll call – and try to picture – you. ■

(High Life)

3

1 Look at the following words/phrases taken from the two texts. What do you notice about the way in which they are formed?

satellite links	lie-detector
wrong number	read-out
front door	household appliance
close-up	peephole
ear-pieces	videophone
civil rights	best-sellers

2 Place each of the words above into one of the following categories:

a noun + noun
b adjective + noun
c derived from phrasal verbs

3 Listen to the way the compound nouns in 1 are pronounced. As you listen mark the correct stress. Listen again and say each one aloud as you hear it, paying particular attention to the stress.

4 Find five more examples from the two reading texts to add to category (a) and five more to add to (b). Think of five more examples of your own to add to category (c).

5 Look at these phrases:

a pictures <u>which are as sharp as a pin</u>
b a phone <u>which transmits only the voice</u>
c a blind <u>which can be pulled down</u>

Find a compound adjective in the reading texts which means the same as the words underlined.

6 Find ten more examples of compound adjectives which were used in the two reading texts.

7 Look back at the categories for forming compound nouns in activity **2**. Write down similar patterns for forming compound adjectives.

Your thoughts

- Would you want to use these two new types of telephone inventions?
- Do you agree that people play games on the telephone?
- Will video and truth phones benefit our society or are there hidden dangers to these inventions?
- Would you accept evidence from video and truth phones in a court of law?

Ways of learning: deducing meaning from context

Both the articles you have just read contain words/ phrases which may be new to you. Some examples are in the list below.

smudge (Text 2, line 44)	warbling (Text 2, line 57)
chirrup (Text 2, line 57)	crossed (Text 2, line 130)
line (Text 2, line 148)	pilfering (Text 1, line 60)
whopper (Text 1, line 36)	

1 You can gather a lot of information about a new word even if you don't know its meaning. What can you learn about the word *smudge* (see line 44) from the second reading text? Fill in the missing words below:

a it's probably a .... because it comes after an adjective

b it can be .... in colour

c it can be found on a .... so is probably a physical object

d it's part of a question in a videophone conversation between two people who may be ....

e the context is that one partner is .... for being delayed at work while the other partner is .... about something red which can be seen on the first partner's collar

f other words which might fit into this position would be .... or .... , but *smudge* is a word that often collocates with 'lipstick'

g the implication must be that the delay has nothing to do with a late business meeting but is probably the result of a meeting with a lady who wears red .... !

h something else that smudges / makes a smudge is .... on paper

Do you now know how *smudge* differs from *mark* or *stain* or *spot*?

2 Choose two or three other words from the list above. Try and work out what they might mean by looking closely at how they are used in the text. Check your answers in a dictionary. Were you right?

3 From each of the reading texts choose a word which is new to you and write a similar set of sentences to get as close to its meaning as you can.

4 When you meet a new word, how do you decide what it means? What advice would you give to another student of English? Make a few notes then discuss your ideas with a partner.

Grammar reminder: order of adjectives

> **Remember:**
> When you wish to use more than one adjective in front of a noun, it helps to break the adjectives down according to type.
>
> e.g. article – an
> adjective of opinion – amazing
> adjective of size – little
> adjective of age – brand-new
> adjective of colour – black
> adjective of origin – Japanese
> adjective of material – plastic
> adjective of type – pocket
> + noun – calculator
>
> In general, the more specific an adjective is, the closer it will be to the noun.

1 Choose three adjectives for each of the following categories and write them down.

opinion	size	age	colour
origin	material	type	

Compare your examples with a partner's. Add two more examples to your own.

2 For each sentence below, put the adjectives in brackets in the correct order before the noun.

1 The international summit meeting was held in a ... castle. (seventeenth century, beautiful, French)

2 Among the gifts presented by the Japanese delegation to their hosts was a set of ... plates. (lacquer, exquisite, black, traditional)

3 A series of ... studies has shown that that tobacco advertising has a powerful effect on the smoking habits of young people. (recent, sociological, important)

4 Truth phones offer a ... approach to checking for lying. (technological, new, clever)

5 The managing director bought himself an ... car. (red, Italian, new, sports, expensive)

3 Write a brief description of an invention or special gadget you have seen advertised which you would love to buy or be given as a present. Use at least five adjectives in your description of it. Compare your item with a partner's.

✳ Writing

Choose *one* of the two new types of telephone described in the texts in this section and write a short article arguing strongly in favour of **or** against its introduction in society. You should include a brief explanation of how it works, what the advantages/ disadvantages are, and why you are in favour of/ opposed to its use. Write approximately 250 words.

(Before)

(After)

B

The art of persuasion

Starter activities

1 Look at these photographs from magazine advertisements. What product is each one advertising? Who do you think each of these advertisements is aimed at? What message do you think is being given to readers by each picture? Compare your answers with a partner's.

2 Describe to a partner an advertisement which has amused you, an advertisement which has shocked you, or one which has directly influenced your buying habits.

Listening

Listen to two actors talking about advertisements. Complete the notes in the table using no more than three words. You will hear each extract once.

	Actor 1	Actor 2
What was the product?	a (1) .... called Heart	a (5) ....
Why was the actor chosen?	• acting/singing/ dancing experience	• suffered from (6)..........
What did he/ she have to do?	• dress up as (2) .... • sing and dance • (3) .... the product	• be filmed (7) .... and (8) .... using the product
Were there any problems in making the advert?	• was (4) .... at the end of the filming	• (9).......... before filming so needed to use (10) ....

We put people in front of cars.

Your thoughts

- **Which of the two advertisements do you think was the better designed, and why?**
- **Do you think the second one distorted the truth?**

Reading

1 Four sentences have been taken out of the text below. Read through the text and then choose the best sentence (**A–G**) to fill each gap. To help you choose the correct sentence, look carefully at the text before and after each gap.

A This means that they also have values.
B Its primary function is, of course, to sell goods and services.
C The purchase of the product becomes the key to entering this mythical world.
D But they do offer a highly selective form of truth-telling.
E Some agencies have come up with what is called lifestyle advertising.
F These images and lifestyles are created mainly by telling stories with a human interest.
G But they can also create dissatisfaction with the way things are.

ADVERTISING AND PERSUASION

Whatever its measurable effects, advertising clearly matters to advertisers, since huge sums are spent on advertising budgets and spending has trebled over the last decade. (1) ....
But since advertising uses powerful images to promote its products, it also incidentally promotes 'lifestyles'. Some advertisements, like those for public utilities and environmentally sensitive industries, are solely devoted to promoting public images of themselves. (2) ....

Advertising stories are not just series of events in time. They involve structures of cause and effect. (3) .... Advertisements for items like cars or computers speak of status, style and success more than the actual features of the products. The kind of values portrayed and the way they are presented are important factors in creating the ideologies which envelop the products.

Advertisements do not lie. At least, not in an obvious way. (4) .... There are clear differences between the frontal 'hard sell' approach which makes direct claims about products and urges audiences to behave in specific ways and the more 'soft sell' which leaves audiences to do more imaginative work themselves. Stories usually demand this kind of imaginative work from audiences, so we need to focus our attention on how they work.

---

2 For each of the statements **1–8**, put a tick in the 'My view' column if you agree and a cross if you disagree.

		My view	Writer's view
1	Advertising often promotes a particular lifestyle.		
2	Advertising usually distorts the truth.		
3	Advertising is incompatible with an environmentally sensitive lifestyle.		
4	Advertisements often project an imaginary world.		
5	Advertising can't sell anything to anyone unless they really want to buy it.		
6	Advertisements can create dissatisfaction with life as it really is.		
7	Advertisements often portray a product as a solution to your problem.		
8	Advertising changes people's behaviour.		

3 Read the rest of the text 'Advertising and Persuasion' on page 84 and put a tick/cross in the Writer's view column according to whether the writer seems to agree or disagree with statements **1–8**. Leave the box blank if you think the writer expresses no opinion.

Discuss your answers with a partner.

4 Find words in the text that carry a positive, negative or neutral connotation in relation to advertising, e.g.

Positive	Neutral	Negative
reliable	lifestyle	self-satisfied

ADVERTISING AND PERSUASION

1 In many cases, advertisements offer their products as solutions to problems. But they can also create dissatisfaction with the way things are. What if you cannot afford what is on offer and what if it fails to fulfil its promise? By offering products to aspire to in a mythical future, advertising may create discontent with the here and now.

2 Advertisements often promote feelings of dissatisfaction or desire amongst audiences which the products claim to remove. This is most often done by the creation of a mythical ('Martini') world which is offered as a superior form of existence. The purchase of the product becomes the key to entering this mythical world. So advertising has effects beyond stimulating the need to buy.

3 Some agencies have come up with what is called 'lifestyle' advertising. In order to create such lifestyle images they need to find out what we as audiences are thinking and feeling. So when market research uncovers new social trends advertisers are feeding back to us versions of ourselves.

4 In the 1980s, images of thrusting, self-satisfied, high-consuming 'yuppies' were rife in advertising. For the 1990s, agencies suggest that the dominant images will be more socially and environmentally sensitive.

5 'Greed', they say, will be superseded by 'Green'. But how can advertising be used for socially desirable ends like promoting green issues? Is there not a danger that concern for the environment is being translated into just another 'lifestyle' label? Some advertising agencies have predicted a number of new labels for the 1990s which are a strange concoction of 'Greed' and 'Green'. They include people who are 'carers' but not 'sharers' and 'money-grabbing ecologists'.

6 The Volkswagen Passat advertisement (1989) is a good example of these paradoxical formulations. It reiterates Volkswagen's long-standing claim for the reliability of its cars, but in a novel way. At the centre of its story is a young Shirley Temple look-alike who is rescued by her father from an inner-city nightmare. The urban jungle is polluted by danger, crime, and exhaust fumes. He leads her away to his powerful car where the mother is waiting to whisk her away. It offers a fairy-tale solution of private security against public squalor. A form of escape is being recommended which only some people can afford and which works to the detriment of others. Ironically, the motor car (which is arguably a major factor in urban migration and inner-city decay) is seen as providing a kind of privileged escape. It presents a contradictory and very private kind of ecology.

(Understanding the Media: A Practical Guide)

Your thoughts

- **What do you feel are the positive and negative aspects of advertising today?**
- **Are there certain styles of advertisement which are unacceptable?**
- **Are there any products for which you think advertising should be restricted, e.g. tobacco products?**

Vocabulary summary

Look back over the first two sections of this unit and write down ten items of vocabulary on a piece of paper. Then divide into pairs and decide who will be A and B. Student A should then define the first word on their own list as quickly and clearly as possible so that Student B can say what the word is, e.g.

Student A: **It's a product that's very popular and that a lot of people buy.**
Student B: **Best-seller.**

Student B then defines the first word on their list so that Student A has to guess. The game continues until each person has defined all their words.

✳ Speaking

1 Work with a partner and decide who will be Student A and who will be Student B. Student A should look at the first picture on page 213 while Student B looks at the first picture on page 218.

At the end you can both compare your pictures.

2 Now carry out the same task with different pictures. Student B should look at the second picture on page 218 while Student A looks at the second picture on page 213.

Grammar analysis: cleft sentences

1 Look at the following pairs of sentences. What is the difference in meaning between **a** and **b** in each case?

a Most advertisements project an imaginary world.
b What most advertisements do is <u>project an imaginary world</u>.

a Advertising affects people's value systems, not their buying habits.
b It's <u>people's value systems</u> that advertising affects, not their buying habits.

a Advertising distorts the truth.
b What advertising does is <u>distort the truth</u>.

a Advertisements can create dissatisfaction with ordinary life.
b It's <u>dissatisfaction with ordinary life</u> that advertisements can create.

In sentence **b** in each case the underlined phrase is being given a strong emphasis or focus. By structuring a sentence in this way it becomes possible to place the focus or emphasis on a particular aspect of what we are saying. The focus or emphasis may be on a person/thing, an action, or the circumstances of an action such as the time/place/etc.

This type of sentence structure is called a 'cleft' sentence. Two common forms of cleft sentence structure are:

1 What + clause …
2 It is + noun phrase + that …

In sentence **1** the information which is being emphasised moves to a position at the end of the sentence. In sentence **2** the information which is being emphasised is brought forward to a position near the front of the sentence. Note that 'what' is sometimes placed in the middle of the sentence and that this also brings the emphasised information to the front, e.g. *An imaginary world is what most advertisements project.*

2 Here are some more examples based on the reading texts in Section A of this unit. Match the first half of each cleft sentence in list A to its second half from list B and write out the whole sentence, e.g.

What office videophones may well need are …
… <u>curtains or some sort of pull-down modesty blind.</u>

A **1** What telephone engineers are working on now is …
 2 What is clearly going to be needed as a matter of urgency is …
 3 It's in the business world that …
 4 It's personal privacy which is …
 5 What people could be measuring is …

B **a** a videophone equivalent of the answering machine.
 b an issue as much as anything.
 c the implications of the truth phone could be devastating.
 d a compact version of the videophone for the home.
 e your emotional response without you knowing.

Underline the words being emphasised in each complete sentence as shown in the example.

3 Change the structure of sentences **1–5** to place the focus on the underlined phrases, e.g.

Advertisements offer their products <u>as solutions to problems</u>.
What advertisements do is offer their products as solutions to problems.

You may find you can do this using more than one type of cleft sentence structure.

1 Advertisements offer their products <u>as solutions to problems</u>.
2 Market research <u>uncovers new social trends</u>.
3 Market research uncovers <u>new social trends</u>.
4 Advertisers <u>feed back to us versions of ourselves</u>.
5 Advertisers feed back to us <u>versions of ourselves</u>.

4 Read these two short texts and decide which of the suggested sentences **a** or **b** best completes each text.

1 Most advertisements for products tell you about the various characteristics of the product being advertised; its newness or convenience, its taste or low price, etc. Advertisements for cars, however, are slightly different …………………………
 a Advertisements for cars speak of status, style and success more than the actual features of the product.
 b What advertisements for cars speak of is status, style and success more than the actual features of the product.

2 Recent years have seen a subtle change in the images presented by advertising agencies in their campaigns. ……………………… Nowadays, the same agencies prefer socially and environmentally sensitive images. Concern for the environment has been translated into another 'lifestyle' label which is often a strange mixture of 'greed' and 'green'.
 a It was images of successful, high-consuming young executives that were dominant in advertising in the 1980s.
 b It was in the 1980s that images of successful, high-consuming young executives were dominant in advertising.

Discuss with a partner the reasons for your choice in each case.

C

Paper 1 (Reading): Multiple matching

Introduction

In Unit 1 we looked at the multiple choice format which is used to accompany a reading text in the CAE exam. In this unit we shall focus on another format used in the Reading Paper – the multiple matching format.

What does a multiple matching exercise look like?

1 Here is an example:

Read the following short descriptions of five different optical inventions and choose the correct name for each invention from the list of options **A–H**.

What do you call …

1 spectacles which have dark-coloured glass in them to protect your eyes from bright sunlight?
2 small plastic lenses placed onto the surface of the eye so that you can see properly?
3 an instrument which magnifies very small objects so that you can look at them and study them in detail?
4 an instrument consisting of two small telescopes joined together side by side which help you to see things in the far distance?
5 a piece of glass, usually in a frame with a handle, which makes objects appear bigger than they really are?

A sunglasses	**C** contact lenses	**E** microscope	**G** magnifying glass
B telescope	**D** binoculars	**F** opera glasses	**H** spectacles

Typically, in this type of exercise you match each of the definitions to its correct name, chosen from a set of related answer options.

2 Here is another example of a multiple matching task based this time upon a reading text.

Look at the text entitled 'Contact lenses'. The short questions **A–K** below can be used as headings for the numbered paragraphs **1–9** in the text.

A	Is it difficult to put them in?	**G** Can you wear them to play sport?
B	Can anyone wear contact lenses?	**H** Can they get lost in your eyes?
C	Are they comfortable to wear?	**I** How long does it take to get used to them?
D	Which type is best for your eyes?	**J** Can you wear eye makeup?
E	Are they difficult to look after?	**K** Do you get rid of your spectacles?
F	Do they ever fall out?	

What is the best heading for paragraph 1 of the text?

Option D is the best heading question for paragraph 1. The connections between the heading and the paragraph are illustrated below.

Heading: **Which type is best for your eyes?**
(Option D)

Paragraph 1

Your optician is the best expert. He or she will examine your eyes and will then be able to advise you. They will take into account any special considerations you might have. For example, if you work in a particularly dusty environment, play a lot of very active sport or only intend to wear the lenses occasionally. Generally, however, soft lenses are the most popular because they're the easiest to get used to and the most comfortable to wear.

---

2 From options **A–K** choose the best heading question for paragraph 2 of the text about 'Contact Lenses' and underline the relevant words/phrases in the text as for paragraph 1.

3 Complete the task by choosing the most suitable headings from **A–K** to suit the remaining paragraphs **3–9**.

CONTACT LENSES

Contact lenses were first manufactured at the end of the 19th century using glass. Since then, the invention of versatile and hard-wearing materials has meant that today many more people wear contact lenses in preference to spectacles. Nowadays there are different types of lens from which to choose – hard, soft and gas permeable, and it's even possible to select a tinted contact lens which will enhance the natural colour of your eyes! There are a number of questions people commonly ask about wearing contact lenses, so here are some answers to set your mind at rest.

1 Your optician is the best expert. He or she will examine your eyes and will then be able to advise you. They will take into account any special considerations you might have. For example if you work in a particularly dusty environment, play a lot of very active sport or only intend to wear the lenses occasionally. Generally, however, soft lenses are the most popular, because they're the easiest to get used to and the most comfortable to wear.

2 A common misconception is that the lenses can get stuck round the back of the eye. This is totally impossible. They can slip slightly out of place but they are easily manoeuvred back again.

3 This really depends on the type of lens you choose. With soft lenses your optician will probably recommend you wear the lenses for around four hours for the first day and then gradually build up the wearing time every day. After four or five days you should be able to wear them all day. But this can vary from person to person so don't worry if it takes a little longer, it's better to under- rather than over-wear them.

4 Some people worry about not being able to touch their eyes with their fingers. But after a couple of goes nearly everyone finds that it isn't a problem. When you first get your lenses, someone who understands these worries will show you how to put the lenses in and how to take them out. You will only be allowed to take them home when you are completely happy with doing this.

5 No, we recommend you keep them. Many contact lens wearers find that they still feel like wearing their glasses from time to time.

6 It's far easier to play sport with lenses than with glasses. They can't steam up, get knocked off or broken. They are ideal for all sports, from contact games like rugby to fast games, like tennis, that require rapid eye movements. Swimming is the only sport where they could be difficult. Some opticians say not to wear them in the pool at all, others say you can wear them as long as you don't open your eyes under water or dive. To be absolutely sure, it's best to wear goggles.

7 Hard and gas permeables can very occasionally fall out but this is quite rare. However, with soft lenses it's virtually impossible, as the edges of the lenses are under the eyelids.

8 No. But it is very important to care for them properly. The process for doing this varies for the different types of lenses. For most lenses the care system takes only a few minutes every day. You'll soon find it easy to follow the recommended cleaning routine.

9 Yes, of course, but it's important that you put your lenses in first. It will also be a lot easier to apply when you can see what you're doing. And if you've been used to wearing glasses then you will be able to make a lot more of your eyes.

Exam practice

Answer the questions **1–9** by referring to the text 'Blind to the dangers'. The text describes problems experienced by people who wear disposable or reusable soft contact lenses.

What problems are associated with the following two types of contact lens? Choose your answers from the list of problems **A–D**. You may choose any of the problems more than once.

1 disposable soft lenses

2 reusable soft lenses

A loss of vision

B corneal ulcers

C low oxygen exchange

D conjunctivitis

Which opinion is expressed by the following people in the text. Choose your answer from list **A–G**.

3 Jean Brown

4 Prof Nathan Effron

5 Miss Susie Forbes

6 Dr Sudi Patel

7 Mr John Dart

A Gas permeable lenses are better for the eyes and carry a lower infection risk than soft lenses.

B Wearers of soft contact lenses can actually suffer a slight reduction in vision over a period of a few months.

C Wearing soft lenses for more than ten years will probably result in permanent damage to the eyes.

D It's easy to think that you don't have to worry about keeping disposable lenses really clean and free from germs.

E It's hardly surprising that ulcers occur when you discover how easy it is for germs to breed on the lens surface.

F We're currently developing a lens which covers a larger surface of the eye and has hundreds of tiny holes to allow the eye to breathe more oxygen.

G It's obviously safer to change your soft lenses once a year rather than every few years as I have been used to doing.

From your reading of the text, which two pieces of advice (**A–E**) are given to contact lens wearers?

8 ....

9 ....

A change to gas permeable lenses

B avoid wearing eye makeup

C replace lenses on a more frequent basis

D leave lenses out occasionally

E ensure regular and careful cleaning

Blind to the dangers

With more than two million contact lens wearers, experts are increasingly worried about poor hygiene. **Christine Doyle** discovers those most at risk of damaging their sight

WHEN Susie Forbes swapped her spectacles for disposable soft contact lenses, she was delighted. However, within a few months she started to get sore eyes and severe light-sensitivity. "When I put in my lenses, my eyes watered and it was as if I was temporarily blinded."

Like others with similar problems, Miss Forbes, who is features editor of *SKY Magazine*, went to the casualty department at Moorfields Eye Hospital, London. "I was told I had a corneal ulcer, though fortunately it was on the mend because I had left the lenses out for some time." She was advised to return to spectacles for several months. A corneal ulcer is a bacterial infection, which can advance quickly and may damage sight permanently.

Miss Forbes, 26, is among 2,000 contact-lens wearers, who are being studied by Mr John Dart, consultant ophthalmologist, and colleagues at Moorfields and the Institute of Ophthalmology. This investigation, which finishes next month, is expected to confirm a smaller pilot study last year, which showed that wearers of disposable soft lenses are at greater risk of infection than wearers of conventional reusable soft lenses.

Those wearing disposables during the day may be up to four times more likely to suffer a corneal ulcer than those wearing reusable soft lenses. Continuous wear of both disposable and reusable soft lenses at night increases the risk of infection with about one in 500 likely to suffer an ulcer. While wearing lenses for 24 hours a day and changing them each week is still popular in the United States, most British eye specialists and contact-lenses practitioners advise against it for most people.

With more than two million people wearing all types of contact lenses in this country, the Moorfields' study focuses fresh attention on the safest use of all types. Soft lenses, which many say are more comfortable to get used to than

rigid, gas-permeable lenses, are worn by four in five contact-lens users; about one in 14 wear disposables. According to one estimate, the incidence of corneal ulcer is one in 2,500 for reusable soft lenses worn daily, against one in 10,000 among gas-permeable lens wearers.

Although relatively the risks are small, specialists stress that the sheer numbers of people wearing lenses have led to an increasing stream of sufferers from infections and from 20 or so other possible complications. Many problems are due, says Mr Dart, to poor hygiene or using disposables for longer than the recommended two weeks or so.

Miss Forbes pleads guilty. "I blame myself. There seems to be an impression that you do not need to bother with disinfecting or cleaning them – it is enough to soak the lenses in saline each night. I am now wearing them again but am careful about cleaning daily and weekly and have not had any more trouble."

However, some eye specialists, including Mr Dart, do not blame wearers entirely. When disposables were first marketed it was believed infection risks might be lower. Advice from many optometrists on cleaning was not initially as rigorous as for reusable lenses.

Prof Nathan Effron, director of the European Centre for Contact Lens Research in Manchester, says: "It could have been predicted that ulcers would occur. Some of these lenses are made of material that easily attracts protein deposits, an ideal sticky breeding ground for bacteria."

Mr Dart says: "The eye is not a sterile environment, We have pictures of bugs growing in slime on the lens surface."

Concern over disposables has led to more intense scrutiny of all lenses. While good hygiene is crucial, emphasis has grown on replacing conventional soft lenses more frequently than in the past, as Jean Brown, a 25-year-old graphics editor, found. "After wearing soft lenses for 10 years, I developed a capillary conjunctivitis. My eyelids became red with lumps inside and the veins looked like crazy paving. I was lucky it was caught early. Otherwise there might have

been permanent damage and I would not be able to wear lenses at all."

To her astonishment, she was advised to renew her soft lenses every 12 months after previously changing them every three or four years. Now, it emerges, not only may slight damage to the surface over several years lead to increased irritation, dryness and discomfort, but vision may also be marginally impaired. Dr Sudi Patel, of Caledonian University in Glasgow, who has carried out a two-year study of 150 lens wearers, says: "There is a measurable loss of contrast vision after six months. It happens so slowly that you may not be aware of it but, reading say restaurant menus in low light might become harder. Put in a new lens and the vision is fine again." The same may happen to a lesser extent, he believes, with gas-permeable lenses.

In the final analysis, Mr Dart now recommends that those considering switching from spectacles to contact lenses are advised first to try gas-permeable lenses. "They may take a little longer to get used to, but physiologically they allow the cornea to breathe with much more oxygen exchange than soft lenses, which cover a larger surface of the eye. The infection risk is also less."

For the future he believes disposable soft lenses will come into their own only when they are truly able to be thrown away every night after wearing during the day.

Many manufacturers are piloting such a lens, but they are unlikely to be introduced until the price can be comparable with present lenses.

One British laboratory is working on a way to introduce hundreds of tiny holes into the outer rim of soft lenses. This development, which is being followed closely by manufacturers around the world, would mean more oxygen exchange and lower infection risk.

Not least, several researchers talk of adding some kind of self-destruct mechanism into disposable lenses to make sure people throw them away when recommended. Prof Effron says: "One idea is for a red ring to appear after a certain number of days' exposure to tears in the eye." That would give another meaning to the term 'pink eyes'.

'Some lenses are an ideal sticky breeding ground for bacteria'

What techniques help you to complete multiple matching reading exercises?

A multiple matching task usually involves matching one item of information to another. This may be done in different ways:

a you may be given a set of text-based answer options and asked to match one of the options directly to a gap in the text; e.g. task on page 83

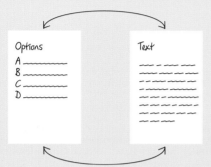

b you may be given some text-based questions/statements and asked to match one (or more) different section(s) of the text to each question/statement; e.g. task on page 65

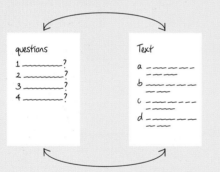

c you may be given some text-based questions/statements alongside a set of text-based answer options and asked to match one (or more) of these options to each question/statement; e.g. task on page 60

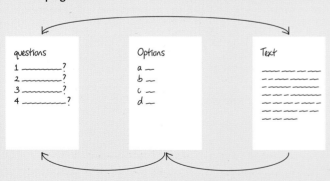

In each case you will need to refer directly to the text, but you may not need to read the text all the way through in great detail.

> **Remember:**
> - **sometimes some of the options may not be used at all**
> - **sometimes the same option can be used more than once**
> - **sometimes an answer may consist of more than one option**

Always check the instructions to the task carefully!

Reflections

1 In this unit we have looked at some of the many types of multiple matching exercise and at some of the techniques which help you to answer them. Tick the types of information-matching you have practised in Unit 6.

- matching a person to an opinion/comment/attitude
- matching a paragraph to a heading
- matching a paragraph/short text to a name/content description/ name
- matching specific details to a set
- matching a person/object/event to a factual detail
- matching cause to effect
- matching a problem to a solution
- matching a person/object to an attribute
- matching a text/caption to a picture

2 Look back at the reading texts and activities in Units 1–5 and find other examples of multiple matching formats. Can you add any more ticks to your list in **1**?

Seven

A

What about getting a job?

Starter activities

1 Here are ten ways of categorising different types of jobs:

1 administrative, e.g. *insurance clerk*
2 literary, e.g. *journalist*
3 health, e.g. *dentist*
4 construction, e.g. *builder*
5 agricultural, e.g. *farmer*
6 computational, e.g. *accountant*
7 scientific, e.g. *pathologist*
8 artistic, e.g. *designer*
9 sales/services, e.g. *sales representative*
10 leisure, e.g. *sports centre manager*

Classify the following jobs in the same way by writing the appropriate category number (1–10) against each one.

optician	engineer
pharmacist	policeman
barman	librarian
author	architect
interpreter	solicitor
translator	secretary
economist	actor
chemist	advertiser
dustman	draughtsman
shop assistant	systems analyst
customs officer	sales representative
speech therapist	

2 Think of ten other jobs and put them into the categories.

3 How are the jobs pronounced? Work with a partner, using a dictionary if you wish, to mark the stressed syllable in each word, e.g. fàrmer, dèntist. Then say the words out loud to one another with the correct stress.

4 Tick those jobs you could be interested in. Which of the ten kinds of job do you generally prefer? Discuss your answers.

Reading

You are going to read an extract from the beginning of a science fiction story in which someone called 'Dorcas' takes on a new job.

1 Read quickly through the extract to decide whether you think Dorcas is right for the job.

Granny thought it a perfectly horrible idea; but then, she could remember the days when there were *human* servants.

'If you imagine,' she snorted, 'that I'll share the house with a monkey, you're very much mistaken.'

'Don't be so old-fashioned,' I answered. 'Anyway, Dorcas isn't a monkey.'

'Then what is she – it?'

I flipped through the pages of the Biological Engineering Corporation's guide. 'Listen to this, Gran,' I said. '"The Super-
10 chimp (Registered Trade-mark) *Pan Sapiens* is an intelligent anthropoid, derived by selective breeding and genetic modification from basic chimpanzee stock –"'

'Just what I said! A monkey!'

'"– and with a large-enough vocabulary to understand simple orders. It can be trained to perform all types of domestic work or routine manual labour and is docile, affectionate, housebroken, and particularly good with children –"'

'Children! Would you trust Johnnie and Susan with a – a
20 *gorilla*?'

I put the handbook down with a sigh.

'You've got a point there. Dorcas is expensive, and if I find the little monsters knocking her about –'

At this moment, fortunately, the door buzzer sounded. 'Sign, please,' said the delivery man. I signed, and Dorcas entered our lives.

'Hello, Dorcas,' I said. 'I hope you'll be happy here.'

Her big, mournful eyes peered out at me from beneath their heavy ridges. I'd met much uglier humans, though she
30 was rather an odd shape, being only about four feet tall and very nearly as wide. In her neat, plain uniform she looked

just like a maid from one of those early twentieth-century movies; her feet, however, were bare and covered an astonishing amount of floor space.

'Morning, Ma'am,' she answered, in slurred but perfectly intelligible accents.

'She can speak!' squawked Granny.

'Of course,' I answered. 'She can pronounce over fifty words, and can understand two hundred. She'll learn more as
40 she grows used to us, but for the moment we must stick to the vocabulary on pages forty-two and forty-three of the hand-book.' I passed the instruction manual over to Granny; for once, she couldn't find even a single word to express *her* feel-ings.

Dorcas settled down very quickly. Her basic training as Class A Domestic, plus Nursery Duties – had been excellent, and by the end of the first month there were very few jobs
50 around the house that she couldn't do, from laying the table to changing the children's clothes. At first she had an annoy-ing habit of picking up things with her feet; it seemed as natural to her as using her hands, and it took a long time to break her of it. One of Granny's cigarette butts finally did the trick.

She was good-natured, conscientious, and didn't answer back. Of course, she was not terribly bright, and some jobs had to be explained to her at great length before she got the point. It took several weeks before I discovered her limi-
60 tations and allowed for them; at first it was quite hard to remember that she was not exactly human, and that it was no good engaging her in the sort of conversations we women occupy ourselves with when we get together. Or not many of them; she did have an interest in clothes, and was fascinated by colours. If I'd let her dress the way she wanted, she'd have looked like a refugee from Mardi Gras.

The children, I was relieved to find, adored her. I know what people say about Johnnie and Sue, and admit that it contains some truth. It's so hard to bring up children when
70 their father's away most of the time, and to make matters worse, Granny spoils them when I'm not looking. So indeed does Eric, whenever his ship's on Earth, and I'm left to cope with the resulting tantrums. Never marry a spaceman if you can possibly avoid it; the pay may be good, but the glamour soon wears off.

By the time Eric got back from the Venus run, with three weeks' accumulated leave, our new maid had settled down as one of the family. Eric took her in his stride; after all, he'd met much odder creatures on the planets. He grumbled about the
80 expense, of course, but I pointed out that now that so much of the housework was taken off my hands, we'd be able to spend more time together and do some of the visiting that had proved impossible in the past. I looked forward to having a little social life again, now that Dorcas could take care of the children.

For there was plenty of social life at Port Goddard, even though we were stuck in the middle of the Pacific.

There was a constant flow of distinguished visitors and travellers from all parts of the Earth – not to mention remoter points.

2 Now read the extract again, in detail, to complete this imaginary 'Employment record form' about Dorcas.

Employment record form	
Species:	
Name:	
Type of work undertaken:	
Qualifications:	
Training:	
Personality:	
Competence for job: strengths/ weaknesses	

3 The following words are from the extract. What do they mean? Work out their meaning from the extract, then write a definition for each one.

1 snorted (line 3)
2 flipped (line 8)
3 slurred (line 35)
4 squawked (line 37)
5 butt (line 54)
6 wear off (line 75)
7 took her in his stride (line 78)
8 was taken off my hands (line 81)

Discuss your answers, then check them in a dictionary or with your teacher or a partner.

4 Find five words in the extract related to the topic of 'jobs'. Compare your answers with a partner.

5 Do you think this story has a happy ending? How do you think it might end? The following text is the last paragraphs of the story about Dorcas. Read it and fill in the missing words in the blanks with one word only.

The house was utterly still; there was (1) .... sign of life. With a sense of mounting apprehension, I tiptoed through the drawing room, the dining room, the kitchen, and out into the back. The garage (2) .... was open, and I peered cautiously through.It was a bitter moment of truth. Finally freed (3) .... my influence, Dorcas had at last developed a style of her (4) .... She was swiftly and confidently painting – but not in the way I had (5) .... carefully taught her. And as for her subject ...

   I was deeply hurt when I saw the caricature she was painting. After all that I had (6) .... for Dorcas, this seemed sheer ingratitude. Of course, I know now that no malice was (7) .... , and that she was merely expressing herself. The psychologists, and the critics who wrote those absurd programme notes for her exhibition at the Guggenheim Art Museum, say that her portraits (8) .... a vivid light on man-animal relationships, and allow us to look for the first time at the human (9) .... from outside. But I did not see it *that* way when I ordered Dorcas back to the kitchen.

   For the subject was not the (10) .... thing that upset me: what really rankled was the thought of all the (11) .... I had wasted improving her technique – and her manners. She was ignoring everything I had (12) .... told her, as she sat in front of the easel with her arms folded motionless on her chest.

   Even then, at the (13) .... beginning of her career as an independent artist, it was painfully (14) .... that Dorcas had more talent in either of her swiftly moving feet than I had in (15) .... my hands.

Your thoughts

- **How would you have reacted to Dorcas? like Granny? like the children? like Eric? like the narrator?**
- **How suitable would you be for a job like Dorcas's, for example doing domestic chores and dealing with a family?**
- **What might Dorcas's vision of the human race be like?**

Writing

Imagine you are the narrator in the above text. At some time in the future when Dorcas no longer works for you, you receive a request from an employment agency for a reference for Dorcas. They want you to comment on how suitable she is for domestic work. Write the reference using the 'Employment record form' to help you with ideas. Don't forget to think about who you are writing for, and whether your style should be formal or informal.

Grammar reminder: words for linking sentences/clauses

Here are some words and phrases used in English to join sentences. They express four different meanings:

contrast   exception   comparison   addition

1 Which of these words or phrases express which meaning? Write **con** (contrast) or **exc** (exception) or **com** (comparison) or **add** (addition) against each.

apart from	**in relation to**	**along with**
except for	**despite**	**besides**
although	**even though**	**furthermore**
in comparison with	**in spite of**	

2 Complete these sentences about Dorcas by using the appropriate word or phrase from the list above. N.B. You will not need to use all of them.

1 .... human servants, Dorcas didn't seem very bright.
2 No one objected to Dorcas .... Granny.
3 .... her domestic skills Dorcas was also very easy to get on with.
4 .... the children, their mother much appreciated Dorcas.
5 The narrator thought that .... some humans Dorcas wasn't particularly ugly.
6 .... helping with domestic tasks Dorcas also took care of the children.
7 .... her limited knowledge of language Dorcas learnt very quickly.
8 .... her problems with cigarette butts Dorcas settled in easily.

3 Write four sentences about yourself and work using a different category of linking word in each.

Compare your sentences with a partner.

Listening

1 You are going to hear two young people Lisa Green and Keith Walker talking about their first jobs. Listen to find out (a) what jobs they talk about and (b) whether or not they enjoyed them.

✱ **2** Which of the things in the table below do you think are important to Lisa and Keith? Listen again and tick the appropriate column.

	Lisa	Keith
a good salary	✓	
interesting work	✓	
good promotion prospects	✗	
a good pension scheme		
acceptable working hours	✗	
good people to work with	✗	
a good physical environment		
job security	✗	
status and prestige	✓	
freedom	✓	

✱ Speaking: ways of comparing

1 Look at the list in Listening activity **2** and number the items, 1–10, according to what you (would) look for in a job. (1 = most important, 10 = least important).

2 Here are some expressions which are used to make comparisons. How emphatic are they? Number them: 3 = very emphatic, 2 = quite emphatic, 1= neutral.

It's much more important ...	**It's more important ...**	**It's so much more important ...**
It's not half so important ...	**It's nothing like so important ...**	**It's not so important ...**
There's no comparison ...	**You just can't compare them ...**	

Discuss your answers to activity **1** with a partner using as many of the expressions in **2** as appropriate. Tell other classmates what your conclusions were.

Your thoughts

- **Does either Lisa's or Keith's job appeal to you?**
- **Are young people usually interested in job security?**
- **Should your first job be one you could do all your life?**

RICH PARENTS

GOOD LOOKS

SUCCESS AT SCHOOL

B

Will I get a job?

Starter activity

Look at these ten pictures. Which attributes do you think help people most to get a good job ? Rank them 1–10, then discuss your answers.

$10 \times 7 =$
$10 \div 5 =$
$A B C D E$

GENERAL INTELLIGENCE

POOR PARENTS

DETERMINATION

FLAIR

HARD WORK

LUCK

TALENT

Reading

1 Read quickly through the article 'So you want to be a success' and note down at least nine things it mentions as contributing to success. Compare your answers.

2 Here are some words taken from the text. In groups of three or four work out the meaning of the words you don't know. It will help you to look at them in the text.

haphazard	a correlation
to inherit	affluent
to capitalise	plain
a peer	to rise through the ranks
awkward	a high-flier
to cope	a self-help manual
to forge your way to the top	

Listen to the words and repeat them paying particular attention to their pronunciation.

3 Read the article in detail and decide which paragraph mentions each of the following.

A Good looks help you in early life.
B It doesn't work to 'try, try and try again'.
C Motivation is the key to success.
D Many successful entrepreneurs leave school early.
E Entrepreneurs tend not to fit in.
F Rich people very often have rich parents.
G You can often predict the success of intrapreneurs.
H A hard life as a child can help you later on.

4 These are the final three paragraphs of the article. Some phrases have been removed from them. Decide which phrase belongs in which gap. You will not need to use all the phrases.

But what none of these self-improvement techniques do is to look at the quality of your life, or consider whether the price of success is too high. Professor Cooper describes the entrepreneur as 'an anxious individual, a non-conformist, poorly organised and not (1) ....'. Twenty-five per cent of top executives were unhappy with the long hours they worked (2) ....

In his best-selling book *The Seven Habits of Highly Effective People* Stephen Covey points out that concentrating exclusively on your own effectiveness leads to (3) .... To build a successful life you need to be able to behave in a way that meets the needs of others and yourself.

True success turns out to be founded on more than just chest-thumping motivational rituals. There is a need for harmony (4) .... *Jerome Burne.*

A achieving the right balance between work, creativity and relationships
B in need of organisational support
C negative results for all concerned
D balanced development
E and the destructive effect on their family
F a stranger to self-destructive behaviour
G greater feelings of self esteem

Your thoughts

- **Is it worth making sacrifices to become successful?**
- **Are successful people usually neurotic?**

Listening

1 You will hear an extract from a radio programme about three unemployed graduates, Richard, Jo and Gary. Listen to find out what is mentioned about who.

1 Richard
2 Jo
3 Gary

A previous job
B qualifications
C attitude to unemployment
D how unemployment has affected him/her
E their efforts to overcome unemployment

2 Look at these words. Tick those you remember hearing on the cassette.

unemployment	application form	friends
broke	career	graduate
rejected	degree	qualification
confidence	lonely	on the dole
social security	give up	lifestyle
ambition	experience	failure
self-esteem		

Compare and discuss your list with a partner. Can you remember the context in which you heard the word. Listen again to check your answers.

Your thoughts

- **Who do you feel most sympathy for – Richard, Jo or Gary?**
- **What would you do if you were in Richard's situation?**

So you want to be a success

We live in a society increasingly obsessed with material success.
2 We are exhorted to "Get on!" "Get ahead!" "Get a step on the ladder!" "Make it to the top!" If you don't prosper, it's easy to feel like a flop, that you've wasted your life and failed your family.

3 But is such success open to all? Do we all have the potential to be millionaires, and can success be taught? What can we learn from those who do make it to the top?

4 Becoming a millionaire is a surprisingly haphazard affair. At school we are told that if we work hard and pass exams we will do well. But a recent study by Professor Cary Cooper, of the University of Manchester Institute of Science and Technology, refutes this advice. When he studied the lives of successful entrepreneurs, he found that nearly 60 per cent left school early either because they were thrown out or were "bored". Other studies suggest there is little correlation between how well children do at school and the salary and job satisfaction they achieve as adults.

5 The most certain route to riches is to start out wealthy. Over half the people in the most recent *Sunday Times* survey of the richest 200 people in the country inherited money. Twenty-five per cent of those who head large corporations were born into affluent families.

6 If you're not born wealthy, you may be able to capitalise on another advantage: good looks. "Good looks make early life easier. Teachers and other children will expect you to be kinder, cleverer and to do better than plainer peers," explains Dr

Raymond Bull of Portsmouth University, expert on the effects of facial appearance.

7 Being tall is also an advantage. Other qualities being equal, employers are more likely to select taller and more attractive people. However, unless you want to work with children, it can be a handicap having too pretty a baby face. You are likely to be regarded as kind, but not very efficient. You may fare better by taking to crime – juries are far more likely to acquit you.

8 In a new book, *Business Elites*, Professor Cooper compares a number of successful entrepreneurs with people Cooper calls intrapreneurs. He defines intrapreneurs as those who rise through the ranks to the top of large corporations.

9 Cooper found major differences between the two groups. "Intrapreneurs tended to be the kids everyone thought would do well. Over half went to university, they are good organisers and get on well with people."

10 But the entrepreneurs often had early reputations as trouble-makers. "They probably left school early, had several business disasters and are awkward personalities. They are also intuitive and very determined."

11 The most dramatic difference between entrepreneurs and corporation high-fliers was that only five per cent of Cooper's entrepreneurs had both parents present throughout childhood, compared with 91 per cent of the intrapreneurs. In some cases the parent had died, in others they had been absent for long periods. "Coping with disaster early in life appears to give people vital resilience later on," suggests Cooper.

12 Nearly half of Cooper's entrepreneurs also felt that they had been the victims of discrimination early on – some were Jewish, some were immigrants, some were just physically small.

13 But even if you are born poor and ugly to parents who refuse to absent themselves from you, there's still plenty you can do to influence your chance of success. A range of courses and self-help manuals are available to help you forge your way to the top.

14 Go into any large bookshop and you'll find a section with titles such as *The Magic of Thinking Big*, or *Riches While You Sleep*. There's even a magazine called *Personal Success*, filled with ads for courses that will "unleash the power within" or "transform your thinking, behaviour and relationships".

15 "Successful people," says Breen, an organisational consultant, "are the ones who, when something doesn't work, try something else. Unsuccessful people keep on doing the same thing, only harder."

16 Most of today's courses on positive thinking originate in America. Many start by advising you to try "positive affirmations" such as this one from *Success Magazine*. "Look in the mirror every morning and say to yourself: 'You are rare, unique and different. You were designed for accomplishment, engineered for success.'" Sounds embarrassing? Don't forget that self-belief is crucial for success.

17 In his training programmes, Breen shows people how to banish negative thoughts and put themselves in a more productive frame of mind. Motivation is the key. Working in a big organisation can provide motivation (if only because the boss shouts at you), but entrepreneurs have to learn to "gee" themselves up.

18 Breen gets students to concentrate on immediate specific tasks that need attention, rather than allowing themselves to be overwhelmed by a mountain of things waiting to be done.

19 "We get them to imagine getting one thing done, and

how good it will feel when they've finished," says Breen. "If you really concentrate on those thoughts for just two or three minutes you'll find you can't wait to start work instead of dreading it."

(Foresight Magazine)

Grammar reminder: more words for linking sentences/clauses

In the three sentences below, the underlined parts relate in different ways to the main part of the sentence. The type of relationship expressed is given in brackets.

She sent off an application form *because she needed a job.* (reason)

He went back to studying *so that he could make himself better qualified.* (purpose)

She just couldn't find a job – *she got really depressed.* (result)

1 Now put the words below into the correct column according to their meaning.

since	so	owing to	in order to
so that	so as to	due to	seeing as
in order that	because	because of	as

Reason	Purpose	Result

2 Match the sentences on the left to those on the right as in the example, e.g. **a – 5**

a	He started painting pictures	1	so as to cheer himself and his mates up.
b	He started an unemployment club	2	he decided to emigrate.
c	He nearly gave up trying	3	seeing as he never had any success.
d	She went out to celebrate	4	no one was ever interested in him.
e	She began to do crossword puzzles	5	to get some money.
f	Although he had excellent references	6	to keep herself busy.
g	Due to the unemployment situation	7	since she'd just got a job.

3 Change the above sentences in as many different ways as you can while keeping the meaning the same, e.g.

He started painting pictures to get some money.
He started painting pictures so as to get some money.
He started painting pictures in order to get some money.
He started painting pictures in order that he should get some money.

There may be some differences in style in the sentences you make. What are those differences?

4 Write three sentences about unemployment in your country, one containing a result, one a purpose, and one a reason. Compare and discuss your sentences.

Vocabulary summary

1 Get into teams of three or four then listen to the questions on cassette. The first person to guess the answer correctly gets a point. The team with the most points at the end is the winner.

You may like to revise the vocabulary in the first two sections of this unit before doing the quiz.

2 In this unit, there are many examples of collocations (words that are frequently found together), e.g. job satisfaction, good looks. All the words below are taken from this unit. Match two words, one from each list, to make common collocations, e.g. cigarette butt

cigarette	balance
manual	face
instruction	butt
baby	sided
non	help
lop	organiser
good	flier
high	labour
self	conformist
right	manual

Read through the unit and find three more examples.

3 Think of some people you know (famous or not) who these collocations remind you of. Write their name against the collocation then explain your answer to a partner.

C

Paper 2 (Writing): Section A

Introduction

1 In Section C of Unit 2, you looked at the content of CAE Paper 2, Section A. What can you remember about this section? Make notes then compare them with a partner's.

2 Below is an example of a Section A task. Don't do this task yet but read it through and decide why you need to read each text to do the writing tasks. Make notes then discuss your answers.

A 19-year-old friend of yours, David Creusz, has recently written to you, and so has the Simmons au-pair agency. Write the letter of reference for David that the Simmons Agency requests and then a brief postcard to David to let him know what you've done. To write your letter and postcard, make use of any relevant information from the letters below and from the ad.

Your letter should be approximately 250 words long and your postcard about 30 words long.

**Live in with a British family
Au pair needed**

Month of August
To look after 2 young boys aged 6 and 8
Some domestic work required
Edinburgh, Scotland, U.K.
Free board and accommodation plus pocket money

Dear _____,

I've just applied for a job, and guess what… I've put your name down as a referee – I hope you don't mind, but I thought you could say what a great person I am, how I've got exactly the right personality for the job, etc., etc.! If they ask you what experience I've got of looking after children, don't forget I've done stacks of babysitting and there's my three younger brothers, so I've done a lot of babysitting there too.

I'd love to go to Britain for a month, especially Scotland. It'd be really good to stay with a family too and I'm sure I'd enjoy looking after two young boys – they're great fun at that age.

Thanks so much for your help. Maybe you can come and visit me if I get the job!

Love, David

Simmons Au pair Agency
Request for reference

Dear_____

re. references for Mr. David Creusz

We have recently received an application from Mr. David Creusz for an au pair job, an ad. for which I enclose.

He has put your name down as a referee and I would be grateful if you could please provide references. Could you please include the following points in your reference:

1   How long you have known the applicant and in what capacity
2   His/her personality
3   His/her experience of and relationship with children
4   His/her ability to adapt well and quickly to a new environment

May I thank you in advance for your help.

Yours sincerely,

P. Simmons

P. Simmons

How to approach Section A tasks

There are three basic steps to take when preparing to write a Section A task. These are:

1 identify **2** select **3** connect

> **1 Identify**
>
> You need to identify
>
> - what kind of text(s) you must write.
> - why you are writing.
> - who you are writing to.
> - what style you must write in.
>
> **2 Select**
>
> You need to decide what information you need to carry out the task.
>
> Go through the instructions and the texts in the example. Underline the information you need to carry out the task. Use your imagination too and note down any other information you are going to use in the exercise.
>
> **3 Connect**
>
> You need to connect the information in your answer by putting it in a suitable order, joining it with appropriate joining words and writing it up in an appropriate style.

1 Note down as a series of points the information you selected in the example. Then put it in the order you wish to present it in. Write a list of joining words that could be useful to join these points, e.g. words for sequencing (firstly, secondly, etc.) or making contrasts (but, however, etc.) or adding information (and, besides, in addition to, etc.).

2 Discuss and compare ideas with a partner until you come up with an order of points and range of joining words that you are happy with.

3 Look at the style of the letter and the postcard in the example. Which one is formal and which one is informal? Use the following questions to help you decide.

1 Why do you sometimes write informally and other times formally?
2 What different impressions are given by formal and informal writing?
3 Which text contains shorter sentences?
4 Which text contains more contracted forms?
5 Which text contains looser punctuation?
6 Which text uses less precise vocabulary?
7 Which text contains more specialised words?
8 Which text contains more complex sentence grammar?
9 Which text is more personal?

4 Look at your answers to questions 3–9 and use them to complete the following boxes:

Features of formal language	Features of informal language

Compare your answers.

Exam practice

Write the reference letter and postcard described on page 99, using all the notes you have made so far.

Ways of learning: self-evaluation

Self-evaluation means being able to assess and give your own opinion about how good you are at something. The purpose of it is to help you to recognise your strong and less strong points, so that you can know more clearly what you have to improve and what you can be pleased about. If you can evaluate your own abilities rather than have to ask someone else to do so, it enables you to learn more independently.

We can apply self-evaluation to the Paper 2, Section A writing tasks. How good are you at the Section A steps? Complete the table below by ranking yourself 1, 2 or 3 for each step. (1 = good, 2 = average, 3 = poor) Then complete the other columns.

Section A steps	Your ranking	Your reasons for your ranking	How you could help yourself improve
Identifying the task			
Selecting the relevant information			
Connecting the relevant information			

Discuss your ideas on how you could help yourself improve.

3 Read the article again in detail and answer the questions which follow:

1 The 17-year-old youth was accused of
   A possessing a handgun without the correct licence.
   B endangering another person's life with a gun.
   C driving a car in a dangerous manner.
   D being drunk and disorderly in a public place.

2 The father of the 11-year-old victim appears to have
   A questioned his son at length about the incident.
   B made an immediate complaint to the local police.
   C forced the teenagers involved to go to the police station.
   D chased after the young men in his car to get an explanation.

3 The police apparently found a loaded air pistol
   A in the 17-year-old youth's pocket.
   B at the home of the 17-year-old youth.
   C in the boot of his car.
   D at the home of one of his friends.

4 Apparently, the 11-year-old boy
   A is still receiving professional help.
   B is now too afraid to go out alone.
   C will no longer ride his bicycle.
   D has finally recovered from the experience.

5 The 17-year-old boy was
   A sent to prison for six months.
   B ordered to pay a large fine.
   C given probation and community service.
   D found not guilty of the crime.

4 **1** The newspaper report mentions the youth on trial several times throughout the article, but refers to him in different ways. Look at the text again and tick the descriptions in the following list which the writer uses to refer to the youth.

a young man	**an adolescent**
a Colwood-area teenager	**the accused teenager**
the 17-year-old boy	**the young male**
he	**her client**
the young offender	**the boy**

2 Look more closely at each of the descriptions you have ticked. Why do you think the writer has chosen to use each one? Is it because:

a it is the first time the character has been mentioned to the reader?
b it replaces a longer description with a shorter one?
c it adds some extra information to what we already know?
d it emphasises a different aspect of the character?
e it helps to avoid boring repetition?
f it helps to distinguish between two similar characters?

Discuss your answers.

3 Choose two of the following characters/objects in the story and note down the different ways the writer refers to them as the article progresses.

pellet pistol	**defence counsel**
an 11-year-old boy	**a car**
three young males	

Your thoughts

- **What do you think of these people in the article?**
  the 11-year-old boy
  the boy's father
  the judge
  the 17-year-old teenager
  the teenager's friends
- **Do you think that 17-year-olds should be allowed to carry guns?**

Listening

1 You will hear five short news reports about different crimes. For questions **1–5**, match the extracts with the crimes **A–H**.

1	**A**	murder
2	**B**	theft
3	**C**	arson
4	**D**	smuggling
5	**E**	rape
	F	assault
	G	dangerous driving
	H	manslaughter

2 Listen to the five extracts a second time. For questions **6–10**, match the extracts with the punishments given.

6 (1)	**A**	exile
7 (2)	**B**	execution
8 (3)	**C**	imprisonment
9 (4)	**D**	probation
10 (5)	**E**	fine
	F	hard labour
	G	flogging
	H	community work

Speaking

1 Which of the crimes **A–H** listed in listening activity 1 do you consider to be the most serious? Put them in order. (1 = most serious)

1	**4**	**7** ....
2	**5**	**8** ....
3	**6**	

2 Compare your answers with those of a partner. What sort of punishments are given for these crimes in your country? Together agree on the three *most* serious crimes and report your views to the rest of the group.

Grammar reminder: reporting orders/requests/advice

> **Remember:**
> **To report an order, a request or a piece of advice, you normally need to**
> **a** choose an appropriate reporting verb, e.g. *order, instruct, command, tell, urge*
> **b** include an object for that verb, e.g. *the gang ordered the bank clerks*
> **c** complete the sentence using a to + infinitive clause, e.g. *the gang ordered the bank clerks to put their hands above their heads*
>
> **Remember you may need to make changes to other parts of the original sentence, e.g. verb tenses, pronouns (*your* becomes *their*), etc.**
>
> **To make the reported orders negative, you need to**
> **d** insert 'not' after the object and before the verb, e.g. *the leader of the gang warned them not to touch the alarm.*

1 Look at these sentences.

a The gang ordered the bank clerks to put their hands above their heads.

b The leader of the gang warned them not to touch the alarm.

c The judge told the youth that his behaviour had been stupid and dangerous.

For each sentence, underline the 'reporting verb' and put a circle round the object of that verb. Now write down the actual words that you think the speaker(s) used.

2 Change the following sentences into reported speech using the words in brackets. The first example has been done for you.

1 'You will serve a 6-month period of probation.' (judge/order/young man)

The judge ordered the young man to serve a 6-month period of probation.

2 'The jury should disregard the evidence of this witness.' (judge/instruct/jury)

3 'Please don't shoot!' (bank clerk/beg/gunman)

4 'Open the safe and put the money in the bag.' (thieves/command/shopkeeper)

5 'Lock your bicycles whenever you leave them anywhere.' (policeman/advise/students)

6 'Do report the theft to the police.' (friend/urge/me)

7 'No possession of guns, ammunition or explosives for five years.' (court/forbid/young man)

8 'Don't touch anything until we've dusted for fingerprints.' (detective/warn/his men)

B

Crime and the writer

Starter activities

1 Have you ever read a novel and later seen a film or TV version of the same story? What was your reaction to it? What do you think are the difficulties of turning a book into a film or TV drama? Discuss your views with a partner.

2 Look at this photograph. Who is the woman and why is she famous? Read the paragraph to find out.

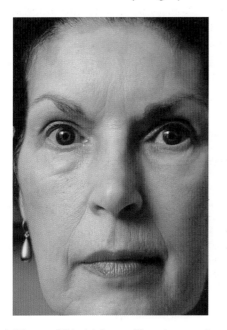

Ruth Rendell is one of Britain's best selling crime novelists. She has written many novels and won many awards. Her novel *A Fatal Inversion*, which she published under the pseudonym Barbara Vine, won her the Crime Writers' Gold Dagger Award in 1987 and was subsequently made into a television programme.

3 Read the 'blurb' for *A Fatal Inversion*.

In the long hot summer of 1976, a young man inherits a large country house and its contents following the death of a distant relative. He decides to spend the summer there and is joined by a group of other young people. They manage to live by stealing and selling some of the items from the house. Ten years later, the bodies of a woman and a child are accidentally discovered in the grounds of the house. Which woman? Whose child?

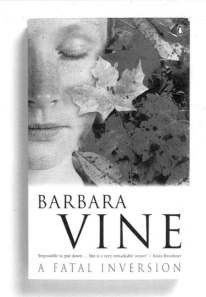

Would the picture and the blurb on the jacket encourage you to read *A Fatal Inversion*? Discuss your answers.

Reading

1 Read Ruth Rendell's own account of how she came to write the novel and how it felt to see her novel brought to life as a television series. Was she satisfied or disappointed with the final results? Why?

Summer of love
AND DEATH

Two days before I sat down to write I had no idea of a subject or characters. A young man who was designing a conservatory and called to talk about it came to my rescue. Not that he knew it. He sat in my kitchen, drinking tea and talking about old houses, more particularly about the old country house a friend of his had inherited at the age of 19 and had lived in for a few months with a group of friends until their money ran out.

2 I had my idea. I had my setting, too – my own garden that I could see from my window as I wrote: that view plus the enhancements of wish fulfilment. There was no walled fruit garden out there but Ecalpemos, the fatal inversion (it is "someplace" backwards), should have one; my pond is only a pond but Ecalpemos should have a lake; my bit of gravel and my stone vases on a low flint wall were transformed into a terrace with statues.

3 My own house I didn't use. Mine was too old for my purposes and too much a farmhouse. I never saw Ecalpemos except inside my head until I went to the large house in the country that had been picked as the setting for the television production. And there it was, perfect, as if I had created it myself and put it there, or had visited the house years before, forgotten it and seen it only in dreams. Perhaps I had.

4 *A Fatal Inversion* was a successful book and won the Crime Writers' Gold Dagger award for the year of its publication. That may be part of the reason why it was chosen as the first Vine novel to be adapted for the small screen, for there have been three more since. What also appeals, I think, is its contemporary setting, a high level of suspense in the plot and the youth and vitality of the characters.

5 The lazy summer days in which this plot unfolds, the atmosphere of paradise, I hoped would be captured in the production. When I drove up to see some

Crime writer Ruth Rendell tells how it felt to see her thriller, *A Fatal Inversion*, brought to life.

Actors Jeremy Northam and Clara Salaman: "The young cast had tremendous enthusiasm"

of the shooting it was cold and grey, but the garden was there and the peace and remoteness. The young cast had a tremendous enthusiasm for what they were doing. They liked the characters they were playing, they appreciated the story they were telling and enjoyed being in the unspoilt British countryside, in spite of having to wear shorts and swimming costumes in the bitter May weather.

6 I had taken pains to get the meteorological records for that particular July and August from the Weather Centre

> *'I shivered once or twice at the way the actors became the people who had tumbled out of my imagination, and sometimes uncannily more so…'*

while I was writing the book. It was important to me that it should at any rate look hot on screen. Later on, of course, our late hot weather arrived and turned into much the kind of summer I had in mind.

7 Immense pains had been taken to get the house just right. I was shown over the 18th-century house with ten or eleven bedrooms. It is a strange feeling to see the product of your own imagination take concrete form. This was very nearly exactly as I had conceived the house and its setting. People with sensitivity had inferred what I meant and rendered that impression back in carpets and curtains and pictures and ornaments, in disorder and cobwebs and rags and dust. And they had made a garden so near an Eden that you could understand my young people preferring to stay there rather than go to Greece.

8 The acting in this country is the best in the world, I wasn't surprised by the performances of the young actors, though I shivered once or twice at the way they conjured up reality, at the way they became the people who had tumbled out of my imagination, and sometimes uncannily more than those people. But that was at the shooting. For all my pleasure I was apprehensive when the video came and I settled down to watch it. After all, I have been disappointed before. What author hasn't?

9 I was pleased.
The worst fate I can imagine befalling a book of mine in adaptation, apart from obvious misrepre-sentation, is that the result turns out bland, stereotypical and pedestrian; that it should be "safe", not alarming and not provoking viewers to wonder and to question their own motives and assumptions.

10 *A Fatal Inversion* is very unsafe, very provocative and, as well as exciting, likely to arouse in a good many people a nostalgia for their own youth and that past time.

(Radio Times)

2 Read the text again and answer these questions:

1 Where did the idea for the story first come from?
2 Where did the author find the setting for the story?
3 What name did she give the house and why?
4 What does she think is the attraction of the novel for TV?
5 What efforts were made by the TV production team to be faithful to the original book?

3 1 Read the text again and collect all the words and phrases relating to

   a the original novel 'A Fatal Inversion', e.g. *subject, characters*
   b the television version of the novel, e.g. *TV production, setting*

2 The following nouns were all taken from the text. Can you add to each one any other nouns, verbs, or adjectives formed from the same root?

adaptation	film	production
performance	setting	actor

Your thoughts

- **Do you think this is a story you would enjoy?**
- **What crime novels or stories have you read or seen in English or in your own language?**
- **Do you have a favourite crime writer?**
- **Is there a popular crime writer in your own country?**

Grammar analysis: relative clauses

1 Look at these phrases:

1 ... a young man who was designing a conservatory ...
2 ... a terrace on which there were statues ...
3 ... the country house that had been picked as the setting ...

In each phrase underline the relative pronoun, i.e. the word(s) linking the first part of the phrase with the second, e.g.

first part	relative pronoun	second part
a young man	who	was designing a conservatory

2 Relative pronouns are normally used to attach essential information to a noun which has gone before. Make a list of all the relative pronouns which you know can be used in this way. Compare your list with a partner's.

3 Match a phrase from list **A** with another from list **B** to make a complete sentence. Use a relative pronoun to link the phrases together as in activity **1**.

A
1 The idea came from a young man
2 He described an old house
3 The old house
4 The story was set at a time of year
5 The actors actually became the people

B
a had tumbled out of my imagination.
b the weather was particularly hot and oppressive.
c he and a group of friends had lived for a few months.
d friend had inherited an old house at the age of 19.
e they did the filming was set in the countryside.

4 Look at these two sentences:
a The young actress who recently played the part of Juliet on stage got the part in the film.
b The young actress, who recently played the part of Juliet on stage, got the part in the film.

In sentence **a** the relative clause is a defining relative clause, i.e. it carries important information which clearly distinguishes 'the young actress' in question from any other young actress. In sentence **b** the relative clause is a non-defining relative clause, i.e. it provides additional rather than essential information about 'the young actress'. For this reason it is enclosed in commas within the sentence.

Discuss with a partner the differences in meaning in these pairs of sentences:

1 a An old house, which stood in remote countryside, was chosen as the setting for the drama.
  b An old house which stood in remote countryside was chosen as the setting for the drama.
2 a The novel in which she described her own childhood was published last year.
  b The novel, in which she described her own childhood, was published last year.
3 a The wood where the murder took place was owned by a local farmer.
  b The wood, where the murder took place, was owned by a local farmer.

5 Write your own pair of sentences – one with a defining and one with a non-defining relative clause. Ask a partner to explain the difference in meaning between the two.

Listening

1 Listen to the opening section of *Good Shot* and then answer the questions below.

1 Who do you think the man is?
2 What does he pick up from the table?
3 How do you think the story will continue?

2 Now listen to section 2 of the story. As you listen, note down anything you learn about the man's *feelings*. Compare your notes with a partner's.

3 Work with a partner and listen to section 3. One of you should note down what we can learn about *Dorothy* while the other one notes down any information about *Jim*. Share your information and discuss the following questions.

1 How old do you think Jim and Dorothy are?
2 What do you think their relationship to one another is?

Give reasons for your answers.

4 Now listen to section 4 and try to decide where Jim is and why he is there.

5 *'She had become totally vindictive, seeming to delight in all the heartache and unhappiness she'd caused.'* This is an important line in the story. Think about all the information you have gathered from the story so far and then discuss the following questions with a partner.

1 Who is the 'she' referred to?
2 In what way has she affected Jim's life?
3 How do you think the story will end?

6 Listen to the final section of the story to see how it ends.

What is your reaction to the story ending? Check with a partner that you know the answers to the following questions.

1 Who were the characters in the story?
2 Why did they behave as they did?

7 Now listen to the whole story once again for pleasure.

Writing

Your college/place of work produces a regular English language magazine and invites readers to contribute reviews of books and films. Choose a book you have read or a film you have seen recently and write a review for the magazine. Explain what the book/film is about, what you consider to be its strengths and weaknesses, and why you enjoyed (or didn't enjoy) it. You should write approximately 250 words.

Vocabulary summary

1 Choose the correct words to complete the text.

witnesses trial sentence prosecution
jury defence evidence judge
crime defendant

Anyone accused of a serious (1) .... has the right to a (2) .... by (3) ...., a group of men and women (usually twelve) chosen by chance. A (4) .... lawyer tries to convince the court that the (5) .... is guilty. A (6) .... lawyer sets out to prove the accused person's innocence. (7) .... tell the court what they know about the crime. After listening to all the facts or (8) ...., the jury must decide whether the prosecution has proved guilt. The (9) .... helps the jury understand the laws relating to the trial and passes (10) .... if there is a guilty verdict.

2 Work in small groups. One person in the group should secretly choose a word used in Sections A and B of this unit and write down the same number of dashes as there are letters in the chosen word. The other members of the group must then start guessing the letters in the word, calling out one letter at a time.

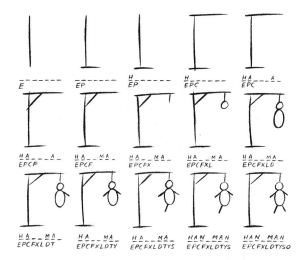

If a guess is successful, the first player writes the letter above the appropriate dash (if it appears more than once in a word, the letter must be written in as often as it occurs). If the guess is incorrect, the first player starts to draw a picture of a hanged man and continues to draw one line of the picture for each incorrect letter.

The other players must try to guess the secret word before the first player can finish the picture of the hanged man. The first player to guess the secret word chooses the next word in the game.

C

Paper 3 (English in Use): Section B

Introduction

Read the description of Section B of CAE Paper 3.

In Section B candidates will be expected to recognise and correct errors and inappropriacies of various kinds. This section is specifically designed to evaluate the candidate's ability to proofread and refine samples of written English. As such, this is a test of the real-life skills of correction and editing required in study and work.

Section B of CAE Paper 3 usually contains **two** tasks. In one you have to **identify and correct errors in a text,** while in the other you have to **choose the appropriate words and phrases** to use in a text.

Identifying and correcting errors in a text

1   This short text contains a number of errors. The first two have been identified for you. Read the text and identify the remaining errors by putting a circle round them.

A mother, aged 32 attacked a deputy headmistress, grabbed a secretary's hair and bite a teacher's leg after demanding to see the headmistress at her sons school, bournemouth Crown Court was told yesteday. She had become angry when the boy's junior school sent her a form to update. She was given a two year probation order.

2   Make a list of the errors you found in the text and write the corrected form alongside each error, e.g. *aged 32* → *aged 32, bite* → *bit*

3   What kind of errors does the text in activity 1 contain? Tick from the following:

*   missing comma
*   capital letter missing in name
*   missing apostrophe in contraction
*   missing full stop
*   missing speech marks
*   missing letter in a word
*   missing possessive apostrophe
*   missing hyphen
*   wrong form of verb

4   The text below has a different type of error to be identified and corrected. Read the text to find out what it is.

A man who snapped after he a year of being kept awake by the noisy neighbours was given a conditional discharge by a judge who said he did understood why he had threatened to burn down their house. Hull Crown Court was told that all Peter Plummer had moved to Bridlington to be recover after illness but was tormented when by all-night parties.

How did you identify the errors? Make a list of any clues you used.

5   Correct the text in activity **4** by removing the unnecessary words.

The task in this part of Section B of CAE Paper 3 may focus on any of the following types of textual error:

*   use of punctuation
*   spelling conventions
*   agreement of verbs
*   word formation
*   phrase and sentence structure
*   unnecessary words

Remember that a few of the lines in the text will not contain any errors – you need to be able to identify correct lines as well as incorrect lines!

Exam practice

1   In most lines of the following text, there is either a spelling or a punctuation error. For each numbered line, write the correctly spelled word(s) or show the correct punctuation in the space at the end of each line. Indicate any correct lines with a tick.

Motorists near Chicago stuffed there pockets with cash	1 ....
after hundreds of thousands of dollars fell out the back	2 ....
of an armoured van as it sped down a motorway with its	3 ....
doors open. "It was chaos People with car doors open –	4 ....
they didn't care if they were going to be hit, said Brandon	5 ....
hatch, an ambulance worker who scooped up a sack	6 ....
containing $120,000 and deliverd it to a police station.	7 ....
An aditional $30,000 was turned in, bringing the total	8 ....
recovered to £150,000.	9 ....

2   In most lines of the following text, there is one unnecessary word which does not fit in with the sense of the text. For each numbered line, write the unnecessary word in the space at the end of each line. Indicate any correct lines with a tick.

Barely 24 hours after the murder of an American student, the eight	1 ....
people were shot and wounded yesterday when by gunmen who	2 ....
ambushed a coach on a regular overnight journey from between	3 ....
Cape Town and Johannesburg. The ambush which happened just	4 ....
after midnight as the double-decker coach, carrying 52 passengers,	5 ....
was approached Beaufort West, 180 miles from Cape Town	6 ....
in the semi-desert Karoo region of. The gunmen, using South	7 ....
African army issue assault rifles, opened fire at as it slowed outside	8 ....
a stretch of road that flanked by townships. The coach was riddled	9 ....
with 39 more bullet holes.	10 ....

Choosing appropriate words and phrases to use in a text

1   Read these four short texts. Match the texts into two pairs by matching a more formal text with a more informal text on the same topic.

A   You wouldn't believe it, but they actually wrote to tell me if I didn't pay up and clear the bill straight away, they would take me to court! I was furious, I can tell you.

B   The security of any vehicles belonging to visitors is the responsibility of the individual concerned. We cannot accept liability for any loss or damage.

C   This is to notify you that unless there is an immediate settlement of this longstanding account, legal proceedings will be initiated.

D   Park in car park when you come – make sure car's out of the way and locked up – College won't want to know if it gets bashed or pinched. Chris

2   For all four texts decide as much of the following information as you can:

- where you would expect to read the text
- what the purpose of the text is
- who the text is written for
- whether the style is formal or informal

3   What different words and phrases have been used within each pair of texts to reflect different styles? Find more examples to add to those given below.

Formal	*Informal*
to notify	to tell

Look back at Unit 7 page 100 for more information about general features of formal and informal language.

4 Read part of this informal letter to a friend.

> *... You probably heard from my mother that we were broken into last week so it's been quite chaotic here. I couldn't believe it. I got home from work as usual around half five and I knew something was wrong 'cos I found the back door wide open. They'd smashed the lock and got in that way. They must've gone straight to the desk to look for loose cash. My cheque book and credit cards, £25 in notes and a gold watch belonging to my father had all gone. They took the TV, video and Peter's computer which is worth over £1500, and they made a terrible mess of the lounge – drawers pulled out, cupboards emptied, things scattered all over the floor, some of them broken in the process. The same thing happened upstairs in our bedroom; some of my bits and pieces were gone – a couple of rings, a brooch, even the pearl necklace my grandmother left me. Apparently a neighbour saw a couple of characters hanging around in the street at*

about 4pm that afternoon so the police think they could've had something to do with it. They've put out a description and hope it'll bring them one or two leads but they're not very hopeful about getting any of our stuff back ...

A
broken into, got home, found, 'd smashed, got in, cheque book and credit cards, £25 in, worth, couple of rings and a brooch, gone, a terrible mess, put out, had something to do with, a couple of characters

B
stolen, issued, been involved, gained access to, considerable damage, had forced, valuables, valued at, discovered, two young males, arrived home, £25 worth of, items of jewellery, burgled

A house in Tunwell's Lane, Great Cheshunt was (1) .... last week. The crime is thought to have been committed some time between 4pm and 5.30pm last Tuesday afternoon. The owner (2) .... after work and (3) .... that thieves (4) .... a door at the rear of the house and (5) .... to the premises. They escaped with a TV, a video and a computer (6) .... £1,750 as well as other (7) .... including a cheque book and (8) .... cash. Certain (9) .... were also (10) .... The property suffered (11) .... Police have (12) .... a description of (13) .... who were seen acting suspiciously in the vicinity earlier in the afternoon and who they suspect may have (14) .... in the burglary.

Exam practice 2

The following text is an advertisement for jobs in Scotland. Read the advertisement and use the information it contains to complete the numbered gaps in the informal letter. Use no more than two words for each gap. The words you need do not occur in the advertisement. The first example (**0**) has been done for you.

Advertisement

WANTED: GOOD LISTENERS

Mediation UK is currently seeking one or two individuals to join its mediation group in Scotland.

What is mediation?

Mediation is now being used increasingly to resolve the kinds of disputes which, if unchecked, can result in violent crime. It aims to bring people together so that they can discuss and resolve their grievances in a civilised manner. Although the group's present work involves mediation in neighbourhood disputes, an exciting new scheme has recently been initiated to develop the role of mediation in exchanges between criminal offenders and the victims of crime.

How do we operate?

The group responds directly to pleas for help – either from a member of the public or via an official body. Trained mediators discuss the dispute separately with both parties and, if both agree, arrange a meeting on neutral territory. The mediator's role is to enable the dispute to be discussed in a controlled environment and to encourage the parties towards a resolution of their problem which is acceptable to all concerned.

Who do we want?

Applications are invited from interested individuals who have a mature and varied experience of life. They should be committed to respect for the rights of the individual and be concerned for the well-being of the community as a whole.

For further details, please contact Maria Leibnitz on Glasgow 79684.

Informal letter

Dear Sophie,

I promised I'd fill you in about the work done by our local mediation group. The official advert to say we're (**0**) looking for new people will be in next week's paper. In this area most of our work is to do with (**1**) .... between neighbours although more and more we're being asked to help in other ways. We've recently (**2**) .... a project to develop positive communication between burglars and victims of burglary.

Calls for help can come from (**3**) .... or through (**4**) .... like the police or Citizen's Advice Bureau. We generally (**5**) .... a call for help directly and meet both (**6**) .... separately first of all to find out what the problem is and how they each see things. Then we try and (**7**) .... a meeting on safe ground (ie not in their homes!) when we can (**8**) .... the problem all together. The (**9**) .... of the mediator is to (**10**) .... under control at all times and not let them get out of hand! Hopefully we can find (**11**) .... which (**12**) .... everyone, although sadly that doesn't always happen.

I think what the group is really after in a mediator is someone who has a rich experience of life and people in general, and who is (**13**) .... to see the needs of the individual balanced against the needs of the many. If you'd like (**14**) .... on what's involved then please do give me (**15**) .... at home on Glasgow 59937.

Best wishes, Maria

Nine

A

Recognising feelings

Starter activities

1 Look at the faces and posture of the woman in the photos. How do you think she is feeling? Match the photos to the feelings listed below them.

frightened	**lonely**	**confused**
downhearted	**reluctant**	**furious**
elated	**aggressive**	**fascinated**
bored		

2 You will hear eight people expressing feelings. Which of these feelings are they expressing?

frustration	**delight**	**depression**
anger	**sadness**	**jealousy**
desperation	**irritation**	**weariness**
uncertainty	**determination**	**indifference**

Listen to the extracts again. Listen and repeat them paying particular attention to your intonation.

3 Can you make nouns from the adjectives in activity **1** and adjectives from the nouns in activity **2**?
e.g. *frightened* → *fright* , *frustration* → *frustrated*

1

2

3

4

5

6

✳ Speaking

Look at the feelings listed below. In your opinion, which of these feelings is most beneficial/productive ? Number them 1–10. (1= the most beneficial one)

jealousy	**contentment**	**bitterness**
guilt	**depression**	**self esteem**
indifference	**boredom**	**happiness**
desperation		

Discuss your answers with a partner, then discuss the following points:

- **Is it good for people to experience negative feelings?**
- **Do feelings get in the way of success?**
- **How important is it to listen to your feelings?**

🔲 Listening

1   You will hear some people having a row. Listen and decide (a) who the people involved are, (b) what the row is about and (c) what each person wants.

✳ **2**   Look at the opinions (**1–9**). Listen and match the opinion to the speaker who expresses it. Put **M** for mother, **D** for daughter and **F** for father. More than one person may express the same opinion.

1   The holiday will cost a fortune.
2   The bus trip might be dangerous.
3   The daughter needs some freedom.
4   The mother is a snob.
5   Clare isn't the wisest companion.
6   The daughter can stay in one place.
7   There's lots to do in Los Angeles.
8   The bus trip is well-known.
9   They need to talk about the trip again.

3   Look at these adjectives. Of the three speakers you have just heard, whose behaviour do they describe?

rude	**firm**	**frustrated**
angry	**resentful**	**furious**
appalled	**reasonable**	**worried**

4   Listen to these extracts from the same conversation and repeat them paying particular attention to your intonation.

Your thoughts

- **Which of the three people in the conversation do you agree with?**
- **Do you think rows can ever be useful?**
- **Do you prefer to avoid arguments?**

Reading

✳ **1**   Look at the extract from a book on page 115. It discusses why we feel feelings. Read the text through quickly to see which of the following its authors would agree with:

Our feelings are caused by:

a	our bodies	**d**	social factors
b	our memories	**e**	all of these
c	events		

2   Here are ten key words from the extract. Find them in the text, and then in groups explain their meaning to one another.

1	physiological (line 3)	**6**	saline (line 16)
2	adrenaline (line 9)	**7**	stooge (line 24)
3	flushed (line 11)	**8**	euphoric (line 31)
4	sweaty (line 11)	**9**	trigger off (line 55)
5	placebo (line 15)	**10**	take into account (line 57)

Now discuss the register of these words, i.e are they technical, formal, informal, etc.

Two psychologists called Schachter and Singer performed
a series of experiments designed to investigate just how
much physiological changes *do* matter in emotions, and
also how much our knowledge of what's going on is
important.

   In 1962, they performed experiments that involved
injecting people with adrenaline, and noting how they
reacted. They had three groups of subjects. One group
was given an injection of adrenaline and told what it was,
10 and the sort of reactions that they could expect from
it. (A flushed face, slight tremblings, and sweaty hands.)
A second group was also given an adrenaline injection,
but they were misinformed about the symptoms: they were
told that it might give them a slight headache, or other
things like that. The third group had a *placebo* – that is, they
were given a harmless injection of saline solution, which
wouldn't have any effect at all. So this would show up any
'imaginary' effects from being given what they thought was
a drug.
20   Schachter and Singer told their students that it would
take some time for the injection to have its full effect, and
asked them to wait in a waiting room in the meantime.
In the waiting room, each subject (they were tested
individually) met a 'stooge', who said that he was also
waiting for the second part of the experiment. The stooge
was really an actor, who was instructed to act either happy,
or angry. With the angry condition, he would become
increasingly impatient, complaining about the experimenters
and the waiting period, and eventually showing every sign of
30 becoming really angry. With the happy condition, the stooge
would appear euphoric, making jokes, and playing with
paper aeroplanes.
   Schachter and Singer found that the mood that their
real subjects fell into matched the mood of the stooge.
If the stooge was angry, the subjects would get angry; but
if the stooge was euphoric, the subjects, too, would start
to become happier. So it seemed from these findings, that
the emotions people experience can depend on the *social*
factors around them.
40   But another thing which Schachter and Singer found,
was that the *degree* to which their subjects reacted,
depended on the injections that they had been given. The
subjects who had been given adrenaline, and misinformed
about its effects, reacted very extremely – they either

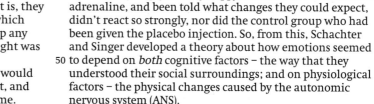

became very angry, or very happy. But the ones who had had
adrenaline, and been told what changes they could expect,
didn't react so strongly, nor did the control group who had
been given the placebo injection. So, from this, Schachter
and Singer developed a theory about how emotions seemed
50 to depend on *both* cognitive factors – the way that they
understood their social surroundings; and on physiological
factors – the physical changes caused by the autonomic
nervous system (ANS).

   From their studies, then, Schachter and Singer's theory
was developed as follows: a stimulus triggers off the
physiological response, and at the same time, the stimulus
is *interpreted* in the brain, taking into account previous
experiences of similar situations. The brain produces the
actual emotion that the subject experiences, through
60 cognitive factors, and the ANS produces the degree
to which that emotion is felt. So emotion is a mixture of
both cognitive and physiological factors.

   Although criticism can be made of this study, it does
seem to be likely that both cognitive and physiological
factors play their part in the emotions that we feel. One
theory argues that, in fact, we can divide the influences on
emotion into three groups of factors, and that we receive
information from each group. When we put all the
information together, then this makes up the emotion
70 that we experience.

   The three groups of factors are: physiological factors,
like the emergency reaction; stimulus factors – the actual
event which has caused us to react; and cognitive factors in
the form of the memories we have of previous events and
experiences.

(A First Course in Psychology)

3   Read the text in detail to find the best answer, **A**, **B**, **C**
or **D** to the following:

1   The subjects in the experiment
   A   all knew the drugs would alter their moods.
   B   were all told the truth.
   C   were all treated in different ways.
   D   received one of three different kinds of treatment.

2   In the waiting room
   A   each group met a different stooge.
   B   the stooge behaved angrily or happily with each subject.
   C   the stooge and the subject both had to wait.
   D   the subjects had to wait a long time.

3   From their experiment, Schachter and Singer concluded that
   A   our emotions are very dependent on who we are with.
   B   our physical state strongly affects our emotions.
   C   interpretation of a stimulus follows a physiological
          response.
   D   our nervous system determines how much we feel.

4   From the extract we can conclude that its authors
   A   fully agree with Schachter and Singer conclusions.
   B   thought their experiment was poorly designed.
   C   developed Schachter and Singer theories.
   D   believe Schachter and Singer's theories were probably
          correct.

Discuss your answers in small groups.

Your thoughts

- **Is it wrong to mislead subjects in experiments?**
- **From your own experience do you agree with the
  conclusions drawn in the extract?**

Grammar analysis: phrasal and prepositional verbs

1 Each of the following sentences contains a verb + a preposition. Some of these verbs are phrasal verbs and the others are prepositional verbs. Read the sentences then do the exercise below them.

1 Her demanding job broke up her marriage.
2 He was always hoping for an improvement in their relationship.
3 His tears broke down her indifference.
4 The two states have recently broken off diplomatic relations.
5 She shouted loudly for help when she realised how nasty the accident was.
6 Her fresh approach brought about a big improvement.
7 They called on their friends late last night.

Decide if the sentences below are true or false.
Mark them T or F as appropriate. Correct the false ones.

a Phrasal and prepositional verbs are made up of a verb and a preposition.
b Phrasal verbs and prepositional verbs can look exactly the same.
c You can separate the verb and the adverb in a phrasal verb, but you can't separate the verb and the preposition in prepositional verbs, e.g. *he gave the book away; *she ran the stairs up; she called her friend up; *he called his friend on.*
d Phrasal verbs generally occur in formal language.
e The preposition is normally stressed in prepositional verbs.
f You can put an adverb between the verb and its preposition in prepositional verbs, but you can't insert an adverb between the verb and the adverb particle in phrasal verbs, e.g. *she ran quickly up the stairs, *she rang quickly up her friend.*

2 Write 'phrasal' or 'prepositional' against sentences **1–7** in activity 1 depending on the kind of verb they contain.

3 Here are some phrasal and prepositional verbs that can be connected to feelings or emotions. Which feelings would you connect them with? Write the feelings beside the verbs. Then compare your answers.

to break down	**to liven up**	**to burst out**
to be down	**to give up**	**to talk over**
to care for	**to object to**	**to resort to**

Now go through the list of verbs and note beside each what kind of verb they are.

Vocabulary summary

1 Read through this section to make a list of ten feelings it mentions, then write the opposite of each feeling. Compare your list with a partner's.

2 Complete this table where possible:

Noun	Adjective	Adverb	Verb
happiness	happy	happily	——
delight			
	determined		
		irritatedly	
desperation			
			bore
	guilty		
frustration			
contentment			
fright			
			depress

Tick five vocabulary items that match how you feel/have felt recently. Using the words explain your answers to a partner.

B

Expressing your feelings

Starter activity

Opposite is a questionnaire that tries to find out how emotional you are. Do the questionnaire, then check your score and how to interpret it on page 118.

Compare your answers.

How emotional are you?

Are you uptight or are you loose, cool and ready to let it all hang out? Complete the questionnaire below to find out. Just write 'yes' or 'no' answers.

1 Do you feel guilty if you cry in public? 1 _____
2 Do you think that crying is a sign of weakness? 2 _____
3 Do you think that men and boys should be encouraged to hide their tears? 3 _____
4 Do you feel embarrassed if you find yourself crying while watching a film or reading a book? 4 _____
5 Would you try to hold back your tears if you attending a funeral? 5 _____
6 Would you distrust a politician who shed tears in public? 6 _____
7 Do you think that tears are an unnecessary expression of emotion? 7 _____
8 Would you allow someone to comfort you if you were found crying? 8 _____
9 Do you get embarrassed if you see grown men crying? 9 _____
10 Would you pretend that you had something in your eye if you were unexpectedly found crying? 10 _____
11 Do you always try to hide your anger? 11 _____
12 Do you always try to hide your disappointment? 12 _____
13 Do you ever lose your temper? 13 _____

14 Has your temper ever got you into trouble? 14 _____
15 Do you believe that it does you good to get rid of your anger? 15 _____
16 Do you tend to brood about things which have made you angry? 16 _____
17 Do you get cross quite easily? 17 _____
18 Do you touch someone you love at least once a day? 18 _____
19 Do you enjoy physical signs of affection? 19 _____
20 Do you ever get broody when you see small babies? 20 _____
21 Would you happily hold hands in public with someone you cared for? 21 _____
22 Do you enjoy being massaged? 22 _____
23 Do you regularly tell those whom you love how you feel? 23 _____
24 Have you ever had a pet of which you were very fond? 24 _____
25 Do you enjoy being kissed and hugged by people you love? 25 _____
26 Do you ever laugh out loud when you are watching funny films? 26 _____
27 Do you ever tap your feet while listening to music? 27 _____
28 Do you often have the last clap at concerts, sports events and the like? 28 _____
29 Do you ever shout encouragement to sports or TV heroes? 29 _____
30 Can you remember when you last really laughed and enjoyed yourself? 30 _____

(Know Yourself by Vernon Coleman)

Check your score

1 yes 0 no 1	16 yes 0 no 1
2 yes 0 no 1	17 yes 1 no 0
3 yes 0 no 1	18 yes 1 no 0
4 yes 0 no 1	19 yes 1 no 0
5 yes 0 no 1	20 yes 1 no 0
6 yes 0 no 1	21 yes 1 no 0
7 yes 0 no 1	22 yes 1 no 0
8 yes 1 no 0	23 yes 1 no 0
9 yes 0 no 1	24 yes 1 no 0
10 yes 0 no 1	25 yes 1 no 0
11 yes 0 no 1	26 yes 1 no 0
12 yes 0 no 1	27 yes 1 no 0
13 yes 1 no 0	28 yes 1 no 0
14 yes 1 no 0	29 yes 1 no 0
15 yes 1 no 0	30 yes 1 no 0

Total =

Interpret your score

If you scored between 17 and 30, your attitude towards your emotions is a healthy one. You aren't ashamed to let your emotions show occasionally, and you will undoubtedly be much healthier because of this attitude.

If you scored between 8 and 16, you know how to let your emotions show but you still find it difficult to do so as often as you should. You should be prepared to let your emotions out more often. When you feel sad, let yourself cry. When you feel angry, let your anger show. When you feel happy, allow a smile to cross your face. Allowing your emotions out in this way will do wonders for your physical and mental health.

If you scored 7 or less, you are definitely very uptight. You really do need to let your emotions hang out a little. There really isn't anything wrong in allowing people to know how you feel. The more you struggle to retain your natural impulses, the more likely it is that those impulses will damage your health.

Your thoughts

- **Do you agree with what the questionnaire told you about yourself?**
- **Are questionnaires like this a reliable way of finding out about yourself?**
- **Is it better to express rather than suppress your emotions?**
- **Do men find it harder to express their emotions than women?**

Listening

1 Listen to the story 'Looking Lost'. Do you think it is sad, ridiculous, sentimental, happy or tragic?

Discuss your answers with a partner.

2 Listen to the story again and put the events **A–I** in order.

A Amy asked a boy about her daughter.
B Amy went to the newsagent's.
C Amy tried to move towards her daughter.
D Amy went to her daughter's school.
E A policeman arrived.
F Rosie died.
G Mr Phillips found the child's drawing.
H Amy was happy.
I Amy started panicking.

3 The following verbs are all taken from the story. Discuss their meaning and try to remember when they are used in the story.

spill out	peer	drum	jolt
scan	stir	glisten	swirl
shimmer	mumble	frown	gaze down

Now listen to the story again to check your answers and to enjoy the story.

Grammar reminder: *as* and *like*

As and *like* can both be used to introduce descriptions of manners or ways of doing things. In these cases, generally speaking, *as* is used to introduce clauses or in comparative phrases, whereas *like* introduces noun phrases.

Fill in the gaps with *as* or *like*.

a His reply was as quick .... lightning.
b She always reacted to events .... her mother did.
c He cried .... a baby would, just howling and howling.
d They looked just .... clowns, comical and sad at the same time.
e It is said that men can behave .... aggressive animals.
f The children solved their dispute by talking it through sensibly .... adults.
g Scientific evidence suggests that men don't react .... women.
h In the interview she was treated .... a naughty girl.
i They always expressed their emotions freely .... young children do.
j We believe, ... do all the scientists involved in gender testing, that their findings are only tentative.

Speaking: speculating

Here are pictures of six difficult situations. Imagine yourself in each in them.

1 Complete these sentences about yourself and these situations.

If I were ...	**Were I to ...**
Should I ...	**If that were me in ...**
If I were in /their/ shoes ...	**In that sort of situation ...**
In a case like that ...	

Compare your answers.

2 With a partner:

- **describe what you would do and how you would feel in each situation.**
- **say which situation you would react best in and why.**
- **advise one another on the best course of action for each situation.**

Reading

1 Read the headlines and captions for the article below. What do you think the article will be about? Discuss your answers. Read the article for gist to check your answers.

2 Read the article in detail and list the arguments it contains for suggesting that 'male and female thought processes are different'.

Men, the emotional sex

Even before birth, the brains of men and women operate differently. Now new research shows that intuitive responses of the sexes are pre-programmed too

Equal opportunists will be confounded by the evidence that, in fact, male and female thoughts processes are different.

EVER since Neanderthal man evolved into a creature with feelings, he has been trying to conceal them. But hiding the giveaway clues isn't easy. The smile that doesn't follow through to the eyes, the hint of a quaver in the voice, the merest suggestion of a furrowed brow – all conspire against people who don't wear their hearts on their sleeves ... and society has always believed that when it comes to picking up such clues, women have the edge on men.

However, a study released last week by scientists at the University of Pennsylvania indicates that it is men who have the stronger emotional response to other people's feelings. It throws a whole new light on to the male psyche and is one of the first investigations conducted into the differences in male and female ability to process emotions.

During the research, male and female 'guinea pigs' were shown photographs of actors and actresses making a range of facial expressions. They were then asked to describe the emotion portrayed. In virtually all areas, men consistently outperformed women – especially when it came to detecting sadness.

The findings are the latest to add weight to a theory that has confounded the equal opportunists. Quite simply, it proposes that men's and women's thought processes are fundamentally different.

The theory remains highly controversial in the medical world. But the evidence behind it has been accumulating for the past decade to the point where it can no longer be ignored – however politically incorrect its implications.

A catalogue of studies now strongly suggests that while there is no actual difference in male and female levels of intelligence, the sexes have markedly different patterns of ability and perception.

Numerous scientists have now come to the conclusion that men are more decisive, aggressive and driven by money and status than women. They also believe they tend to be more mechanically minded, better at targetting objects and better at activities which require spatial reasoning – such as playing with Rubik cubes.

Women, on the other hand, are thought to have greater verbal fluency than men, though the sexes have equal vocabularies. They prefer amicable solutions to problems and perform better in non-competitive situations. They also outperform men in arithmetic calculation, can store more random information, and are far better than men at identifying matching items in a hurry.

The reason for the differences is thought to be largely due to levels of the hormone testosterone in both men and women.

Scientific evidence from all over the world supports this belief – including research conducted by Melissa Hines, a Los Angeles behavioural scientist. Dr Hines contacted a group of women born with a rare genetic abnormality which caused them to produce elevated levels of the hormone.

She found they had all developed skills traditionally thought of as 'male', and had entered fields such as architecture, mathematics and mechanics. It seems hormones create a mental divide between men and women even before puberty. Recent research by Professor Doreen Kimura, of the University of Western Ontario, has come down heavily in favour of the theory that babies are born with mental gender differences – because sex hormones have affected the brain as it develops in the womb.

It has been fashionable to insist that any differences in the intellectual thought processes of the sexes are only minimal and the result of different experiences during the development of a child. But, says Professor Kimura, the bulk of evidence now indicates that sex hormones take effect so early in life that, from the very start, the environment is acting on differently wired brains in girls and boys.

Professor Kimura has conducted extensive tests which show that three-year-old boys are better at targetting objects than girls of the same age. Animal studies she looked at confirmed these early differences.

Her studies show that major differences in the intellectual function appear to lie in patterns of ability rather than in the overall level of intelligence.

Scientists believe that the specific area of the brain affected by sex hormones is the hypothalamus, which is situated at the base of the brain and stimulates feelings of rage, hunger, thirst and desire.

As well as creating differences in the thinking processes of the sexes, the same area of the brain appears to influence sexual orientation. Last summer, San Diego scientist Simon LeVay announced the intriguing discovery that part of the hypothalamus was twice as large in heterosexual men as in women or homosexual men.

3   Here is the last part of the article. The paragraphs A–E have been removed. Match the paragraphs to the numbered gaps in the article. There is one extra paragraph which does not belong in any of the gaps.

PROFESSOR Kimura has now discovered that homosexual men tend to do worse in targetting tasks, but are superior in other areas, for
120 example, listing things that are a particular colour. This goes one step further towards supporting the theory that part of the brain is pre-programmed.

But despite all the differences that appear to have emerged between male and female brains, Professor Kimura's studies indicate that the sexes still have something quite striking in common: both, it appears, are sensitive to hormonal fluctuation throughout their lives.

Women tested by scientists at Canada's York University have been found to score much better on spatial reasoning tests during
130 menstruation, when their oestrogen levels are low. Now Professor Kimura has discovered that males perform best on mental-rotation tests in the spring when, contrary to popular belief, male levels of the hormone testosterone are at their lowest. Autumn, when testosterone levels are high, is when her male subjects fare worst in tests.

1 [   ]

Moreover, weaknesses in certain skills are not fixed immutably. Extra training in weak areas for both sexes can go far towards rectifying the gender balance.

2 [   ]

It's a good step forward towards greater harmony between men
140 and women. It means they can work towards understanding and helping each other, even on the most basic level.

3 [   ]

FURTHERMORE, says Dr Apter, the latest findings mean that women need no longer force themselves into activities for which they have no natural gift – just for the sake of equality. 'They don't have to feel guilty or inferior about doing feminine things.' With childcare, for example, women have developed the skills of attending to babies and noticing what they need and when they need it. This is partly social because they spend more time with them, but women do also tend to be quicker at learning how to
150 respond to the young.

4 [   ]

A   But Dr Terri Apter, a social psychologist at Cambridge University, welcomes the recognition that the sexes have different intellectual abilities.

B   'If women want to stay at home looking after their children, they should do so. They happen to be very good at it.'

C   What's more, the experts acknowledge that in spite of some evidence to the contrary women generally recognise their superiority in this field.

D   'If a man finds his wife is not very good at map-reading and realises that it may be genetic, he will not only be more patient but he can teach her how to do it better.'

E   Of course, as all scientists involved in gender testing are at pains to point out, their results are only averages. Some women will be better at football than most men, and some men will be better at Russian than most women.

Compare your answers with a partner's.

4   The article contains these idiomatic expressions. Read the article again to try and work out their meanings then write a definition of each one.

1 a giveaway clue (line 5)
2 the hint of a quaver in the voice (line 7)
3 a furrowed brow (line 8)
4 wear your heart on your sleeve (line 9–10)
5 have the edge on (line 12–13)
6 throw a new light on (line 18–19)
7 guinea pigs (line 24)
8 add weight to (line 31–2)
9 target an object (line 52)
10 from the very start (line 93)
11 rectify the balance (line 137–38)

Compare your definitions with a partner's and decide which definitions are best or how they could be improved, then check your definitions with a dictionary or with your teacher.

Your thoughts

What do you think about the following statements?

- **Men and women's thought processes are fundamentally different.**
- **There is no real difference in male and female levels of intelligence.**
- **Men are more decisive, aggressive and driven by status than women.**
- **If women want to stay at home looking after their children, they should do so.**

Writing

You have been asked by your classmates to write a letter to the English newspaper that published the article 'Men, the emotional sex' outlining your objections to/support for it. Write the letter in about 250 words. You should say why you are writing, outline your reactions to the article and say why you agree/disagree with it.

Vocabulary summary

1   Look through the unit and find at least five words that a) remind you of yourself, b) you like and c) remind you of someone you dislike.

Compare your lists and explain your answers.

2   Get into teams of four or five and choose ten fairly 'difficult' words from the unit. Then write a clue, like a crossword clue, for each word. When all the teams are ready, hold a quiz. Each team reads out a clue in turn; the first team to guess the correct word wins a point, etc. The team with the most points is the winner.

C

Paper 4 (Listening): Section C

Introduction

Read the information below about Section C of Paper 4 and underline anything that isn't clear to you. Discuss your queries with a partner.

> *What you listen to:* a conversation of approximately four minutes that you hear twice.
>
> *What kinds of things you listen to:* interviews / meetings / announcements / radio broadcasts / recorded telephone messages.
>
> *What skills are being tested:* understanding of gist, attitude and directly stated information.
>
> *What you have to do:* transfer information / complete notes / sequence information by writing in or ticking boxes / multiple-choice questions, etc.

An example of CAE Paper 4, Section C

Try this example of a Section C task.

You will hear a radio extract which describes something special a woman did. Read the questions and circle the correct answer, **A**, **B**, **C** or **D**. You will hear the piece twice.

1 The extract is about
  A a fight.
  B a robbery.
  C an act of bravery.
  D an injustice.

2 Yvonne
  A caught the first raider with her gun.
  B trapped the second raider by her legs.
  C raced after the second raider.
  D hit the second raider with her shopping bag.

3 When the police arrived Yvonne
  A gave up hope.
  B was terrified.
  C kept calm.
  D got frightened.

4 The police
  A put the raider in their van.
  B pointed a gun at the raider.
  C found the raiders' getaway car.
  D dropped the post office cash box.

5 Yvonne is
  A proud of her deed.
  B embarrassed by her weight.
  C positive about her weight.
  D worried about her children.

6 Yvonne's bravery
  A worried the police.
  B was admired by all concerned.
  C angered the police and her children.
  D was praised by the police and the post office owner.

Ways of learning: different ways of listening

There are many different ways of listening – how you listen will depend on your role as a listener, e.g. you may be listening for detailed information or simply overhearing a conversation which you are not participating in.

1 Write some brief notes about what you would pay attention to in the following situations:

1 An airport announcement:
  a if you were about to catch a flight?
  b if you were at the airport just to have a look around?

2 An upset child's report of having seen a car accident:
  a if you were the child's parent?
  b if you were a policeman?

3 News of a small earthquake:
  a if you lived in the earthquake area?
  b if you lived on the other side of the world and knew nobody from that area?

4 A parent rowing with their teenage child about coming home late:
  a if you were the teenager?
  b if you were a neighbour listening through the wall?

Discuss your answers with a partner.

2 Note down some occasions on which in your everyday life you

- listen for gist
- listen for detail
- listen for attitude
- listen for a mixture of these

Compare your answers with a partner's.

3 Think about these questions.

- What are our reasons for listening in different ways?
- Which of the above situations involves listening for (a) gist (b) attitude (c) detail?
- Would it be a good idea to always listen to things in the same way? Why / why not?
- Is it different carrying out these different kinds of listening in your own language and in a foreign language? Why / why not?

Listening in the exam

- Which of the questions in the example on page 122 required you to listen for gist, attitude or detail?
- Can you tell from looking at multiple-choice questions what kind of listening might be required of you?
- Is it better to listen generally the first time and only concentrate on answering the second time or answer whenever you can?

Exam practice

Do this task as you would in the CAE exam.

You will hear a radio interview with a pop star whose hobby is parachuting. For questions **1–8**, complete the sentences with an appropriate word or short phrase. You will hear the piece twice.

Jason did his first parachuting when he (**1**) .... the air cadets. Now he belongs to (**2**) .... where he goes most weekends. Jason can afford to parachute because (**3**) .... He thinks the most frightening moment in parachuting is (**4**) .... and that you feel very (**5**) .... just after you jump. He says that when the parachute opens you feel you've been (**6**) .... He once had a problem when his parachute and (**7**) .... got tangled up. He plans to jump off (**8**) .... next year.

Ten

A

What is assertiveness?

Starter activities

1 Decide which of the following adjectives apply to the people in the cartoon.

threatening	clear	angry
respectful	equal	uptight
rejected	defensive	direct
rebellious	self-confident	fed-up
victimised	humiliating	

2 Mark the stress on the adjectives (use a dictionary if you wish), then say them to one another.

3 Would you describe the people in the cartoon as assertive, passive or aggressive?

4 In small groups write definitions for assertive, passive and aggressive.

5 How assertive are you? Answer this questionnaire to find out. Circle the answers which are right for you.

> ## What would you do if...
>
> 1 someone sold you rotten fruit?
>   A say nothing   B create a scene
>   C calmly ask for some D other
>   decent fruit
>
> 2 someone smoked in a non-smoking compartment you were in?
>   A call an inspector   B ask the person not to
>   smoke
>   C suffer in silence   D other
>
> 3 a waiter ignored you in a restaurant?
>   A walk out noisily   B wait patiently
>   C go and get the waiter D other
>
> 4 your boss criticised your work?
>   A sulk   B get angry with your
>   boss
>   C discuss the matter   D other
>   with your boss
>
> 5 a friend asked to borrow a new record of yours that you loved?
>   A lend it to them   B tell them to get lost
>   C come to a compromise D other
>
>

Now read through your answers and classify them into passive, aggressive or assertive. Discuss your answers with a partner. Are you generally passive, aggressive or assertive?

Reading

1 Look at these three definitions of 'assertiveness'.

a Making sure you always get what you want
b Standing up for your own rights
c Respecting your own rights and those of others

The following text is an extract from a book about assertiveness. Read through the extract and decide which of the three definitions best describes the author's point of view?

Assert yourself

1 The most self-assured and sophisticated of people can find themselves unable to deal satisfactorily with certain situations – cold food in a restaurant, angry neighbours, stroppy shop assistants, uncommunicative teenagers – from time to time. And for many of us, attempting to deal with such irritations without either losing control and our tempers, or being wimpish and ineffectual, is too common an occurrence.

2 The usual reason for such maladroit behaviour is an inability to express ourselves clearly and straightforwardly. We beat around the bush endlessly before, if ever, we reach the nub of the argument. Failing to communicate clearly what you want and/or what you feel, means, at one end of the spectrum, that you fail to persuade the shop to exchange a faulty garment or fail to have your cold dinner replaced in a restaurant; and at the other extreme, that you're unable to negotiate with your boss or your juniors calmly, or that you spend far too many evenings in grumpy silence because you cannot express your feelings to your partner.

3 We usually fail to communicate what we want, how we feel about something, because we are anxious about the way our views or requests will be received. And when we feel anxious, we tend to become aggressive, or manipulative, or passive allowing ourselves to be trampled upon. By being aggressive, we are often over-reacting and alienating others. Being manipulative may bring immediate success but it's hardly a basis for an honest strong relationship – and deviousness can backfire. Needless to say, being passive makes you feel even smaller, and may also result in abject failure.

The assertive way

4 Over the past few years, many people have learned another way of behaving, a middle course between being aggressive or passive, the assertive way. It is a way of communicating clearly one's wishes, needs and/or feelings while at the same time respecting the needs, wishes and feelings of others. It is *not* about winning all the time, rather more about negotiating life without constant anxiety or lack of self-confidence. It is usually a more appropriate and a more effective form of communication.

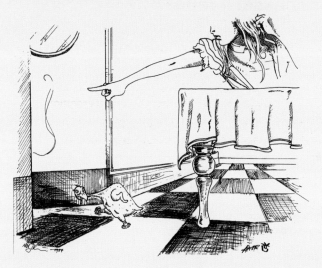

5 Helen was having dinner with friends in a small local restaurant. When her main course – roast chicken – was served, she discovered it was undercooked. Before she learned some assertiveness skills, she would have screamed at the waiter and caused an embarrassing fuss. This time she drew a deep breath and calmly asked to speak to the manager. He looked scornfully and commented: 'Our cook is excellent and no-one has ever complained before.' 'Well, I'm sure your cook is excellent,' said Helen, 'but I'm complaining because this chicken isn't cooked properly. Please can you give me some that is cooked.' He blustered a little more but Helen refused to be side-tracked, nor did she lose her temper. She just repeated her request. Eventually her meal was replaced.

6 By handling her complaint assertively, Helen avoided an embarrassing scene, which would have spoiled the evening for everyone, and was given what she wanted – a properly cooked meal.

(Channel Four Television)

2 Look at these twelve adjectives which describe people's behaviour (and reactions). Find their opposites in the text on page 126. You may find more than one for some of them.

powerful	strong	effective
communicative	calm	easy
good-tempered	appropriate	at ease
passive	aggressive	respectful

With a partner discuss occasions on which any of these adjectives (positive or negative) could have been used to describe you.

Do any of these adjectives remind you of anybody else? Write their names beside the adjective, then explain the connection to a partner.

3 For questions **1–6**, read the text through carefully and match each paragraph with one of the summaries **A–F**.

1 .... **A** an example of assertive behaviour
2 .... **B** assertive behaviour
3 .... **C** how common lack of assertion is
4 .... **D** the negative effects on relationships of lack
5 ....   of assertion
6 .... **E** the positive effects of some assertive
                 behaviour
          F situations brought about by lack of assertion

For questions **7–11**, match the items with one of the descriptions **A–D**, according to the view given in the passage.

7 a stroppy shop assistant   **A** a difficult situation
8 clear communication   **B** a negative emotion
9 repeating a request   **C** assertive behaviour
10 being manipulative   **D** unassertive behaviour
11 being unable to exchange
    goods

Your thoughts

- **Do you think that behaviour can be classified into these three types: assertive, aggressive or passive?**
- **Do people need to learn to be assertive?**
- **Did Helen behave correctly in the restaurant?**

Grammar analysis: modal verbs for speculation and deduction

1 Some of the modal verbs in the sentences below are being used to speculate. Write the numbers of those sentences.

1 Helen could have been aggressive in the restaurant.
2 The cook can't have cooked the chicken properly.
3 The cook mightn't have been very good.
4 Managers ought always to accept their customers' complaints.
5 The waiter should have replaced Helen's chicken straight away.
6 The manager must have been telling lies.
7 Undercooked meat might poison you.
8 The chicken must have been undercooked.
9 You should never accept poor quality food in a restaurant.
10 Assertive behaviour may not always do the trick.
11 After two hours in the oven, chicken must be cooked.
12 Restaurant managers shouldn't be scornful of their customers.

2 Use the above sentences to complete these rules for the use of modal verbs for speculation.

In English the following modal verbs can be used to express speculation: (a) ....
....

To speculate about past events you need to add (b) ....
to the form of the modal verb.

There is a difference in meaning between 'must' and the other verbs when used for speculation.

'Must' implies (c) ....
....

whereas the other verbs imply (d) ....
....

3 Look at the four following situations. Speculate on how they may have come about, what may be happening and what may happen.

1 A woman is standing in a line of traffic looking astonished. She looks alternately at a stopped car and at a car disappearing into the distance.
2 A man and a woman are having a furious row. A dog is lying beside them, wounded.
3 A secretary in tears, a fuming boss, a broken photocopier.
4 A train seat, a newspaper, two angry passengers.

4 Note down two past occasions when you behaved unassertively and two current situations in which you react/behave unassertively. Discuss them with a classmate, speculating on the reasons for your behaviour.

🔊 Listening

1 You will hear an extract from a lecture on how to be assertive. Listen and decide on a title for the extract. Discuss your answers with a partner or in groups.

✳ 2 Listen again and complete the notes from the lecture.

- One of the results of our realising the importance of assertiveness has been an increase in the number of (1) .... and pressure groups.
- It can be (2) .... to rely on professional workers to defend us.
- We often don't act assertively because we unconsciously hear unpleasant (3) .... in our minds.
- With the *Broken Record* technique you keep on (4) .... your message until eventually the other person (5) .... or (6) .... you.
- *Broken Record* is easy to use because the words (7) ....
- You're recommended to use *Broken Record* when you're short of (8) ....
- *Broken Record* involves using the same or (9) .... words each time.

Compare your answers with a partner's.

Speaking: making your point

1 Here are some phrases which are used in English when people want to reinforce a point they've made. Read through them, then use as many of them as appropriate in the exercise below.

What I mean is ...
Let me put it another way ...
What I meant was ...
The fact of the matter is ...
What I was trying to say was ...
But my point is ...
Don't misunderstand me, but ...

2 Divide into small groups of three or four and choose an appropriate situation in which to practise the skill of 'Broken Record'. Use one of your own scenes or select some from this list :

taking bad fruit back to the greengrocer's
refusing a date from a persistent admirer
refusing to work overtime / do extra homework
saying 'no' to an invitation to a party

Take turns in practising the technique, firstly repeating exactly the same sentence. Secondly, try slightly altering your words but ensure that the message is exactly the same.

When you have mastered the technique, practise using it together with a sentence which empathises with the other person. For example, 'I can appreciate that you are in a difficult position (*empathy*) but I would like a refund now, please'.

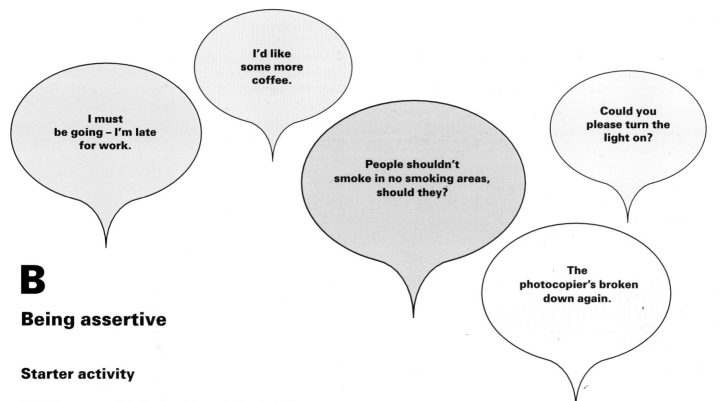

B

Being assertive

Starter activity

Get into groups. Say the sentences in the bubbles aggressively or passively or assertively. The others in your group should listen to tell you how you said them.

Listening

1 You will hear extracts from nine conversations. Listen and note down what each extract is about.

2 Listen again and tick the columns in the table below which best describe each extract.

	Formal	Informal	Assertive	Passive	Aggressive
1 command		✓			✓
2 description					
3 complaint					
4 complaint					
5 refusal					
6 refusal					
7 criticism					
8 request					
9 request					

3 Listen once more and repeat the extracts.

Speaking

Imagine the following situation:

Someone bought a pair of shoes last week. He/She wore them twice and then the heel fell off. He/She returns to the shop where the shoes were bought to get them replaced.

In pairs act out this situation as customer and shop assistant, first aggressively, then assertively, then passively. As you do so, pay special attention to your voice, eye contact, posture and gestures.

Discuss anything you noticed about your behaviour while you were acting.

Reading

Assertiveness is a question not only of maintaining your message, but also of adopting the right style for your message, a style that won't give offence or in any way be out of place or ineffectual in a particular context. The following extract talks about achieving and maintaining the right style. Read it and carry out the exercises.

A sense of occasion

Police Constable Plod has been given the task of addressing an infant school on how to cross a road safely. As this is his first attempt at such a task, he has written out his talk. What do you think of it?

> To ascertain whether any motor traffic is approaching, adopt a stationary position near the edge of the pavement, facing forward. Direct your attention to all the relevant points of the compass; if no oncoming vehicles are perceived, proceed across the road in an orderly manner, maintaining due vigilance.

And what about Sir Reginald Chump's efforts? Sir Reginald has been asked to write a speech for the prime minister to deliver on television to acknowledge defeat in the general elections.

> Well folks, it's been really great working with you all, and yeh, it's a real shame you've kicked us out of office. But that's the way the cookie crumbles. Anyway, here's hoping we stay good mates, and I guess it'd be good to see you some other time. Cheers!

'Correctness' and context

Is there such a thing as correct English? If there is, who decides what it is? Would you use the same kind of English in your own private diary as in a letter to your employer? Would the kind of English you are taught for an English composition be of any use to you in a street argument?

In this short 'thank you' letter, there are points along the way where you are offered a choice of expression. Copy out the letter. When you come to the first point, choose whichever phrase you like. After that, your choices should all *match* this first expression.

Dear ...

Thank you for a
- really fantastic
- very enjoyable
- most entertaining

evening.

I think everyone else who was there
- had a ball.
- was quite enchanted.
- had a good time.

The music was
- particularly agreeable,
- lovely,
- smashing,

and what a
- great
- nice
- charming

place you have.

You really are
- very lucky.
- a lucky so and so.
- most fortunate.

I hope you'll
- look us up
- come and see us
- allow us to return your hospitality

when we've settled in here.

We're planning to hold a housewarming.

It should be
- a lot of fun.
- quite a riot.
- a pleasant little occasion.

- Warmest regards
- All the best,
- See ya!

Being consistent

Good English is simply the English that is best suited to the job you are doing. Choose the language that is appropriate to the sort of speaking or writing you are involved in – and to the likely audience. An anecdote you tell a friend in a letter requires a different tone from a short story written for an English examiner.

Once you have chosen the appropriate tone or level of language – keep to it. Avoid words and expressions that are clearly out of place.

From each of these, copy the word or phrase that destroys the chosen tone. Next to it write a suitable alternative.

1 'You creep!' Perkins yelled at the vanishing thief. 'When I get hold of you I'll break your bloomin' neck! Then you'll be sorry for the damage inflicted on my property – you little brat!'

2 Gazing pensively across the barren, windswept landscape, Caroline reached into her handbag, took out a fag and carelessly handed it to Charles to light for her.

3 Milkman: 2 extra pints please plus one carton of orange juice. Furthermore, I require ½ lb butter.

4 The new English Bible, while O.K. for accuracy, perhaps lacks the grace of the older translations.

5 The two bunnies arrived at the edge of a huge cabbage field. What a treat! But just as they were about to tuck into a a fresh, juicy cabbage, they were startled by the clump! clump! of heavy footsteps. Oh dear! It was Farmer Jones tramping across the field towards them. They were possessed by a feeling of intense consternation – so away they scampered down the dusty little lane.

(Write better English)

✳ Writing

Read the following informal letter (A) of complaint about a computer bought through a mail order catalogue and use the information to complete the numbered gaps in the more formal letter (B).

A

Dear Sir or Madam

I'm really fed up. It took me ages to save up to buy a computer. And then what happens? The wretched thing goes wrong almost as soon as I got it.

I ordered a computer from your catalogue a month ago and I got it yesterday. I set it up OK, it worked for about five minutes and then just gave up. I can't get anything out of it for the life of me.

I want my money back please – immediately – and some compensation for all this bother. Can you please fix this up as quickly as you can.

Yours sincerely,

B

Dear Sir or Madam,

I am writing to make a (1) .... about a computer which I purchased (2) .... weeks ago from your mail order catalogue.

On (3) .... of the computer, I plugged it in and (4) .... to get it to work satisfactorily. (5) .... , this was the case for no more than five minutes, after which it (6) .... and refused to work again.

The situation is (7) .... unacceptable. It has taken me a (8) .... amount of time to save up for this computer.

I insist on an immediate (9) .... of my money as well as some compensation for the (10) .... this has caused me.

I look forward to your prompt action.

Yours sincerely,

Grammar reminder: adjectives + prepositions

As you know, adjectives in English can be followed by prepositions, e.g. keen *on*, enthusiastic *about*. The problem comes in deciding which prepositions should follow which adjectives. This is sometimes a question of collocation and sometimes a question of meaning, which may mean that different prepositions can combine with a word, e.g. I'm bad *at* maths; I feel bad *about* the way I treated him.

1 Below is a series of adjectives. Put the adjectives into groups according to the prepositions which follow them (with, at, for, to, about, of, in). N.B. Some adjectives may go in more than one group.

indignant	astonished	reluctant
rude	sensitive	angry
right	discontented	fed up
responsible	doubtful	pleased
hostile	kind	interested
capable	ashamed	thankful
bad	deficient	

Does there seem to be any common meaning in each preposition?

2 Look at the cartoon. Give the people names, then use the adjectives and the correct preposition to talk about the cartoon, e.g. He's not very pleased about his friend's request.

3 Make up sentences about yourself using some of these adjectives. Compare your answers.

Vocabulary summary

1 Go through the unit and list six adjectives or nouns describing feelings or attitudes you approve of and six you disapprove of. Compare your answers with a partner's.

2 Make nouns out of the adjectives you have listed.

C

Paper 5 (Speaking): Phase B

Introduction

Below is a description of the different stages of CAE Paper 5, Phase B. Read it and tick the parts of it you think you would enjoy doing. Put a cross next to those you would dislike doing. Say why.

In Phase B:

- you work with a partner
- you are each given a different visual prompt (a photo or a cartoon or a diagram, etc.)
- you describe, for approximately one minute, your visual prompt to your partner
- your partner listens and at the end of your description makes a reply
- you then listen while your partner describes his/her visual prompt
- you make a reply to your partner

How should candidates behave?

Below is a list of ways in which candidates might behave during Phase B. Write **ag.** for aggressive, **as.** for assertive or **pa.** for passive, against each one.

The candidate:
1 doesn't understand the instructions, but doesn't ask the examiner to repeat or clarify them.
2 asks his/her partner to speak up.
3 interrupts his/her partner's description.
4 asks his/her partner if the description is clear.
5 asks his/her partner to clarify what they said.
6 pretends to understand his/her partner.
7 finds alternative ways of describing difficult or unknown words.
8 tries to dominate the whole conversation.

Discuss your answers and decide what, if any, better ways there might be of behaving in each of these situations.

Your thoughts

- **How might assertiveness help you in each of the Phase B stages outlined in the Introduction above?**

What are the examiners looking for?

These are the criteria used by examiners to assess candidates in all phases of the CAE interview. Read and discuss them.

Fluency: i.e. naturalness of rhythm and speed, coherence of spoken interaction; pauses that indicate the marshalling of thoughts rather than language.

Accuracy: correctness of grammatical structures and vocabulary. (Major errors would be those which obscure the message; slips of the tongue are not penalised.)

Range: evidence of a range of structures and vocabulary to maintain communication in all contexts.

Pronunciation: control both of individual sounds and of prosodic features such as stress, rhythm, intonation and pitch. First language elements will not be penalised as long as they do not affect communication.

Task achievement: participation in each phase of the test, covering the following areas:

- appropriacy of contributions to the task
- fullness of contribution
- independence in carrying out the tasks
- the organisation of contributions
- flexibility/resourcefulness in task management

Exam practice

In groups of four (two examiners and two candidates) take it in turns to do four Phase B tasks. If you wish, use the assessment criteria to discuss or evaluate or improve your performance. When you are taking the examiners role note down the language the candidates use to:

- ask for clarification
- start
- hesitate
- ask their partner to speak more slowly
- ask if they've been understood

1 **Examiners:** Look at pages 214 and 219
   Candidate A: Look at page 214
   Candidate B: Look at page 219

2 **Examiners:** Look at pages 214 and 219
   Candidate A: Look at page 214
   Candidate B: Look at page 219

3 **Examiners:** Look at pages 215 and 220
   Candidate A: Look at page 215
   Candidate B: Look at page 220

4 **Examiners:** Look at pages 215 and 220
   Candidate A: Look at page 215
   Candidate B: Look at page 220

Ways of learning: situations in which we use different styles of language

Language appropriacy and style is tested in various ways in the CAE examination. Several exercises in this unit have concentrated on the use of appropriate language, and the characteristics of formal and informal language were outlined in Unit 7. To use language appropriately you must not only know what language to use but recognise the situations in which different styles of language seem appropriate.

1 Note down situations in which you use (a) formal (b) neutral (c) informal language in your own language in both written and spoken forms. Compare and discuss your notes with a partner's.

2 In pairs try to identify what factors in a situation affect the kind of language you use, e.g. the status of the person you are talking to can be one factor.

Revision Exam Practice 2

Paper 1 (Reading): Multiple matching

Answer questions **1–14** by referring to the article on page 136 about different designs for kites. Choose your answers from kite designs **A–F**.

Note: Where more than one answer is required, these may be given in any order. Some choices may be required more than once.

Which kite or kites
 1 had a single-line design?
 2 proved difficult to assemble?
 3 were easy to get into the air?
 4 had good instructions?
 5 were difficult to fly?
 6 resisted damage on crashing?
 7 lacked speed and manoeuvrability?
 8 are best for children under seven?
 9 will easily fit in your pocket?
10 cost the least?
11 is unsuitable for strong winds?
12 were good for stunts?
13 are unsuitable for beginners?
14 won top marks in the trials?

Remember to put your answers on the separate answer sheet.

TRIED & TESTED

HIGH AND FLIGHTY

IF KITE FLYING spells childhood memories of struggling to get a flimsy paper and wood diamond into the air, you'll find that things are very different today. Kites have gone technical, with enthusiasts willing to pay several hundred pounds for power, speed and manoeuvrability. To understand some of the latest designs, a degree in aeronautical engineering might be useful, but the fundamental thing to appreciate is the difference between one-string and two-string kites. The first are easy to fly but considered less exciting, while the second can perform acrobatic stunts but require a degree of skill to control them.

Whether you've advanced to swoops, skims and dives or would simply be thrilled to see your kite fluttering in the sky at all, which designs are the best to try? We asked three young, less experienced kite flyers and an expert from a kite club to take to the air with a selection. The results demonstrate that you don't need a two-string stunt kite to have fun.

THE PANEL

Eric Poultney (age 11) and family; Jessica Blackstone (12) and friends; John Levis (13) and family; Tony Gilbey, of the Essex Kite Group, and other group members. They flew the kites in both light and stronger winds.

THE TEST

Panellists gave the kites marks for how easy they were to assemble, how clear the instructions were, how easy they were to get up in the air, how robust they seemed, for speed, manoeuvrability and looks, and for how much fun they had overall.

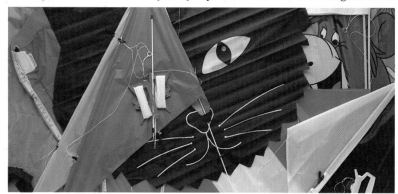

Kite fantastic: the panel decided that the Brookite Stunt Kite was best for beginners and the Windy Cat the most entertaining

A * * * * WINDY CAT

Spinnaker nylon/wood frame, one-string, £28, for age 10+

This kite was extremely popular and voted as much fun as the Brookite Stunt Kite despite being a single-line design and so not suited to tricks and stunts. The striking cat design, described as 'a crowd-puller' by one panellist, was the easiest to assemble and get in the air. It also had excellent instructions. "Great kite, great design, really easy to get up and fly. The holes in the eyes make a meowing sound," said Jessica Blackstone. But despite its immediate appeal you might find the novelty wears off after a while. "It was a bit boring standing there, but it would be lovely for onlookers," said nine-year-old Judith Poultney. It can fly in only a light wind – in fact, Tony Gilbey thought a strong wind might break the spars, though they could easily be replaced from a DIY store.

B * * * WORLDS APART POCKET ROCKITE

Rip-Stop nylon, no frame, one-string, £12.99, for age 6+

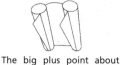

The big plus point about this kite is that you can just stuff it in your pocket if you're going out for the day, in case the chance comes up to fly it. With no frame, it's very simple to assemble and the panel found it very easy to get it into the air and fly, if not terribly exciting. "A real goer but no stunting. Everyone liked to go back to this each time the others got too complicated," the Poultney family said. Tony Gilbey's expert view was: "It flew well with an attractive dancing motion but collapsed when the wind rose. Robust enough to stand crashing due to fold-up when the wind blows too hard."

C * BROOKITE BOX KITE

Spinnaker nylon/glass fibre and wood, one-string, £10.10, for age 6+

This is a traditional single-string kite, fairly easy to assemble and get into the air. But it doesn't have the speed and manoeuvrability of other designs. "It went up very well but just stayed there," said Jessica Blackstone. Tony Gilbey's expert view was: "A 'good fly at the seaside' kite, easily carried and assembled. It flew well in light to moderate winds but went wild in strong winds and crashed. It was robust enough, though, not to be damaged."

D * * * WORLDS APART RAPIDO

Rip-Stop nylon/glass fibre, two-string, £14.99, for age 8+

COMPILED BY STELLA YARROW

The panel found this stunt kite, in the popular delta shape, fiendishly difficult to put together. But once it was in the air, most found it fast and easy to manoeuvre. Tony Gilbey said: "Small stunter with very good performance in light and up to strong winds. The flying and control were impressive. But Jessica Blackstone found it impossible to fly. "This kite is probably very good if you have know-how, but we didn't. The instructions were very unclear. Even Dad couldn't understand it. A no-no for beginners."

E * * WORLDS APART SUPER STUNTER

Polythene/glass fibre, two-string, £5.99, for age 8+

The panel found this kite, decorated with Disney characters, complicated to assemble and not very easy to get up in the air. One member of the panel, John Levis, couldn't get it to fly at all. Once the kite was up in the air, Eric Poultney enjoyed flying it: "It was easy to control. One of the most enjoyable kites." Tony Gilbey found an over-long spine made it flap about and thought the instructions too difficult for an eight-year-old: "Despite this, it did fly, it did steer, it did survive strong winds without damage and I am sure a young flyer could enjoy it after Dad or Mum had put it together."

F * * FLEXIFOIL STACKER POWER KITE

Rip-Stop nylon/glass fibre polyester resin, two-string, £59.95, for age 12+

You'll need some muscle and probably a bit of expertise to fly this powerful kite, which looks very different from a traditional design: "More like a sleeping bag than a kite," said John Levis. Its design, which works on the same principle as an aeroplane wing, means that it has a very strong pull. One family could not get it to fly. Jessica Blackstone, who did, found it the hardest of all. "I think I'll leave it to the pros. We could barely keep it up for 15 seconds." But Tony Gilbey was rhapsodic about it: "A thrilling, exhilarating experience, superb speed, acceleration and control. Will fly in a light wind or a howling gale if you have the strength, stamina and nerve. Not for the young – or the irresponsible old."

Paper 2 (Writing): Section A

You've been thinking what to do for your holiday this summer and a friend has just sent you the postcard below from the USA and this advertisement from a newspaper. You're quite interested in the job and would love to spend a month in America. You don't particularly want a tough holiday, though.

Reply to the advertisement in about 200 words giving all the information they request and inquiring about the things that worry you, e.g. money, accommodation and working hours. Then write a quick postcard of no more than 50 words to your friend thanking him/her and letting him/her know your plans.

Well, here I am in the USA working on a summer camp. It's fabulous – beautiful place, lots of sport, easy work – just organising people doing games and sports and things, nice people – what more can I say except come and join me? I'm sending you an ad. for the vacancies they've got here in case you're interested.

Hope to see you soon

P.S The pay is pretty hopeless, you sleep in bare dormitories and there's hardly any free time, so don't come if you want to get rich quick or have a luxurious, relaxing holiday.

US Summer Camps

Are you interested in

spending a month in the mountains of Vermont, USA?
organising and supervising adults doing games and sports?
free board and lodging?

Applicants should be aged 18–30, energetic, good at/qualified in a number of sports.

Apply by letter giving relevant details of experience, qualifications and personality to:
The Recruitment Manager, Vermont Summer Camps, 189 Wilton Way,
Vermont 10098, USA.

Paper 3 (English in Use): Section B

1 In most lines of the following text there is one word which is not in the correct form. For each numbered line **1–14**, write the correctly formed word in the space on the answer sheet. Some lines are correct. Indicate these lines with a tick. The exercise begins with two examples (**0**).

0	Crime preventing is as crucial in the workplace as it is in the home or
0	neighbourhood. Reducing crime is as much a part of good management
1	as prompt delivery, good staff relations, and other acceptable management
2	functions. Losses from shops through shoplifting are extremely high,
3	and ultimately, those losses are payment for by all of us in high prices.
4	There are many opportunities for shopkeepers themselves to reduction
5	shoplifting. As with all types of criminal, prevention is better than cure.
6	The best deterrent is the present of staff properly trained in how to
7	identify potential shoplifters. There are also many secure devices now
8	available. Video camera surveillance is a popular system, even with
9	quite small retailers. In clothes shopping, magnetic tag marking systems that
10	set off an alarm if they are taken out of the shop have proved their worthless.
11	However, there are many simpler measures that retailers should consider.
12	Better lighting and ceiling-hung mirrors can helpfully staff to watch all parts of
13	the display area. Similarly, simply arrangement shelves and display units to
14	allow clear fields of visible is a good deterrent.

Do not forget to put your answers on the answer sheet.

Examples:

0	prevention
0	✓

2   Read the informal memorandum below and use the information it contains to complete the numbered gaps (**15–28**) in the more formal version for an information booklet. Use no more than two words for each gap. The words you need do not occur in the informal memo. The first example has been done for you (**0**).

INFORMAL MEMO

Dear Geoff,

I think it's about time we updated the page on security issues in the College Information Booklet for students. I've jotted down the main points to include as follows:

— *all students living in college accommodation are responsible for their <u>own</u> belongings – we <u>can't</u> take any responsibility for things getting lost, broken, etc.*
— *it's not always easy to tell who's a genuine visitor and who isn't, so students <u>must</u> lock their rooms when they leave them empty.*
— *remind them <u>not</u> to leave handbags, wallets, expensive items like cameras, etc. lying around for anyone to pick up.*
— *it's <u>their</u> job to arrange their own insurance cover.*
— *they should keep all outside doors locked at all times and <u>only</u> let in people they know.*
— *if they see/hear an intruder, they must let the Security Officer know at once.*
— *the new rules mean <u>all</u> bikes will have a college number from now on – they can get it from the Secretary – it's also a good idea for them to buy a good strong lock.*

Could you please draft the above into a suitable format for the Booklet?

Many thanks,
Susannah

INFORMATION BOOKLET

College Security

The security of (**0**) .... belonging to all persons (**15**) .... in College premises is the responsibility of such residents. The College does (**16**) .... liability for loss or damage.

Petty theft is common in the College premises mainly because it is difficult (**17**) .... whether visitors are genuine or not. It is therefore (**18**) .... that rooms should always be locked when left (**19**) .... , and (**20**) .... should never be left (**21**) .... in public rooms. Adequate insurance cover is (**22**) .... responsibility.

Members of the college should be on their guard at all times against intruders in college premises. External doors should be kept permanently locked and (**23**) .... permitted only to known persons. Intruders should (**24**) .... immediately to the Security Officer.

College (**25**) .... now require that all students have their bicycles marked with a college number, which can (**26**) .... from the Secretary. Since theft of bicycles is very common, it is (**27**) .... not only to mark them but also (**28**) .... a sturdy lock!

Do not forget to put your answers on the answer sheet.

Example: | **0** | **property** |

Paper 4 (Listening): Section C

Listen to the conversation between three people and match the speaker to the opinion by putting the correct letter against the appropriate opinion. Write
B for Mr Buckhurst, the personnel manager,
P for Mrs Petts
F for Flora.
You will hear the piece twice.

Flora has had lots of opportunities at work.		1
Flora may not be interested in promotion.		2
Flora's qualifications are good.		3
Training doesn't lead to promotion.		4
Flora is getting too angry.		5
Your job description decides your duties.		6
Promotion comes through impressing your managers.		7
Flora has an attitude problem.		8
Lack of challenge leads to lack of motivation.		9

You will now hear the piece again.

Transfer your answers for questions 1–9 to the answer sheet.

Paper 5 (Speaking): Phase B

Task 1

Examiner: Candidate A, I'm going to give you a drawing and Candidate B a sheet of paper. I'd like you to describe your drawing to Candidate B so that he/she can try to draw a picture exactly like yours. You mustn't show your picture to your partner, by the way. Candidate A, your drawing is on page 216.

At the end of one minute, Candidate B, you can ask questions if you want to, then you can compare your drawings.

Task 2

Examiner: Candidate B, you have a set of four holiday houses. (Look at page 221.) Your partner has photos of five houses – four of them the same as yours. I'd like you to describe them to Candidate A so that he/she can decide which one he/she has extra.

Candidate A, I'm giving you five photos of some houses. (Look at page 216.) Your partner has four of these photos. He/She will describe the photos he/she has so you can decide which extra photo you have.

After a minute, you can ask questions if you want, and I'll ask you to say which one you think is missing.

Eleven

A

Learning at school

Starter activity

Look at these students coming out of school. What do they think school is for? Discuss your answers with a partner. Who, if any, do you agree with most?

Reading

Here are two articles about two kinds of schooling that are a little unusual.

1 Read the articles quickly to find out why the schooling is unusual.

2 Read the articles in more detail to find out which article refers to the issues **A**–**J** below. If the issue is referred to in the United States article mark it with 1; if it is referred to in the boarding school article mark it 2. Some of the issues may be referred to in both articles.

A homesickness
B food
C the cost of the scheme
D learning languages
E discipline
F bedtime
G parental help
H crying
I settling in
J timetables

Going to school far from home

The challenges faced by young Brazilians who choose the U.S. to complete high school.

By Rita Borges
Photos by Rossana Gobbi

Flight 830. Departure 10.45 p.m. At first glance, just another routine flight to Los Angeles, California. Yet for 38 young passengers between 15 and 18 years of age, it is the start of a new experience: they will spend 10 months of their lives studying abroad, far from their families. Every year the United States is host to an average 78,000 foreign high school-level students, of which 3,000 are Brazilian. They all go for the same reasons – to become fluent in English, complete high school, and understand everything they can about the American way of life.

For the majority, the decision to study abroad is taken only after a period of careful planning, at least six months. "For me," says 17-year-old Gloria Marcato, "it's more important to learn to speak English and live through this experience than it is to receive a diploma from the American government." Others, more ambitious, dream of continuing on to college. "I want to be a conductor, and I've already chosen the best American music school," enthuses Sandro Rodrigo de Barros.

Things, as they say, are not always so easy. Even young students who plan on staying in the United States just long enough to finish two semesters of high school have difficulty finding a host family. Very few arrive in the country with all the details worked out. Gloria Marcato is one of the lucky ones. Before leaving, she had received two letters and some photos of her new "parents." "I think it all depends," says Gloria, "on how you answer the questionnaire sent by the overseas study company here in Brazil. For example, I didn't economize on words. I even wrote about my four dogs, and said I went to church every Sunday." She hit the target. Americans are quite religious (the majority being Protestant) and have a special place in their hearts for pets.

Each student is expected to cover his or her own expenses with articles for personal use, entertainment, long distance telephone calls and clothing. Towards this, they should budget between US$ 200 to US$ 300 a month. American families which host foreign students are not reimbursed, though they are allowed a small income tax deduction.

In the event of illness, each student has a medical assistance card. Health insurance does not cover AIDS, abortion and suicide, nor dentist and optometrist bills. At the end of each semester, as long as the student passes final exams, American authorities grant a certificate which is recognized in Brazil. One important regulation of the foreign study program has to do with the curfew stipulated by the host "parents" to be at home on weekend nights. "They're really tough," says Juliana Martini, who just finished her first semester – "You have to be in by 10.30 p.m., and if you disobey, you get punished."

Another moment of tension descends as students await the domestic flight that will take them to their temporary home. From then on it's everyone for himself. No one really knows how he or she will adapt to such new customs. Though most foreign students remain in California, some are sent to Texas, Arizona, Idaho, Oklahoma or Virginia.

After a few days, the general complaint is about the food. "Even though I adapted easily, I really miss rice and beans. The food here doesn't look too nourishing," pines Fernando Andrade. Another big problem encountered by most youngsters is homesickness.

A few arrive in the United States with little command of English. In such cases the only recourse is private language study. This in turn pushes up the cost of the program, estimated at about US$ 3,800, including air fare.

On the whole, most students leave knowing they will have to do without their accustomed parental protection and learn to take care of themselves. However no one packs his or her bags alone. Parents always give suggestions, or even take on the task themselves. The kids frequently show their lack of practice at such things. They take along unnecessary items. One student from the Brazilian South succeeded in cramming two enormous suitcases to the brim, and had to contend with her carry-on luggage as well. As a result, she couldn't lug them around by herself.

For many the departure at the airport is the worst moment. Even though friends and family support the idea of going, it is difficult to say good-bye at this moment. "It's not easy to leave behind the people you love, especially a boyfriend. I cried at the departure and I cried on the plane too," tells Patricia Caglian, 16.

(Icaro)

A training for life in the day of a boarder

HELEN TAYLOR, 11
St Christopher School, Letchworth
350 pupils aged 11–18

HELEN TAYLOR lives with 24 other boys and girls in a large white suburban house called Little Arundale with beehives and a vegetable garden. House-parents Mike and Jill Clement try to recreate family life in the boarding house, one of eight at St Christopher School, Letchworth.

Helen's day begins at 7.30am when Mike comes in to "Woodpeckers", the cosy room she shares with her fellow pupils Louise and Zoë, and opens the curtains. The girls put on jeans, rugby shirts and trainers and go downstairs for breakfast. Then, picking up
10 a vinyl shopping bag full of books and a baggy green cardigan, Helen walks to school to see Penny, her personal advisor, to plan the day's activities around the set lessons.

Helen, daughter of an army lieutenant-colonel, swears she has not been homesick since the day she arrived five months ago with her twin sister Caroline, "It's brilliant here, the most magnificent school in the world! And I've been to seven schools so I know," she says.

"I haven't cried once yet – well, I cried when Caroline had tonsillitis and I cried when I had a cold and didn't feel well, but I haven't cried because I miss home. If you have a problem here you
20 can speak up and people will listen to you. You are treated like a person, and not just a body or a £5 note."

Having her sister there obviously makes it easier to settle away from

home, but it did not help at the strict prep school where the two began to board at the age of nine. "It was really terrible. We weren't allowed to ring our mum, and she could ring us on Thursdays only. Every Thursday we cried all night. We used to ask her to take us away. The matron wouldn't let us go to the loo at night or see the nurse when we were sick. If you didn't get up they poured cold water on your face."

St Christopher was a good choice of senior school for Helen and
30 Caroline because it gives special help for problems such as the twins' spelling difficulties. After a morning of academic lessons and a vegetarian lunch of salads, wholemeal pudding and custard, Helen's friends try to persuade her to come to netball practice instead of one-to-one tutoring in spelling. Sensibly, she refuses.

"Oh great!" says spelling coach Anthea when she looks at Helen's English homework. "You're not behind any longer, in fact you're ahead, but there is still a gap between this and what you will be able to do." The rest of the afternoon is spent making pottery with Mike in a large studio. Today's theme is totem poles.
40 "We are going to assemble geometric shapes in an interesting way, because it pleases you," says Mike, who is dressed in khaki denim, handing out wet brown clay. "That's wicked," says one boy. "I wish it was chocolate," says another. The girls are already hard at work sculpting pyramids, cylinders and trapezoids.

Soon it is 3.40 and the children are free. Suddenly the grounds are full of children wheeling on bikes, careering on roller-skates and skate-boards. Helen has a medical examination and then goes back to Little Arundale for vege-burgers and chips. At 5.30 there is a mass exodus to watch a soap. For homework Helen and other girls go to
50 Caroline's room, "Skylarks", a triangular room in the attic with ship's bunks. Instead of doing homework the girls gossip and eat illicit fruit gums.

Mike comes in to see if they have done their prep. It's time for swimming. In the bus to the local leisure centre, where the main attractions are wave-machines and crisp-machines, the children shout, scream and howl at the moon like werewolves. Fortunately Tony, the teacher on duty, is very tolerant.

Back home at 8.00pm. Plum tart and fresh lemonade are laid out for supper in the kitchen. Everyone puts on their night clothes.
60 Helen's mother phones, for the fourth time that week. Older boys play snooker with Mike while the little boys appear with teddy bears and furry slippers and beg to be allowed to phone their mums. While they are waiting, they hang around Jill in the kitchen on the pretext of helping to clear up.

Helen's last chore of the day is to throw away cold lumpy custard. Then at 9pm, to squeals of protest, Mike shepherds them all to bed where Helen quietly reads *Peter Pan*.

(The Independent on Sunday)

3 The words below appear in one of the two articles. With a partner, look at the words and mark them with 1 if you think they are in the United States article, or 2 if you think they are in the boarding school article.

Now find the words and phrases in the articles to check if you were right and try to work out what the words mean if you don't already know. You can use a dictionary to help you if necessary.

a soap	budget	cramming
gossip	wave-machines	strict
host family	curfew	roller-skates
tough	the loo	economize
clay	lug	snooker
the target	trainers	
a chore	reimbursed	

Your thoughts

- **Of the activities mentioned in the two articles which would you enjoy? Which wouldn't you enjoy?**

 Writing

Imagine you are a student at St Christopher's boarding school or one of the Brazilian students in the United States. Write your first letter home after your arrival, giving details in about 250 words of how you feel, what you have seen and done and how you are settling in. Enquire too about your family. Remember to think carefully about who you are writing to and how that will affect the style and content of your letter.

Grammar reminder: indirect questions

Remember that to report a question you must:
- **Decide whether you need to insert 'if' or 'whether'. You must do this if the question in direct speech does not begin with a question word, e.g. Are you coming to the cinema tonight?**

N.B. 'Whether' tends to be used in rather more formal language than 'if' which is neutral or informal.

- **Change the verb tense to one further in the past if the action or state referred to is no longer happening or no longer true and the introductory reporting verb is also in the past tense.**

- **Get rid of the interrogative word order of the original sentence and replace it by the order of words used in statements, e.g. 'When did you see him?' the teacher asked me, becomes, *The teacher asked me when I saw/had seen him*.**

1 Now complete the letter below by using the words in brackets to make indirect questions.

Dear Mum and Dad,
Just a quick note as I'm in a tearing hurry. Guess what – today I was interviewed by a journalist who asked me lots of questions about how I'm getting on here in America. There's going to be an article about me in the local paper. Fame at last! I'll send you a copy when it comes out. Anyway, the journalist asked me (1) .... (are you enjoying your stay?) and (2) .... (how long have you been here?). He also asked me a rather embarrassing question: (3) .... (do you like American food?). You know I can't stand it! He also wanted to know (4) .... (why did you come to the States?) and (5) .... (what will you remember most and best about the States?). I found those difficult to answer as I've only been here two weeks. Don't forget to show the article to everyone!

Love, João

2 Write down four questions to ask a partner about their schooling. Ask and answer the questions in pairs, then tell another partner what questions you were asked. (Use indirect speech!)

Listening

1 In Britain, secondary school students sometimes do 'work experience' during their school hours as part of their education. You will hear two people speaking about their 'work experience'. Listen to find out what each speaker did.

2 Listen again and decide who said what. Match the statements to each speaker. Write **W** (for woman) or **M** (for man) or both **W** and **M**.

Work experience was
A boring
B better than school
C a rather negative experience
D enjoyable
E useful socially
F a way of learning
G a way of finding out what you don't like

Your thoughts

- **Do you think work experience is a good idea?**
- **Have you done any work experience as part of your education? Do you intend to?**

Speaking: what makes a good school?

1 Look at these pictures which illustrate factors that help to make a good school. In pairs decide which picture(s) you would choose to accompany a magazine article on 'What makes a good school?'

2 Now discuss one or more of the following:

- **School can never provide the learning each individual needs.**
- **Living teaches you more than school does.**
- **School should be a choice not an obligation.**

B

What makes us learn ?

Starter activity

Look at the illustration above. What do you think is happening to the baby? Now look at the text and the dictionary extract below. What do you think about the Workgroup and 'hot housing'?

---

hot-house/'hɒt-haʊs, $'hɑːt-/ *n* [C] **hothouses**/ £'hɒt.haʊ-ziz, $'hɑːt-/a usually large heated glass building in which plants are grown • *hothouse tomatoes* • *Cucumbers and tomatoes ripened in her hothouses* • *(fig.) He was attracted by the hothouse* **atmosphere** *of Britain's top schools* (= in which children are forced to develop quickly). • *(Am)***Hothouse children** are children who are protected from experiencing the more unpleasant parts of life and society by their parents.

ExcelAcademy Institute
Post-natal Stimulation Workgroup

Dear Parent

Dr Rosemary Williams, founder and Chief Executive of the Williams Institute of Human Growth Potential, will be conducting a workshop designed to equip parents with the skills and the knowledge that they need to maximise the potential of their newborn baby. Dr Williams will address the following topics:

Intellectual Development strategies
Parent-child bonding
Balanced nutrition

The Williams Institute utilises the DOMAN Developmental Profile to help stimulate the intellectual development of a child. Dr Williams, herself a mother of four children, is a member of the Californian Institute for the Attainment of Potential, USA, and ExcelAcademy Institute, USA.

Details
Date:
Time:
Venue:
Admission:

Includes course pack, lunch and coffee.

Call: 02 3885 4765 to reserve places.

Listening

1 Listen to an extract from a radio programme and decide what the connection is between the extract and the illustration in the Starter activity.

2 Listen again and fill in the details below.

A portrait of Edith Stern

1 Father's name:
2 Father's occupation:
3 Mother's name:
4 Methods employed by father to 'develop' his child:
5 Age at which accomplished the following:
   read:
   read the Encyclopaedia Britannica:
   spoke in full sentences:
   played music:
   played chess:
   went to college:
   became an assistant professor of mathematics:
6 IQ:
7 Current job:
8 Physical description:
9 Character description:
10 Age:
11 Marital status:
12 Interests:

Compare your answers with a partner's then listen again to check if you were right.

Your thoughts

* **Would you bring up a child in this way?**
* **Can hot-housing produce 'better people'?**
* **Should parents have high expectations of their children?**

Is there a gene for genius?

1 DR HOWARD GARDNER of Harvard University believes that geniuses are largely made. He has banned television from his home because he fears it might rot the minds of his family. He makes time every day to listen to his seven-year-old son, Benjamin, play the piano – even if it is no more than a few minutes during a transatlantic phone call while he is away at a conference.

2 Dr Sandra Scarr of Virginia University, president of the Society for Research in Child Development, believes geniuses are largely born. She says parents should not worry too much about whether to take their kids to a ball game or to a museum. Talent will out.

3 It seems psychologists are as divided as ever over the issue of nature versus nurture. This may, however, be about to change. A conference organised earlier this year by the Ciba Foundation brought to London some of the biggest names from both sides of the debate. Startling results from unpublished work were revealed – and the beginning of a consensus could be discerned.

4 The most exciting results came from those working on the biology of individual differences. Dr Robert Plomin of Penn State University, working with a team from Cardiff University, hopes to announce within the next few months that he has tracked down one of the genes that plays a part in determining intelligence. An unnamed gene has been identified but the results have yet to be confirmed.

5 At present, it is believed that genes account for at least half of what researchers call "g" – the general cognitive ability that IQ tests are supposed to measure – while environmental influences account for the other half. But so far the evidence for a genetic component has been purely statistical, being inferred from comparisons of twins and other such hereditary studies. Plomin's method makes use of new gene mapping techniques and promises to provide direct evidence of the role that genes play.

6 Plomin stresses that the discovery of a first gene does not mean the riddle of intelligence has been solved. A single gene will code for only one of the many neurotransmitters and cell proteins that are the building blocks of the brain. This means that hundreds, if not thousands of genes must be involved in intelligence. The identification of even one gene does, however, have immense implications for the nature/nurture debate.

7 Another innovation, the computerised brain scanner, has led to a second discovery by those seeking the biological component of mental abilities. Professor Camilla Benbow of Iowa State University is head of a long-term study of the mathematically gifted. For many years she has been puzzled as to why so many of the children in her study should be boys – at the top level, boys outnumber girls by 13 to one. In a soon-to-be-published paper, Benbow reveals that the gifted boys' brains appear to process spatial information in a very different way from those of average boys and even of gifted girls.

8 The children in the study were scanned while being presented with a simple visual puzzle. The boys of average ability and the gifted girls showed strong activity on both sides of their brains as they thought about the puzzle. However, the gifted boys responded very differently. There was a sudden drop in activity in their left hemispheres – the side of the brain most involved in language – and an exaggerated reaction on the right, the side strongest at spatial thinking. It seems that the brains of boys with mathematical talent operate in a way that is physically distinctive.

9 Benbow says she was surprised that the gifted girls should lack this pattern of response. The only explanation she has is that male brains have a tendency to become more lateralised during development; when this lateralisation is taken to an extreme, unusual spatial abilities result.

10 Because females do not have this tendency (lateralisation is known to be hormonally governed), girls who perform well in mathematics are doing so because of a more general mental superiority. And because statistically such all-round ability is less common, this would be the reason for there being fewer mathematically gifted girls.

11 Benbow is quick to add, however, that cultural expectations probably exaggerate the imbalance. In China, where girls are more likely to get encouragement in mathematics, the number of gifted boys exceeds that of gifted girls by four to one rather than the 13 to one seen in the United States.

12 Both Plomin's and Benbow's findings would seem to give ammunition to the argument that exceptional mental abilities are largely innate. But the Ciba conference heard equally strong evidence for the role that environmental factors play in creating genius. A theme repeatedly heard from the speakers was that special children invariably have special parents.

(The Independent on Sunday)

Reading

1 Read the article on page 147 quickly to find out which it says is stronger, 'nature' or 'nurture'?

2 All the words in list A below are taken from the article. Find them in the article, then match their meaning to the explanations in list B.

A

talent will out	startling
to discern	to track down
determining (adj.)	a mapping technique
a riddle	innate
a brain scanner	distinctive
lateralisation	all-round
to give ammunition to	

B

amazing	deciding
a way of showing where things are	general
	inborn
to hunt	to strengthen
to notice	a puzzle
special abilities will reveal themselves	special
a machine that reads cerebral activity	
a process involving the development of one side of the brain	

3 True or False? Read the following statements and decide if they are true or false. Correct them if they are false.

According to the article:
a Dr Gardner believes your brain develops by being active.
b Dr Scarr believes study and sport help talent.
c Dr Plomin has found the intelligence gene.
d The G factor is 'general cognitive ability'.
e The genetic component of the G factor has only been statistically established.
f Professor Benbow has proved that gifted boys process spatial information better than gifted girls.
g Lateralisation helps both boys and girls to do better at mathematics.
h Chinese girls are better at maths than Chinese boys.
i The Ciba conference was presented with arguments on both sides of the nature/nurture debate.

4 Look at the second half of the article on page 149. Some of the paragraphs have been removed and placed below it. Read the article and decide which of the paragraphs **A–F** fits each gap. There is one paragraph too many.

5 Complete this paragraph about the second half of the article by filling in the blanks with one missing word.

The article claims that the parents of many great prodigies (1) .... a lot of time with them. It also states that there are two kinds of (2) .... stimulation: supportive and stimulating. It goes on to state that parents who only stimulate their children may (3) .... them to suffer from burn up. The best kind of parental style is said to be (4) .... supportive and stimulating. The article adds that parents who don't talk to their children much may bring about a narrow-minded (5) .... of thinking in them. (6) ...., parents shouldn't just talk a lot with their children. They need to make (7) .... that their talk is constructive. The article concludes that it's more difficult to guarantee a beneficial environment than to (8) .... biological fulfilment.

Compare and discuss your answers, then read the article again to check them.

It is a popular myth that great prodigies – the Einsteins, Picassos and Mozarts of this world – spring up out of nowhere as if touched by a divine finger. The archetype is Karl Friedrich Gauss, born into a supposedly illiterate family of labourers, who grew up to become the father of modern mathematics.

Professor William Fowler of the Massachusetts Centre for Early Learning has attacked this myth, saying that when he looked into Gauss's childhood, he found that Gauss's mother had been teaching him numerals at the age of two. His father had been a foreman, not a labourer, and played calculation games with him. Furthermore, Gauss had an educated uncle who taught him sophisticated maths at an early age.

1

But what sort of parental stimulation should it be? The conference heard plenty of evidence that, too often, parental pressure and attempts at "hot-housing" children result in burn-out rather than giftedness. Professor Mihaly Csikszentmihalyi of the University of Chicago reported on a study which identified two kinds of parental style – the supportive and the stimulating.

2

Csikszentmihalyi's study followed four groups of children: one with supportive parents, one with stimulating parents, one whose parents combined both qualities and a final group who offered neither. The children were given electronic pagers; when these buzzed at random intervals during the day, they had to make a note of what they were doing and assess how happy and alert they felt.

The not too surprising result was that the children whose parents were simply supportive were happier than average but were not particularly intense in their concentration when studying or working on an interest. The children who fared best were those whose parents were both supportive and stimulating. These children showed a reasonable level of happiness and a very high level of alertness during periods of study.

3

Another crucial factor stressed at the Ciba conference is the need for parents to have proper conversations with their children. Through having the chance to talk with adults, children pick up not only language skills but also adult habits and styles of thought. One reason why prodigies such as Picasso and Einstein had a head start in life was that they had parents who demonstrated how to think about subjects like art or physics at a very early age.

Professor Fowler said a survey in Holland showed that a typical father spent just 11 seconds a day in conversation with his children. A more recent study in America produced a somewhat better result, but the fathers in question were still talking to their children for less than a minute a day.

4

Fowler is attempting to show this experimentally with a study in which groups of parents are taught how to have constructive conversations with their toddlers. Fowler says these children have shot ahead of their peer group in language ability, intellectual ability and even social leadership skills. While the study is not yet complete, the children appear to have been given a lasting advantage.

So what is the outlook for parents who do everything right, those who manage to be both supportive and stimulating, who are good at demonstrating thinking skills to their children and successful at fostering a self-motivated approach to learning? Would such parents be guaranteed to have a gifted child?

There was general agreement at the conference that there is no denying that genuine biological differences exist between individuals; geniuses need to be lucky in both their genetic make-up and their parents. The most significant implication would seem to be that while most people are in a position to fulfil their biological potential – that is, barring serious illnesses or dietary deficiencies, they can be certain their genetic capacities will be fully developed – there can be no such certainty that they will grow up in the environment necessary for that development.

5

A

Supportive parents were those who would go out of their way to help their children follow their pet interests and praised whatever level of achievement resulted. Generally, such parents created a harmonious home governed by clear rules. Stimulating parents were more actively involved in what their children did, steering them towards certain fields and pushing them to work hard, often acting as a tutor.

B

So although knowing more about the biology of genius is all very interesting, it is research into better parenting and educational techniques that will have lasting significance.

C

It seems as though what counts may not be quantity so much as quality. How parents engage their children's interest may be a crucial factor in determining the attitude of mind and general disposition to learning that a person grows up with. Nobody can afford to undervalue quality of time.

D

Children whose parents were stimulating without being supportive were candidates for burn-out. These children did work long hours, but their alertness and happiness during study time was far below that of children in more balanced family environments.

E

It is the same story with other prodigies. Einstein's father was an electrical engineer who fascinated his son with practical demonstrations of physics. Picasso's father was an art teacher who had young Pablo copying still lifes at the age of eight. Mozart's father was a court composer who was teaching his son to sing and play almost before he could walk. "In every case, when you look into the backgrounds of great people, there is this pattern of very early stimulation by a parent or mentor figure," Fowler says.

F

It is not just the time spent that counts, Fowler says, but also the way in which a parent talks. A parent who brushes off a child's questions or gives dull answers will be imparting a negative, narrow-minded style of thinking. On the other hand, parents happy to take a child step by step through an argument, encouraging it to explore ideas, will foster an open and creative thinking style.

Grammar analysis: the present perfect and present perfect continuous tenses

1 Read these sentences and use them to complete the gaps in the rules for the main uses of the present perfect and the present perfect continuous tenses.

1a I've been going to the cinema a lot.
1b I've been to the cinema a lot.
2a You've been having too many late nights.
2b You've had too many late nights.
3a I've been studying hard.
3b I've studied hard.
4a This book has been ruined.
4b You've been eating too much.

The **present perfect** tense generally refers to:

a A state or event leading up to the (1) .... time.
b A habit in the (2) .... leading up to the present time.
c A past state or event with (3) .... in the present time.
d A state or event in an undefined period leading up to the present time.

The **present perfect continuous** tense refers to:

e States or events of limited (4) .... leading up to the present time.
f Recently (5) .... past states or events with results in the present time.

N.B. The difference in meaning between the two tenses is sometimes very fine or non-existent. The present perfect continuous tends to emphasise the duration or frequency of an event/action over a period of time.

2 Complete these sentences by putting the verbs in brackets into the correct tense: present perfect or present perfect continuous.

1 I .... (study) at this school since last term.
2 I .... (never read) anything about hot-housing before.
3 She seems to .... (really enjoy) the intensive tutoring she's getting at her new school.
4 His upbringing .... (mark) him significantly.
5 She .... (always have) a very high IQ.
6 I .... (send) my child to a special school, but I can't afford it any longer.
7 He .... (always believe) in the importance of education.
8 I .... (study) hard of late. I've got exams next week.

Vocabulary summary

All these words are from this unit. In two minutes write down the opposite of each one, then compare your answers. If you can't think of a 'one word opposite' use more than one word to describe what you mean.

ambitious	tough	temporary
cosy	strict	ahead
tolerant	dull	fresh (of food)
protest (*n*)	ban	gifted
exaggerated	distinctive	innate
stimulating	alert	clear
shoot ahead	fascinate	
narrow-minded		

With a partner, compare and explain your answers. Why may you sometimes have different answers which are both right?

Ways of learning: different reasons for reading

1 List all the things you have read in the last three days (in whatever language), then note down against each how you read, i.e. for general information, for selective information, for detail, for pleasure. Discuss your answers. What makes you decide which way to read?

What might be the dangers of always reading in the same way?

2 In the reading sections in this unit you carried out various reading tasks. Write down the page and number of the task(s) in which you needed to:

• **understand the general meaning of the text**
• **understand each word in the text**
• **understand the details of particular parts of the text**
• **understand the general meaning of particular sentences**

Did you read in the same way in each case?

Can you explain to one another how your reading differed for certain tasks?

C

Paper 1 (Reading): Gapped paragraphs

Introduction

In CAE Paper 1 you are required to do a gapped paragraph exercise. This means that you are presented with a text from which certain paragraphs have been removed and placed after the text in jumbled order. You then have to decide where in the text the jumbled paragraphs belong. This is a similar task to the one you did earlier in this unit, in **Section B Reading,** activity 4.

The purpose of this kind of task is to see if you can understand the structure of texts, i.e. the logic of their sequence and development. Understanding the structure of a text helps you understand the meaning of a text.

Using lexical and grammatical clues

Texts always contain words, groups of words and grammatical patterns that link up with other words or grammatical patterns in the text. It is these links that help you carry out this kind of task. They provide lexical or grammatical clues.

1   On page 152 there is a gapped text followed by jumbled paragraphs on page 153. Decide which paragraph belongs where and write the letter of the paragraph in the correct numbered gap. **N.B.** In this text and in the exam too there is one extra paragraph that does not belong in any of the gaps. As you carry out this task, note down the strategies you use to do so.

2   Underline anything that gave you a clue to the answer. Discuss your clues with a partner.

3   On page 155 you will see the complete text. In it some of the clues which link back and forward to something else in the text have been circled. Can you decide what they link to? If you take example 1 *Three years later* you have to ask yourself the question '*Later than what?*' *Later* suggests a link back to a previous point in time – so you have to find this point earlier in the text.

4   Answer 'yes' or 'no' to the questions below:

When you do a gapped-paragraph exercise do you think it is a good idea to:

a   read the text in detail beforehand?
b   work out the meaning of each word in the text?
c   try to understand the general meaning of the text?
d   always work through the text in order?
e   make final decisions on each gap as you do it?
f   underline clues?
g   look for one clue for each gap?
h   look for clues before and after each gap?
i   put arrows on the question paper between the paragraph and its probable gap?
j   read the text again from the beginning before you go on to each new paragraph?

List any other tips you think might be useful for the completion of these kinds of exercises. Discuss your answers.

Ways of learning

Design a poster with the following title:

> # TIPS ON HOW TO ANSWER GAPPED PARAGRAPH EXERCISES.

When they are complete, display your posters in the classroom. Whose is the best poster? Why?

Schedule for passing the test of time

Andrew Northedge on the most vital skill to learn at college – managing your study time.

I was in a student coffee bar during my first week at university soaking in the atmosphere when another student announced calmly that he intended to get a first in classics. He would work 25 hours a week, study five hours a day on weekdays and leave the weekends free. That would be sufficient.

I was vaguely committed to endless hours of work. I imagined that at some point I would spend weeks of intensive study.

Nevertheless, when I came to look back I realised he had studied more than anyone else I knew. Through sticking assiduously to a modest but well defined, realistic plan, he had achieved a great deal. He had enjoyed work much more, too.

2

I was too inexperienced at looking after my own affairs to realise I was already failing one of the major tests of studenthood, the organisation of time. I thought that success in studying was to do with how brilliantly clever and original you were: I had yet to discover that one of the central challenges of adult life is time management.

At school the work timetable was defined for us and teachers made sure we fitted all that was required into the school year. At university I was at sea. Time came in great undifferentiated swathes. What to do with it all? With 168 hours in a week – or 105, allowing nine a day for sleeping and eating – how many was it reasonable to spend on study? Individuals vary and different subjects make different demands. Nevertheless with a target you can plan your studies, not just stumble ahead in hope.

Sticking to a modest but well-defined plan, he achieved a great deal

The sketchiest of weekly timetables, setting aside 40 hours to cover all study is an invaluable aid in defining time. Then you can divide it into segments and use it strategically, rather than let it dribble away.

3

I would sit in the library for a whole day, dipping into one book after another, often with glazed-over eyes. What was my purpose / how would I know when I had finished? Although my lecture notes weren't up to much, I could tell myself I had accomplished something, which would bring down my anxiety level.

4

Dividing big jobs into smaller sub-tasks helps to bring work under control, allows you to set targets and check your progress. There is so much pressure to be ambitious – to go for the long dissertation, to read the huge tomes. Yet achievement arises out of quite modest activities undertaken on a small scale. The trouble with the big tasks is that you keep putting them off, their scope and shape is unclear and we all flee from uncertainty. The more you can define your work as small, discrete, concrete tasks, the more control you have over it.

5

There are few reliable guidelines. Essentially you have to keep circling round a self-monitoring loop; plan an approach to a task, try it out, reflect afterwards on your success in achieving what you intended and then revise your strategy.

6

A

Three years later he sailed to his first while other friends struggled to very modest achievements. As I discovered when sharing his lodgings, he worked more or less to the plan he had outlined. He slept late in the mornings, only stirring himself if there was a lecture to attend. He played cards with the rest of us after lunch. Then he moved to his desk and stayed there until around seven. The evenings he spent more wildly than most, hence the late mornings.

B

Organising tasks into the time available can itself be divided into strategy and application. It is useful to think of yourself as 'investing' time. Some tasks require intense concentration and need to be done at a prime time of day, when you are at your best and have time to spare. Others can be fitted in when you are tired, or as 'warm-up' activities at the start of a session. Some, such as essay writing, may best be spread over several days. Some need to be done straight away.

C

Defining what to do is harder. Take the book lists. How many books are students expected to read? How long should a book take? It took me so long just to read a few pages that I felt defeated when I looked ahead. Should I take notes? How many? What would I need them for?

D

Much later I discovered I could learn a great deal from close reading of selected sections; that taking notes could sometimes be very satisfying and at other times was not necessary. The trick was to take control: to decide what I wanted to find out – something specific – and then work at it until I had taken in enough to think about for the time being.

E

He argued that it was not possible to work productively at intensive intellectual tasks for more than a few hours at a time. I aimed to do much more. But I was easily distracted. By the time it was apparent that stretches of a day had slipped away, I felt so guilty that I blotted studies out of my mind.

F

It is extremely important to always keep to a rigid timetable of study. This is clearly demonstrated by his success and my paltry achievements.

G

Once you start to think strategically, you begin to take control of your studies rather than letting them swamp you.

Exam practice

For questions **1–4**, you must choose which of the paragraphs **A–E** match the numbered gaps in the newspaper article. There is one extra paragraph, which does not belong in any of the gaps.

THE FIRST few weeks of a university course can seem dangerously elusive and intangible. The initial euphoria of finding that you've got only 12 lectures a week and Fridays are free soon dissipates in the 10-page reading list. Lecturers will toss around conflicting ideas and a bewildering array of interpretations, where school teachers would lead you comfortably through the syllabus. And suddenly it's up to you to decide when, where, how much and even how to study.

1

"The important thing is to find out what's right for you. You should ask yourself am I a morning person or an evening person and for how long can I concentrate? Do I work best in my own room or in the library and what conditions do I need? You may work best with a bit of music or you may need perfect quiet. Working a nine-to-five day – filling in the chunks of time between lectures – suits some people, but others prefer working early in the morning."

2

In lectures it helps to develop an abbreviated style of note-taking. Ms Crookes says: "You need to ask yourself why you are taking notes. They should be a complement to listening to the lecture, recording the most important points, not a substitute for listening." It may also reinforce your understanding and memory of the lecture, if you go through the notes after each lecture, underlining key points and making summaries.

3

Tutorials and seminars provide the opportunity to get to grips with fundamental ideas, question and try out ideas that you could use in essays. But often it is wasted as people sit in embarrassed silence, thinking that their suggestion or idea is too silly to mention. Overcoming such shyness can be liberating not only for you, as you will usually find your idea is taken seriously, but also for other students who may be encouraged to express their views.

4

She says the best policy is to try to strike a balance between the two levels. "Most of the literature points towards deeper level learning being both more satisfying for the student and more successful at internalising the material but bear in mind that there are still games to be played. You've got to be very clear about what's required in exams and coursework and you should get hold of as many past exam papers as you can and talk to your lecturers to get pointers as to what's coming up in exams," she says.

Student poverty and overstretched libraries mean that obtaining books is likely to be one of your most persistent problems. Some libraries are limiting reservations for key texts to 24 hours per student, which makes it even more important to read effectively. It's a good idea to approach second-year students for second-hand textbooks. Some groups of friends pool book budgets and share books.

A
Ms Loder has done a study in which she grouped students as surface-level and deeper-level learners according to the approach they took to studying and then compared their success rate in exams and coursework. "Most common was for the mid-line, deeper-level student to do well both in coursework and exams and surface-learners not to do so well. Surface-level learners could do well in exams if they were good at cue spotting and bending the lecturers' ears but in general they tended to get through but not to excel, mainly because they didn't take in broader ideas so well. However, some of the deeper-level students had big psychological problems with exams, because they didn't agree with the whole concept of exams," she says.

B
It also helped if people were encouraged to volunteer for things they had a flair for and if they overcame their fear of giving the presentation of what the group had done. "Presentations are a very good way of reinforcing what you have learnt," she says.

C
Many universities issue students with booklets on study skills and use of the library and you should ask your course co-ordinator, personal tutor or student counsellor for their advice. Effective reading is the key to success to both essay writing and exam performance and it starts with identifying clearly the question you are trying to answer. You need to find the most relevant books; use the index to find the relevant section and read selectively with the question in mind, picking out key passages, taking down notes and quotation. In essay writing, this needs to be married with a logical structuring of the answer, perhaps by labelling notes that go with each part of the argument.

D
As the workload builds up, some students are gripped by a growing sense of panic. But Shirley Crookes, a counsellor at Warwick University, says that by paying careful attention to how you manage your time and realising that studying involves simple skills that can be learnt the situation can be defused. 'You need to recognise there are 168 hours in a week and that you can work hard, play hard and relax in that time. It's a question of how to balance your use of time to get the full potential out of it,' she says.

E
Cari Loder, a lecturer in the Centre for Higher Education Studies at London University, says: "Researchers at Lancaster University have done a lot of work on how students learn and they are pushing the difference between surface-level learning and deeper-level learning." Surface-level learning is absorbing and retaining detail and being able to reproduce it later, deeper-level learning involves engaging with fundamental principles and adjusting your own beliefs accordingly.

Schedule for passing the test of time

Andrew Northedge on the most vital skill to learn at college – managing your study time.

I was in a student coffee bar during my first week at university soaking in the atmosphere when another student announced calmly that he intended to get a first in classics. He would work 25 hours a week, study five hours a day on weekdays and leave the weekends free. That would be sufficient.

I was vaguely committed to endless hours of work. I imagined that at some point I would spend weeks of intensive study.

1. (Three years later) he sailed to 2. (his) first while other friends struggled to very modest 4. achievements. As I discovered when sharing his lodgings, he worked more or less to the plan he had outlined. He slept late in the mornings, only stirring himself if there was a lecture to attend. He played cards with the rest of us after lunch. Then he moved to his desk and stayed there until around seven. The evenings he spent more wildly than most, hence (the late mornings.) 3.

Nevertheless, when I came to look back I realised he had studied more than anyone else I knew. Through sticking assiduously to a modest but well defined, realistic plan, he had achieved a great deal. He had enjoyed work much more, too.

He argued that it was not possible to work productively at intensive intellectual tasks for more than a few hours at a time. I aimed to do much more. But I was easily distracted. By the time it was apparent that stretches of a day had slipped away, I felt so guilty that I blotted studies out of my mind.

I was too inexperienced at looking after my own affairs to realise I was already failing one of the major tests of studenthood, the organisation of time. I thought that success in studying was to do with how brilliantly clever and original you were: I had yet to discover that one of the central challenges of adult life is time management.

(At school) the work timetable was defined for us and teachers made sure we fitted all that was required into the school year. At university I was at sea. Time came in great undifferentiated swathes. What to do with it all? With 168 hours in a week – or 105, allowing nine a day for sleeping and eating – how many was it reasonable to spend on study? Individuals vary and different subjects make different demands. Nevertheless with a target you can plan your studies, not just stumble ahead in hope.

Sticking to a modest but well-defined plan, he achieved a great deal

The sketchiest of weekly timetables, setting aside 40 hours to cover all study is an invaluable aid in defining time. Then you can divide (it) into segments and use it strategically, rather than let it dribble away.
Defining what to do is harder. Take the book lists. How many books are students expected to read? How long should a book take? It took me so long just to read a few pages that I felt defeated when I looked ahead. Should I take notes? How many? What would I need them for?

I would sit in the library for a whole day, dipping into (one book) after another, often with glazed-over eyes. What was my purpose / how would I know when I had finished? Although my lecture notes weren't up to much, I could tell myself I had accomplished something, which would bring down my anxiety level.

Much later I discovered I could learn a great deal from close reading of selected sections; that taking (notes) could sometimes be very satisfying and at other times was not necessary. The trick was to take control: to decide what I wanted to find out – something specific – and then work at it until I had taken in enough to think about for the time being.

Dividing big jobs into smaller sub-tasks helps to bring work under control, allows you to set targets and check your progress. There is so much pressure to be ambitious – to

go for the long dissertation, to read the huge tomes. Yet achievement arises out of quite modest activities undertaken on a small scale. The trouble with the big tasks is that you keep putting them off, their scope and shape is unclear and we all flee from uncertainty. The more you can define your work as small, discrete, concrete tasks, the more control you have over it.

Organising tasks into the time available can itself be divided into strategy and application. It is useful to think of yourself as 'investing' time. Some tasks require intense concentration and need to be done at a prime time of day, when you are at your best and have time to spare. Others can be fitted in when you are tired, or as 'warm-up' activities at the start of a session. Some, such as essay writing, may best be spread over several days. Some need to be done straight away.

There are few reliable guidelines. Essentially you have to keep circling round a self-monitoring loop; plan an approach to a task, try it out, reflect afterwards on your success in achieving what you intended and then revise your strategy.

Once you start to think (strategically,) you begin to take control of your studies rather than letting them swamp you.

Twelve

A

Time off

Starter activities

1 Look at the photos below and list the different leisure activities they illustrate.

2 Think of five different leisure activities and add them to your list.

3 Tick what you consider to be the five *most* popular activities. Compare your answers with those of a partner.

Speaking

1 Discuss with a partner what are typical leisure activities for each of the following age-groups:

a 16–24 years   **b** 25–44 years
c 45–64 years   **d** 65 +

Compare your views with the table below.

The leisure ages of men and women in Britain		
Age-group	Emphasis	Leisure activities
16–24	away from home	social activities, listening to records, eating and drinking out, active sport, formal entertainment
25–44	more at home	DIY, gardening, open-air outings, family holidays in UK
45–64	renewal of away from home	sightseeing, clubs, holidays abroad, gardening
65 +	at home and away	reading, sightseeing, clubs, holidays

2 Discuss some of the following statements about 'leisure'. Which do you agree with, and why?

Leisure is the opposite of work.
Leisure is essential to good health.
Leisure is a modern concept developed during the 20th century.
Leisure is big business nowadays.

Listening

1 Look at the times of day below and circle the period *you* like best.

dawn	**morning**	**noon**
afternoon	**sunset**	**evening**
midnight	**the small hours**	

2 Listen to five people talking about their favourite time of day. For questions **1–5**, match the speaker with their favourite time of day **A–H**.

1	....	**A**	dawn
2	....	**B**	morning
3	....	**C**	noon
4	....	**D**	afternoon
5	....	**E**	sunset
		F	late evening
		G	night
		H	the small hours

For questions **6–10**, listen again and match the same extracts (**i–v**) with the aspects of personality **A–H**.

6 (i)	....	**A**	enjoys being at home with family/friends
7 (ii)	....	**B**	prefers a well-ordered life
8 (iii)	....	**C**	content to be different from others
9 (iv)	....	**D**	has plenty of energy
10 (v)	....	**E**	tends to worry about things
		F	needs peace and quiet to think
		G	lacks personal confidence
		H	inclined to be restless

Your thoughts

- **Find out from two other people which is their favourite time of day and why.**
- **What kind of personalities do they have?**

Reading

1 What sorts of people do you think find it especially hard to take time off and relax? What advice would you give someone who finds it difficult? Read quickly through the text 'Easy does it' on page 159 to find out the writer's views on these two questions.

2 Find ten words and phrases in the text associated with each of the following:

the world of work   leisure activities

✳ 3 Read the text again in detail to complete the following statements.

1 Top executives often find it difficult to take time off because
  A it would cause them financial problems.
  B they need to protect their jobs.
  C they have never really learnt how to relax.
  D they simply don't have the time.

2 For many executives the worst thing about going away on holiday is
  A having to stay in a hotel or holiday home.
  B having to lie on a beach in the sun.
  C being out of touch with the office.
  D being unable to escape the telephone.

3 The main role of a leisure adviser is to
  A teach an executive a new leisure activity.
  B give an executive a full medical check-up.
  C help an executive alter his approach to life.
  D organise a holiday for an executive.

4 The author believes executives need to be convinced of the
  A psychological benefits of a holiday.
  B financial benefits of a holiday.
  C commercial benefits of a holiday.
  D social benefits of a holiday.

5 If the initial training is successful, an executive might then be persuaded to
  A have regular holidays abroad.
  B take up an exciting new activity.
  C spend more time at home.
  D reorganise his business.

Your thoughts

- **What do you think of the idea of a 'leisure adviser'?**
- **How easy is it for you to relax?**

Grammar reminder: *would* and *used to*

> **Remember:**
> *Would* and *used to* are often used to talk about things that were true in the past, but the two are not always interchangeable.
> **a** If you want to describe *a state or situation which existed* in the past but which no longer exists today, it is best to use *used to*, e.g.
> *A hundred years ago people <u>used to have</u> far fewer leisure activities available to them than we have today.*
> **b** If you want to talk about an *activity or habit that happened regularly* in the past but which no longer happens today, you can use *would* or *used to*, e.g. *A lot of families <u>would/used to</u> create their own entertainment. They <u>would/used to</u> gather round a piano at home and sing songs.*

1 Complete the following sentences using *would* and/or *used to* as appropriate.

1 When I was a child I .... live in the centre of London.
2 My parents .... take me to London Zoo at least once a month.
3 The zoo .... have a giant panda called Chi Chi.
4 We .... visit her every time we went.
5 I was very interested in wild animals at that time so I .... collect all sorts of books and posters on the subject.
6 I even .... be a junior member of the World Wildlife Fund.

2 Complete the questionnaire below for yourself.

MY LEISURE PROFILE		
Age 7–12	Interests:	....
	Sports:	....
Age 13–16	Interests:	....
	Sports:	....
Age 17–20	Interests:	....
	Sports:	....
Age 21–25	Interests:	....
	Sports:	....
Age 25+	Interests:	....
	Sports:	....

3 Compare your completed questionnaire with a partner's and discuss any differences using *used to* and *would* as appropriate.

Easy does it

1 RELAXING ISN'T EASY. I know – I have tried it.

2 I can see, therefore, why Japan's Ministry of International Trade and Industry should want corporations to have full-time "leisure advisers". It seems an idea worth copying.

3 A start should, perhaps, be made at the very top. Captains of industry often find it hardest of all to relax.

4 Workers at least have the excuse that they need to protect their job and pay off the mortgage. Many tycoons have all the money they could ever hope to spend. So why don't they ease up?

5 Some buy a luxurious yacht, a beach house, or even an island, but seldom make use of these expensive leisure facilities. "I don't have time for a holiday," they insist.

6 What they usually mean is that they *could* find the time, if pressed, but that they don't *want* to.

7 Some consider themselves so indispensable that their business would collapse if they were not around to supervise every detail.

8 Some are prisoners of their own success: they sit on so many boards of directors, and have such a heavy schedule of appointments, that they "haven't a moment to spare".

9 But more often than not the plain truth is that they don't know how to ease up. No-one has ever told them how to do it.

10 You can't be a frantic executive one day and a leisurely beachcomber the next: the contrast is too great. The bronzed young drifters who make it look simple have had years of practice.

11 Put a captain of industry on a beach and he tends to

get bored and restless. He misses the pace, the action.

12 Invite him to play tennis and he will probably decline, because he fears that he will look foolish – he prefers to play games in the office, where he is a proven winner.

13 If he has a holiday home, or stays in a plush hotel, he will be on the telephone six times a day, doing what he does best. Relaxing is for wimps.

14 So what can a "leisure adviser" do for him – or, increasingly, her?

15 The basic task is to change attitudes, and *gradually* to introduce him to various leisure activities.

16 Some experts believe in playing what is known as the "fear card". The executive is warned of the risk of "burnout" and told that, if he doesn't take care of his

health, the business will suffer.

17 Does he realise what it would cost if he had to go into hospital? More, much more than a holiday. That is the bottom line.

18 But I believe in a more positive approach. A good start is to persuade him that holidays are a "psychological investment", and that it is perfectly feasible to combine business with pleasure.

19 This has to be done step by step: the cold turkey treatment is rarely effective.

20 They can take work with them. (A recent survey by the Hyatt Corporation showed that nearly half of the executives questioned do so.) For a captain of industry, holidays are ideal for strategic planning.

21 They can call the office, though the aim must be to

reduce the number of calls as the holiday progresses.

22 They can have faxes sent to them, though the staff should try to cut down on the rolls of fax paper: one should be sufficient after a while.

23 They can be persuaded to take up golf. It is not only a pleasant (and healthy) way of going for a leisurely walk, but it can also be good for business.

24 Some of the biggest deals of the past decade have begun with a casual remark on the golf course, and bankers have acquired some of their most lucrative clients while blasting their way out of a bunker. It no doubt helps to explain why golf has become the favourite sport of senior executives throughout the world. If he needs that little extra push, show him the formula developed by a British leisure expert:

$$RP = \frac{T}{2} + (Z - 4) = CD = CA$$

25 The RP stands for rest period, and you needn't bother with the other stuff. The formula proves convincingly that a few days on the golf course are absolutely vital.

26 There are plenty of courses in the sun. Executives should be reminded that this is the time of the year when it becomes imperative to embark on inspection tours of overseas subsidiaries in places like Florida, Australia and Jamaica.

27 Once the initial leisure training period has been completed you can try to hook him on other activities which are every bit as challenging as a take-over bid. He can climb mountains, ride river rapids, go scuba diving. He may well end up making a happy discovery: leisure *can* be fun. ■

Illustration: Tony Simpson

(High Life)

B

Moving images

Starter activities

1 Ask three people the following questions:

1 How many hours do you think you spend watching television per day/week?

2 Do you watch TV mainly to
   a relax?   b escape?   c learn?

2 Some psychologists say that 'we are what we watch'. What do you think they mean by this?

Reading

1 Read the set of quiz statements and put a tick alongside all those which you feel apply to you.

The what-you-watch-is-what-you-are-quiz!

Turn on, tune in and reveal yourself! What you watch and how you watch can tell a lot about the inner you. Are you shy? Are you tense? Are you lazy? With the help of clinical psychologist Dr Robert Sharpe, PAMELA TOWNSEND has devised 32 loaded questions to help you find out.

Tick the statements you feel apply to you. And be honest – there are no right or wrong answers! Your final score matters to no one but YOU!

1 I like to settle down to the soaps with a box of chocolates or a snack to keep me company.
2 No matter what I'm watching, when it gets to a certain point in the evening my eyes glaze over.
3 I like to watch the credits at the end of programmes because I am interested in how TV shows are put together.

4 I dislike being interrupted while watching my favourite programmes.

5 I have a remote-control unit so that I can change channels easily.
6 Watching late-night TV is the easiest way for me to get off to sleep.
7 When watching documentaries I always keep a pen and paper handy so I can jot down the interesting facts.
8 I love to watch TV in bed and often fall asleep while it's still on.

9 I like to time my evening meal between the programmes I wish to see.
10 I look forward for weeks to the return of my favourite series.
11 Documentaries are my favourite sort of programme and I may remember them for months afterwards.

12 I like to flick between the sports programmes on Saturday afternoons so that I see as much action as possible.
13 I often find myself day-dreaming during programmes and have to ask someone else to bring me up to date with the plot.
14 Watching a thriller late at night can have me jumping at the tiniest noise in the house.
15 When watching a debate or audience discussion, I often work out what I'd say if I had the chance.
16 I am annoyed when my favourite programmes are shown at the same time on different channels.
17 I prefer short programmes or quiz programmes to those where I have to concentrate for a long time.
18 When I watch a travel or holiday programme I'm transported into another world and feel I'm actually there.

19 I usually send off for fact packs or leaflets if they are advertised in conjunction with particular TV programmes.
20 I usually have the television on in the background while I do jobs around the house.
21 I read as much as I can about the actors and their roles in the series I follow.
22 Westerns are the only thing I really enjoy because they remove me completely from ordinary life.
23 Social and political programmes give me great insight into current affairs.
24 I often bring work home with me and finish it off while watching TV.
25 I prefer watching snooker or darts to boxing or football.
26 I enjoy watching TV with my children and seeing them absorbed in programmes made specifically for them.
27 I am addicted to health and family problem programmes.

28 I'll do anything, including cancel social engagements, to make sure I don't miss an instalment of my favourite serial.
29 Thrillers and crime programmes set my imagination running.
30 A comedy programme that really gives me a thoroughly good laugh always leaves me feeling much more relaxed.
31 I watch a lot of quiz shows and panel games to try to increase my general knowledge.
32 People are often amazed that I can follow a television programme and have a conversation at the same time.

(TV Times)

2 Make a note of the numbers of the statements you have ticked and give each one a letter using the scoring system below.

- **If you have ticked 1, 4, 10, 14, 18, 21, 22, 29, mark each with E.**
- **If you have ticked 2, 6, 8, 13, 17, 25, 26, 30, mark each with R.**
- **If you have ticked 3, 7, 11, 15, 19, 23, 27, 31, mark each with L.**
- **If you have ticked 5, 9, 12, 16, 20, 24, 28, 32, mark each with J.**

Add up the number of ticks for each of the letters. Decide which are your highest and lowest scoring letters and then look at the analysis.

3 1 Look at these sentences:

> *I like to settle down to the soaps with a box of chocolates.*
> *When it gets to a certain point in the evening my eyes glaze over.*

The quiz uses a large number of phrasal verbs. Make a list of all the other examples you can find in the text.

2 Divide your list into
  a those phrasal verbs you feel you know well.
  b those which are less familiar to you.
  Check their meaning with your partner.

3 Mark the stressed syllables in each phrasal verb from list b and practise saying them aloud.

4 For four or five of the verbs in b, write a sentence to show its meaning.

Your thoughts

- **Compare your results on the personality quiz with those of a partner.**
- **How are your personalities similar/different?**
- **How accurate do you feel the analysis of your personalities is?**

DR SHARPE'S ANALYSIS

You will probably find you have some ticks in three, even four, sections but you should also find that most of your ticks fall into just one or perhaps two groups. For example, you may have six Es and only one L but two Rs. Use your highest scoring letter, or letters, for your main analysis. But the low scores are important as well and should be read in conjunction with the analysis of your main group.

E – THE ESCAPER
If you have scored between 5 and 8 then many TV characters must seem like old friends and relations. You tend to want to escape from everyday life and join the fictional world of television. This may indicate that you neglect some areas of your social life in favour of the ready-made world of telly. This could be because you are shy, unassertive and lack the will to confront your problems. Try to be more selective in your choice of viewing, mix more with other people, consider joining a club or group and put your energy into getting out and about. And don't worry! It won't stop you from enjoying the telly when you do watch.

If you scored between 1 and 4 you're showing a hint of laziness! You probably think nothing of lying back in your comfy chair and watching TV while someone else does the work. You're a fairly passive spectator but you should guard against getting too involved in the emotions of the characters on the screen.

R – THE RELAXER
If you scored between 5 and 8 it probably means your average day is quite exhausting and that there's nothing you love more than flaking out in front of the box. It may help you unwind and there's nothing wrong with that – in moderation. But, if you find you do nothing but flop in front of the screen night after night, and if you also find you are nodding off to sleep, then you'll probably also find you're becoming unpopular with those you live with! If when you *do* leave the screen you can't actually secure a soothing, natural sleep in bed, then you've got problems. Don't sit glued to the screen! Before bed, take a nice hot bath, persuade your other half to give you a massage and do some deep-breathing exercises. When you feel those eyelids drooping, go to bed, preferably with a sleep-inducing non-alcoholic drink in hand.

If you scored between 1 and 4 you also use the TV as a way of unwinding and probably find that up to an hour of relaxing in front of a good programme does the trick. Tremendous. Keep doing just that.

L – THE LEARNER
If you scored between 5 and 8 then you certainly see TV as a way of increasing your world knowledge. Perhaps you should consider improving your qualifications, because you seem to have a deep desire to improve yourself. Does an Open University course or evening class appeal?

If you scored between 1 and 4 you have a balanced approach to viewing, realising that it's a source of information, but only one of many.

J THE JUGGLER
If you scored between 5 and 8 you probably infuriate your family by trying to watch three programmes at once, switching between them to find out what's going on on one and missing the crucial part in another! This behaviour shows you have an alert, flexible mind, but it could also mean you're edgy, can't relax or are frightened of missing out on something.

If you scored between 1 and 4 then you probably like to have several things on the go. You probably watch TV while doing something else and the commercial breaks probably find you rushing off to get jobs done. You don't like wasting time, that's for sure!

If your ticks are divided evenly between all groups, you are a real rarity. Do the quiz again another day. If it happens again, it may be that you live for what's on screen. But if you scored low in all sections, you are a very practical viewer. You probably use a video recorder a lot, so that television doesn't interfere with the important things in your life.

(TV Times)

Grammar analysis: time clauses

1 Look at these sentences:

1 I often fall asleep <u>while</u> the TV is on.
2 I usually watch TV until I go to bed.
3 When it gets to a certain point in the evening, my eyes glaze over.
4 Before I go to bed I like to relax with a long, hot bath.
5 I like to sit and watch the news with a cup of coffee after I've finished supper.

In each sentence, underline the word which provides a link in time between the first half of the sentence and the second half. The first example has been done for you.

2 Match the sentences in activity **1** with the following categories:

a one thing happening before another
b two things happening at the same time
c one thing happening after another
d things happening at a specific time when
e two things meeting at a point in time

3 Here are some of the most common link words and phrases used in time clauses.

when	after
before	while
as	since
whenever	immediately
prior to	as soon as
the moment	until
till	once
by the time	during
at the same time	subsequently
whilst	

Match the words above to the categories in activity **2**.

4 Time clauses normally explain when something happens by referring to a period of time or to another event/activity. The time relationships in a sentence can often be drawn as a diagram, e.g.

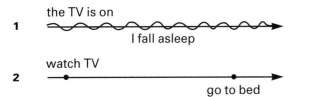

Draw similar diagrams to show the time relationships for the other three sentences in activity **1**.

5 Look back at the quiz and find more examples of sentences containing time clauses. Draw a diagram to show the time relationship for each example you find.

6 Choose a word from each of the categories in activity **2** and write five sentences about your own or your family's behaviour where watching television is concerned.

Listening

1 Look at the opinions in the table below on the subject of violence in films. Tick those you agree with and then discuss your answers.

Opinion	My view	Speaker's view
1 It's better to know if a film contains scenes of violence before you go and see it.		
2 Cowboy films don't usually show the real effects of violence.		
3 Violence on screen encourages violent behaviour in society.		
4 A good film is one where the audience is encouraged to use their imagination.		
5 Young people need to be protected from seeing certain films and videos.		
6 Censorship is unfair on both film-makers and the viewing public.		
7 There is a case for banning all pornographic and violent films.		
8 Censorship can simply make things appear even more attractive.		

2 Listen to a discussion among three friends about screen violence. Listen the first time to decide whether they are talking mainly about violence

a on television   **b** in videos
c in films   **d** in computer games

3 Listen a second time and tick the opinions in the table above which are expressed by one or more of the speakers.

4 Listen again and tick any phrases below which the speakers used when hesitating.

um	er	well
the thing is	kind of	in fact
you see	you know	how shall I put it
let's see now	sort of	I mean
I think	so to speak	

Hesitating is a very natural part of native speaker English and hesitating 'properly' can actually make you sound more fluent.

Ways of learning: checking back over written work

1 Here are some aspects which will be taken into consideration by someone who has to mark written work for the CAE exam:

- range/choice of sentence structures
- accuracy of grammar
- use of an appropriate style and tone
- accuracy of spelling
- range/choice of vocabulary used
- meaningful use of punctuation
- coherent linking of ideas and information
- use of an appropriate layout
- clear organisation and development of content
- legible handwriting

Do you think any of these aspects are more important than others?

2 Look at the following piece written by a learner of English for the writing task in this section. What sorts of errors do you notice?

Dear TV Manager!
I'm writting with serious complaint about a film you have shown last night on your television chanel. It was named "Funny Business" and was given out at seven-thirty pm. In your TV magazine this film was marked as OK for all people in the family to watch. Because of this I and my 10-year-old cousin watched together. I had a great shock when I saw moments in the film that were very violent and I think it wasn't apropriate for him to see. It's not good. If films are very violent for children it can be frightened and damage their minds. The television must be responsable to show these such films only late in the night when the children are sleeping. You must not show these films again so early in the evening. Another way is making clear in the TV magazine what is the subject of the film so we can chose better.
Thank you, Laurence.

With a partner, give the writer a score of 1, 2 or 3 for each of the following features (1 = poor, 2 = average, 3 = good).

- content
- style
- task achievement
- vocabulary range
- accuracy
- organisation

3 Collect three examples of different writing tasks you have done recently. Make a list of the sorts of mistakes or problems which seem to occur frequently in *your* written work. What steps could you take to prevent these recurring in future written work?

4 With a colleague design a ten-point 'Writing task checklist' which you think could be copied and distributed for the benefit of all students preparing for CAE, e.g.

1 Check your spelling carefully, especially those words you often make mistakes on.

Speaking

In pairs try to rank from **1–10** which of the following forms of entertainment may require greater censorship than others. 1 = needs extensive censorship. If you hesitate try to use the expressions in Listening activity **4**.

film	video	television
books	radio	newspapers
computer games	telephone	chat lines
theatre		

Writing

Imagine that early yesterday evening you sat down to watch a film on television with your 10-year-old cousin. Although the film had been advertised as suitable for family viewing you were shocked to discover that it contained several scenes of violence. Write a letter to the television channel expressing your concern and making suggestions as to how a similar occurrence might be avoided in the future. You should write approximately 250 words.

Vocabulary summary

1 Look back over this unit and collect all the words you can find related to the topic of leisure. Divide them into the appropriate categories below.

a homebased activities

b creative activities

c sports activities

d cultural activities

Mark the stress on these words, then say them to one another.

2 Read the following short text and then decide which word, A, B, C or D, best fits each space.

Leisure is generally seen as an (1) .... which takes place outside (2) .... hours. The peak leisure time for most people is between 6.00 pm and 12.00 am, although in recent years there has been an increase in people working (3) .... hours and shifts, together with more 'flexitime'.

Leisure is often thought of purely as a (4) .... activity, i.e. playing sport. Although many people use their (5) .... time in this way, there are plenty of other leisure opportunities that are more (6) .... in nature, such as watching television or sunbathing on a beach.

It's important to realise that leisure can embrace a whole range of experiences and activities, although personal choice may be limited due to factors such as age or provision of local (7) ....

The leisure emphasis will normally change at different (8) .... of one's life-cycle. Different types of leisure activities tend to be popular with varying age groups. It's probably true, however, that some members of the older (9) .... are more capable of pursuing active (10) .... than they are sometimes given credit for!

1	**A** event		**B** incident	
	C experience		**D** affair	
2	**A** labour		**B** working	
	C employment		**D** job	
3	**A** unsocial		**B** unreasonable	
	C unsociable		**D** unsuitable	
4	**A** cultural		**B** social	
	C physical		**D** mental	
5	**A** rest		**B** free	
	C unoccupied		**D** empty	
6	**A** creative		**B** selective	
	C productive		**D** passive	
7	**A** conveniences		**B** facilities	
	C capacities		**D** capabilities	
8	**A** parts		**B** levels	
	C sections		**D** stages	
9	**A** generation		**B** era	
	C age		**D** period	
10	**A** entertainments		**B** occupations	
	C pastimes		**D** games	

C

Paper 2 (Writing): Section B

Introduction

Read the following description of Section B of the Writing paper and then fill in the missing information in each of the statements below the box.

> Candidates will be required to write one piece of approximately 250 words. A choice of four specific tasks will be offered based on a range of writing activities such as: articles, reports, letters, instructions and expanded notes. Task descriptions will outline the content required and specify purpose and intended audience.

There will be a total of (1) .... different writing activities to choose from.

You will have to choose (2) .... of them.

You will be told what to include as far as (3) .... is concerned.

Both the (4) .... for which you are writing and (5) .... for whom you are writing will be made clear.

You will be expected to write about (6) .... words in all.

To complete the writing task, you will need to do the following:

1 Identify the task   **2** Select the format
3 Connect the ideas

(See also Unit 7 Section C.)

Identifying the task

1 Remember to consider the following points when you set about any writing task.

- audience / target reader
- purpose for writing
- content
- organisation
- style/tone

For each of these points, think of a question which you might ask yourself when preparing a writing task.

2 Look at the writing task below. Do not do it yet.

Ask yourself the five questions you wrote in activity **1** and write an appropriate answer to each question.

3 What sort of ideas would you expect to find in the letter of reply for the task in activity **2**? With a partner sort out which ideas should go into the same paragraphs. Discuss how many paragraphs you are likely to need and what would be the best order to put them in.

> An English friend is considering taking time off between finishing school and going to university in order to travel around your part of the world for a year. He/she has written to you to find out what you think about his/her idea and to ask for your advice on which regions/countries he/she might visit, what would be the best way to travel, where he/she might stay and what sort of temporary jobs he/she might be able to get to earn some money. Write **a letter** of reply to your friend.

Selecting the format

1 Different writing tasks are likely to require different formats, e.g. brochures, leaflets, columns. The following short extracts A, B and C are all about the same topic but are very different in the way they have been written.

Read each extract and then decide which of the following sources it was taken from:

1 a public information leaflet in a supermarket
2 a page from a geography textbook
3 the label on a food packet

A

How to cook:
1. Allow 50g of rice per person.
2. Place in a large saucepan of boiling water.
3. Boil for 15 minutes.
4. Drain through a sieve and serve.

B

There are several varieties of rice–white polished rice, brown unpolished rice and wild rice. In addition, parboiled rice and instant rice are now widely available.

White and brown rice
White and brown rice both come in three grain sizes – long, medium and short grain – and are named after the areas in which they are grown. Long grain rice is suitable for savoury dishes, medium grain rice is most suitable for stuffings and short grain rice is best used for sweet puddings.

Parboiled rice
Because it is steamed by a special process before milling, parboiled rice retains much food value.

Instant rice
This has been fully-cooked and then dehydrated before packaging. It is prepared by soaking it in hot water for 5 minutes, and then cooked according to the manufacturer's directions. Instant rice may be used for quick dishes.

C

Lowland or swamp rice is an important food crop that is well adapted to monsoon climates. It probably originated in South-East Asia thousands of years ago. When the monsoon rains arrive, the paddy fields are flooded. Workers transplant young rice plants in the flooded fields and the plants grow in water until they start to ripen. The fields are drained at harvest time. The world's leading rice producers are China, India, Indonesia and Bangladesh.

2 Listed in these tables are some of the layout features which a writer can use. Look again at the three rice texts in activity **1** and for each text tick the layout features which you think the writer has deliberately used to create a particular effect.

Layout features	A	B	C
section headings			
numbering			
shorter paragraphs			
longer paragraphs			

Layout features	A	B	C
instructions			
letter layout			
note form (rather than full sentences)			
short, simple sentences			
longer, more complex sentences			
illustrations/diagrams			

3 Discuss with a colleague which of the layout features listed might be appropriate when writing the following types of text:

1 a report on a recent overseas visit
2 a set of instructions to accompany a camera
3 a formal letter of complaint
4 a review of a TV programme
5 an information leaflet on your college
6 notes to a friend on using your kitchen

4 Which of the layout features are relevant to the following writing task?

> You have been asked to write **an article** for your college magazine recommending two different places to eat in your local area – one at the lower end of the price range and one which is more expensive. Your article should include information about the menus available, the quality of the food, the standard of service, the atmosphere and decor, the prices and whether the restaurants are more or less suitable for certain types of occasion.

5 In groups of three or four, decide what would be the best format for the writing task in activity **4**.

Connecting the ideas

1 In groups, discuss and plan in detail each paragraph of the writing task in activity **4**. Make notes on the content and structure of each paragraph as in the example below:

Paragraph 1: **introduce the topic and explain purpose for writing**

Paragraph 2: **refer to 'Jade Fountain', Chinese restaurant, in city centre ...**

Paragraph 3: **simple decor, excellent quality esp. Peking duck, service good but leisurely ...**

Paragraph 4: **rather expensive, good place for special occasions ...**

Paragraph 5: ....

2 Each member of the group should then take responsibility for writing a first draft of one or more paragraphs of the text, using the overall plan and the detailed notes agreed by the group.

3 When the first draft is complete, each paragraph should be checked and edited by another person in the group.

4 The various draft paragraphs should be assembled for the whole group to see. The group can then discuss and make any necessary changes before assembling the paragraphs into the final complete text.

Make sure that the finished text doesn't look as though it has been written by four or five different people. Together check to see that the style is consistent. If words are repeated, can you replace the second word with a pronoun? Are there enough linking words in the text to link paragraphs smoothly? Is the information consistent from one paragraph to another?

Ways of learning: understanding the instructions for a task

The instructions (or exam rubric) for a CAE Writing Paper Section B task are designed to give plenty of guidance about what and how to write, so it is important to read them carefully before you begin.

1 Section B of the Writing paper begins:

Choose ONE of the following writing tasks. Your answer should follow exactly the instructions given. Write approximately 250 words.

Write down the three important messages contained in this rubric.

2 Read the following task rubric and decide why certain words have been printed in bold type.

A good friend has offered to come and stay in your flat for a few days to look after things while you are away. Write a set of **notes** for your friend giving **useful information** on **where to find** various household items, **how** to look after your pet animal, **where** the nearest shop is, **who to contact** in the case of an emergency and **anything else** you think your friend will find it **helpful** to know.

3 Read the following task rubric and underline any words or phrases which you think are essential to successful completion of the task.

A local magazine has announced a competition on behalf of an English TV channel.

Be a guest presenter on our top TV travel and holiday programme!

We are currently looking for new holiday destinations for inclusion in our regular TV travel programme and this is your chance to be chosen as a guest presenter. Simply choose a place in your own country which you think would make a good holiday destination. Write an account of it giving details of how to travel there, where to stay, what to see and anything else which might be of interest to potential holidaymakers. We shall be offering a prize for the the best 250-word account and the winning writer will be invited to produce and present the television report.

4 Look back at the words and phrases in bold type in activity **2** and at those which you underlined in activity **3**. What sort of things do they draw your attention to about the task?

Exam practice

Choose one of the writing tasks which have been included in this section and complete it. When you have finished, check your work using the Writing task checklist you designed in **Ways of learning** in section **B**.

Thirteen

A

It's a weird world

Starter activities

1 Fact or fiction? Look at these pictures and news clips. Tick the ones you think are 'fact'.

Compare your answers with a partner. How do you explain these weird phenomena?

2 Do you know of any 'weird phenomena' or has anything weird ever happened to you or anyone you know? Tell one another.

In 1972, a strange creature – about five foot tall, silver coloured, bipedal, with enormous ears and scaly skin – emerged from Thetis Lake, British Columbia, and chased two boys.

TORNADO 25 April
OKLAHOMA:
This twister killed seven and injured over 90 when it tore through Tulsa (where it wiped out a church) and moved on to Cartoosa, seven miles to the east. Cars and trucks were blown off Interstate 44 and 242 houses and mobile homes were destroyed. An area a mile wide and two miles long was completely flattened. Damage was estimated at $100 million.

Colin Hill went on holiday to Torquay in Devon in 1976, arriving at the harbour just as skin divers surfaced with a pair of spectacles he had lost there on his last visit seven years earlier.

Armin da Broi, 23, sold his Alsatian, Barry, when he became too big for his flat in Bari, southern Italy. Armin then moved to Solingen, West Germany, and a year later, on Christmas Eve, the dog was found whimpering outside his flat. Armin vowed they would not be parted again.

Reading

1 The article on page 171 is a factual account of a 'weird' happening. Read it through selectively to find out what the 'weird' phenomenon is.

2 Find the words in the text which mean the same as the following:

a by the side of the road
b angled
c shaking with cold
d fascinated/puzzled
e a deep / holy cave
f to be present during / to see
g a sacred place associated with a saint
h rocking to and fro
i drawing up of the shoulders to show indifference or doubt
j unusual
k lessened
l a short, sharp intake of breath

3 Read the account again to find the correct way **A**, **B**, **C** or **D** to complete these statements.

1 The shrine is situated
  A outside Ballinspittle
  B near a cave
  C up a hill
  D near a disco
2 On the early occasions when the statue moved
  A a policeman shrugged when told
  B someone was pushing it
  C Clare O'Mahoney showed no interest
  D interest was immediate
3 When he was at the shrine, the author
  A remembered catholic ritual
  B felt ill at ease at first
  C quickly saw the statue's face changing
  D was interested mainly in the crowd
4 The author
  A claims he saw the statue move
  B has seen the statue move twice
  C doubts that the statue really moved
  D has seen pictures of the statue moving
5 The tone of the account is
  A balanced
  B exaggerated
  C casual
  D mystifying

Your thoughts

- **Do you find this account convincing?**
- **Do you know of any similar events?**

Grammar reminder: cohesion through substitution

Can you remember what you learnt about 'substitution' in Unit 5? Carry out the following exercises to check.

1 Find the following words in the text on page 171 and underline them.

a it (line 8)   **f** it (line 21)
b her (line 12)   **g** did (line 35)
c they (line 16)   **h** is (line 40)
d so (line 16)   **i** did (line 40)
e such (line 18)   **j** it (line 42)

What words or phrases is each of these words substituting?

What is the language function of these words?

2 How can you substitute the underlined parts of each of the sentences below to avoid the repetition they all contain? Make the necessary changes to each sentence.

a It's difficult to believe in the paranormal unless you've experienced the paranormal.
b When the crowd was questioned the crowd claimed to have seen a miracle.
c I believe in miracles and I know lots of people who believe in miracles.
d The author saw the statue move and other people saw the statue move.
e He took photos of the statue. I don't know how he took photos of the statue.
f Perhaps I'll try the experiment. If I try the experiment I may learn something.
g The Loch Ness Monster exists. My friends say it exists.
h If you don't try things you'll regret not trying things.

What seems to be the main words or kinds of words used for grammatical substitution in English?

The summer of 1985 was windy and wet. In south-west Ireland, where I live, that's normal.

Ireland has been Christian since the fourth century, but has an even longer tradition of pilgrimage. The countryside is decorated with wayside shrines.

The shrine standing on crossroads just outside the village of Ballinspittle is typical. It consists of a life-size concrete statue of the Virgin Mary
10 (mother of Jesus Christ) in ground-length white plaster robes, her hands raised with fingertips touched in prayer, her head looking upwards, slightly tilted to one side. She stands in an ivy covered cave about twenty feet above the road with a 100 watt halo of little lights above her head. Passers-by, if they feel so inclined, join the plaster child in a personal act of worship.

Seventeen-year-old Clare O'Mahoney felt no such inclination. She was walking past on her way home
20 that Monday, thinking of the disco she had been to in Bandon, when the statue began to rock backwards and forwards, as though someone were pushing it from behind. Alarmed, she went to fetch her mother, Kathrine, who saw the same thing and climbed up to make sure that nobody was interfering with the shrine. The next evening several dozen local people turned up and reported that the monument was 'swaying to and fro' or 'shivering'. On Wednesday the crowd grew to hundreds, including police sergeant John Murray from Cork, who saw the head and shoulders 'shrug'. And by Thursday Ballinspittle was besieged by thousands of pilgrims who blocked the narrow roads with their cars. They were rewarded when, at 3.30 am, the Virgin seemed to open both her hands in benediction.

August was wet even by our standards, producing the heaviest rains this century. But despite the floods, an estimated quarter of a million people came to witness the phenomenon.

30 I went to watch in early September, intrigued as much by the crowd as by the chance of observing a paranormal phenomenon. By now it was necessary to park half an hour's walk from the shrine and to stand with a mass of pilgrims on a roped-off slope some fifty yards from the statue. Prayers were broadcast every twenty minutes and there was the constant distraction of flashing cameras and torch lights wandering over the grotto. But the atmosphere was electric. Six or seven thousand people were gathered there for the same purpose, to witness a miracle, and many did. Myself included, I think.

It was a cool night with constant gentle rain; the sort of weather the Irish describe as 'soft' and hardly seem to notice. There must have been a good proportion of tourists and casual sightseers in the crowd, many like myself non-Catholic, but there were enough church-goers who knew the rituals to lend real cohesion and energy to the prayers. And between the rosaries and the responses there was a growing hum of people telling each other what
40 they could see: 'Look, look, she's moving her head.' 'She *is*!' 'She *did*!' 'I didn't see anything.' 'Oh God, her face, it's changing.' 'I think she's going to fall!' 'Mummy, can we go home now ...?'

I found it a little confusing. I had brought my binoculars and, through them, could see nothing untoward, just a plaster statue with crude features and a very vacant expression. But then something happened to change my mind.

Around midnight the crowd thinned a little and the loudspeakers took a rest. There were still thousands of us there and the air was charged with interest and emotion, but some of the early tension had dissipated. We were more relaxed. Or at least we were until there was a collective gasp, then wonderful confusion as everyone compared notes. And the wonder was that we had all seen the same thing. The statue had, very deliberately, looked down and around to her left, slightly spreading her hands in a gesture of acknowledgement.

I am left, as one always is in such things, without easy answers. Debate about whether or not the statue 'really
50 moved' is pointless, though Jim O'Herlihy in Blarney has a series of photographs, taken in rapid succession with a long lens on a tripod, which seem to show the hands in several different positions. I have visited the grotto on other occasions since, by night and day, usually on my own – and have seen nothing out of the ordinary. There are few reports these days of anything much happening in Ballinspittle.

Listening

You are going to hear an extract from 'The Hound of the Baskervilles', about the famous detectives Sherlock Holmes and Dr Watson. Here is the story so far:

> Holmes and Watson have gone to a moor near a country house with another detective, Lestrade. They are trying to capture a 'monster' which haunts these moors. They send out a decoy, Sir Henry, as bait to attract it.

1 Listen to find out if their plan is successful.

2 What did you think of the story? Tick the most appropriate adjective(s) below and/or add your own.

frightening	exciting	exaggerated
boring	realistic	gripping
terrifying	interesting	cruel
ridiculous		

Discuss your answers and your reasons for them.

3 The words below are all taken from the story . Underline the ones you know, then with a partner work out the meaning of the others. Try to remember how they are used in the story.

drifting	orchard	hound
glowed	savage	moor
patter	leap	apparition
vulnerable	mortal	wound
trigger	swirl	

4 The three drawings below illustrate parts of the Baskerville story. Listen to the extract again and take notes on what is happening in each drawing. Then compare your notes with a partner's and tell the story to one another. You may then wish to listen to the story again just for enjoyment.

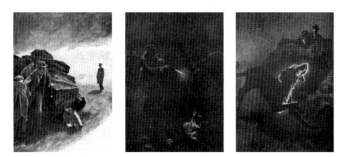

Writing

Imagine that the notes given below were written by Lestrade to help him prepare his report of the incident on the moor. Using the notes for guidance, write the full report in approximately 250 words, giving details of the setting for the events and the background to the events, explaining what happened and giving your conclusions on the mystery.

Remember to think carefully about the information you are going to include, who you are writing for, whether you should be formal or informal, and the range of vocabulary and structures you should use.

> *Place of incident: Grimpen Moor*
> *Time of incident: Night Time*
> *People involved: Detectives Sherlock Holmes and Dr. Watson, Sir Henry Baskerville, myself*
> *Type of incident: Identification and shooting of 'The Hound of the Baskervilles'*
> *Description of Events: went to moor; waited in hiding positions, weather very foggy, Sir Henry went past, heard terrible panting sound, caught sight of monster; Holmes shot it as it was attacking Sir Henry*

Speaking: illustrating your point

Look at the list of weird phenomena below. Against each write ✓ if you think they exist, **?** if you don't know and X if you think they don't exist.

aliens	The abominable snowman
ghosts	The Loch Ness monster
magic spells	Good luck charms
lucky numbers	

Compare and discuss your answers. In your discussion make use of any of these expressions for introducing examples to illustrate the point you are making.

For example ...	For instance ...
For one thing ...	Take the way (he) ...
Just to give you an idea ...	Just think of ...
Look at the way ...	Let me give you an example ...

2 Which adjective best describes your class's attitude to weird phenomena? Support your opinion by using appropriate expressions from activity **1**.

cynical	romantic	sceptical	sensible
open-minded	foolish	superstitious	other...
hard-headed	naive	indifferent	

B

It's a damaged world

Starter activities

1 In one minute, list all the pollutants and pollution you can think of. Compare your lists.

2 Listen to a list of kinds of pollutants and pollution. Tick the ones you noted and add any extra ones.

3 Listen again to some of the words and repeat them, paying attention to their pronunciation.

🔲 Listening

1 You are going to hear a fable describing an idyllic country scene. First look at the picture above, and label as many of the features as you can. Then listen to the first part of the fable and label the remaining features using one or two words only.

✳ **2** Now listen to the second part of the fable which describes how the idyllic scene was destroyed. Complete the following chart by filling in the numbered blanks in the columns with one, two or three words only.

What was affected	What happened?
chickens	maladies
cattle and sheep	1 ...
people	2 ...
birds	3 ... / dying / sick
young animals	not born/too weak to survive
4 ...	no pollination
5 ...	lined with brown and withered vegetation
streams	6 ...

Compare your answers.

Your thoughts

- **How would you feel if your home town was destroyed in this way?**
- **Do you think this fable is exaggerated or realistic?**

Grammar analysis: the future

1 In English all the following verb forms can be used to refer to the future.

- **going to**
  I'm going to find out more about that as soon as I can.
- **will/shall**
  I think it will run out fairly soon.
  I think I'll start recycling newspapers.
  Christmas will be on a Sunday next year.
- **the present continuous tense**
  We're leaving school next week.
- **the present simple tense**
  The plane leaves at 10 o'clock next Tuesday.

Each verb form expresses a way of viewing the future. From the examples above, decide which verb form expresses which of the following views.

a an intention or something bound to happen in the near future because of something present
b a timetabled or otherwise unalterable event
c the results of a plan or arrangement
d a prediction
e an 'on the spot' decision
f a simple statement about the future

2 Below are ten sentences referring to the future. Complete them with an appropriate form of the verb in brackets.

1 The government ban on the use of CFCs .... (come in) as from the year 2000.
2 From now on, ... (I/recycle) all the glass things I buy – I've decided.
3 The hole in the ozone layer .... (get bigger) in the next few years judging by the evidence available.
4 I think there .... (not/be) any rain forest left in 50 year time.
5 I .... (take part in) a fund-raising event tomorrow.
6 What's the fuss about? The world .... (go on) for ever.
7 The panda .... (become) extinct in 10 years or so.
8 Factories .... (stop) discharging their wastes into the river next year.
9 I imagine they .... (ban) cigarette advertising.
10 All cars .... (change) to lead-free petrol at the end of next month.

Compare your answers. You may find differences between them. Discuss the reasons for these differences.

3 Read the sentences in **2** again and beside each write which view of the future they express.

4 Note down some future events connecting your life with the environment. Think about:

- **on the spot decisions**
- **plans/arrangements**
- **timetables**
- **predictions**

Compare the events you have mentioned and your attitudes towards them.

Reading

1 The diagram on page 175 illustrates and explains different kinds of environmental pollution. One sentence has been removed from each paragraph. Read the diagram and match the sentences (**A–I**) to the paragraphs. There is one extra sentence.

1	....	**A**	which is potentially lethal to trees
2	....	**B**	produces serious pollution
3	....	**C**	which may reach the ground water reservoirs
4	....		
5	....	**D**	leading to severe damage
6	....	**E**	while nuclear power threatens air, water and land
7	....	**F**	water disperses contaminants
8	....	**G**	one which over the last two decades has grown enormously
		H	grown with the aid of
		I	by dissolved chemicals which are washed through the ground

Compare and discuss your answers.

2 According to the text, what causes what? Read the text again selectively to match the following:

1	fossil fuels	**A**	damage to trees
2	agricultural chemicals	**B**	pollution of the ground
3	water	**C**	dispersal of contaminants
4	acid rain	**D**	damage to our food supplies
5	dissolved chemicals	**E**	contamination of deep water sources
6	household waste	**F**	contamination of the atmosphere

3 How much do you know about the environment? In groups of three or four, take it in turns to ask questions to each other, based on the information in this unit. The first to give the correct answer to each question gets one point. The person with the most points at the end may be the most 'environmentally friendly'. Here are a few example questions to start you off.

- **Where does much of the world's fresh water lie?**
- **What creates acid rain?**

Your thoughts

- **Which of the above kinds of pollution do you take seriously. Why?**
- **What do *you* do to help ease pollution?**

Vocabulary summary

You will hear some questions checking whether you remember some of the vocabulary of this unit. Divide into teams and listen to the questions. The first member of any team to answer the question correctly gets a point. The team with the most points is the winner.

The Environment Under Attack

The global environment can be broken down into three main elements – land, water and air. Through our daily activities, we manage to pollute and contaminate all three different elements. If it continues, the damage caused by this may become irreversible.

POLLUTION FROM ENERGY PRODUCTION
The need for larger supplies of energy generates pollution on a huge scale. Energy derived from fossil fuels contaminates the atmosphere 1 .....

INDUSTRIAL AIR POLLUTION
The manufacture of many of the products we use in our homes – especially plastics – 2 ....., as industrial chemicals are released into the atmosphere.

WATER POLLUTION
Water is polluted both by industrial and domestic users. Like air, 3 ..... so that they affect a wide area and reach places far from their point of origin.

POLLUTING THE SOIL
The burial of household waste pollutes the ground and also produces a chemical run-off 4 ..... that are used for public water supplies.

ACID RAIN
This relatively new form of pollution is a by-product of atmospheric contamination. The gases that are released into the air from cars, factories and power stations, react with the atmospheric moisture to form rain 5 .....

TRANSPORT POLLUTION
Fossil fuels provide the chief sources of energy for transport. They are a major source of air pollution, 6 ......

AGRICULTURAL CHEMICALS
The food we eat is prepared from crops 7 ..... a wide range of agricultural chemicals. These chemicals may end up in our food and in the water supply.

GROUNDWATER CONTAMINATION
Much of the world's fresh water lies in natural reservoirs deep underground. These are slowly becoming contaminated 8 .....

(Blueprint for a green planet)

Ways of learning: remembering vocabulary

The quiz you did in section **B** is one way to help you remember vocabulary. What other ways do you use? Make a list of these different ways and compare your list with a partner's. What ways seem most efficient? What aspects of vocabulary do they help you remember?

C

Paper 3: Section C

Introduction

Section C of CAE Paper 3 contains 2 different exercise types: gap-filling at phrase or sentence level and notes expansion.

Gap-filling at phrase or sentence level

1 Here is an example of a gap-filling exercise. Complete it and note down the strategies you use.
Note: In the CAE exam, there are always more sentences to choose from than there are gaps.

For questions **1–6**, read through the following text and then choose the best phrase or sentence to fill each of the blanks, from **A–J**. One answer has been given as an example (**0**).

From the poles to the tropics, weather determines the way we live. Most cultures have developed technology to conquer the elements – using clothing, housing and food to adapt to extremes of climate. Eskimos have learnt to cope with temperatures that drop to –50°C. They pile on layers of clothes and (**0**) ....

The average Eskimo male has a metabolic rate thirty per cent higher than the average European. But this is the result of a diet low in carbohydrates and high in protein and fat, not because they are born with this advantage. It is quickly lost if the diet is changed. Eskimos have also evolved short arms and legs (**1**) .... People living in the tropics who are acclimatized to heat have a larger blood volume, (**2**) ....

In a hot, dry climate sweating is the best way for the body to lose excess heat. But in the tropics, where there is high humidity, increasing sweat production may offer no advantage (**3**) .... Studies of indigenous Nigerians have found that they have no more sweat glands than British men, but when they start physical work (**4**) .... This is because with repeated stimulation the sweat glands become larger and more efficient.

Acclimatization to heat encourages a tendency (**5**) .... Nigerians, for example, lose significantly less salt through sweating than British men. This specific adaptation to the climate is due to increases in the concentration of a hormone called aldosterone in the blood, which acts on the sweat glands and the kidneys (**6**) ....

A to aid the conservation of **salt**

B as it doesn't make a difference

C **enabling them** to radiate heat **more** effectively

D so **they** have **less surface area** to radiate heat

E so as to help evaporation

F because **sweat** does not evaporate

G although diet contributes to this

H **they start sweating more** quickly

I **for salt** concentrations in **sweat** to decrease

J **retreat** to the insulation of their igloos for **warmth**

Example: | 0 | J |

2 In pairs compare your answers and decide how you might complete the following advice on how to do gap-fill exercises.

- **Reading the whole text through first is helpful because ...**
- **Reading for gist at paragraph level is helpful because ...**
- **Detailed reading of specific sentences is also helpful because ...**
- **Lexical and grammatical clues to the answer can be found in ...**

3 Now look at the words printed in bold in the removed sentences in activity **1** above. These words give lexical and/or grammatical clues to how the sentences link with the rest of the text. Find what these words link to in the text.

Exam practice

For questions **1–8**, read through the following text and then choose from list **A–J** the best phrase or sentence to fill each of the blanks. One answer has been given as an example.

Note: Some of the suggested answers are extra.

Example: | 0 | C |

Geoff Slater of Haverfordwest in Wales was testing a metal detector in his garden when he found a gold wedding ring. With the help of the hallmark he was able to trace and return it to Viv Stoddard **(0)** .... and was delighted to celebrate this reunion on the twentieth anniversary of her wedding.

There are times when metal detectors seem to exceed their design specifications and behave more like high-tech divining rods: **(1)** .... a treasure ten years after it was lost on a picnic site. Pat Knapton of Humberside in England was reunited with her wedding ring on the day of her fifteenth anniversary.

Sometimes the agency is human rather than mechanical, but the timing is none the less extraordinary. Brenda Rawson lost her diamond engagement ring on the beach at Lytham St Annes in Lancashire in 1961. She got it back in 1979 after her husband, Christopher Firth, was asked to help trace **(2)** .... John Firth was discovered in the neighbouring county of Yorkshire. And, during a casual conversation about Lancashire, he mentioned that his last visit there eighteen years before had been made memorable **(3)** .... It was the same one, identifiable by a jeweller's mark, found by the one person among hundreds of thousands using the beach that summer who would ever be able to return it.

By far the most common and recurrent of all tales of returning treasure **(4)** .... A recent example: John Cross of Newport News in Virginia lost a ring while crossing Hampton Roads during a storm in 1980. Two years later it turned up inside a fish served at his favourite restaurant in Charlottesville. There is nothing too surprising **(5)** .... Fishermen rely on such behaviour for the design of many of their most successful lures. But there is something in all these accounts of homing objects which seems to carry **(6)** .... There are hints of mythical connections and suggestions of some kind of unconscious human involvement. Folklore in almost every nation, for example, has its version of the ring-found-in-a-fish story.

The thing about fish, apart from their tendency to swallow tiny things, is that they are heavily symbolic of motherhood and the womb – 'from which all treasures flow' – and it is no surprise to find them involved in the restoration of wholeness and acts of reunion. Such archetypal reinforcement is bound to encourage the reporting of these events, **(7)** .... , bringing old myths back to life in today's newspapers. Hence a piece given prominence in the *New Sunday Times* of Malaysia, about dozens of fish caught with jewellery in their stomachs, just three weeks after the sinking in 1980 of the Philippine ferry *Don Juan* **(8)** ....

A	significance beyond that of outrageous coincidence	**F**	from which more than a hundred bodies were still missing
B	are those which involve the mediation of a fish	**G**	another one was instrumental in returning
C	who lived twenty miles away in Milford Haven	**H**	a long lost cousin John to share in an inheritance
D	the moon acts as a powerful magnet	**I**	by the discovery of a ring on the beach
E	about fish being attracted to bright objects	**J**	giving them deep credence even now

178

Notes expansion

Below there is a set of notes followed by a written up (expanded) version of the notes. Read both the notes and their expansion and answer the following questions.

1 Does the expansion contain abbreviations or symbols?
2 What kinds of words tend to be missing in the notes?
3 How many sentences are there in each note expansion?
4 Are the words in the expansion always in the same form as in the notes?
5 Does the expansion contain extra information that isn't in the notes?
6 What style is the expansion written in? Why?
7 Is the information in each expansion always presented in the same order as in the notes?

You are designing a poster about vehicle pollution. You've written the notes below to help you draft your final text for the poster. Use the notes to draft the final text.

Notes

Facts
1. Unleaded petrol = 40% of petrol sold; 3 years ago = 1%
2. Car travelling 100 km. per hour uses 30% more petrol than at 80 km. per hour
3. 17% all vehicles cause more than 50% all road pollution
4. ¼ full bus = twice more efficient family car

Action
1. Buy unleaded petrol = cheaper, cleaner
2. Look after car – increases fuel efficiency
3. Walk / cycle when possible / safe
4. Use public transport – reduces congestion

Expanded Notes

Facts
1. Unleaded petrol makes up 40% of all petrol sold, whereas three years ago it only made up 1%
2. A car that travels at 100 kilometres per hour will use up 30% more petrol than a car travelling at 80 kilometres per hour
3. 50% of all road pollution is caused by only 17% of the vehicles on the road
4. A bus which is only a quarter full is still twice as efficient as a family car

Action
1. Buy unleaded petrol if you can; it is cheaper and cleaner
2. You should look after your car; doing so increases its fuel efficiency
3. Try to walk or cycle whenever this is possible or safe
4. Use public transport as it reduces road congestion

Exam practice

Use the following notes to write part of an article for your school magazine in which you explain your class's plans for helping to improve the environment.

Write one **complete sentence** for each numbered set of notes, using connecting words and phrases as appropriate. You may add words and change the form of words where necessary. The first point has been expanded for you as an example.

WHAT CAN WE DO TO SAVE THE ENVIRONMENT ?
CLASS 7 HAS MADE UP ITS MIND. THIS IS WHAT WE ARE GOING TO DO:

(**0**) recycle all paper/glass/aluminium – put in containers around town

(**1**) at home – turn out lights + avoid spray cans

(**2**)   7 in class smoke = harmful to them + others – give up!

(**3**) no more lifts from parents – walk/cycle/public transport = better for health too!

(**4**) litter – sweet papers/drinks cans/burger wrappings, etc. bin it !

(**5**) tell others about environmental dangers: posters/debates/articles/campaigns

(**6**) collect £££££ – send to environmental projects short of £££££

We want to enjoy the earth. We want our children to enjoy the earth too. We must help.

COME AND JOIN US. YOU CAN HELP TOO!

(**0**) *We've decided to recycle all the paper, glass and aluminium we use by putting it in the recycling containers round town.*

(**1**) ....

(**2**) ....

(**3**) ....

(**4**) ....

(**5**) ....

(**6**) ....

Reflections

Compare your expanded notes with a partner's to see what differences there are between them and discuss which ways of expanding seem more successful.

What advice would you give to someone who hadn't done a notes expansion exercise before? Write up your advice as a list of helpful points.

Fourteen

A

Personal relationships

Starter activities

1 How many words to do with weddings do you know? e.g. bride, wedding presents, etc.

2 How much do you know about different wedding customs from around the world? Answer these questions by matching each custom to a country from the list below.

In which country ...

1 is a song or poem specially composed for the bride and groom?

2 do the bride and bridegroom feed each other cake?

3 does the bridegroom pay money to the bride's friends and relatives before passing through a cloth barrier to his bride?

4 do the bride and groom stand under a canopy?

5 do the bride and groom give presents to the wedding guests?

6 do the wedding guests pin paper money to the clothes of the bride and groom?

7 do the bride and groom walk seven times round a sacred fire?

8 are the bride's family seated on one side of the church while the groom's family are seated on the other?

a Japan
b Greece
c India
d Britain
e Denmark
f America
g Myanmar (formerly Burma)
h Israel

Do you know of any other traditional wedding customs from around the world?

Reading

1   Complete the following statements about marriage in your country by using the words 'is increasing', 'is decreasing', or 'remains stable'.

In my country ...
1   the number of people getting married ...
2   the number of people getting divorced ...
3   the number of remarriages ...
4   the number of people living together ...
5   the number of children born outside marriage ...

Compare your views with those of a partner.

2   The text below contains information about the state of marriage in British society today. Read the statements below and then read the text selectively to find the missing information. Choose your answer from **A**, **B** or **C**.

A   is increasing   **B**   is decreasing   **C**   remains stable

In Britain ...
1   the number of people getting married ...
2   the number of people getting divorced ...
3   the number of remarriages ...
4   the number of people living together ...
5   the number of children born outside marriage ...

Marriage

Between 1971 and 1975, a researcher called Mark Abrams, at the Social Science Research Centre, conducted a complicated series of studies designed to gauge people's satisfaction with various domains of their lives.

Throughout the series, marriage emerged as by far the greatest source of satisfaction – ahead of 'family life', health, standard of living, house, job and much more. The obvious inference, that marriage makes you happy, is widely accepted among those who specialise in marital studies. So is the view that marriage, like happiness, is good for your health, a view borne out by a number of studies.

Some of these studies present a confused picture because they compare the health and life expectancy of married people with the health and life expectancy of the divorced, separated and bereaved. (The latter group invariably come out worse, but should that be blamed on the termination of their marriages or on the fact that they married, perhaps unhappily, in the first place?)

But other studies have specifically compared the married with the single and reached similar conclusions. Even these are slightly ambiguous. Are single people more susceptible to serious illness because they are single? Or is their single status a result of their susceptibility?

None the less, the general message seems incontrovertible: marriage is not as bad as it seems. It is certainly not bad for you and almost certainly good for you. Few sociologists, doctors or statisticians would dispute the statement that married

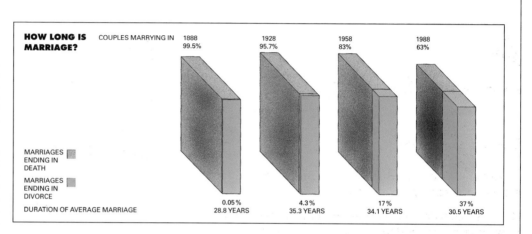

HOW LONG IS MARRIAGE?

COUPLES MARRYING IN

| 1888 99.5% | 1928 95.7% | 1958 83% | 1988 63% |

MARRIAGES ENDING IN DEATH
MARRIAGES ENDING IN DIVORCE
DURATION OF AVERAGE MARRIAGE

| 0.05% 28.8 YEARS | 4.3% 35.3 YEARS | 17% 34.1 YEARS | 37% 30.5 YEARS |

people live an average of five years longer than the unmarried and are significantly less susceptible to strokes, ulcers, cancer, heart attacks, depression, mental illness and high blood pressure.

Nor is the institution of marriage as beleaguered as it is sometimes made out to be. As well as having the second highest divorce rate in Europe (Denmark's is highest), Britain has the equal-highest marriage rate (along with Portugal). The divorce rate seems to have levelled out since 1985, and the huge long-term increase in the twentieth century probably owes as much to changing legislation as it does to worsening marital relations. The total numbers of marriages and of married people are much the same today as they were in 1961 (although both increased briefly in the early 1970s).

Since 1891 the proportion of the population who are married has increased significantly, while the proportion who are single has decreased. Today, around 85 per cent of men and 91 per cent of women will marry at some point in their lives.

That said, marriage is clearly under threat, both from divorce and from the growing trend for unmarried cohabitation. The divorce rate is increasing, even since the last significant changes in the divorce laws: from 11.6 per thousand in 1978 (143,667) to 12.8 per thousand in 1988 (152,633). The marriage rate is declining, from 14.9 per thousand in 1978 (368,258) to 13.8 per thousand in 1988 (348,492).

And a growing proportion of marriages – about one in three – are remarriages (partly because the number of people in a position to marry again has increased so much). Unmarried cohabitation has never been more popular. The proportion of women aged 18 to 49 who are cohabiting almost tripled between 1979 and 1988, from 2.7 per cent to 7.7 per cent. The proportion of children born out of wedlock in the UK has increased from 5.8 per cent in 1961 to 26.9 per cent in 1989. And according to Gallup three adults in four no longer think that becoming pregnant is a reason for a single woman to marry.

One problem is that marriage is increasingly perceived, in popular culture, as lacking the spontaneity of unstructured love. Does reality bear this out? According to the *Observer*/Harris poll, people who cohabit are two-and-a-half times more likely to be 'madly in love' with their partners than married people (25 per cent to 10 per cent).

Yet most other indicators suggest that married couples derive more happiness from their relationships than non-married couples, and people's perception of their own marriages remains optimistic. The 1991 *Observer*/Harris poll showed that 91 per cent of married people expect their own marriages to last until death. Their negative feelings about marriage are reserved for other people – 66 per cent rate the average marriage's chance of succeeding as 50:50 or worse.

Last year the Family Policy Studies Centre caused a great stir by predicting that, based on existing trends, 37 per cent of new marriages would end in divorce – an all-time high. Another way of looking at this, as several advocates of marriage have pointed out, is to say that nearly two-thirds of marriages will succeed.

3 Read the text again to find the answers to the questions below. Choose your answers from the list of percentages **A–I**.

A 10%	**D** 33%	**F** 66%	**H** 85%
B 25%	**E** 37%	**G** 75%	**I** 91%
C 27%			

In Britain ...
1 what proportion of the male population marry during their lifetime?
2 what proportion of the female population marry during their lifetime?
3 what proportion of marriages are remarriages?
4 what proportion of married people expect their marriage to last until death?
5 what proportion of marriages are expected to end in divorce?
6 what proportion of children are born outside marriage?

4 **1** The following expressions with numbers are all taken from the article. How do you say them?

in the early 1970s	348,492
since 1891	between 1979 and 1988
85% of men	from 2.7% to 7.7%
91% of women	50:50
11.6 per 1000	$2\frac{1}{2}$ times
14.9 per 1000	$\frac{2}{3}$ of marriages
143, 667	

2 Listen to the cassette to check your answers, then repeat the expressions paying particular attention to the stress and intonation.

3 Write down at least ten different fractions, numbers or percentages and ask a partner to say them aloud.

5 Complete the following text using only one word for each space.

Modern marriage is in chaos. Most men and women seek a relationship (1) .... a member of the opposite sex and we still have (2) .... idea of a perfect partner. But that won't immunise you against the fact (3) .... married life is difficult in the late 20th century. Society today no longer has a clear concept of (4) .... marriage means. Most people would never enter a marriage (5) .... they didn't think there was something mystical in it. The trouble (6) ...., we have overplayed the romantic notion and ideal of love. Modern couples talk about marriage (7) .... togetherness. Men and women use the same word but very often they mean different things and they may want different things. Women want togetherness (8) .... the sense of doing things together. Men like (9) .... wives somewhere for them, but not necessarily with them. The evidence is that (10) .... subtle differences are important. If they're not addressed they can produce a gulf.

(The Independent on Sunday)

Your thoughts

- **Do you agree that marriage brings the benefits suggested in the article?**
- **What do you consider to be the disadvantages of marriage?**
- **Do you think all societies are preoccupied with a notion of romantic love?**
- **Is it true that men and women look for different things in a marriage relationship?**

Speaking

1 Personal relationships can be very demanding and may even cause stress. Discuss with a partner how each of the following life events can be stressful and which are particularly stressful.

family reunions	**breaking up with a**
leaving home	**boyfriend/girlfriend**
getting divorced	**a family row**
the arrival of a new baby	**getting married**

2 Report your conclusions to the rest of the group.

Grammar analysis: 'empty' *it*

1 Look at these sentences:

a It's very annoying if the phone rings while you're in the shower.

b I find it useful switching on the answerphone if I don't want to be interrupted.

c It doesn't cost much nowadays to buy yourself an answerphone.

In which of the three sentences above does *it*

- refer to a clause acting as the subject of the sentence?
- refer to a clause acting as the object of the sentence?
- combine with an adjective to describe a clause acting as the subject of the sentence?

For examples **a–c**, underline the part of the sentence to which *it* refers in each case.

2 *It* can be used

- to indicate a sentence subject which is a clause rather than a compact noun phrase, e.g. *It takes a lot of commitment to stay married to the same person all your life.* (i.e. *To stay/Staying married to the same person all your life* takes ...)
- to indicate a sentence object which is a clause rather than a compact noun phrase, e.g. *Some people think it better to live together than to marry one another.* (i.e. Some people think *living together rather than marrying one another* is ...)
- in combination with an adjective to describe the subject (a fact, an action, an activity) where a clause is used rather than a simple compact noun phrase, e.g. *It's difficult to know exactly what makes people happy or unhappy.* (i.e. *Knowing exactly what makes some people happy or unhappy* is difficult.)

In the following sentences either the subject or object is in the form of a clause. Rewrite each sentence using *it* so that the sentence sounds less clumsy.

1 The getting of a divorce is much easier now than it was fifty years ago.

2 For children to be born outside marriage has become much more common in recent years.

3 To see so many marriages ending in divorce is worrying to the Family Policy Studies Centre.

4 That on average married people tend to live longer than unmarried people is widely accepted by the experts.

3 Now practise using *it* in this way by making up some sentences of your own about your thoughts and feelings on the subject of personal relationships. Use the following phrases to help you.

I prefer / like / hate it if ...
It would be a good idea for ...
It's ... if / when ...
It takes / costs ...
It's amazing / important / doubtful that ...

 ## Listening

1 Listen to two speakers, Claire and Philip, each talking about someone they feel has strongly influenced their own life. Listen to find out who they are talking about.

Is it:

a a close relation?   **c** a famous personality?
b a family friend?   **d** a teacher?

2 Listen again and complete the notes using not more than three words for each answer.

Claire recalls meeting a man called Simon Hardcastle when she was (1) .... He worked as a (2) .... for a national newspaper and his work meant that he often travelled to (3) .... This made him a very (4) .... in Claire's eyes and she believes that he was instrumental in her decision to study (5) .... at university so that she could go on and follow a career in (6) ....

Philip recalls the influence of someone he met when he was (7) .... He believes that for the first time in his life he was encouraged to (8) .... institutions such as school and family, instead of just (9) .... what he was told. He believes that this relationship introduced him to a new way of (10) .... He was also encouraged to develop his (11) .... talents which gave him a new (12) ....

Your thoughts

- **Describe to a partner someone who you feel has been an important influence in your own life, and explain why.**

B

Working relationships

Starter activities

1 Look at the above pictures. Who do you think the people are in each group?

2 What helps the people in each picture to work together successfully as a team?

Speaking

1 What sort of personality do you have? Are you a good team member? For each pair of boxes below, tick the one you feel best reflects your personality.

Extroversion ☐	**Introversion** ☐
prefers action energised by what is going on focus on world around them	prefers ideas energised by quiet reflection focus on inner world
Sensing ☐	**Intuition** ☐
interested in facts emphasis on what will work adopts step-by-step approach	interested in possibilities good at making links in problem solving likes new projects
Thinking ☐	**Feeling** ☐
analyses impersonally counts the cost of stragegies sticks to ground-rules and principles	analyses personally weighs up alternatives as to how deeply felt they are sticks to values and how people feel
Judging ☐	**Perceiving** ☐
decisive orderly controlling	flexible spontaneous understanding

2 Compare your personality profile with a partner's. In what ways are you different?

3 What contribution do you think you would make to a team? What difficulties might you have as a team member?

Listening

1 Listen to an extract from a radio discussion in which two young people, Pam and Neil, are interviewed about being part of a team. Complete these sentences:

a Pam describes being part of a team when she did ...
b Neil describes being part of a team when he did ...

2 Listen again. Indicate which of views **1–10** are expressed by Pam and which are expressed by Neil. Write P (for Pam) or N (for Neil). You may write both letters if you think both Pam and Neil express the same view.

1 Some team-members can end up displaying surprising leadership skills.
2 The barriers between people in a team soon disappear.
3 Being in a team means that everyone is in the same position.
4 Sometimes personal interests must give way to those of the group.
5 Certain people have a very caring attitude towards weaker team-members.
6 You can be anxious about whether you're making a positive contribution.
7 People often find themselves confronting their fears in these situations.
8 Taking important decisions for other people can be quite a challenge.
9 Being in a team with strangers is very different from being with people you know.
10 It's important to be a good listener and to say what you think.

Your thoughts

*   **Have you ever been part of a team? Tell your partner what you learned from the experience.**

Reading

1 What sorts of problems can arise in relationships between people who work together? Discuss your ideas.

2 Read the text quickly and decide which of the following titles would suit it best:

A Dealing with conflict
B Rules of relationships
C Managing your staff

Getting on well with colleagues, as anyone who works in an office knows, is a vital element in our working lives. Many office jobs involve a great deal of time spent talking. One British study of 160 managers, for example, found that they spent between one third and 90 per cent of their time with other people.

'Working relationships,' write social psychologists Michael Argyle and Monika Henderson, 'are first brought about by the formal system of work, but are elaborated in several ways by informal contacts of different kinds… It is essential for such relationships to develop if co-operation at work is to succeed.' And good relationships at work, research shows, are one of the main sources of job satisfaction and well-being.

Are there any 'rules of relationships' that might be useful as general markers of what to do and what not to do in your dealings with others?

'Universal' rules

Michael Argyle and his colleagues have found that there are such rules. Through interviews with people they generated a number of possible rules. Then they asked others to rate how important those rules were in twenty-two different kinds of relationships. These included relationships with spouses, close friends, siblings and work colleagues as well as relationships between work subordinates and their superiors.

The researchers discovered five 'universal' rules that applied to over half of all these relationships:

1. Respect the other's privacy.
2. Look the other person in the eye during conversation.
3. Do not discuss what has been said in confidence with the other person.
4. Do not criticize the other person publicly.
5. Repay debts, favours or compliments no matter how small.

This doesn't mean that nobody breaks these rules, as we all know – it just means that they are seen as important. The 'looking in the eye' rule, for example, is a crucial aspect of good social skills. It is very uncomfortable to have to talk to someone who never, or hardly ever, looks at you during the conversation. One needs to look at the person one is talking to to see if they're still attending and to monitor their reactions (if they've completely stopped looking at you and appear transfixed by the flowers in the window-box, it means shut up). To signal interest, the listener has to look quite frequently at the person who is speaking.

Work rules

As well as these general guidelines for keeping good relationships, Argyle and his associates questioned people about rules that apply very specifically to work settings. In addition to the 'universal' rules they came up with nine 'rules for co-workers':

1. Accept one's fair share of the workload.
2. Be cooperative with regard to the shared physical working conditions (e.g. light, temperature, noise).
3. Be willing to help when requested.
4. Work cooperatively despite feelings of dislike.
5. Don't denigrate co-workers to superiors.
6. Address the co-worker by first name.
7. Ask for help and advice when necessary.
8. Don't be over-inquisitive about each other's private lives.
9. Stand up for the co-worker in his/her absence.

Again, these make a lot of sense. And number 4 is an interesting one – it raises the big problem of colleagues with whom you simply don't get on.

In one of their studies, Monika Henderson, Michael Argyle and co-workers defined four categories of work relationships:

1. *Social friends*: 'friends in the normal sense who are known through work and seen at social events outside the work setting'. Research shows that up to a quarter of friends are made through work.
2. *Friends at work*: 'friends who interact together over work or socially at work, but who are not invited home and do not engage in joint leisure activities outside the work setting'.
3. *Work-mates*: 'people at work seen simply through formal work contacts and with whom interactions are relatively superficial and task-oriented, and not characterised by either liking or dislike'.
4. *Conflict relations*: 'work colleagues who are actively disliked'.

Disliked colleagues

Argyle and Co. have come up with a special list of endorsed 'rules for people we can't get on with'. The main ones are:

1. Respect each other's privacy.
2. Strive to be fair in relations with one another.
3. Don't discuss what is said in confidence.
4. Don't feel free to take up as much of the other's time as one desires.
5. Don't denigrate the other behind their back.
6. Don't ignore the other person.
7. Repay debts, favours or compliments no matter how small.
8. Look the other person in the eye during conversation.
9. Don't display hypocritical liking.

Argyle and Henderson also suggest: 'Another approach to resolving interpersonal conflicts is increasing the amount of communication between those involved, so that each side comes to understand and to trust the other more. Suspicion and hostility are increased by ignorance of what the other is up to.'

Trying to get to know the other person a bit more, if you can manage it, is really quite a good approach. You might find they're really not so bad after all.

(All this and work too)

*   **3**   Read the text again in more detail. Which of the social skills mentioned in the article and listed below as **A–I** apply to:

1   relationships in general
2   relationships in the workplace
3   relationships with working colleagues you don't like very much

A   respect for personal privacy
B   ability to be fair
C   maintenance of eye contact while talking
D   avoidance of public criticism
E   repayment of debts, favours, etc.
F   willingness to ask for and be asked for help
G   respect for confidentiality
H   use of first names
I   recognition of the other person

4   **1**   Look at the vocabulary items below and sort them into two groups according to whether they normally carry a positive or negative connotation.

hypocritical	ignorance	willing
conflict	compliment	cooperation
satisfaction	interesting	well-being
denigrate	suspicion	problem
superficial	criticise	fair
hostility		

e.g. *Positive:* interesting, ...
Negative: problem, ...

2   Change each of the following adjectives by adding the appropriate negative prefix. Would you use any of the adjectives to describe yourself to your partner?

interesting	essential	personal
comfortable	frequent	social
fair	satisfied	formal
specific	normal	cooperative
willing	possible	important

Your thoughts

*   **Do you agree with the rules mentioned in the article?**
*   **Are there any which conflict with cultural traditions in your country?**

Grammar reminder: conditional sentences

> **Remember:**
> **Conditional sentences often follow one of three main patterns:**
> **a**   **the first conditional which uses if + simple present + will/shall, e.g. *If you use people's first names, you will find that they respond more positively.***
> **b**   **the second conditional which uses if + simple past + would/should, e.g. *If the office manager simply said thank you more often, he would get on much better with the staff.***
> **c**   **the third conditional which uses if + past perfect + would have/should have, e.g. *If I had known the working conditions were so bad, I wouldn't have taken the job in the first place.***
> **However, the three sentences below show that conditional sentences in English can sometimes follow other patterns (referred to as 'mixed' conditionals).**
> **d**   *If their relationships at work are good, people are normally more satisfied and content in the job.*
> **e**   *If you told the secretary anything in confidence then she just passed the information straight to her boss.*
> **f**   *If you have found it difficult to get on with someone in the past, you could try getting to know them better.*

1   Match each of the example sentences **a–f** with one of the uses of the conditional described below:

1   a common occurrence in the present
2   a common occurrence in the past
3   a possible situation in the present
4   a possible future occurrence
5   an unlikely situation
6   something which might have happened but didn't

2   In the following sentences put the verbs in brackets into an appropriate tense.

1   If they got to know him better they (find) he's not so bad after all.
2   You will see an improvement in your working relationships if you (follow) some basic rules.
3   If he (look) me in the eye when we talked, I'd have a much better idea of what he really thought.
4   If they'd both made more of an effort, they (get on) much better together.
5   You spend a lot of your time talking to people if you (work) in an office.
6   If the boss (not criticise) his secretary in public, she never would have left the company.
7   If I lost interest in what she was saying, I (transfer) my attention to the photograph on the wall behind her.
8   Life can very difficult if you (share) an office with someone you dislike.

Writing

1 In most lines of the following text there is either a spelling or a punctuation error. For each incorrect line write the correctly spelled word(s) or show the correct punctuation in the numbered spaces below. Indicate any correct lines with a tick.

1   In your dealings with people its essential to realise how very important it is to us all ....

2   to think well of ourselves. We have, as social psychologist john Turner puts it, a ....

3   'need for positive self-esteem. You will get on best with people if you try not to ....

4   damage their self-identity, and to afirm it when you can do so genuinely and ....

5   believably. So if you think your own behaviour might be perpetuating an ....

6   unfortunate cycle of dislike, try gradually not too suddenly or it'll look extremely ....

7   false and thoroughly suspicius) to change it to a warmer, more rewarding and less ....

8   defensive style. The evidence is that we usualy like those people who seem to like ....

9   us, and we don't like those who we imagine don't like us. And none of these things is unalterable. ....

2 In groups of three, discuss some possible rules for relationships in the classroom. Agree on ten rules and write them out in leaflet form to be displayed for the whole class to see.
For example:

Rules of relationships in class
1   Always listen to other people and value their opinions, even if they are different from your own.
2   If you are late to a lesson, try not to interrupt the work of the class.
3   ...

Vocabulary summary

All the words below are taken from this unit. Match a word from each list to form collocations used in the unit, e.g. serious illness

A

social	working
vital	life
dramatic	popular
close	divorce
single	serious
significant	family

B

rise	parent
rate	friends
culture	expectancy
illness	proportion
conditions	skills
element	life

C

Paper 4 (Listening): Section D

Introduction

📼 **1** Listen to a description of the task for CAE Paper 4 Section D and fill in the missing information.

> **Paper 4, Section D**
>
> – a series of (**1**) .... extracts
>
> – each extract approx. (**2**) .... seconds
>
> – (**3**) .... pauses between extracts
>
> – all extracts (**4**) .... in some way
>
> – whole series heard (**5**) ....
>
> – questions test identification of:
>
>   (**6**)............., (**7**)............., (**8**) .... , (**9**) ....

2 Discuss with a partner what you think could be the most difficult aspect of this type of task.

Identifying the topic

1 Imagine that you have switched on your radio and change from one radio station to another looking for something interesting to listen to. What clues would you use to identify what each programme is about so that you can decide whether to listen to it or not?

📼 **2** Listen to a short radio extract. What is it about?

3 Tick the clues in the following list which helped you to decide on the topic in activity **2**:

- I understood everything the speaker said
- I used my knowledge of the world
- I noticed the intonation of the speaker
- I recognised some key words related to a single idea
- I analysed the grammar of what was said

📼 **4** Listen to a short sports report and decide which sport is being described. Are there any keywords which help you decide your answer?

Identifying the speaker

📼 **1** Listen to an extract from a sports report and decide whether the speaker is:

a   **a sports commentator**
b   **a sports coach**
c   **a competing athlete**

2 Tick the features that helped you to identify the speaker in activity **1**.

- recognition of sex
- choice of words
- awareness of age
- relationship to the topic
- role within a conversation
- style of speaking

📼 **3** Listen to another short extract and decide whether the speaker is:

a   **a parent**
b   **a teacher**
c   **a youth club leader**

Identifying a speaker's attitude or opinion

1 How might the following features of speech help you identify the opinion or attitude of a speaker?

- **speed of speaking (fast /slow)**
- **intonation (rising/falling)**
- **loudness (loud/soft)**
- **voice pitch (high/low)**
- **precision (precise/slurred)**
- **use of pauses**
- **choice of words**

📼 **2** Listen to two of the previous extracts again and identify the speaker's attitude.

Extract 1
Does the speaker sound:
a   surprised?   b   proud?   c   relieved?

Extract 2
Does the speaker sound:
a   furious?   b   annoyed?   c   depressed?

Identifying purpose or intention

1 Listen to a short extract and answer these questions:

a What is the topic of the conversation?
b What is the purpose of the conversation?

What sorts of clues helped you to decide the purpose of the conversation?

2 Note down the words and phrases you might expect to hear if you overheard the following:

1 someone describing a new car they'd bought, e.g. 'I'm really pleased, it's a dark blue Toyota, a couple of years old, one owner, loads of room in the boot, etc.'
2 someone arranging to borrow a car from a friend
3 someone apologising for damaging a friend's car
4 someone explaining the reasons why a car won't work
5 someone persuading someone to buy a car

3 Listen to two more extracts on the topic of cars. Which of **2–5** in activity **2** is the speaker trying to do in each extract?

4 Which of the words or phrases you thought of in activity **2** were actually used in the extracts in activity **3**?

Exam practice

You will hear five short conversations in which different people are talking about various instruments for telling the time. You will hear the series twice.

For questions **1–5**, match each conversation to one of the pictures **A–H**.

1 ....
2 ....
3 ....
4 ....
5 ....

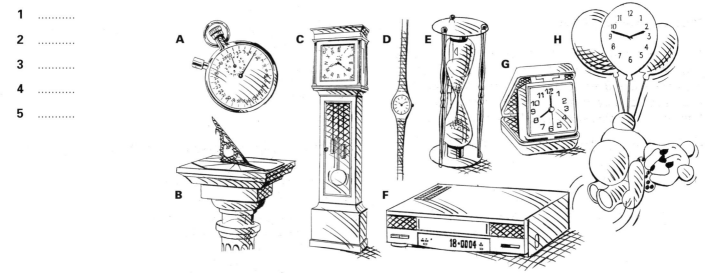

For questions **6–10**, match each conversation to one of the purposes **A–H**.

6 (1)........... **A** arranging for something to be repaired
7 (2)........... **B** checking something is suitable
8 (3)........... **C** complaining about something
9 (4)........... **D** apologising for a mistake
10 (5).......... **E** persuading someone to buy something
F expressing gratitude for something
G explaining how something works
H confirming the value of something

Ways of learning: focusing attention in Section D Listening Tasks

There are different ways of approaching the CAE Paper 4 Section D task. You could either:

a fill in the answers to the first block of questions on the first listening, and the answers to the second block of questions on the second listening

or

b fill in the answers to the second block of questions on the first listening, and then go back to complete answers to the first block of questions on the second listening

or

c write draft answers to both blocks of questions on the first listening, and then check your answers on the second listening to confirm or revise them

Discuss what you think might be the advantages and disadvantages of each approach? Which approach did you find yourself using in the exam practice task? Did you find it helpful, or would you wish to alter your approach in some way?

Fifteen

A

Let's peoplewatch

Starter activities

1 What does peoplewatching mean?

- **being a spectator at a sports event**
- **spying**
- **observing other people**
- **being nosy**

2 When you peoplewatch what do you look at most?

- **clothes**
- **way of moving**
- **facial features**
- **behaviour**
- **relationships to others**
- **character**
- **anything else**

Why? Discuss your answers.

Speaking: generalisations and exceptions

1 Some peoplewatchers think they can tell people's characters from their facial features. Match the descriptions below to the facial features on the right. Check any vocabulary you don't understand with a partner or a dictionary.

upper lip thicker than bottom lip
thin, angular nose
straight/horizontal nostrils
narrow notch
shifty, watery gaze
crooked mouth
joining eyebrows
heavy upper eyelids
elliptical eyes
nostril apertures slanting upwards towards nose tip

very thin lips
pointed high and prominent cheekbones
wide notch
nostrils slanting down towards nose tip
deep-set, extremely narrow eyes
middle zone longer than other two zones
smooth, wide, high and deep forehead

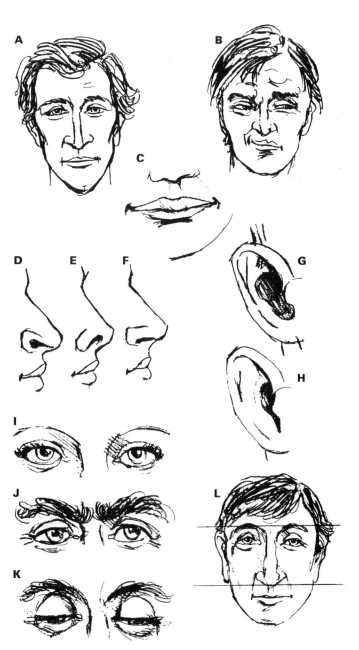

2 Which of the following expressions are used to generalise and which to talk about exceptions?

Generally speaking ...	In general ...
By and large ...	The exception is ...
There are exceptions ...	Apart from ...
As a rule ...	You can't really say that about ...

3 In pairs discuss which, if any, of the facial features in the drawings are associated with the following character traits. Use appropriate expressions from activity **2**.

patience	friendliness / sociability
patience before explosion	jealousy
impatience	chilliness / coldness
generosity	meanness
great intelligence	untrustworthiness
unfaithfulness	

4 Now read some psychologists' opinions and discuss whether you agree with them, again using the expressions as appropriate.

Facial feature	Its meaning
nostril apertures slanting up	impatience
straight nostrils	patience
nostrils slanting down	patience before explosion
eyebrows joined or copious hair between brows; heavy upper eyelids; elliptical eyes	jealousy
shifty, watery gaze; deep-set, extremely narrow eyes; crooked mouth	untrustworthiness
upper lip thicker than lower lip	unfaithfulness
a good forehead	great intelligence
very thin lips; thin, angular nose; pointed chin and high, prominent cheekbones	chilliness/coldness
middle zone longer than either the top or the lower zone	friendliness/sociability

Reading

1 Here is a famous face. Who is she? Describe her face to one another. Is there anything special about it? Just judging by her looks, would you like to get to know her? Why / why not?

2 These are some words or phrases used in the passage on page 193 to describe Mona Lisa. They describe her character or her physical appearance. Use a dictionary or a colleague to see if these are positive qualities or not. Write **P** (positive) or **N** (negative) or **?** (it depends) beside each word.

enigmatic	sinister	lose her temper
a glint in her eyes	bawdy	callousness
a mole	flab	an unflinching gaze
plump	greedy	a spendthrift
fickle	witty	

3 Now read the passage about Mona Lisa and decide whether you would still like to get to know her or not. Note down those character traits that attract you and those that put you off.

4 The passage suggests various modern day jobs that Mona Lisa might be good at. Look at these jobs and briefly list the qualities you think they require, then read the passage again to see if Mona Lisa would be suitable for the jobs. Note down your reasons.

a teacher	a secretary	a politician
a mother	an engineer	an actress
a housewife	a lawyer	

Discuss your answers.

There is endless speculation as to who Mona Lisa was and what her character might have been. It has even been suggested that the lady with the enigmatic smile could be a self-portrait of the artist Leonardo Da Vinci dressed as a woman. Her smile is the most famous in the world. Some see it as having a sinister aspect, described by the psychologist Sigmund Freud as expressing contrast between 'the most devoted tenderness and a sensuality that is ruthlessly demanding'.

It is a slightly crooked smile because it is stronger on *her* left (on the right of the painting). The smile suggests that she told lies and traded insults whenever it best suited her or when she lost her temper, which probably occurred frequently.

The hint of a smile playing around those much-admired lips and the distinct glint in her eyes attest to her fun-loving ways and a bawdy sense of humour. But the fact that these lips are 'bloodless' warns the face watcher of her callousness.

If you examine her lips in the portrait, which hangs in the Louvre in Paris, you will notice a small mole on her top lip. A mole anywhere on the lips or immediately above the corners of the mouth signals indigestion and flatulence. Whatever embarrassment this might have caused it does not detract from the appeal of her pretty, elongated rosebud mouth, a shape which normally testifies to a romantic, dreamy lover.

Mona Lisa holds her head and face straight and as erect as a pillar, her steady and unflinching gaze affirming her dominant personality and worldly ways. She was probably a woman of high status, a gifted abstract thinker, and would therefore in modern times be considered eminently employable.

It would appear from the angle of her jaw that it 'dropped' straight and below the ears. No face reading can be complete without a thorough study of the ears, which in her case are hidden, but Mona Lisa's jaw suggests that she would have been very successful in a sales career, or in publicity, public relations or in the hotel or travel industry. Moreover, a deep, smoothly rounded jaw such as hers exhibits firmness and optimism, but the beginnings of flab developing below the chin together with those plump cheeks, disclose her fondness for pasta, rich Italian food, and the local, full-bodied Italian wines. Yes, she was definitely greedy.

That she was a spendthrift is evident from her nostrils, for nostrils which are visible when the face is viewed full-on, indicate their owner has a scant understanding of money, and so she should not have been given the control of the family (or company's) budget. The nostrils, moreover, are narrow and the sides of her nose are flat, both features pointing to a rather untidy woman, who probably dropped her clothes, shoes, hairnets (in the portrait she wears one that flattens the top of her head) all over the parquet floor in the bedroom of a townhouse or palace near to Leonardo's hometown of Vinci, between Pisa and Florence, in Tuscany.

Because the hairnet sweeps the hair off her forehead, we can see how smoothly rounded and curved her hairline grows. This type of perfectly rounded hairline spells out a clear message: Mona Lisa was fickle, an unreliable 'friend'. Her forehead is longer and wider than the part of the face known as the low zone, which consists of the area between the nose tip and the jawline. This facial trait tells us that she had an IQ above average, that she was a fast learner, but being impractical and not wanting to spoil her elegant hands, she would not have been able to mend a broken vase or set a mousetrap.

A nose that is straight, long, thin and with a high bridge in addition to Mona Lisa's peculiar type of nostrils generally belongs to a witty and engaging conversationalist, but one who is impatient with those unable to keep up with the wide range of topics discussed.

A final word about her eyes: very few of us have identically-shaped eyes, but she is an exception. The eyes are narrow and elliptical, signalling jealousy, and if she suspected that another woman was after her lover (or husband), she would punish the enemy by any means, foul or fair. Mona Lisa was most definitely a sneak, but one who needed at least nine hours' sleep each night, judging by the puffy eyelids which are clearly shown in the Leonardo portrait.

(The Naked Face)

Writing

Choose a photo or picture of a person (famous or not) and use it to write a description of about 250 words of the person in the same way as in the passage on Mona Lisa.

or

Write a letter of approximately 250 words to the author of the passage on Mona Lisa saying what you think of her interpretation of Mona Lisa's character, and why.

Remember to think carefully about who you are writing for and how this will affect the style and content of your writing.

Grammar analysis: verbs taking two objects

1 Look at the following sentences and tick those that are grammatically correct.

1 I lent to her a record.
2 She gave some chocolates to me.
3 I showed her my present.
4 He brought the book to her.
5 They offered a drink them.
6 We promised our friend some help.
7 I read him a story.
8 They saved me some chocolate.
9 She handed the ticket to him.
10 He found me a job.
11 I asked to him a question.
12 We owe to them some money.

2 Correct the incorrect sentences. How were they incorrect?

3 Which of the following verbs can take two objects like the ones above?

search	write	stare	play (music)
take	point	teach	send
speak	grant	forget	allow

4 Below are some sentences containing 'two-object verbs' in the passive. Match them to their active equivalents in **1** above. N.B. Remember that there are two ways of making the passive with these verbs. Then write two passive sentences each for sentences **6–12**.

a The book was brought to her.
b My present was shown to her.
c They were offered a drink.
d A drink was offered to them.
e She was brought the book.
f A record was lent to her.
g Some chocolates were given to me.
h She was lent a record.
i She was shown my present.
j I was given some chocolates.

5 Use your work above to write a description of:

• 'two-object verbs'
• the rules for the use of 'two-object verbs' in English

Compare and discuss your answers.

Listening

1 You are going to hear four people talking about peoplewatching. Listen and match each speaker to what they watch or notice in particular. Tick the appropriate boxes.

Speaker	1	2	3	4
feet				
faces				
arguments				
hands				
scratching				
people watching other people				
people getting drunk				
mannerisms				

2 Listen again and match the speakers to the things they like or dislike about peoplewatching by ticking the appropriate boxes.

Which speaker likes or dislikes watching...?	1	2	3	4
people's disgusting habits				
people pretending not to notice something embarrassing				
people watching other people				
people on trains				
people avoiding your glance				
faces that tell stories				
people's mannerisms				

Your thoughts

• **Which of the above speakers do you agree with most?**
• **What is your favourite place for peoplewatching?**

a   b   c   d

B

Reasons for peoplewatching

Starter activities

1 Tick the statements that you agree with.

- **The casual way people dress nowadays tells us little about them.**
- **The main function of clothes is to provide cover and comfort.**
- **Our moods affect the way we dress.**
- **Gestures, facial features and posture tell us more about a person than clothing.**

Compare and discuss your answers.

2 Look at the photos of four women and four men. Which of the following adjectives would you match with which person?

e   f

big-headed	**casual**	**intimidating**
ridiculous	**mysterious**	**friendly**
natural	**approachable**	**smart**
relaxed	**feminine**	**submissive**
scary	**high-powered**	**mature**
classy	**sedate**	**well-groomed**
trendy	**off-putting**	**comfortable**
vain	**aggressive**	**attractive**

Discuss your answers.

g   h

✳ 🔲 Listening

1 Listen to five people who were asked which of the people in the photos they would like to meet. Match the speaker (**1–5**) to their preference **a–h**.

2 Listen a second time and match the speakers (**1–5**) to the features (**A–H**) that attract them to people. You may need to give more than one answer for some speakers.

Speaker

1	....	**A**	lack of pretension	**E**	mystery
2	....	**B**	smartness	**F**	informality
3	....	**C**	challenge	**G**	confidence
4	....	**D**	intelligence	**H**	femininity
5	....				

Your thoughts

- Would you be particularly put off by or attracted to any of the people in the photos? Why / why not?
- How much does someone's appearance affect whether you want to get to know them or not? Should it?

Grammar reminder: indirect statement

1 Can you remember the rules for 'indirect statement' in English? Read them, then carry out the activities.

---

1 In indirect speech the tense of the reported statement goes one further step back into the past, e.g.

'He looks rather nervous', she said – She said that he looked rather nervous.

The exceptions to this rule are the following:

- **If the tense is already in the past perfect, then the tense doesn't change,** e.g.
'He had come before me', she said – She said he had come before her.

- **If what was said is still happening or applicable at the time of reporting the tense doesn't change,** e.g.
'The earth goes round the sun', he said – He said the sun goes round the earth.

2 Pronouns (e.g. I, we), possessive pronouns (e.g. my, ours) and adverbs of time (e.g. now) and place (e.g. here) may need to change to make sense, e.g.

'My jewels are here in my handbag at the moment', she told the insurance clerk.
She told the insurance clerk that her jewels were there in her handbag at that moment.

🔲 **2** Say these sentences (from the cassette) to one another and after each, tell one another what each person said. Start *He/She said (that) …*

Speaker 1: *I love the cool dude in the waistcoat.*
I can't stand shoes that are too shiny.
Speaker 2: *I wouldn't mind the number of her mobile phone.*
Speaker 3: *My girlfriend will be here in a minute.*
Speaker 4: *I'd be quite happy to go out with him*
Speaker 5: *She isn't trying to be anything other than who she is.*

3 Ask several of your classmates what the appearance of their 'ideal partner' would be like, then report their answers to others.

Reading

1 Read the passage on page 198 quickly and decide which of these would be the best title for it.

A Changes in clothing
B What clothes to wear
C Clothes
D Clothing Signals

2 Read the passage again, in more detail to match these paragraph summaries (**A–F**) to their paragraphs.

Paragraph
1 .... **A** The rise and fall of skirt lengths.
2 .... **B** The reasons why we follow fashion.
3 .... **C** Why skirt lengths rise.
4 .... **D** Whether we like it or not all our clothes send signals about us.
5 .... **E** The way we dress nowadays is still governed by rules.
6 .... **F** Most of us put on our 'normal' clothing only once a day.

3 Read the passage in detail again to answer the following multiple-choice questions.

According to the author:
1 People who dress very casually
   A take no interest in clothing.
   B talk a lot about clothing.
   C don't transmit clothing signals.
   D are signalling something.
2 The act of dressing is
   A practised only by people who wear specialized clothes.
   B a once a day activity.
   C is more common than it used to be.
   D done more often by rich people.
3 A young man wearing jeans
   A is following rules.
   B is disobeying new rules.
   C is being formal.
   D is casual.
4 The author believes
   A skirts lengthen in times of need.
   B midi skirts are very expensive.
   C women wear short skirts confidently.
   D the future may tell us the meaning of skirt lengths.
5 We all use clothes to
   A display our wealth.
   B keep up to date.
   C measure change.
   D communicate.

4 What are you wearing today? What message do you think the clothes you have on convey? On a piece of paper, complete this information about yourself.

I think my clothes today show that I ...
You can see this from ...

Get into groups of four or five and shuffle your pieces of paper, then read them out loud and try and guess who is being talked about. Do you agree with one another?

Vocabulary summary

1 Divide into teams of four or five, choose ten words from the unit and then make up clues for each word.

2 Hold a quiz. Each team takes it in turn to read out their clues, while the other teams try to guess the words. The team with the most points at the end is the winner.

1   It is impossible to wear clothes without transmitting social signals. Every costume tells a story, often a very subtle one, about its wearer. Even those people who insist that they despise attention to clothing, and dress as casually as possible, are making quite specific comments on their social roles and their attitudes towards the culture in which they live.

2   For the majority of people, Clothing Signals are the result of a single daily event – the act of dressing, performed each morning. At the top and bottom of the social scale this activity may lose its once-a-day frequency, with rich socialites changing several times daily as a matter of course, and poor vagrants sleeping rough in the same clothes they wear by day. Between these two extremes, the once-a-day routine is usually only broken for the donning of specialized clothing. The man who gets dirty wears working clothes, the sportsman wears high-activity clothes. People attending special ceremonies – weddings, funerals, garden parties, dances, festivals, club meetings, formal dinners – change into the appropriate costumes. But although these pursuits mean the doubling of the once-a-day act of dressing, the change is nearly always from 'everyday' clothes into 'special' clothing. The old pattern, in which social rules demanded the changing from 'morning dress' to 'afternoon dress' to 'evening dress', as a matter of regular routine, has now virtually vanished.

3   The modern trend in dressing behaviour is usually referred to as one of increased informality, but this is misleading. In reality, there is no loss of formality, merely the exchange of old formalities for new. The wearing of a pair of jeans by a young male today is as much of a formality as was the wearing of a top hat by his equivalent in a previous epoch. He may feel that he is free to wear anything he pleases, and is rid at last of the suffocating rules of costume etiquette that once dominated social life, but what he wears is as much a uniform today as the costumes of his predecessors were in earlier times. The written rules of yesterday may have been scrapped, but they have rapidly been replaced by the unwritten rules of today.

4   There are many interwoven trends that can be observed in the complex world of Clothing Signals. Some are long-term, lasting for whole decades, while others are short-term, surviving only for a season or two. Not all are easy to explain. One of the most mysterious is the relationship between female skirt-length and economic conditions. During the present century, ever since the First World War, there has been a rather precise correlation between the length of female skirts and the periods of boom and depression. On the surface, one would expect long skirts, employing greater quantities of material, to be related to the boom periods, and the skimpier, shorter skirts to be made when money also was short. But an analysis of the facts reveals that the exact opposite is the case. As the stock market rises so too do the skirts, and when it falls they descend with it. Attempts to change this relationship have met with disaster. For example, in Britain back in the boom period of the 1960s, the fashion houses tried desperately to increase the amount of cloth used in skirt-making by the introduction of the 'midi', a skirt almost twice as long as the 'mini skirt' then in favour. The midi-skirt project was an expensive failure and skirts went soaring on upwards. Only with the recession of the 1970s did the longer skirt edge its way back into fashion.

5   Exactly why females should want to expose more of their legs when the economy is healthier, it is hard to understand. Perhaps the general atmosphere of financial activity makes them feel more physically active – a condition favoured by shorter, less hampering skirt-lengths. Hopefully, future fluctuations will give us a clearer explanation.

6   More short-term variations are at work in a hundred different ways, as fashion trends diffuse themselves rapidly around the globe. Many of these are no more than 'novelty changes', based on the need to signal up-to-dateness by the wearers. Displaying the latest mode indicates not only the social awareness of the individual but also the ability to pay for new clothes at regular intervals, and therefore has its own special status value. Each new minor trend of this type modifies or reverses the fashion of the previous season, and can often be measured with precision. The width of male lapels, for example, has been growing during the last few years, as has trouser-bottom width, tie-width, shirt-collar height, and shoe-heel height. By measuring these changes, and hundreds of others like them, it should be possible to plot graphs of shifting Clothing Signals and demonstrate the ways in which first one element and then another is modified to produce a constantly varying costume display system. Unconsciously, we all plot such graphs, all the time, and, without knowing quite how we do it, we read off the many signals that our companions' clothes transmit to us in every social encounter. In this way clothing is as much a part of human body-language as gestures, facial expressions and postures.

C

Paper 5 (Speaking): Phases C and D

Introduction

The last two parts of CAE Paper 5, Speaking are Phases C and D. Here is a description of these phases.

Phase	Target Skills	Input	Formats
C	• negotiating and collaborating; reaching agreement or 'agreeing to disagree'	• visual prompt (photo, cartoon, diagram, map etc.) and/or written prompt to set up a problem solving task	• two-way interaction between candidates, examiner assisting as and when necessary • candidates work together on one shared task, involving for example: sequencing, ranking, comparing and contrasting
D	• reporting, explaining, summarising, developing the discussion	• this phase is based on the output from Phase C	• four-way conversation, candidates are asked to present their decisions from Phase C and to clarify and/or elaborate on points arising

(Adapted by permission of the University of Cambridge Local Examinations Syndicate)

Ask your teacher any doubts or queries you have about this description, then in pairs, and without looking at the description, act out this role-play. One of you takes the role of the teacher and the other takes the role of the student.

Student: **You don't know what phases C and D are about, what you have to do in them, or what their purpose is. You ask your teacher questions to try to find out.**
Teacher: **You try to explain all about Phases C and D to the student.**

Useful language for Phases C and D: Interacting with other speakers

In phases C and D you may need to use language for the following purposes **A–D**:

A keeping talking
B inviting others to talk
C encouraging others to go on talking
D interrupting

Match these expressions (**1–12**) to the purposes **A–D**:

1 hold on a minute
2 I'd just like to say something else
3 just to finish, I'd like to say
4 what do you think, Maria?
5 please let me finish
6 go on, Takako

7 what about you, Christian?
8 as I was saying…
9 right, right
10 no, I'm sorry but
11 would you like to say anything else, Alex?
12 yes, that's right

Useful language for Phase D: Reporting your decisions

Below are some examples of language that can occur particularly in Phase D. Match the examples (**1–17**) to the language purpose (**A–D**) they are used for.

A reporting
B summarizing
C clarifying
D developing the discussion

1 what I mean is
2 we thought that
3 to sum up
4 so
5 go on
6 something else
7 I'd like to say something else
8 what I was trying to say was
9 we decided that

10 we agreed that
11 so, in the end
12 you see
13 yes, I think you're right to a certain extent but
14 we didn't really agree with one another
15 the point we were trying to make was
16 then the next thing we decided was
17 the next point we discussed was

Exam practice

Here are two Phase C and D tasks. Do them in groups of four, taking the roles of the two candidates, and the two examiners. Change roles after the first task so that everyone has a turn at playing the role of the candidate. The examiners could use the assessment criteria on page 133 of Unit 10 if they wish.

Task 1

Phase C (3 or 4 minutes)
The best places for peoplewatching

Examiner: Together look at these four pictures of Britain. If you were tourists in Britain which place(s) do you think would be best for peoplewatching and finding out about the British? Discuss your ideas with your partner. Make sure that you understand your partner's opinion. At the end of three minutes I will ask you to report your decision to me, and take part in further discussion.

(The Phase C discussion takes place)

Examiner: O.K., would you like to tell me now what you have decided? Why did you come to that conclusion?

Phase D (3 or 4 minutes)

The examiner asks for clarification, if necessary, e.g.

- What did you mean by X?
- Do you really think X?
- Why did you decide X?
- Can you tell me more about X?

And then asks more general questions from the following, as appropriate to the discussion:

- Why do people enjoy watching one another?
- What interests you most about a foreign country?
- Does the way people behave in public vary much from one country to another?

Task 2

Phase C (3 or 4 minutes)
Which photo to send?

Examiner: Together look at these four photos of a young woman. She has applied for a job as a teacher of English and has been asked to send in a photo of herself along with her application. Which one do you think she should send? Discuss your ideas with your partner. Make sure that you understand your partner's opinion. At the end of three minutes I will ask you to report your decision to me and take part in further discussion.

(The Phase C discussion takes place)

Examiner: O.K., would you like to tell me now what you have decided? Why did you come to that conclusion?

Phase D (3 or 4 minutes)

The examiner asks for clarification, if necessary, e.g.

- What did you mean by X?
- Why did you decide X?
- Do you really think X?
- Can you tell me more about X?

And then asks more general questions from the following, as appropriate to the discussion:

- Should employers consider appearance when employing people?
- Would you always wear your smartest clothes to go to a job interview?
- In which jobs is it essential to 'look right' for the job?

Reflections

In your groups, discuss how you got on with the tasks, e.g.

- What did you find easy/difficult?
- What could have been improved? How?
- Did you learn anything from acting as an examiner?

Write down some adverbs on the best ways to carry out Phases C and D, e.g. reasonably, patiently.

Ways of learning: interactional language

The expressions often used for interactional language (see Useful language for Phases C and D on page 200) tend to be colloquial. They are an important ingredient in helping to make communication flow smoothly.

1 Look at the 'Functions' column in the Map of the book, and in pairs tell one another as many of these expressions as you can remember.

2 From now on, listen out for, and even note down, the interactional language expressions you hear, e.g. on TV, on the radio, on cassette or in conversation.

Revision Exam Practice 3

Paper 1 (Reading): gapped paragraphs

For questions **1–6** you must choose which paragraphs **A–G** on page 204 match the numbered gaps in the newspaper article. There is one extra paragraph which does not belong in any of the gaps. **Indicate your answers on the separate answer sheet**.

What's the score, girls?

Anne Smith reports the latest IQ research and wonders if we should have our heads examined

BACK IN 1912, psychologists Cyril Burt and R. C. Moore tested 130 children in Wallasey schools to try to find out if there is any difference between the general intelligence of girls and boys. They found none.

1

This year Dr Halla Beloff of Edinburgh University, has published the results of a similar study of groups of first-year students over five years, stimulated by a report in The Guardian in 1987 of research carried out by Louise Higgins in Chester College. None of her subjects, 502 women and 265 men, had been IQ tested before. They were asked to estimate their own and their parents' IQ. Women put their own IQs on average at 120.5, their mothers' at 119.9 and their fathers' at 127.7. Men put their own IQs at 126.9, their mothers' at 118.7 and their fathers' at 125.2.

2

To test this, she asked them to generate 20 statements about themselves, all beginning: "I am …" These were sorted into three categories: positive, eg "I am using my brain all the time," negative, eg, "I am fat," and neutral, eg, "I am an only child."

3

"Girls," she says, "have a more dynamic adjustment to make growing up than boys do. Their lives are more precarious. Precariousness is a theme in one's life as a female." The caution they learn spills over into their whole perception of themselves.

4

For women success equates with effort, but failure is the result of stupidity. Men, on the other hand, take success as proof of talent and attribute their failures to lack of effort.

Beloff points to research in California which concluded that because men are more competitive they tend to focus on their successes. Women monitor both successes and failures more carefully, and draw a balance overall.

5

The difference between the two sexes' estimates of their IQs can be attributed to a variety of interlocking causes, from the low status traditionally given to what are regarded as "female" occupations to the dominance of men in our culture.

6

In the next stage of her research she will study fewer students in greater detail, to try to determine how they reached their judgement of their intelligence, asking questions like: "What is the cleverest thing you've done?" and "What intellectual tasks have you tried at and failed?" She will then get them to relate this to their other skills, to sketch out a hierarchy of the personal attributes considered most important in our society.

A

She believes, however, that no training or encouragement will ever induce women to rate themselves as highly as men, in spite of all evidence to the contrary.

B

In 1977 H. Wayne Hogan of Tennessee Technological University carried out 11 separate studies on 881 white males and 1,021 white females. He asked them: "What do you estimate your own IQ score would be should you take one of the standard objective tests?" He found that women invariably underestimated their IQs compared to men, and that both men and women, but especially women, thought their fathers' IQs were higher than their mothers'.

C

Women proved more positive than men. On the IQ test, the women were found to have assessed themselves more realistically than the men. Beloff believes this may be because girls are brought up to be more modest about themselves, and to be careful, because they are so vulnerable sexually.

D

Because they take their successes as evidence of talent, men have the edge over women when it comes to self-confidence. Beloff points out that confident people are more likely to join activities that have high demands, and at a higher level and are likely to persevere longer with problem-solving.

E

"Where women make positive statements," Beloff has observed, "it's in areas they themselves control." When they do well in an exam, they will say: "That's because I worked hard," or "They were very easy questions."

F

Over the five years the patterns of results did not change. "The women's movement still has not managed to sabotage women's perception of their relative intelligence," Beloff says. "It seems to be ingrained in them that there is this differential."

G

Beloff concluded that the young women students regard themselves as intellectually inferior to the young men, which of course they are not. So she asked herself: "Is it that in general male students think they're terrific and women students do themselves down?"

Paper 2 (Writing): Section B

Choose *one* of the following writing tasks. Your answer should follow exactly the instructions given. Write approximately **250** words.

1 You have a friend who teaches in a secondary school and who is trying to collect information about different festivals around the world to use as teaching material with her classes. She has asked you to provide an **account** of a traditional festival in your country. You should describe when the festival takes place, what is being celebrated, who takes part and what happens (e.g. special food, costumes, activities, etc.). Do **not** write the accompanying letter to your friend.

2 The librarian in your college wants to make it easier for English-speaking students to use the college library. You have been asked to write an **information leaflet** which can be handed out to students on their arrival, describing where the library is situated, when it is open for use, how to find and borrow books, and what additional facilities are available (e.g. videos/cassettes, daily newspapers/magazines).

3 Tragedy strikes: thousands forced to flee their homes

Your country was recently hit by severe bad weather which caused extensive damage and even some loss of life. Having seen exaggerated reports about this on TV and in the newspapers, a friend overseas has written to you expressing great concern. Write a **letter** reassuring them that you are all right, and describing what has happened and how people are coping with the difficulties.

4 The company you work for is attempting to improve security in the workplace following a number of incidents (missing handbags, car removed from car park, unauthorised person found on the premises, etc.). Write a **set of instructions** which can be displayed on the staff noticeboard and which will provide all employees with appropriate advice on how to protect both personal and company property.

Paper 3 (English in Use): gap-filling and notes expansion

1   For questions **1–7**, read through the following text and then choose the best phrase given below it to fill in each of the blanks. Write one letter **A–J** in the correct box on your answer sheet. **Some of the suggested answers do not fit at all.** the exercise begins with an example (**0**).

One hot Sunday afternoon in 1906, a merchant vessel was steadily plying its way round the coast of Brazil, bound for Montevideo. On the bridge, two officers were keeping watch while the rest of the crew rested in the heat. A sailing ship passed by in the distance. It was then that the creature appeared.

"I was still standing in the middle of the bridge (**0**) .... when the helmsman suddenly shouted 'Sir! Sir! Look over there, on starboard!'."

Officer J Koopman later reported, he spun round to see a 60 metre-long beast, (**1**) .... "It was overtaking our ship, which appeared to be standing still, with the speed of an arrow off a bow." Through the telescope, he could see its enormous head and dorsal fins (**2**) .... Koopman never doubted that he had seen a sea serpent.

But was it all an optical illusion, or another tall tale from a mariner too long at sea? Or do we really share our planet with creatures so bizarre that they seem to have stepped straight from our nightmares?

After years of hearsay, fuzzy photographs and blatant fraud, science is now turning its attention to the likes of sea serpents, the "Loch Ness Monster" and the "Abominable Snowman".

Cryptozoology – from the Greek for "hidden animals" – is becoming a respectable field of research, as the cranks give way to researchers using highly sophisticated equipment (**3**) ....

There is now an International Society of Cryptozoology, based in Tucson, Arizona, directed by professional scientists from universities (**4**) ....

Some of their targets are creatures thought to have become extinct only recently: the Tasmanian tiger, the last example of which died in captivity in 1936, or the flightless Moa bird of New Zealand, (**5**) .... But other targets are far more dramatic: giant squid so large they can attack and sink ships; huge apes that stalk the remote mountains of China; a dinosaur-like creature reported to be lurking in the lakes of central Africa.

But far larger creatures seem to be out there. In the winter of 1896, a huge mutilated corpse of a creature was (**6**) ....

Baffled by its origin, scientists bottled up tissue samples and forgot about it. In 1971, the samples were tested using modern techniques, (**7**) .... Calculations suggested that the original animal could have measured 60 metres across.

A   washed up on a beach in Florida
B   who coordinate findings from around the world
C   racing through the water 100 metres from the ship
D   to track down their elusive quarry
E   whose shape intrigues investigators
F   and found to belong to an octopus
G   rising high out of the water
H   worn out by the passage of time
I   which died out in the 17th century
J   with my telescope pointing at that sailing ship

Do not forget to put your answers on the answer sheet.

Example: | 0 | J |

2 Your local school is organising an exhibition on 'Our weird world'. It has asked you to write a leaflet to give out to the public during the exhibition. The subject of the leaflet is:

THE APE MAN – OUR RECENT ANCESTOR

Use the following notes to complete the leaflet.

Write one **complete sentence** for each numbered set of notes, using connecting words and phrases as appropriate. You may add words and change the form of words where necessary. The first point has been expanded for you as an example.

THE APE MAN – OUR RECENT ANCESTOR

What do you know about the APE MAN?

Read these facts and help us save our ancestor from extinction.

0. Spotted in America, Himalayas, Russia and China
1. Description, similar all over world = usually approx. 2 m. tall and about 300 kg
2. Different names in different places: e.g. abominable snowman, yeti, wild man, Sasquatch
3. Proof/existence = footprints in snow/ mud and sightings in different places
4. Best evidence = Russian scientific expedition/Lake Balkhash; report = 2 sightings + footprints + smashing sounds
5. Problem = no photos/videos of them yet
6. Expedition leaving soon; need ££££; please give

---

(0) *They've been spotted in all different kinds of places : America, the Himalayas, Russia and China.*

(1) ....
....

(2) ....
....

(3) ....
....

(4) ....
....

(5) ....
....

(6) ....
....

Paper 4 (Listening): Section D

You will hear five short extracts in which different teachers are talking about the same student. You will hear the series twice.

For questions **1–5**, match the extracts with the speakers **A–H**.

A music teacher   ☐ **1**

B geography teacher   ☐ **2**

C maths teacher   ☐ **3**

D chemistry teacher   ☐ **4**

E sports teacher   ☐ **5**

F French teacher

G art teacher

H history teacher

For questions **6–10**, match the extracts with the speaker's attitudes **A–H**.

A encouraging   ☐ **6**

B disappointed   ☐ **7**

C cautious   ☐ **8**

D complimentary   ☐ **9**

E confident   ☐ **10**

F dismissive

G supportive

H critical

Transfer your answers to questions 1–10 to the separate answer sheet.

Paper 5 (Speaking): Phases C and D

Examiner: I'd like you to both look at these photos of seven different people. You'll see that each of them is dressed differently. I'd like you to decide between you what order you would put them in for 'The most nicely-dressed' to 'The least nicely-dressed'.

A

B

C

D

E

F

G

(Candidates carry out task for 3–4 minutes)

Examiner: Now I'd like you to tell me what you've decided.

(Candidates carry out task)

Examiner: (Asks questions from among the following:)
How should people decide what to wear?
What does 'nicely-dressed' mean for you?
Would you ever dress casually for a wedding or a job interview?
Do you think we pay too much attention nowadays to what people wear?

Exam tips

Examiner recommendations on doing your best in the CAE exam

The CAE Examination Reports produced by Cambridge University Local Examination Syndicate (UCLES) contain recommendations to candidates on how to do best in each of the papers in the CAE exam. Here is a summary of the main recommendations made in these reports.

Paper 1

- Prepare for the paper by reading widely. Include in your reading texts from a wide range of different sources (e.g. magazine articles, newspaper articles, leaflets, brochures). Make sure too that you get used to reading long texts.
- Read the exam texts purposefully; your purpose for reading the text should be dictated by the task accompanying the text.
- Read the text in the way required by the task, i.e. use the reading strategy (reading for gist or specific information or detail or inference or cohesion, etc.) that is most suitable for the task.
- Don't worry about unfamiliar words or trying to understand every word; your purpose in reading should be to complete the task, and it isn't necessary to understand each word in order to do this.
- Be aware how texts 'hang together'. They do this through using 'grammatical glue words', 'lexical glue words', logical organisation and development.
- Make yourself familiar with the answer sheet and how to complete it. In the exam make sure you complete the answer sheet accurately.

Paper 2

- Prepare for the paper by reading widely. When reading, look out for collocation and idioms that you could use in your own writing.
- Before the exam, practise writing a range of task types. Make sure you can write a letter as well as a leaflet, a brochure, a report, a review, a note, instructions, etc.
- Read all the details of the exam instructions and reading input very carefully. This is particularly important for Section A of the paper where there is a large amount of reading input. Your answers are expected to respond to and pick up on all the detail that the instructions and input contain. Pay particular attention to anything on the paper that is written in bold.
- Try to imagine yourself as fully as possible in the situation of the writer of the task. This will help make your answer relevant, comprehensive and well targeted to its purpose and intended reader.
- Write for your intended reader. Keeping your reader fully in mind helps you use the right register and style. Register and style are important factors in the assessment of this paper.
- Keep the text type you are writing well in mind. The text type has a strong influence on the layout and style of your writing, e.g. the style and layout of a leaflet are usually quite different from those of a letter.
- Choose the question you will answer carefully. This applies only to Section B. Make sure you have enough knowledge of the situation outlined in the task to be able to answer the question well.
- Plan and organise your writing carefully.
- Write clearly, i.e. make sure your handwriting is legible. The examiners don't mark your handwriting as such, but the legibility of your writing does affect how well your answer communicates. An answer in

beautiful English that is illegible doesn't communicate well.

- Once you have written your answers, check them thoroughly for any inaccuracies of grammar, vocabulary, punctuation, register or style.
- Keep in mind the points that the examiners will be assessing when they mark your answers. These are: the relevance of the content, accurate and appropriate use of vocabulary, grammar, good organisation of the answer, the use of appropriate register, sensitivity to the intended reader.

Paper 3

- Prepare for the paper by reading widely so as to develop your knowledge and use of vocabulary and structure.
- Prepare for question 3 by doing lots of proof reading of your own and other people's work, before the exam.
- For questions 2, 4 and 5 (the open cloze, the rewriting, and the sentence gap tasks) look for clues to the answer not just in the words immediately surrounding the blank, but across the whole text.
- Remember that what language you use depends greatly on who you are addressing (your intended reader) and why you are writing (your purpose). This applies particularly to question 4 (the rewriting/editing task).
- Check your work carefully after you have completed your answers. This applies especially to questions 2 (open cloze), 4 (rewriting/editing) and 6 (notes expansion). Check especially that you have been accurate in your spelling, punctuation and grammatical endings (e.g. verb endings).
- For question 6, make sure you are familiar with a wide range of English abbreviations, and when carrying out the task in the exam, make use of a good range of appropriate linking words to join sentences. Don't just rely on 'and' and 'but', for example.

Paper 4

- People often worry a lot about the listening paper. Don't! Statistical analysis of candidates' performance shows that they don't find its level of difficulty significantly different to that of the other papers.
- Don't worry about not having enough time to do everything the paper requires of you. Again statistical analysis of candidate performance shows that candidates generally complete the paper easily.

- When doing note-making tasks, don't write too much. Better answers tend to follow the instructions 'write in a few words'. If you write long answers you waste time and risk making mistakes. Concentrate on writing keywords for your answers to this kind of question.
- Check the spelling of your answers carefully. Remember that you are expected to spell all answers except proper nouns accurately.
- Make sure you transcribe your answers from the question paper to the answer sheet accurately.

Paper 5

- Before the exam, get as much practice as you can of doing speaking tasks in pairs or in groups.
- Speak clearly and as much as the task requires. Remember that an examiner can only judge what they see and hear.
- Don't worry if you can't remember or don't know a particular word. Paraphrase it. What matters is communicating effectively.
- If you don't understand something ask for it to be repeated or clarified. You won't lose marks for doing this.
- Don't rehearse Phase A. It's meant to be genuine interaction.
- Remember there are no 'right answers' to Phase B tasks. If, for example, you think your partner has described picture A whereas in fact they have described picture B, neither you nor your partner will lose marks for this.
- Don't try to dominate the interaction. The test is planned in such a way as to allow both people enough time to speak. If you interrupt your partner inappropriately you will in fact lose marks for interactive communication.
- If you have a partner who doesn't say much, try to draw them out. This will help your assessment as it gains you marks for interactive communication.
- Remember that you are assessed on your own performance; you are not assessed as a pair.
(Adapted by permission of the University of Cambridge Local Examinations Syndicate)

(Adapted by permission of the University of Cambridge Local Examinations Syndicate)

Speaking activities

Unit 5 Section A: Speaking activity 1

Student A

Describe your picture as fully as possible to Student B. You should talk for about one minute.

Unit 5 Section A: Speaking activity 2

Student A

Listen carefully to Student A's description and decide which picture from your set is being described. If you need more help, you may ask some questions.

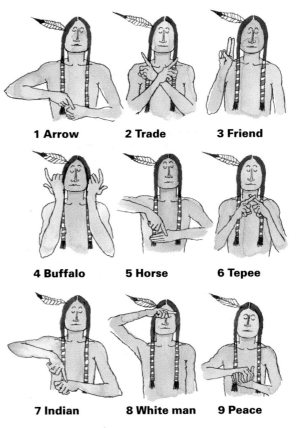

1 Arrow 2 Trade 3 Friend

4 Buffalo 5 Horse 6 Tepee

7 Indian 8 White man 9 Peace

Unit 6 Section B: Speaking activity 1

Student A

Describe your picture as fully as possible to Student B.
You should talk for about one minute.

Unit 6 Section B: Speaking activity 2

Student A

Listen carefully to Student B's description and decide
how your picture might be related to Student B's
picture. If you need more help you may ask some
questions.

Unit 10 Exam practice: Task 1

Candidate A

Examiner: Candidate A, I'd like you to describe your photos to candidate B who has the same photos as you but in the wrong order. Your description should help candidate B to number the photos 1–8 in the right order. You should then try to reach agreement with your partner.

1 2 3 4

5 6 7 8

Unit 10 Exam practice: Task 2

Candidate A

Examiner: Candidate A, I'd like you to describe your picture to candidate B who has a picture which is related to yours in some way.

At the end of one minute, I'll ask candidate B to say what the relationship between your two pictures is. You should then try to reach agreement with your partner.

Unit 10 Exam practice: Task 3

Candidate A

Examiner: Candidate A, I'll ask you to describe two of the six photos below to your partner, who has the same photos as you. At the end of one minute, I'll ask your partner to say which photos you were describing.

Unit 10 Exam practice: Task 4

Candidate A

Examiner: Candidate A, I'll give you some photos of five different pairs of trainers. Your partner also has these photos but in a different order. Your partner will describe the photos to you and say which ones he/she prefers and why. At the end of one minute I'll ask you to say which pair you think he/she prefers.

Revision Exam Practice 2
Paper 5 (Speaking): Phase B

Task 1

Candidate A

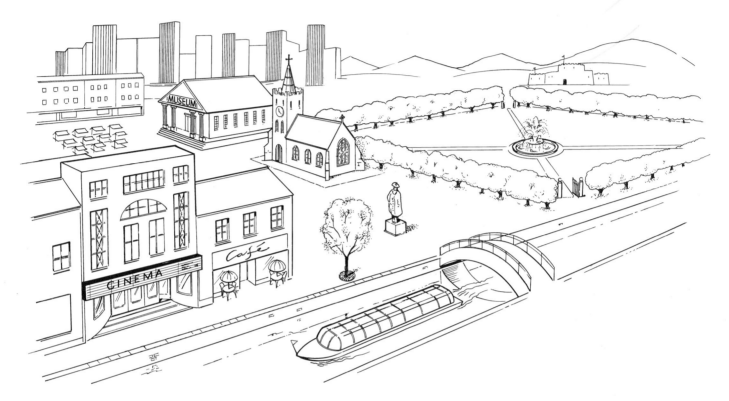

Task 2

Candidate A

Unit 5   Section A: Speaking activity 1

Student B

Listen carefully to Student A's description and decide which picture from your set is being described. If you need more help, you may ask some questions.

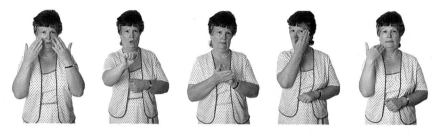

Unit 5   Section A: Speaking activity 2

Student B

Describe your picture as fully as possible to Student A. You should talk for about one minute.

Unit 6 Section B: Speaking activity 1

Student B

Listen carefully to Student A's description and decide
how your picture might be related to Student A's picture.
If you need more help you may ask some questions.

Unit 6 Section B: Speaking activity 2

Student B

Describe your picture as fully as possible to Student A.
You should talk for about one minute.

Unit 10 Exam practice: Task 1

Candidate B

Examiner: Candidate B, your partner has the same photos as you but yours are in the wrong order. Your partner will describe the photos to help you to put your photos in the right order and number them 1–8.

Unit 10 Exam practice: Task 2

Candidate B

Examiner: Candidate B, I'll ask your partner to describe a picture to you. The picture below is related to your partner's in some way. You should listen, and at the end of one minute, ask short questions if you wish/ if necessary. You should then try to reach agreement with your partner on the relationship between your pictures.

Unit 10 Exam practice: Task 3

Candidate B

Examiner: Candidate B, I'll ask your partner, candidate A, to describe two of the six photos below, to you. At the end of one minute, I'll ask you, candidate B, to say which photos your partner was describing.

Unit 10 Exam practice: Task 4

Candidate B

Examiner: Candidate B, I'll give you some photos of five different pairs of trainers. I want you to describe them to your partner and describe particularly the ones you would prefer and why. At the end of one minute your partner will say which pair he/she thinks you prefer.

Revision Exam Practice 2
Paper 5 (Speaking): Phase B

Task 2

Candidate B

Self-Study Guide

Starter unit

This unit focuses on the contents of language learning, communication and the CAE exam to help you become more aware of what the course and the exam involve and so work out your learning goals for your course of learning.

A

Ways of learning

2 These descriptions are used by researchers to describe different kinds of learners. After you have decided which description best suits you, think about what could be the possible advantages or disadvantages of different learning styles. NB More than one description may be suitable for any one person.

Tapescript

Man: I'm thinking of learning Italian. (Oh) Are you erh…? Don't you speak…?

Woman: Well, I did, I used to go to erm…adult classes… to do Italian.

Man: Yeh. Really!

Woman: Oh, I loved it. I loved it. It was wonderful.

Man: Is it easy?

Woman: Well, erm, erm, it…it is quite easy because I think particularly in Italian, they have one word that means an awful lot of things, and it's such an expressive language (yes) that, that the way that you say a word means all sorts of different things.

Man: Yes, what about the grammar? I mean is that…? I've heard that's quite tricky and…

Woman: Well, it's not, it's not…I mean the truth is I've forgotten an awful lot, which is the awful thing because I haven't, I mean I used to go to Italy quite a lot and I haven't been for a long time, so er, when I'm there I find I pick it up really quickly.

Man: So you find it easier actually in the country?

Woman: Oh, much easier. I mean I, I, I have kind of worked there very briefly, but well, for a couple of months and by the time I came back I was w…, I mean I was really excellent.

Man: The thing is I want to, I want to get to know it, to be able to speak it quite well first, so that I don't make a fool of myself when I go out there, because I don't particularly like making mistakes.

Woman: Oh, you shouldn't worry about making mistakes, that's ridiculous…

Man: No, I suppose not really, I should be a bit more adventurous really…

Woman: Well, and I'll also tell you, it's completely different when you're there. (mm) I mean when you hear people talking naturally and at the sort of right speed and everything it sounds so different. And also, and also when you have to, when you have to do things (mm), you know if you go into a shop and you have to buy something you have to communicate (yeh), so you just do it, I mean you just learn how to do it.

Man: And what about, what about, I mean, vocabulary and things? Do you, if they're words you don't know, I mean how do you…do you look them up and then translate them back into…?

Woman: Yeh, yeh. I mean I used to have a wonderful time, I used to always go back and get really frustrated by something I wanted to say and then go home and look it up, and work out how to say it (yeh), and I'd be really pleased with myself, that I'd come up with this phrase that somebody might understand.

Man: When you learnt, did you have…was it one to one? Did you have a teacher and just you or other people in the class…?

Woman: Oh, no, no, it was a big class.

Man: So, you all used to do conversation with each other

Woman: Yes, I mean she'd she'd kind of take…

Man: I think I prefer that.

Woman: Yes, yes. And also, I mean it can be great fun. I mean if they're sort of a nice bunch in the class and everything, I mean it can be very funny. And also when you get it wrong, it's a hoot. I mean, and you get homework. I mean, it's a bit like going back to school, but it's erm. No it's great fun, and they used to do things like you'd go to erm an Italian restaurant, say, and you'd all have to speak, order your food in Italian and do…or cook a meal or something, so that it wasn't just sort of sitting behind the desk, you know, repeating the grammar.

Man: Yes, that's the way to do it, yes.
Woman: Oh, it's lovely, lovely. I think you should do it.
Man: I will.
Woman: Definitely

Key
2   1 C   2 E   3 A   4 B   5 D   6 F
3a) They are talking about evening classes for learning Italian.
 b) The woman definitely enjoys learning. The man too but he has some reservations.

4

Way of learning	Woman	Man
Learning in the country where the language is spoken	✓	?
Learning the language before you go to the country	X	✓
Making mistakes in public	?	X
Being challenged	✓	?/X
Using a dictionary	✓	?
Learning with others in a class	✓	✓
Doing homework	✓	?
Lessons involving real-world activities (e.g. ordering food in a real restaurant)	✓	✓
Repeating the grammar	?	?

The woman would seem to be a risk-taker, possibly a translator and a child-like unconscious learner. The man is possibly a systems person and a teacher depender.

Your thoughts

You will meet 'Your thoughts' sections throughout this book. They are designed to round up your thoughts on a topic or a text and to activate relevant language. It is up to you to decide how many of the points to cover and in which order.

Ways of learning and this book

This introduces you to the 'Ways of learning' sections and to the 'Map of the Book'. The map should be particularly helpful to you as a self-study student. You should get used to using it to direct your learning and to use the book effectively for reference and revision.

B

What does 'communicating' mean?

This section aims to broaden your awareness of the contents of communication.

1 None of the responses are 'wrong'.

2 This is a warm up to the reading text in activity 3.

3 This is a gist reading activity. Set a time limit for reading the text (e.g. 2 minutes). NB The completed sentence summarises the contents of the passage.

4 This is a kind of 'multiple matching' activity.

5 These activities are designed to make you think about your own communicative abilities. You could write a report about yourself using the report here for guidance.

Key
2   Possible answers:
Mother and baby – depend much more on non-verbal signals; baby is learning means of communication, mother has to work at trying to interpret baby's meanings

2–3-year-old at family table – child will try to make sense of what he/she hears, parents will possibly see themselves as still teaching child to talk

School child – learning to talk in more formal settings, learning new vocabulary, learning how to get attention and to take turns in talking

Woman talking at business meeting – probably using quite formal language and possibly specialised language (technical jargon) too; dress and body language probably important elements of communication in this setting; use of appropriate language also important

Boy and girl – non-verbal communication, eye contact and physical gestures, intimate exchanges

3   (1) expression (3) negotiation

4   1   negotiation
    2   appropriate use of language, understanding facial expression, learning intonation, learning to get attention
    3   writing, learning to get attention, stating views, learning to take turns in talking, appropriate use of language
    4   appropriate use of language, awareness of body language, technical jargon, dress
    5   appropriate use of language, understanding facial expression, awareness of body language

Elements of communication and this book

This section gives you a further opportunity to get to know the Map of the Book.

C

The CAE exam

In each unit Section C focuses on part of the CAE exam. These sections contain explicit preparation for the exam, while Sections A and B concentrate on improving your general communication skills to bring these up to the level required. Section C contains an 'exam practice' section in which you have an opportunity to practise tasks in an exam-like situation.

Tapescript

1st woman: Jane (mm), erm, I know you've already taught CAE, isn't that right?

2nd woman: That's right, yes, I've just finished a course actually.

1st woman: Well, I've er, just got my timetable for this term and I've discovered that I've got a CAE class and I've, well, I've never taught towards it before, and I wonder if you could sort of fill me in because I really don't know much about the exam at all.

2nd woman: Well, you know what it stands for, don't you? CAE?

1st woman: Cambridge something or other...

2nd woman: Yes, well, no, actually it is a Cambridge exam, you're right, but it's...CAE actually stands for the Certificate in Advanced English.

1st woman: Right, so, Certificate in Advanced English, O.K.

2nd woman: What else would you like to know about it?

1st woman: Erm, well I suppose really, what sort of level it is, you know, if it's divided up into papers, and what the different papers are.

2nd woman: Erm, sure. Well, it's a fairly high level examination, and I suppose it was really designed as a final qualification in English for people who wanted to use English in their jobs or possibly to go on and use English in a study environment. Erm, it focuses quite a lot on using the language in real world tasks, reading articles or writing letters; that type of thing. So, it has a practical side to it.

1st woman: So, it's not erm...not a sort of academic exam?

2nd woman: No, no, it's...I wouldn't say it's a very high level academic exam, but I would say it has practical application when you're using English in a job or study context. So, it's of relevance to a lot of students who've been studying English for a number of years and want some final qualification which gives an indication of how well they can speak and use the language.

1st woman: Right, so a lot of the sort of work that you do in the classroom...kind of authentic tasks and things like that, they'd be relevant, would they?

2nd woman: They would, yes. In the course that I taught we used a lot of authentic materials from newspaper articles, magazines, listening tasks based on things I'd recorded off the radio; that type of thing. And then, a lot of the writing tasks we did were based around the sorts of writing that you'd very often have to do in, in a job situation or possibly in a study situation; writing a formal or an informal letter, drawing up a short report or writing a description perhaps for a guidebook, that type of thing.

1st woman: So, no composition writing?

2nd woman: Oh, no.

1st woman: Thank goodness, oh, that's a relief. Erm, er, so there's writing in it?

2nd woman: Yes, there's a writing paper.

1st woman: So, there's a writing paper.

2nd woman: And then, there's a reading paper.

1st woman: Hold on, writing, reading, yes.

2nd woman: And, then, of course, the other two skills: listening and speaking.

1st woman: So, then, each of them are papers, are they?

2nd woman: Yes, that's right.

1st woman: How do you have a speaking paper?

2nd woman: Well, it's more like an oral test, I suppose. Erm, in fact, it's quite unusual because er, instead of just the usual sort of interview which you often get in a speaking test where you have an interviewer and one candidate; in this case there are two examiners and two candidates present all at the same time (mm). Which means that it's not just a situation where the interviewer's talking to the candidate, not just sort of that one way type of interaction. But there's the opportunity for the two candidates to talk to each other.

1st woman: Yes, I don't know, but I can imagine that a lot of students would find that a bit more relaxing.

2nd woman: Well, I know the students in my class actually quite enjoyed it because we do a lot of pair work in class anyway, and it just meant that when it came to the exam, they were doing something very similar to what they were used to.

1st woman: Right, so from what you've said, it sort of...the exam doesn't seem to be...the kind of work you'd need to do for the exam doesn't seem to be very different from a lot of the work you'd do in class anyway.

2nd woman: I think that's right, and that certainly made my life a lot easier obviously, in teaching the class, because many of the things the students had been used to doing, they find turn up in the exam in terms of activities.

1st woman: So, there's the four papers?

2nd woman: No, there's actually five (oh). There's a fifth paper, and that's called the English in Use paper.

1st woman: English in Use, right. Grammar?

2nd woman: Yes, it's er, it has grammar in it, but not, it's not rigidly a grammar paper. It includes work on vocabulary as well, so it's grammar in the widest sense. And not just at the sentence level either, but grammar through a text. Erm, it also looks at things like style, choosing the right words to use in the right situation, erm, and all sorts of aspects of English that we use in everyday situations. So, it's not just a matter of students showing how well they can use grammatical rules. And actually, we did some interesting work in class on that, not just going through a grammar book.

1st woman: Right, well, thanks very much. Erm, well, can I come and ask you more questions later on maybe?

2nd woman: Do, yes, yes, and if you want to borrow any materials you're welcome to use them … just let me know.

1st woman: Right, thanks very much.

Key

1   1   **Certificate in Advanced English**
    2   **fairly high level**
    3   **for people who want to use English in their jobs or possibly to go on and use English in a study environment; for people who want a final qualification**
    4   **language in real-world tasks**
    5   **5**
    6

Writing	Reading	Listening	Speaking	English in Use
practical writing e.g. writing formal or an informal letter for a job or study situation; report writing; writing a description for a guidebook etc.; no compositions	articles from newspapers and magazines	listening based on off-air recordings	two examiners and two candidates present; like pairwork	grammar and vocabulary; grammar at sentence and text level; style; choosing appropriate words

One: Introductions

A

The way we live

Starter activities

Key

1   A   Egyptian   B   Aztec   C   Roman   D   Greek

2–3   Give your opinions about these activities out loud or on cassette.

Listening

Tapescript
Excerpt 1

Early schooling was the responsibility of mothers and nursemaids. Most girls and boys went to primary school at seven to learn reading and writing, but primary school teachers were not much respected and most pupils were only taught to learn by heart, with frequent use of the cane.

A smaller number of children went on to grammar school, where the main subject was literature – Greek as well as Latin. A still smaller number of boys finished their education at a school of rhetoric. There they were taught the subjects necessary for a career in public service, such as public speaking and the ability to conduct a debate or legal argument. Most educated citizens could speak Greek as well as they could speak Latin.

Excerpt 2

Each god served a particular need. Some originated in ancient tribal traditions, such as the sacred bulls worshipped at Apis, or the cats dedicated to the goddess Bastet. Others, such as the sun god Ra, developed out of their reverence for nature. Some gods looked human, others had the heads of animals and birds. One important religious belief was the idea of *ma'at*: justice and good order. People believed that the gods ruled the world, and it was people's duty to live according to their will and to maintain *ma'at*, so far as was possible.

Excerpt 3

Demokratia meant government by mass meeting. In Athens an general assembly was held on average once in nine days and every ordinary male citizen was free to attend, speak and vote. In practice, normal attendance at an assembly was about five to six thousand. The city was governed by the votes of this crowd.

Excerpt 4

Understanding time was crucial to them. They needed to know practical things such as when to plant and when to harvest. Much more importantly, these superstitious people wanted to know which days were lucky and which were thought unlucky. They had two calendars. One of these, the solar calendar, was very like ours with 365 days. Five of these days were thought to be very unlucky – it was believed that arguments that started during the 'nothing' days could last for ever, and that children born then would never amount to anything. During this time the Aztecs stayed at home and did nothing.

The other calendar was the sacred calendar, the Count of the Days, which was important for priests and astrologers. This calendar was used mainly for making prophecies and deciding which were lucky days.

Key

1   Excerpt 1: Roman   Excerpt 3: Greek
    Excerpt 2: Egyptian   Excerpt 4: Aztec

2   Possible answers:
    Roman education: early education = responsibility of mothers and nursemaids; most children went to primary school where learnt reading and writing; pupils learnt by heart, cane used; small number of children went to grammar school where studied literature; smaller group of boys went on to school of rhetoric where learnt skills of speaking.

    Egyptian gods and religion: many gods to serve different needs; some gods looked human, others like animals; very important religious belief = *ma'at* i.e. a belief in justice and good order which it was everybody's duty to maintain.

    Greek democracy: mass meetings which any ordinary male could take part in; held frequently and regularly; decisions taken as a result of the meetings' votes.

    Aztecs concerned about time; particularly about lucky and unlucky days; had two kinds of calendar, ordinary one and sacred one; ordinary one helped them to know which days where lucky; sacred calendar was used by priests for making prophecies and deciding on lucky days.

3   There are no correct answers to this activity. They depend on your opinion.

Reading

Key

3   1 T   2 T   3 T   4 ?
    5 F   6 F   7 T   8 F

4   disinclined = unwilling
    lift a finger = help/work
    emerge = be revealed
    take the lead = take on responsibility
    overwhelmingly = above all
    confined = limited
    top the league = come first
    all-round = general
    stoutly maintain = strongly affirm
    fellows = men
    chores = boring/domestic work
    prone = inclined

 Writing

This is the kind of task you might find in Section B of the CAE Paper 2, Writing. Before writing the letter, think carefully about its content and the style of language to use. See page 295 for the assessment criteria used to mark the CAE writing paper.

Grammar reminder – prepositions

The correct use of prepositions is important for the CAE exam. The function, use and meaning of prepositions can vary a lot depending on the context in which they are used.

Key

1   fixed expressions: *to lift a finger <u>round</u> the house; three <u>out of</u> four; <u>in</u> charge <u>of</u>; they left it <u>to</u> women; <u>at</u> their best*

adjective + preposition combinations: *responsible <u>for</u>; confined <u>to</u>; based <u>on</u>; due <u>for</u>*

verb + preposition combinations: *long <u>for</u>; to take the lead <u>in</u>; took part <u>in</u>; looking <u>at</u>; treated <u>with</u>; to care <u>for</u>; to mark <u>with</u>; reconciling <u>with</u>; interviewed <u>about</u>*

noun + preposition combinations: *view <u>of</u>; sort <u>of</u>; availability <u>of</u>; exit <u>from</u>*

passive constructions: *dispatched <u>by</u> Brussels; challenged <u>with</u>; confirmed <u>by</u>; marked <u>by</u>*

prepositions of place: *<u>in</u> the United Kingdom; escort children <u>to</u> playschool, <u>to</u> school; <u>among</u> the most domesticated; <u>in</u> Portugal; <u>at</u> the kitchen sink; <u>in</u> Europe; <u>in</u> Denmark*

2   All the fixed expressions.

Vocabulary

Key

responsible	*irresponsible, irresponsibility, responsibility, responsibly, irresponsibly*
incline	*inclined, disinclined, inclination, disinclination*
liberate	*liberated, unliberated, liberation*
likely	*unlikely, likelihood*
concern	*concerned, unconcerned*
affect	*affected, affectedness, unaffected, unaffectedness, affectedly, unaffectedly*
overwhelm	*overwhelmed, overwhelming, overwhelmingly*
willing	*willingly, unwilling, unwillingly, willingness, unwillingness*
domestic	*domestically domesticated, undomesticated, domestication*
usual	*usually, unusual, unusually*
enthusiasm	*enthusiastic, enthusiastically, unenthusiastic, unenthusiastically*
common	*uncommon, uncommonly, commonly, commonness*
public	*publicise, publicly*
available	*availability, unavailable, unavailability*

hope   *hopeful, hopeless, hopefulness, hopelessness, hopefully, unhopefully, hopelessly*

agree   *agreement, disagree, disagreement, agreeable, disagreeable, agreeably, disagreeably*

B

The way we are

⃞ ✳ Listening

Tapescript

Woman: That's me in the bath with my brother. We loved bath times actually; we normally shared the bath together. I'm surprised I'm sitting at the taps end because erm I was 18 months older than him, and was a much stronger character and could normally force him to sit at the taps end. My mother always used to throw lots of toys in for us and that always sort of took away the pain of having our hair washed which I hated and used to fight against, but it had to be done.

Woman: This is a picture of us at our dance class and looks like some good time is going on. I seem to be day dreaming as normal; my attention has been taken off the camera…mean maybe we were taking a bit of time for it all to happen; I don't know, but I'm not quite there…seem to remember doing that a lot in my childhood, sort of being half there and half not, very taken with my own thoughts, not really paying much attention to anybody else…wasn't nasty, I was just made like that.

Woman: Oh, look at that. I remember that was taken at my friend Susie Wallis' 5th birthday. And whenever I used to go to somebody's birthday party I always used to go straight for the birthday cake, and try and eat it before anybody else got their hands on it. I used to love cake. I mean I'm just eating it there with my bare fingers and my sister's next to me, just watching me sort of hammer away at this cake. I loved food more than anything. I think I loved it more than playing or anything like that. I've sort of grown up quite similar actually. I've a terrible weight problem.

Man: Yes, Smiley, they used to call me or Spotty, but I wasn't then really 'cos I must have been about 5? My hair was lighter; it's darker now; and that's a really dodgy jumper; yeh, I think that was erm, er one of my granny's birthday presents. Yes, 'cos we used to get loads of those. The one my brother's actually in is worse; but, yeh, I don't know, I always seemed to have a grin on me face and be kind of cheeky but I don't know, I paid attention at school when I got older and I kind of grew up quite boring really.

Man: Yeh, this is a picture of me next door with the two little girls who lived next door, being forced to play with paints; and erm, this was sort of a punishment, and also to keep me in check because I was a bit of a wild boy; and, in fact, I've got very short hair in this photo and it's because I'd come off my bike about two months before and had a quite nasty er gash on my head, and erm they just thought I was playing with boys that were older than me and rougher, and erm, so I was forced to play these sissy games, as I saw them next door, and er, that's why I'm not looking very happy, I think.

Key

1 Speaker 1 – picture 2
  Speaker 2 – picture 3
  Speaker 3 – picture 5
  Speaker 4 – picture 1
  Speaker 5 – picture 4

2 Possible answers:
  1st woman: strong character
  2nd woman: day dreaming; not quite there; being half there and half not; not really paying much attention to anybody else
  3rd woman: I loved food; I've a terrible weight problem
  1st man: Smiley; a grin; my hair was lighter, it's darker now; cheeky; grew up quite boring
  2nd man: wild; short hair; gash on my head; not looking very happy

Reading

NB In the 6th paragraph Maeve refers to 'cakes with *hundreds-and-thousands* on them'. These are pieces of multi-coloured sugar which are sprinkled on cakes.

2–4 Magazine and newspaper articles are frequently used for reading passages in the CAE exam. Try and read as many of them as you can. The three reading activities in 2, 3 and 4 require different approaches to reading: reading for gist, reading for detail and reading for specific information.

6 Remember that in English, context/lexical words generally carry the main sentence stress(es) whereas grammatical words tend not to be stressed.

Key

3 Possible answers:
  brought up to think she was centre of the universe; received lots of love and attention; jolly mother; lots of comfort; maid who became a friend; religion; some good teachers; summer holidays

4 **Occupation:** teacher then writer
  Country of origin: Ireland
  Father's occupation: barrister
  Mother's occupation: nurse, then housewife
  Religion: probably Catholic
  Type of school attended: convent
  Physical description: big and fat (as a teenager)
  Personality (as a child): (possible answers) self-confident, goody-goody, extrovert, placid, quick-minded, fanciful, devout, content, innocent, not very academic, lazy

Grammar analysis: the simple past and present perfect tenses

3 Refer to the sentences in 2 for clues to the answers.

Key

1 Present perfect, simple past.

2   1   Both a and b are grammatically correct; b is factually correct.

    2   a is grammatically correct and factually correct; b is ungrammatical and therefore also factually incorrect (it makes no sense).

    3   Both are grammatically correct; we don't know if a is factually true, b cannot be true as it implies that Maeve is dead.

    4   Both are grammatically correct; both are also likely to be factually correct – it is clear that Maeve's childhood is still important to her, so a is correct, and it is likely that she regarded it as important while she was a child, so b is probably true, though we don't know for certain.

    5   Both are grammatically correct; we don't know if a is true; b is true as she says so in the article.

    6   Both are grammatically correct; a is true; b is not factually correct as it implies that she is yet to become a writer, which is not the case.

    7   Both are grammatically correct, a is true but we don't know if b is – it implies that they still spoil her.

    8   Both are grammatically correct; both a and b could be true. a implies that her childhood no longer inspires her writing, while b implies that it continues to do so.

3   (1) actions   (4) past
    (2) time   (5) past
    (3) just   (6) effect

Speaking: asking for personal information

*3   Maybe you could interview a friend or a member of your family.

Key

2   Possible answers:

Name:	What's your name?
Occupation:	What's your job? Do you have a job? What do you do for a living?
Father's/mother's occupation:	What does your father/mother do for a living? What's your father's/mother's job?
Religion:	What religion are you? Are you religious?
Physical description:	What do you look like?
Country of origin:	Where do you come from? Where are you from? What country do you come from?
Type of school: attended:	What kind of school did you go to? Where did/do you go to school?
Personality:	What kind of person are you? What are you like?

Vocabulary summary

Key

Possible answers:

Domestic chores: *shopping, washing up, cooking, cleaning*

Personality: *goody-goody, extrovert, placid, quick-minded*

Physical description: *strapping, big, fat, lovely*

Childhood: *school, birthday parties, homework, summer holidays*

C

Paper 1 (Reading): Multiple choice

Introduction

Multiple choice reading text occurs in each Paper 1. It is usually the second or third part of the paper.

1   Make sure you reflect as you are doing this on *how* you arrive at your answers.

Key

1   1 C   2 D   3 B   4 D   5 A

Exam practice

Do this under exam-like conditions (i.e. timing yourself and with no interruptions) or as homework.

When the examiners mark Paper 1 they add up candidates' scores across sections, so it is not necessary to pass every section.

Key

1 B   2 D   3 C   4 A   5 A   6 D

Ways of learning: approaches to reading

As an introduction to this section, think of some of the kinds of texts you have read recently, in whatever language, and if you have read each in the same way.

Two: Travelling the World

A

Voyages of discovery

Starter activities

1   It doesn't matter if you don't know the exact vocabulary for the types of transport shown in the pictures. Think about what the purpose of each vehicle was/is, and in what ways they are similar.

Key

1   **All the pictures show vehicles which were/are designed and used by human beings for the purposes of exploration.**

Reading

2   Look carefully at the questions *before* you start reading the text so you will know what sort of specific details to look out for *during* your reading. You will not need to read and understand every word.

Key

1   **Christopher Columbus – Italian – 1451–1506 – sailed across the Atlantic – reached the New World in 1492 – undertook three more voyages**

2	1	A	Guanahani, Cuba, Haiti
		B	Jamaica, Puerto Rico
		C	Trinidad, Mainland America
	2	A	Santiago
		B	San Salvador
		C	Trinidad
		D	San Juan Baptista
		E	Hispaniola
	3	A–E	gold, spices, birds, pineapple, tobacco (in any order)

Grammar reminder: *so* and *such*

Key

1   *so* + e
2   *such* + d
3   *So* + b
4   *so* + g
5   *such* + a
6   *so* + c
7   *such* + h
8   *such* + f

Listening

1   Use this introductory activity to help you think about some of the vocabulary you are likely to hear in the listening extract.

2   Check the pronunciation of any new items of vocabulary you add to your list.

* 3   Make sure you understand what sort of detailed information you should be listening for. The pronunciation of the names is as follows: Michael Palin [ˈmaɪkəl ˈpeɪlɪn] and Brian Blessed [ˈbraɪən ˈblesɪd].

Tapescript

V1:   It must be difficult being an explorer nowadays because there're very few places left to explore, but I'd really fancy, I mean would you like to be an explorer, Nigel? I mean would…

V2:   I don't know. I don't think I would really, it doesn't appeal to me. I like home comforts too much. I mean what motivates people to want to go off and discover something no man has found before, you know…

V1:   Yes…

V3:   I think people explore for different reasons these days, I mean for instance they can raise money for charity [mm]…

V1:   Yes…

V3:   Um, you know, every step, um, [it's] a certain [yes] amount of money is given.

V4:   I understand that if you're doing it for a reason but I mean it's the people who, they seem to do things for no reason at all…

V1:   Well, it must [which is] be very exciting, I mean…

V2:   And the desire for fame and wealth, I suppose…

V1:   Well yes, I suppose so, but how many famous explorers are there, really famous, nowadays?

V4:   And how much, you don't really get any – I mean you have to be wealthy to go…

V1:   Mm…

V4:   Now, don't you? I mean…

V3:   You have to be well sponsored.

V4:   It's a wealthy person's game really.

V2:   Well, that TV presenter – um – what's – Michael Palin [mm], you know, he travelled from the North to the South Pole, didn't he? And the camera crew went with him and the TV series was made about it – that would be a good way to do it.

V4:   Well, that'd be great [yeah], be great – you'd get paid as well.

V2:   Yes.

V1:   But imagine the excitement standing on the top of Mount Everest or whatever, compared with most people's lives which is just – you know – going down the pub or whatever.

V4:   Yes I know, but [well], I mean it must be terrifying, must be terrifying [isn't it – mm], climbing a mountain like that, absolutely petrifying.

V3:   But there's some actor at the moment – what's his name – Brian somebody, um…

V4:   Blessed.

V3:   Who wants to…

V4:   Brian Blessed.
Blessed, that's right.
He wants to climb Everest and, um, he wants to be the oldest person ever to climb Everest.

V4:   Yes.

V2: But it's nice to get away from all the kind of, the modern, the modern world and cars and conventional jobs and [escape the, the routine of everyday life] earning money. It's completely different, isn't it [yes, yes]? Well I can see the attraction of that.

V3: Mm, it must be exciting to think that you might be treading somewhere where no-one has ever trod before [mm]. I think that must be [yes]…

V1: And you don't know what you'll find. I mean when they went to the moon they didn't know whether they would find all sorts of cures for sicknesses or…

V3: Yes.

V2: That's true.

V4: But do you think it's because now as well we don't really experience very much physical danger in our lives, do we, because it's all kind of sorted for us [yeah], so to actually go off and really pit yourself against the elements is something [mm] [mm] that we don't in our daily lives do. We're all so protected [yes]…

V2: Go excitement seeking like.

V3: Yes, yes.

V2: Wouldn't appeal to me though, I don't think.

Key

3   1 few places left (to explore)   2 costs (of exploring)

	1 Michael Palin	2 Brian Blessed
Job	TV presenter	actor
Project	travel from North to South Poles	climb Everest
Purpose	make TV series	be the oldest person to do so

Speaking: discussing opinions

1 Play the first phrases on the list and then check your answers before continuing.

2 Practise marking in the intonation and stress on the first two or three examples before continuing.

3 After practising the stress and intonation patterns with the cassette, try using the phrases in longer sentences, e.g. 'it must be difficult being an explorer today because…etc.'

Tapescript

V1: It must be difficult being…
V2: I mean would *you* like to be…
V1: I don't know, I don't think I would really…
V2: I mean, for instance…
V1: It doesn't appeal to me…
V2: well yes I suppose so but…
V1: that would be a good way to do…
V2: well that'd be great…
V1: but imagine…
V2: yes I know but…
V1: well I can see the attraction of that…
V2: that's true
V1: but do you think it's because…
V2: wouldn't appeal to me though I don't think…

Key

it must be difficult being…
I mean would you like to be…
I don't know, I don't think I
    would really…
I mean, for instance…

it doesn't appeal to me…
well yes I suppose so but…

that would be a good way to do…

well that'd be great…
but imagine…

yes I know but…
well I can see the
attraction of that…
that's true
but do you think it's
because…
wouldn't appeal to me
though I don't think…

✱ Writing

This activity gives you practice in writing a Paper 2 type task. Spend some time preparing your article by looking back over the Reading and Listening activities in this section for ideas and vocabulary. Then try writing the article as a timed written exercise.

B

Holiday travel

✱ Starter activities

Tapescript

V1: Well my – perfect kind of holiday is a walking holiday in beautiful, sunny hilltops around the Mediterranean…I'd say the South of France or…er…perhaps Spain or northern Majorca, p'haps the hills round Tuscany. Beautiful, beautiful countryside, walking, drinking, sleeping, lovely…

V2: I like contrasts, so I love sailing and being completely isolated, just the wind blowing and the sea and the colours of the sky, and then arriving somewhere in the evening and having all the bustle and joining in with people and then being able to get away from them again so you can relax in two different environments…

V3: I go to my friend's cabin in northern Vermont, near the Canadian border, park the car, walk about 5 miles in – nearest civilisation is a little country store with a wood stove - storekeeper with a check shirt, and you have to really go out of your way to see people…

Key

	Type of holiday	Reasons
1	walking holiday	beautiful countryside, walking, drinking, sleeping
2	sailing holiday	relaxing in contrasting environments
3	cabin in the countryside	being away from other people and from civilisation

Reading

1–✱2 Set yourself a time limit of about 1½ minutes to make sure you read the short texts quickly and *superficially* when doing these exercises. Then think briefly about the clues you used to decide your answers.

3 You can take more time to read for this exercise.

Key
1 A travel guidebook
   B holiday postcard
   C modern novel
   D advertising brochure

2 1 C 2 A 3 B 4 C 5 D 6 D

3 A –
   B *interesting, lovely*
   C *warm, velvety, beautiful*
   D *beautiful, irresistible, exotic, familiar, luxurious, unpretentious, palm-fringed, lush, scenic, superb, tranquil, undeveloped, bright, delightful, special, world-class, exciting*

Grammar analysis: using the present simple and continuous tenses

3 This activity gives a more detailed analysis of the uses for the present simple and present continuous, based on the novel extract in activity 1. There are a number of verbs which appear more often in a present simple than a present continuous form, e.g. *What do you think?* rather than *What are you thinking?* These are known as 'stative' verbs and usually express a state of affairs rather than a dynamic action. They include verbs of 'being' or 'having', e.g. *You have a one in six chance*…Such verbs can occasionally appear in a continuous form, in which case they indicate that a state is only temporary or incomplete, e.g. *What are you thinking about (right now)? He's having his injection at the moment but he'll be back shortly.* There is intensive practice of the present simple for stative verbs in Section A of Unit 3 (page 42).

Remember too, that both the present simple and the present continuous can be used to refer to the future: *The plane leaves on Tuesday; I'm seeing her after school tomorrow.* This is covered in more detail in Section B of Unit 13 (page 174).

4 Remember that adverbs and adverbial phrases can often give you a strong clue about which tense to use, *at the moment, currently* (indicate present continuous); *normally, always, often* (indicate present simple).

5 Check your example sentences with a native English speaker if possible.

Key
1 is wearing out, are being damaged, enter, are eroding, bring, are rotting, is killing/causing, is, have, swim, are, is, is, aren't enjoying themselves, go, are engaging in, 's, 's.
2 The present simple tense is generally concerned with the characteristic of the permanent nature of things. The present continuous tense is generally concerned with present instances rather than general characteristics.

4 1 present continuous (b)
   2 present continuous (c)
   3 present simple (d)
   4 present simple (c)
   5 present continuous (a)
   6 present simple (b)
   7 present continuous (d)
   8 present simple (a)

C

Paper 2 (Writing): Section A

Introduction

Key
1 Produce one or more pieces of writing
   approximately 250 words
   response to a substantial reading input
   Presentation, register and style should be appropriate
   tasks…set within a context
   purpose and intended audience…made clear

How do I begin?

There is no 'correct' order of steps, but some steps may fit more logically before or after others. Think about what you do when writing in your own language.

Key
Possible answer:
1 read the input to identify the relevant information
2 decide on the reason for writing
3 identify the audience you're writing for
4 organise the information in an appropriate way
5 choose appropriate style and tone
6 produce the final piece of writing

What information is relevant?

Remember that your first task is to identify the issue or problem being raised. Then look for information which could help to address the issue or solve the problem.

Key
1 flying
2 possibility of choosing smoking/non-smoking seats if desired
   papers, magazines, blankets and other useful items usually available on board
   cabin crew always ready to help
   good idea to drink plenty during flight to prevent dehydration (preferably non-alcoholic)
   yawning/swallowing helps reduce discomfort during climb/descent
   don't remove tight-fitting shoes

What is my reason for writing?

There will often be more than one reason for writing. If you can identify your reason(s) at the start, then it is easier to check at the end whether you have achieved your aims.

Key
to reassure, to give advice

Who am I writing for?

It is not possible to be certain of these details, but your writing may be more convincing if you build a mental picture of the person(s) to whom you are writing.

Key
Possible answers:
Sex: female?
Age: 60 +?
Occupation: retired?
Other information: slightly anxious?

How should I organise the information?

Check back over the information you collected earlier in this section. Look at how the different points may be grouped, e.g. advice on smoking/non-smoking, advice on comfort, reassurance about airline staff/facilities. Add your own additional advice/ideas if relevant.

What style and tone should I use for the reply letter?

Remember, choosing an inappropriate style or tone can have a negative effect on a reader. If it is in the wrong style or tone, your letter could upset/anger/amuse a reader so that it fails to achieve its intended purpose.

Key
neutral, reassuring

Exam practice

Try doing this exercise as a timed activity. Make good use of all the preparation work you have done so far.

Key
An adequate letter of reply would probably include the following:
* thanks for the letter
* reference to taxi rank/car rental
* reference to shuttle buses to airport hotels – Gerda may be staying there?
* location of railway station and details of access to it
* regularity of trains to Amsterdam Central Station
* expression of hope for good journey and pleasure at meeting again

Three: Living with other people

A
Family matters

Starter activities

1   Use your imagination and your childhood experience to build a story based on the pictures.

2   'Squabble' is another word for quarrel or argue. People often squabble over unimportant matters.

Listening

✱ 1   Before playing the extract, read through the gapped text about Dave and Celia. Think about the sorts of details/opinions you might expect to hear.

4   Remember that the phrases in 2 and 3 help a conversation run smoothly. Try and practise them on occasions when you use spoken English.

Tapescript
Celia: So Dave, um, have you got any brothers or sisters?
Dave: Yeah, I've got a sister.
Celia: One sister, [yeah] and is she older or younger?
Dave: She's four years younger…
Celia: Right
Dave: …but for a couple of months or something – so, the baby sister.
Celia: Right [laughter] – and do you treat her like the baby sister?
Dave: Well, I suppose I did as a kid, because er [yeah] she was, I used to kind of look after her, you know – but I always used to get in – in trouble; it was always me that got the blame, I think it was because I was older…
Celia: Yes, yes…
Dave: …do you know what I mean?
Celia: I do know what you mean.
Dave: She used to get away with an awful lot.
Celia: Yeah.
Dave: Like she'd hit me [laughter] and it'd be all right because she was, you know, the baby, kind of thing [yes] and if I clumped her back then I was in big trouble which…
Celia: And did she used to blame you for things that you didn't do, as well, or did she never go quite that far?
Dave: Yeah, well, she kind of did naturally [yeah], I don't think she was scheming about it, she just kind of, you know,

the way to get out of trouble was blame big brother [yeah – laughter – yeah]

Celia: And what about when you were a bit older, did you, um, what about like sort of teenage…

Dave: Teenage […years?] was the biggest problem actually.

Celia: Was it?

Dave: Yeah.

Celia: Why?

Dave: Well I hit teenage first – so I wasn't interested in a little sister, as you can imagine.

Celia: Right.

Dave: And then when she hit teenage she was really a rebel, much more than I was…

Celia: Yes.

Dave: …and caused a hell of a lot of trouble, and 'cause I was on my parents' side which was er, you know, 'cause I couldn't believe she was being so naughty…

Celia: Oh, really?

Dave: Yeah.

Celia: So was there a bit of a split between you?

Dave: Yeah – for a couple of years it was really bad; and in fact that's why I left home…

Celia: Oh really!

Dave: 'Cause I just couldn't live with my sister any more.

Celia: Oh, no.

Dave: Yeah.

Celia: So, and are you back, are you…?

Dave: And now we're fine, we get on really well 'cause we don't see much of each other… [right – laughter]

Dave: Have you got any?

Celia: Well I have actually, I've got two sisters; but it's funny the thing you said about like being the oldest and sort of getting blamed…for…

Dave: Are you the oldest as well?

Celia: I'm the oldest as well and so I know. I know exactly what you mean.

Dave: Yeah, you have to guard against that if we have children, you know, you have to [yeah] try and think, yeah, I remember it happened so often.

Celia: What it was like – mm…

Dave: My parents were good I'm sure, you know, you can't blame them but…it's a natural thing.

Celia: Yeah, yeah, absolutely. But um, I mean and I was the same as you, my, I've got two younger sisters and the middle one I was, I think I was very jealous of when she arrived so I used to be horrible to her…

Dave: Oh, yeah.

Celia: …most of the time.

Dave: How many years younger is she?

Celia: She's eighteen months younger, so not very much at all.

Dave: Oh, quite close.

Celia: Yeah, and then er, the youngest one, Suzanne, she's five years younger than me and er, we were very close in the first place, but er…

Dave: Oh, yeah.

Celia: …but we're all very close now, I think you go through, I think everyone probably goes through that patch, don't they, particularly like sort of – ten onwards, perhaps mid-teens…

Dave: It's that growing up thing, isn't it?

Celia: …yeah, exactly

Dave: Changing, and you know,…

Celia: …getting your own personalities together and things…

Dave: …yeah.

Key

(2) *younger*

(3) *into trouble/the blame/ blamed*

(4) *teenagers*

(5) *naughty/rebellious/ a rebel*

(6) *parents*

(7) *leave home*

(8) *(very) little*

(9) *(really/very) well/fine*

(10) *oldest/eldest*

(11) *jealous/envious*

(12) *middle sister*

(13) *close*

(14) *younger*

2–3 *expressing agreement – yes; yeah; absolutely; mm; expressing surprise/shock – oh really?; oh, no seeking further information/explanation – why/ and do you? what about…? who was there? what? checking listener understands – do you know what I mean? you know…? you know the kind of thing; also question tags confirming understanding – yeah; right; I know exactly what you mean; I do know what you mean*

Reading

3 If you have special difficulty with any of these phrases, use a dictionary to help you. Practise the phrases by putting them into full sentences. You might like to keep a list of all the collocations and idioms you meet in this book. To help you learn them, try keeping the two halves of a collocation or idiom on separate cards in two boxes; from time to time take a card out of one of the boxes and try to recall the full phrase to which it can belong. You can check your answer against your list.

Key

1 **sibling rivalry** [ˈsɪblɪŋ ˈraɪvəlri].

2 • **organising an outing, going for a walk, all-age activities**
   • **offer of chocolate/trip to the park/send child to grandparent's/friend's/diversionary activities like drinks/alternative activities/encourage children to sort out their problem between them**
   • **send children to separate rooms/withdrawal of treats/child to tidy up room**

3 *fight like cat and dog* *be at each other's throats*
   retain your sanity *come up with a solution*
   break the rules *take it in turns*
   ease tension *tell someone your side of*
   lose face *the story*

Grammar analysis: stative verbs

1–2   The verbs in activity 1 are all in the simple form, not the continuous. In activity 2 the verbs in sentences 1, 3 and 4 should be in the simple form as in 2 and 5.

3–4   Check the meaning of any listed verbs which are unfamiliar. Note that there may be more than one possible answer for some of the gaps in activity 4.

Key

1   *was, was, had, belonged, don't think, was*

2   1   She *believes* that her parents love her baby brother more than her.
   3   Psychologists *agree* that sibling rivalry is quite normal.
   4   Most parents *love* their children equally.

3   a   *see, hear, smell, sound, feel, taste*
   b   *want, need, mean, like, wish, hope, forget, think, imagine, love, remember, understand, know*
   c   *advise, deny, confess, say, doubt, agree*

4   1   *like/love*
   2   *mean/want/wish*
   3   *confesses/admits*
   4   *believes/thinks*
   5   *advises*

B

Habits and customs

Starter activities

1– ✱ 2   Think about what is actually happening in each cartoon picture before you decide whether you think it is acceptable or unacceptable. Remember that some types of behaviour may be acceptable in some circumstances but not in others. If possible, ask an English-speaking friend for their views.

✱ Listening

Tapescript

Speaker 1 Er, about 3 years ago I was on a, a tour sort of round Africa and er we, we'd already been to several, er, countries, and um this was the fifth country that we visited; and it soon became very clear that Nigerians have a, a great fondness for making speeches at almost er the drop of a hat; um, you could be just going for a cup of tea with somebody, and somebody would have to make a speech about how nice it was to have you for a cup of tea and then somebody else would get up and say how nice it was for them to have made the speech to welcome you and give you a cup of tea and – and

then somebody would get up and say that somebody else would be making a speech later – um – it's very, um, it's a great love of sort of um performance and um sort of making a great formality on any, anything how, however casual it was supposed to be, there would be this feeling that it was a very formal event and this is the way it, it is…

Speaker 2 I'm from Swansea in South Wales, and a couple of years ago I went on a trip, um, around the Greek islands and, er, we ended up on a tiny island called Siphnos; and, um, we stayed in a little village room which was on the back of, a gentleman called Angelos, on the back of his house; and, er, we found out that they were very hospitable and in Greece they have a tradition not only of having, um, a birthday but also a saint's day; and, er, in fact it was the daughter of the house's saint's day while we were there; and, um, what they did was invite us in to, er, their home, and they make a special cake of, er, honey, I think is in it, and almonds, and um also, er, the wife of Angelos, um, she actually produces her own, sort of distils her own wine, um, and er we had a few glasses of this and the home-made cake. So there you not only have, as I say, birthdays but also saints' days as well which they celebrate on completely different…

Speaker 3 Well my first visit to Britain was when I was fifteen and it was with, with a school exchange, I was staying with a family for three weeks, and, well I used to go to school with this girl, she was my penfriend in these days, and, um, well we took a double-decker bus every day to go to school and I was very surprised when I, on the first day, when I saw these girls wearing school uniforms; well at, at school everything was more or less normal and like in my country, but the very funny thing was that they stayed at the school over lunch and had all these sandwiches and crisps with different flavours, vinegar and salt, and things like that, and this white floppy bread, it was really, it was an experience for me because in my country you can, you go home for lunch, and you have cooked lunch because you don't have school in, every, every afternoon, so you can just go home and be, be with your mum who has cooked a fine, very nice lunch for you; so this was something, something very different from what I was used to…

Key

	Country visited	Habit/custom
Speaker 1	Nigeria	making speeches
Speaker 2	Greece	celebrating saint's day
Speaker 3	Britain	school uniforms/lunches etc.

Reading

✱ 1   Before doing the reading activity, it may help you to know that many British magazines contain a section with letters from readers. These letters usually ask for advice on a variety on issues from gardening matters to problems in personal relationships. The four letters in this activity all ask for advice concerning 'good manners'. Set yourself a time limit of about one minute.

✴ 2–3 Try to use vocabulary clues to help you in the matching activity.

Key

1 1a 2d 3c 4b
2 1C 2A 3D 4B
3 1d 2c 3b 4a

Grammar reminder: *-ing* or infinitive?

1–2 Look out for more example sentences showing how these verbs are used to mean different things according to their form. If possible, keep your own list of such examples and add to it as you come across them.

Note that when it is used for making comparisons *prefer* is normally followed by the *-ing* form. Remember that there are also some common verbs which are always followed by the *-ing* form: *enjoy, mind, dislike, adore, finish, can't help*, etc.
e.g. *I don't mind removing my shoes when I visit a Japanese home. Do you enjoy learning about a culture different from your own?*

Key

1 1b 2f 3d 4e 5h 6a 7c 8g

Writing

1–2 It is quite difficult to draw a strict line between what is 'strong' and what is 'tentative' advice-giving. The distinction between the two lists below is only a very general one. Remember that whether advice sounds strong or tentative can be affected by features like intonation, voice tone etc.

✴ 3 Read the instructions for the task carefully and use the phrases practised in 1–2.

Key

Possible answers:

Strong advice	Tentative advice
You ought to...	*If I were you I'd...*
You must...	*You could always...*
You'd better...	*Why don't you...?*
It's best to...	*What about...?*
	It might be a good idea to...

Additional possibilities might include:

You mustn't/shouldn't...	*You might as well...*
Don't...	*It's not such a good idea to...*
Make sure you...	*How about...?*
	Try to...

Ways of learning: talking about grammar and vocabulary

Key

1

1 adjective	7 noun
2 adverb	8 participle
3 conjunction	9 preposition
4 article	10 pronoun
5 infinitive	11 verb
6 modal	12 verbal auxiliary

2

manners – noun	*calmly* – adverb
be – verbal auxiliary	*polite* – adjective
wheeled out – participle	*can* – modal
for – preposition	*or* – conjunction
goes – verb	*it* – pronoun
the – article	*to be* – infinitive

C

Paper 3 (English in Use): Section A

Introduction

Try to find key words in this short passage which identify the important information to remember, i.e. *two blank-filling tasks, authentic texts, vocabulary focus, multiple choice items, structural focus, 15 blanks, 250 words per text.*

Choosing the best words to complete a text

1–3 These activities introduce some of the thought processes which are necessary when you have to select from several options the best word to complete a gap in a text. In activity 2 you should start by drawing on your own knowledge of the meaning of options **A–D**. (Consult a dictionary if you still have difficulty distinguishing between them.) Note that, although all four options fit the gap grammatically and are similar in meaning, there is only one which fits properly in terms of collocation, meaning within the sentence, and meaning across the text as a whole.

Key

1 They are all nouns in the plural form, and they are all words describing people who watch or see something.

2 'Spectators' are people who watch sporting events. 'Witnesses' are people who report in a law court on what they have seen. 'Observers' are people who watch something and comment on it. 'Audiences' are people who watch or listen to a play, film, opera, concert etc.

3 D

Exam practice 1

This gives you an opportunity to work through a longer text with ten items. Use the approaches previously identified and discussed, and try to be aware as you work of the ways in which you select the best option.

Key

1	1	B	6	D
	2	A	7	C
	3	C	8	D
	4	D	9	D
	5	A	10	A

Finding the missing words in a text

1–2 These activities help you to think about different approaches to replacing missing words in a text.

Key

1 (1) *as*   (2) *in*   (3) *more*

Exam practice 2

The text is a continuation of the text used for Exam practice 1 and is another chance to work through a longer text with ten items. Use the approaches previously identified and discussed, and as you work be aware of the ways in which you select the best option.

Key

1	(1)	*as*	(6)	*this*
	(2)	*who/that*	(7)	*what/all*
	(3)	*everyone/anyone*	(8)	*if*
	(4)	*what*	(9)	*and/or*
	(5)	*them*	(10)	*much*

Four: Good and bad health

A

Health on holiday

Starter activities

Key

1 **Possible answers:**
broken arms/legs/limbs, sunburn, sunstroke, skin rashes, stomach bugs (from polluted water), food poisoning (from unfamiliar food), tropical diseases

Listening

1 You should answer these questions quickly.

2 Remember that non-stressed vowels in English often reduce to schwa (ə). Try beating the rhythm of the words out with your hand/foot as you say them.

3–5 In English, sentences normally have only one or two words carrying the main stress. Which words carry stress will depend on the focus of the meaning of the sentence, but they are usually the main content words rather than structural words.

Tapescript

1 1 To stop mosquitoes biting, would you wear dark colours or cover yourself with cream?

2 What would you do if you got sunstroke?

3 Can you fly if you're pregnant?

4 Would you drink tap water abroad?

5 What would you do if you got food poisoning?

6 Would you need a bandage or some elastoplast if you sprained your ankle?

7 When things start going wrong on holiday – for example: losing your passport, having your passport stolen, sleeping in a noisy hotel etc. etc., you can begin to feel quite stressed. What's the solution to holiday stress?

8 Acute sunburn can be very dangerous. How can it be avoided?

9 How would you manage to pay hospital charges after a skiing accident?

10 What diseases should you have injections against before travelling to some countries?

11 What should you do before going on holiday to a place where there's malaria?

12 Do you think it's worth taking out a health or accident insurance before going on holiday?

2 accident, bandage, mosquito, aspirin, chemist, sunburn, insurance, elastoplast, poisoning, injection, medicine, pregnant.

3 **1** You can buy elastoplast at a chemist or supermarket.
  2 Go to see a doctor if you get food poisoning.
  3 You need a bandage if you sprain your ankle.
  4 You shouldn't go in the sun between 12 and 3 o'clock.
  5 Insurance cover can pay for holiday accidents.
  6 You can't get injections against malaria.
  7 Aspirin isn't much good against travel sickness.

Key

1 There is no one correct answer to these questions.

2 The stress on these words is as follows:
'accident in'surance
'bandage e'lastoplast
mos'quito 'poisoning
'aspirin in'jection
'chemist 'medicine
'sunburn 'pregnant

3 **2** *doctor, food*
  3 *bandage, sprain, ankle*
  4 *sun, 12, 3 o'clock*
  5 *insurance, cover, holiday, accidents*
  6 *can't, injections, malaria*
  7 *aspirin, good, travel sickness*

5 Nouns, adjectives, verbs and adverbs (i.e. content words) tend to be stressed more often than structural words (e.g. articles, prepositions, negatives) because content words play a greater role in communicating meaning. Structural words can sometimes be stressed though, e.g. *put it* <u>on</u> *the cupboard not* <u>in</u> *it*

Reading

2 Read for detail in approximately five minutes.

Key

2 The text mentions the following as possible sources of holiday stress:
  • having to deal with problematic relationships in an unknown environment
  • holiday preparations
  • crowded airports, delayed flights, packed hotels i.e. crowds, queues, delays
  • compromising on what you want
  • chores
  • disappointment with the holiday
  • worry about security
  • spending lots of time with the same person/people
  • difficulty in relaxing
  • other people having a better time than you
  • taking holidays at the wrong time

3 *high blood pressure*
family relationships
vicious circle
crowded airports/flights
delayed flights
physical fitness

deeply disappointed
recharge your batteries
tackle problems
high hopes

4 **a** *heart disease, high blood pressure, severe aches and pains (neck and backache)*
  b *cancelling the milk and the newspapers, boarding the family pet, last minute shopping, securing your home from burglars, self-catering, cooking, looking after children, doing chores*
  c *absenteeism, pressure, tense, mini-stresses, a stress factor, strain, over anxious + all the illnesses mentioned.*

✳ Writing

Try to read some real leaflets before this task. They don't have to be in English. Compare their layout, styles, presentation of information and language. NB The language in leaflets can be simple, concise and neutral in tone. Information is often presented as a series of bullet points or paragraphs with headings.

Key
Some possible answers:
  • Tackle your problems before you go. If you're not getting on with someone, talk it through with them.
  • Plan your holiday well in advance and try to get those last minute jobs done early too.
  • If you don't like crowds try going on holiday outside the high season, travel mid-week even if it does mean you miss a day or two of holiday, or simply go somewhere quiet.
  • If there's work to do round the house on holiday, make sure everyone understands <u>before</u> they go that they have to help out. It's everybody's holiday.
  • Don't rely on your holiday to solve all your problems or expect too much of it. What if it's a disappointment?
  • Think hard about who you go on holiday with. You may love someone's company in short bursts, but what if it's all the time?
  • Just relax and enjoy yourself.

B

Health around the world

Starter activities

Key

1 1 North America
   2 Central America
   3 South America
   4 Greenland
   5 Western Europe
   6 Africa
   7 Asia
   8 Australia

Listening

Tapescript

Man: Yes, talking about illnesses, I'm quite surprised to see that in the U.K., illnesses are very different from those in Algeria…to some extent. For instance, in the U.K. people seem to suffer from heart disease and [yes] stress, quite a lot [right, right]; whereas in Algeria they seem to er…suffer from bowel problems more often than in Britain by the sound of it; [hmm] the reason for it being I think erm is diet is connected with diet; in the way people eat, in Algeria they tend to eat hot, spicy food [peppery things]; peppery things, very hot things; which I can't take myself, but the tendency is to eat hot food, and it seems to result in that.

If you look at the pace of life in Algeria and in Britain you'd find that this explains quite a bit of the differences in terms of illnesses. Erm, in Algeria, people, I think, lead a much slower pace, because er life is less hectic [yes], less industrial for a start [yes] erm, so they don't tend to get erm this type of illnesses that are related to stress, such as heart attacks.

Woman: Do you get…what else do you get here? You get quite a bit of cancer.

Man: Cancer? Well, cancer exists there as well; but I think it's more frequent in Britain than it is there. Erm, the reason for it I think is mainly to do with pollution, the levels of pollution that Britain has. It goes again with industry, stress [yes]…Algeria is slightly developed in the North, and that's where we record I think, I'm not an expert in the matter, most cancers; whereas the South is pretty healthy. Erm, so there's that kind of illness that is recorded there, but not very frequent; erm, other types of illnesses that people suffer from, especially young children here is asthma [there's a lot of asthma]. There's a lot of asthma; it's on the increase [yes definitely]. Erm, in Algeria it exists also; but it seems to affect the north, the northern strip, the Mediterranean strip of it rather than the South [yes]. The reason for it is that it's damp. It's also the part of

Algeria that is developed, so if we're to relate it to [to pollution] to pollution then perhaps there is a little bit of that [yeh]. Whereas the South is, is meant to be erm exempt from asthma.

When it comes to other types of illnesses, like er psychological disturbances, psychiatric related problems erm, it appears to me that in Britain people erm are more mad than in Algeria.

Woman: Really?

Man: It seems to be so; in the sense that less people go to the psychiatrist in Algeria than here. Is it a fashion? Is it a true reflection of a state of society? I'm not sure.

Woman: Are there more psychiatrists here?

Man: Oh, far more psychiatrists here than in Algeria, yes. Yes, and people in Algeria would resort to a psychiatrist almost as a last resort for a…for mental illnesses. They tend to rely on the family, because the family structure is again very different from that one in Britain.

Woman: Much stronger.

Man: It's much stronger, so the family would tend to support or even hide in some cases their mentally ill, and try to help them within [yeh]; often by ignoring their illness; saying you are normal, therefore behave normally and that's what's expected from you…seems to work [yeh] seems to work.

But when you move away from these cases of psychological problems, you, you end up, you fall erm into the category of normal medicine, like if you have a broken limb you end up in hospital and you find hundreds of people with broken limbs [yeh], being treated the same way as they would be treated in Britain [right], really. Erm 99% of the cases will be treated the same way as in Britain [the same way].

Yes, perhaps one thing to mention is that people use herbal medicine; or used to use herbal medicine more than in Britain, but I think now Britain uses it quite a lot as well.

Woman: Well it certainly has developed, yes.

Man: It has developed, hasn't it? Yeh, erm, the recipes may differ [mm], people there you know they all seem to have their secret recipes coming down from their granny whatever, but [right] if you analyse them, you'd find that…that the same ingredients for the same cures come and crop up in the books of herbal medicine [yes] yeh [yeh].

Key

a Algeria – bowel problems, some cancer, some asthma in the North
   UK – heart disease, stress, cancer, asthma, psychiatric problems
b The hot spicy food in Algeria causes the bowel problems. The damp in the north of the country causes asthma. The hectic pace of life in the UK, pollution and possibly fashion are given as causes of its illnesses.
c People in both Algeria and the UK go to hospital and use herbal medicines. Algeria uses psychiatry less than the UK.

Reading

1   Read this article for gist in three minutes.

2   Read for specific information in only three to four minutes. Write notes for your answers.

Tapescript

3   a third, ninety one percent, four thousand three hundred and sixteen, thirty nine percent, eight out of ten women, ten percent, seven out of ten men, men aged between sixty five and seventy four, forty percent, the year nineteen eighty, two thirds, a half, forty eight percent, thirty two percent, the year two thousand.

Key

1   c
2   1   men
    2   men
    3   70% men, 80% women
    4   more exercise
    5   using stairs instead of lifts; walking and cycling instead of taking the car

Speaking: agreeing and disagreeing

Key

2   Some possible answers
    agreement: *ok, right, that's right, yeh, I couldn't agree more, I entirely agree*
    disagreement: *that's nonsense, that's not really the case, I don't think so, not really*

Grammar analysis: the definite article

1   This is an exam practice task like those in Paper 3. In the exam this task sometimes focuses on particular areas of language as here.

Key

1	1	✓	9	✓	17	the
	2	✓	10	✓	18	✓
	3	✓	11	the	19	✓
	4	✓	12	✓		
	5	the	13	✓		
	6	✓	14	✓		
	7	✓	15	the		
	8	✓	16	✓		

2   (a)   *before/previously*   (b)   *mentioned/talked about*
    (c)   *specific*   (d)   *in general/generally*
    (e)   *must*   (f)   *countries*
    (g)   *the Amazon/etc.*   (h)   *the Seine/etc.*
    (i)   *ranges*   (j)   *the*

🔊 Vocabulary summary: a quiz

Tapescript

Number 1.	What 'b' do mosquitoes give you?
Number 2.	What nasty 'u.s' can unwashed fruit or vegetables give you?
And number 3.	What 'h.o' means you drank too much alcohol?
Next number 4.	What 'b' do you wrap around a sprained ankle?
Number 5.	What 'v' means you're bouncing with health and energy?
Moving on to number 6.	What 'd' means you're down?
And number 7.	What 'i.r.' can help keep mosquitoes away?
Followed by number 8.	What 'm' is a tropical disease?
And number 9.	What 'i' do cautious people take out before going on holiday?
And number 10.	What 'v.c.' means you're tied up in knots?
Moving right along to number 11.	What 'r.y.b.' keeps you going that much longer?
Followed closely by number 12.	What 'b' is a nasty pain in your back?
That brings us to number 13.	What 'l.m.' means you really should have remembered before?
Number 14.	What 'c' means dreary housework?
Followed by number 15.	What 'o.a.' means you're worrying too much?
And number 16.	What 'h.h.' means you're very optimistic?
And number 17.	What 'c' is a country's money?
Followed by number 18.	What 's' is a study of behaviour or an overview?
And number 19.	What 'q' is a half of a half?
And finally number 20.	What 'b' is a good thing you get from something?

Key

1	*bites*	11	*recharge your batteries*
2	*upset stomach*	12	*backache*
3	*hangover*	13	*last minute*
4	*bandage*	14	*chores*
5	*vitality*	15	*over-anxious*
6	*depression*	16	*high hopes*
7	*insect repellent*	17	*currency*
8	*malaria*	18	*survey*
9	*insurance*	19	*quarter*
10	*vicious circle*	20	*benefit*

C

Paper 4 (Listening): Sections A and B

Introduction

Tapescript
1 Examination information
Sections A and B of Paper 4

Section A
Section A is a monologue so you only hear one voice. You hear the monologue twice and it lasts approximately two minutes. The monologue may be taken from a range of possible text types; for example it could be an announcement or a radio broadcast, a recorded telephone message, a talk or a lecture. You will be tested on your understanding of details of the text as well as the text as a whole. The types of exam exercise that will be used in this section include note-taking, box ticking, multiple choice etc.

Section B
Section B is essentially a monologue, though you may hear short contributions or prompts from a second speaker. You hear this section just once and like Section A it lasts approximately 2 minutes. It also covers the same range of text types as in Section A with the possible addition of conversations. The exam exercises are the same as in Section A.

General information on CAE Paper 4
Timing
You are given time before each section to read it through, and there is a pause after each section. Then at the end of the paper, you are given ten minutes to transfer your answers to an answer sheet.

Writing your answers
You can write your answers in pencil or pen. While you are listening you write your answers on the question paper, then after all the sections of the listening are finished, you transfer your answers from the question paper to the answer sheet. You're given ten minutes' transfer time for the whole paper.

Key
1 (1) *voice*
   (2) *twice*
   (3) *two*
   (4) *broadcast*
   (5) *lecture*
   (6) *details*
   (7) *whole*
   (8) *ticking*
   (9) *prompts*
   (10) *second*
   (11) *once*
   (12) *approximately*
   (13) *conversations*
   (14) *before*
   (15) *pause*
   (16) *ten*
   (17) *answer sheet*
   (18) *paper*
   (19) *transfer*
   (20) *whole*

Exam practice

Tapescript

Section A
You will hear the boy in the photo talking about his illness. As you listen, complete in a few words the information for questions 1–7.

I have haemophilia, which is a hereditary blood clotting disorder. You get bruises inside your body which bleed, but you can't see them. To stop myself having a bleed I inject myself about three times a week. I take bottles of clotting agent to school and, if I need to, I inject myself.

I can usually sort the bleed out before it really starts to hurt. It's a special kind of pain – more than an everyday pain but nowhere as bad as having broken a leg. It's not too bad when it first starts but, after a couple of hours it can really hurt. I used to have bleeds every week, but now it's only once a fortnight.

I don't mind people knowing about it. I think you should be open about these things. After all, no-one's perfect, are they? And I can do most sports. Not rugby and football though. I play tennis and I'm in the chess club at school. And last year I went away with my school to Spain and only had one bleed. We did everything: water skiing, canoeing…If you don't go for it, life can be really boring. Some people are born ugly or get spots. You can't change what you have, so you have to live with it. Some people at school call me 'a little bleeder', but I don't mind. Maybe some of them have learning difficulties and don't understand. Haemophilia has made me really positive. I think it's made me more sympathetic and certainly more determined to enjoy life.

When I'm older, I want to play for England in table tennis which I'm good at. I want to be a 'Grand master' at chess too. And I'd like to help to find a cure to haemophilia; even if it's not for me. I want to help the Royal Free Hospital in London in their work on gene therapy.

Now you will hear the piece again. (repeat)

That is the end of Section A.

Section B

Now look at Section B
You will hear an extract from a radio programme about the voice problems suffered by some famous singers. Listen to the recording and then complete the information for questions 8–14. Listen carefully as you will hear this piece once only.

The radio programme mentions various factors which affect a singer's voice. Tick the correct column, according to whether the programme indicates that each factor is good or bad for the voice.

Presenter: Forget drink and drug abuse. Rock stars now face a new hazard: voice abuse. After last week's announcement that Genesis singer, Phil Collins, might give up touring because live concerts are ruining his voice, doctors are counselling stars about the do's and don't's of voice care. Here in the studio with us today we have Mr. Paul Phillips. Mr. Phillips is a consultant laryngologist at the Highfield Hospital, London and counts many pop and rock stars among his clients. Mr. Phillips: What advice would you give to singers facing voice problems?

Mr. Phillips: If pop singers have got voice problems they really need to be more selective about where they work, they shouldn't work in smokey atmospheres, and, of course, they shouldn't smoke themselves. They also need to think about resting their voices after a show, for instance, they should rest their voices instead of straining them at parties or chatting to fans. Something else they need to be careful about is medicines; aspirin, for example. Singers should avoid aspirin, it thins the blood, and if a singer coughs this can result in the bruising of the vocal cords.

Presenter: And, is it true that some singers use steroids before concerts to boost their voices when they have voice problems?

Mr. Phillips: Yes, this does happen on occasions. They're easily available on the Continent; and they're useful if a singer has inflamed vocal chords and has to sing that night. But if they're taken regularly and long term they cause a thinning of the voice muscle. Most pop singers suffer from three things: lack of training, overuse and abuse of the voice, especially when they're young. They have difficult lives; when they go on tour they do a vast number of concerts, sing in smoke-laden places, and they go off to the next gig in an air conditioned bus or on a plane. Now both of these have low humidity; and this damages the vocal chords. Then they're expected to do very long tours – three months or so; no opera singer would ever dream of doing a tour that long, and they abuse their voices by forcing them so as to be heard over background noise.

Presenter: So what advice would you give to rock and pop singers?

Mr. Phillips: Warm your voice up before a show, and warm it down after.

Presenter: So, whereas late parties, pill popping and cigarettes used to be de rigueur for pop and rock stars, they're now recommended to warm up their voices before a concert and go straight home to bed with a cup of nice hot cocoa after.

Key

Section A

1 Symptoms: pain, bruises inside the body
2 Medicine: clotting agent
3 How medicine is taken: by injection
4 Frequency of illness: once a fortnight
5 Activities not allowed: rugby, football
6 Activities he does/has done: canoeing, water skiing
7 Attitude to illness: positive

Section B

		Good	Bad
8	chatting with fans		✓
9	taking aspirins		✓
10	regularly taking steroids		✓
11	air conditioning		✓
12	low humidity		✓
13	long tours		✓
14	warming your voice down	✓	

Ways of learning

The Cambridge CAE Examination Reports analyse candidates' behaviour on all sections of the CAE exam and give advice for exam preparation. They can be obtained by writing to the Marketing Division of the University of Cambridge Local Examinations Syndicate (UCLES) at the address given on page 5.

Five: Body language

A

Animal communication

Starter activities

Key

1 Grasshoppers rub their back legs together.
Bees dance to inform the hive where the honey source is.
Monkeys make a series of sounds and calls.
Peacocks call and display their tails.
Whales make a series of calls, clicks, etc.
Rabbits drum their back legs on the ground as a warning.

Other examples: Fish use colour, snakes/lizards use smell/taste, insects use sound vibration etc.

2 Possible answers: to attract a mate, to recognise/to warn/to inform other members of the same species, to frighten an attacker

Reading

1 Set yourself a time limit of about 90 seconds to read the text quickly – for gist – the first time.

✱ **2–3** Take more time to read and find relevant details.

Key

1 chimpanzee

2 1 A, B, D, E
2 D, H
3 C, F, G

3 1 *sweet*   2 *funny*   3 *flower*   4 *toothbrush*

4 e.g. *to acquire/teach/learn language*
language development
true/sign/human language

Verb	Noun	Adjective
construct	*construction*	*constructive*
acquire	*acquisition*	*acquisitive, acquired*
understand	*understanding*	*understanding/ understandable/ understood*
speak	*speech/speaker*	*spoken*
mean	*meaning*	*meaningful/ meaningless*
communicate	*communication*	*communicative*

Listening

1 On your first listening don't worry about understanding the details of the experiment. Instead focus on the general results and on the speaker's views.

2 Take a lot of time to look at the diagrams of the experiment. Be sure you know what details to listen for.

✱ Tapescript

V1: (male, radio host): It's obvious that a number of attempts have been made over the years to try and teach dolphins to speak – can you tell us something more about them…?

V2: (female, guest): Well I suppose one of the most interesting experiments with dolphins must be one done by Dr Jarvis Bastian. What he tried to do was to teach a male dolphin called Buzz and a female called Doris to communicate with each other across a barrier. The important thing was that they couldn't actually see each other through this barrier.

V1: So how did he do it exactly?

V2: Well first of all he kept the two dolphins together in the same tank and taught them to press paddles whenever they saw a light. The paddles were fitted to the side of the tank next to each other. If the light flashed on and off several times, then the dolphins were supposed to press the left-hand paddle followed by the right-hand one. If the light was kept steady, on the other hand, then the dolphins were supposed to press the paddles in reverse order – in other words, first the right and then the left. Whenever they responded correctly they were of course rewarded with fish. All right so far…?

V1: Sounds terribly complicated…

V2: I know…well that was the first stage, and once they had learned to do that correctly, Dr Bastian moved on to the second stage. In this stage, he separated the dolphins into two tanks. They could still *hear* one another but they couldn't actually *see* each other. The paddles and the light were set up in exactly the same way, except that this time it was only Doris who could see the light indicating which paddle to press first. But in order to get their fish *both* dolphins had to press the levers in the correct order. This meant of course that Doris had to *tell* Buzz which this was – whether it was a flashing light which meant left-hand and then right-hand, or whether it was a steady light which meant the opposite.

V1: So did it work?

V2: Well – amazingly enough, the dolphins achieved a 100% success rate – even over thousands of attempts at the task. It really did seem that dolphins could talk and that Doris was actually communicating new information to her partner through the barrier.

V1: You sound a bit sceptical – er, do you have some doubts about the experiment?

V2: Yes, I think there *was* a problem, and later it became clear that things weren't quite as the researchers had hoped. You see, while the dolphins were still together in the same tank, Doris had developed the habit of making certain sounds when the light was flashing and *different* sounds when it was continuous [ah]. Um, after the dolphins were separated, she continued the habit. And Buzz had, of course, already learnt which of Doris' sounds to associate with which light. So although it's true to say that they were communicating, you can't actually say that Doris was 'talking creatively'…

Key

1 a The experiment was successful.
  b The speaker is sceptical about the results.
2 (1) *(the) same/one/ (a) single*
  (2) *light*
  (3) *left (hand)*
  (4) *right (hand)*
  (5) *fish*
  (6) *separate/two/ different*
  (7) *Doris*
  (8) *Doris*
  (9) *Buzz*
  (10) *fish*

✱ Speaking

Try to find another English speaker in order to practise these tasks and then go through the instructions. During the activity provide your partner with as full a description as possible; listen carefully to your partner and ask questions if you are unclear.

Key

1 Student A has the second picture in Student B's set of pictures.

2 Student B has the fifth picture in Student A's set of pictures.

Grammar reminder: prepositions of position/direction/time/manner/purpose

Remember that different prepositions can be used to express different concepts, and that sometimes the same preposition can express more than one concept. The examples here are (a) position, (b) reason/purpose, (c) direction, (d) manner, and (e) time.

Key

1 1 *with*
  2 *after/in/over*
  3 *in*
  4 *during/in/over, to*
  5 *on*
  6 *in*
  7 *during/in*
  8 *across/along*
  9 *as, for*
  10 *to, by, on*

B

Reading the signals

Starter activities

Key

3   They have a problem with their body language/the
    way they are standing.

Listening

2   Before listening to the extract read the text and think about
the possible answers. You will only need to write up to three
words for each answer.

4   This is another task of the type found in CAE Paper 5
(Speaking) Phase C.

Tapescript

2   It's generally recognised today that one of our most
important conversational skills comes not from the tongue,
but from the rest of our body. Research over recent years
has shown that, in actual fact, more than 70 per cent of our
communication is non-verbal; in other words, a surprisingly
large percentage of the way we communicate involves the
language of our bodies rather than the language we speak.

'Body language', as it has come to be called, often
communicates our feelings and attitudes to people even
before we open our mouths; and it gives other people a
clear indication of how receptive we are likely to be towards
them. Receptive body language normally involves open
posture (such as keeping your arms and legs uncrossed), as
well as plenty of eye contact, and a friendly smile. Most
people with poor conversational skills don't realise that it is
their non-receptive body language (closed posture, little eye
contact, and no smile) which is often the cause of short
conversations that fail to develop into anything more
substantial.

Whether we like it or not, people very quickly judge us by
the first signals we give; and if the first impressions are not
positive and friendly, then I'm afraid it's going to be difficult
to develop and maintain a good conversation.

Key

2   (1) over/more than 70%   (6)   closed posture
    (2) feelings   (7)   no smile
    (3) attitudes   (8)   short
    (4) eye contact   (9)   positive
    (5) friendly smile   (10) friendly

4   Possible answers: put on a friendly smile, adopt a
more open posture (uncover mouth, uncross arms),
use more eye contact

Reading

1– ✱ 2   Try to read the text quickly, within about two
minutes. These activities require you to find the gist of each
section and then attach a suitable title and illustration.

4   Using the example given in the grid to see how the
information in the text can be rephrased into a personalised
message, write similar messages based on your answers in the
previous activity.

Key

1   A2   B3   C4   D1   E5
2   a5   b3   c1   e2   f4

4

Posture/gesture	Message
smile	'I am keen to communicate.'
arms/legs crossed	'I prefer to keep to myself. Please don't talk to me.'
open posture	'I am interested in establishing contact.'
leaning forward	'I am interested in what you are saying. Please keep talking.'
leaning back	'I do not agree with/I am bored by what you are saying.'
warm handshake	'I want to show you that I have an open and friendly attitude towards you.'
nod of the head/ eye contact	'I am listening and understand. Please continue.'

5   *phony face*
    open/closed posture
    crossed/uncrossed legs/arms
    thinking pose
    warm/firm handshake
    non-verbal gestures
    direct/natural/forced eye contact
    fixed stare
    aggressive behaviour

6   *strong indication*
    friendly/open/positive attitude
    conversational problems
    conversational/positive/receptive/non-verbal signals
    defensive frame of mind
    outside/first contact
    personal space
    social situations
    first step
    brief periods

    Adjectives collocating with *way* and *manner*:
    habitual, casual, natural, safe, positive, suspicious

Grammar analysis: substitution

Substitution is one of the most important ways in which we make connections in written or spoken language. It avoids unnecessary repetition and should make comprehension easier.

Key

1   1 a   2 d   3 a

3   a   *they*   b *his*   c *that*   d *one, another*

4   a   *it, they, she, he, him, them*
    b   *his, her, their, theirs, hers, its*
    c   *this, that, these, those*
    d   *one, such, another, so, some, many, then, there, the*

5   1   *it, he/she/they (are), him/her/them*
    2   *one, they*

6   *this – make connections in language between the things we say*
    they – various ways of doing this
    another – word or phrase
    this – replace or substitute one word or phrase with another

Writing

You could try preparing this task as follows:
1) Plan an outline of the points the speaker might have included. Look back at the Listening and Reading activities for ideas on content.
2) Make a list of four or five examples each of 'good' body language and 'poor' body language. You can then decide which of the 'good/poor' aspects were demonstrated by the imaginary speaker.
3) Write your review, remembering to include: an explanation of who was speaking, when, where and on what; a brief description of the points covered; personal impressions of the speaker's conversational skills; and your conclusion about the value of the talk.

✱ Vocabulary summary

1   This activity provides practice of a multiple choice vocabulary cloze similar to that found in CAE Paper 3 Section A.

Key

1   1 D   2 C   3 A   4 D   5 B   6 B   7 C   8 D   9 A   10 B

C

Paper 5 (Speaking): Phase A

Introduction

1–3   Read the descriptions of Phase A noting any important details.

Introducing yourself or someone else

1–2   Play the first extract and work through it as an example before continuing.

Tapescript

1–2
Extract 1
Juliet: Hello, there.
Nick: Hello, yes, um [hi], we've not met, have we?
Juliet: No, [no] no I don't think so, I don't…
Nick: I'm, I'm Nick.
Juliet: Oh, hello, I'm, I'm Juliet.
Nick: Nice to meet you [yes], um…

Extract 2
CH: Er, Stephen, here's, er, somebody you should meet, this is [oh] Siriol Llewellyn. Siriol, this is Stephen Pacey.
SL: Hello.
SP: How do you do.
CH: You're going to be working on the same account. All right, I've got to leave you, I've got to find some other people. All right.
SP: Fine. I'm sorry, I didn't quite catch your name.
SL: Oh, it's, it's Siriol Llewellyn.

Extract 3
Mike: The street's a bit slippery.
Juliet: Look it's all right, have you got the bottle?
Mike: Yes, I've got it, don't worry.
Juliet: Oh, thank goodness for that, I thought you'd left it behind.
Jenny: Juliet!
Juliet: Jenny!
Jenny: Hi.
Juliet: How amazing to see you [hello], good god, I haven't seen you for ages!
Jenny: No, are you going to Graham and Barbara's?
Juliet: Yes, look [oh, good], this is my husband Mike.
Jenny: Oh, hello, how do you do?
Mike: Hi.
Juliet: This is Jenny. We were at school together, you know, Barbara, the three of us, we were…

3
V1: This is…
V2: Can I introduce you to…
V1: I'd like you to meet…
V2: Hello, I'm…
V1: My name's…
V2: How do you do.

V1: Pleased to meet you.
V2: Nice to meet you.

4

Extract 1

Nick: Nice to meet you [yes], um…
Juliet: …good party.
Nick: It's great, isn't it [yeah, really nice], who do you know here?
Juliet: Er, well, Barbara [oh right], yes I went to school with Barbara [oh, right, well I…], what about you?
Nick: Well I work with her other half, Graham…
Juliet: Oh do you, yeah [laughter].
Nick: He's a laugh, isn't he?
Juliet: Yeah, he is. What, what sort of, what sort of work do you do?
Nick: We work in an insurance office [oh, do you?], but he's a rep so he's out a lot [yes] of the time and I sort of…
Juliet: And what, what about you?
Nick: I work in the office all the time [mm], yeah…
Juliet: Is that, is that interesting work?
Nick: Um, not really, it's not, you know, it's not what I've set my life aside to do but [no], it's good for now and because I've got a young family [yes] and it's quite, it's quite a stable job [mm], I feel quite secure, and, er, we live quite close to the office so it sort of suits me not to be going out and about [yeah] like Graham, but er…I mean, he's very much sort of a free spirit I think, isn't he?

Extract 2

SL: Oh, it's, it's Siriol Llewellyn.
SP: Llewellyn, presumably that's Welsh, is it?
SL: Yes, that's right, both my names are Welsh.
SP: Oh, right, you don't seem to have a Welsh accent.
SL: I suppose that's what comes of being middle class.
SP: Right. You're, you've lived in London for some time, have you?
SL: No, actually I've just been working for a company in Wales and I've been moved up here, [oh, I], promotion, so that's nice.
SP: I see [mm], how long have you been working for Boodle and Boodle?
SL: Well, um, about three years, before that I was working for Jordan and Mason.
SP: I see [mm], well as you know, I work for Ogilvy and Mather [yes] and, um, we're coming together on this project which should be quite exciting.
SL: Two good companies.
SP: Absolutely, yes [yes].

Extract 3

Juliet: This is Jenny. We were at school together, you know, Barbara, the three of us, we were…
Mike: Oh, I see, the famous Jenny.
Jenny: That's right, three little maids from school are we (laughter).
Mike: That's right. You were involved in the incident with taking all the knobs off the doors, weren't you?
Jenny: Oh no, you haven't told him about that…
Juliet: Course I have.
Jenny: …my reputation goes before me.
Mike: You're infamous.
Juliet: So have you seen Barbara recently?
Jenny: Well, I bumped into her at a station actually [did you?] about three weeks ago and that's how I came to be coming to this.

Juliet: Oh, really, so you haven't been in touch with her really?
Jenny: No, well sort of off and on, you know, Christmas cards and sort of we keep in touch sometimes through mutual friends but, but yes so I thought I'd come along tonight…

Key

1

	1	2	3
introducing themselves	✓		
introducing someone else		✓	✓

2   *this is…*   ✓
Can I introduce you to…
Hello, I'm…   ✓
My name's…
How do you do…   ✓
Pleased to meet you…
Nice to meet you…   ✓
I'd like you to meet…
Here's somebody you should meet…   ✓

4

	1	2	3
Family	✓		
Friends	✓		✓
Background		✓	✓
Work	✓	✓	

5 a   *oh, do you? oh, right; oh, really? did you? yeah*
 b   *yes, that's right; yeah, really nice; fine; absolutely, yes*
 c   *I see; oh, right; right*
 d   *not really…; no, actually…; no, well…*
 e   *I'm sorry. I didn't quite catch…*

What should my body language be on meeting someone for the first time?

1   Look back to Section B of this unit to remind yourself of useful tips if you wish.

2–3   These activities provide practice for the Paper 5 (Speaking) test. Practise with, if possible, an English-speaking friend. Sit as you would in the exam situation!

Key

1   **DO:**   lean forward in an interested manner
 maintain direct eye contact some of the time
 shake hands warmly '
 nod your head to indicate understanding/ agreement
 DON'T: sit with your arms and legs crossed (i.e. closed posture)
 cover your mouth/chin with your hand
 stare hard at the other person
 frown too much

What are the important features of speaking ability?

These are the five main assessment criteria used by the CAE examiners when assessing candidates for the CAE Paper 5 Speaking test.

Key
1 B   2 D   3 A   4 C   5 E

How can I improve my speaking ability?

1–2   Remember that there are many practical steps you can take yourself in order to improve your speaking ability – some ideas are given in the table.

3   The annual CAE Examination Report gives some very useful guidance on student performance across the whole examination. See page 5 for details of how to obtain a copy of the most recent Report.

Key
3   Possible answers:

	What I find encouraging	What I should remember
1	Candidates generally appear to work well together.	Ask for clarification or repetition if you don't understand something.
2	Candidates found working in pairs less stressful than a one–to–one interview.	Don't try to over-rehearse or memorise Phase A.
3	Phase A seems to put candidates at their ease.	Try to go beyond small talk and make interesting and original comments on topics raised.

Revision Exam Practice 1

Paper 1 (Reading)

This task is taken from the multiple choice section of the Reading Paper. For information on how to approach this section of Paper 1, see the information and the facsimile questions on pages 26–28. The answer sheet for the Reading Paper is reproduced on page 298.

Allow approximately 20 minutes for this task.

Key
1 D   2 A   3 C   4 B   5 A

Paper 2 (Writing)

This task is taken from Section A of the Writing Paper. For information on how to approach this section of Paper 2, see the information and the facsimile questions on pages 36–38.

Allow approximately 1 hour for this task.

Try doing this exam practice exercise under examination-like conditions (i.e. no notes, dictionary, etc. to help you).

Key
The version below is a suggested answer only, but it incorporates most of the elements that should be included.

Dear Sir/Madam
We are writing to complain about a holiday we recently spent at the Pacific Beach Hotel in Hawaii from September 12th–20th. The holiday was organised for us by your company and we had hoped it would be the "holiday of a lifetime"; instead it proved to be an expensive disappointment for a variety of reasons.

We were especially disappointed to discover that the hotel itself did not match the very positive description of it in your brochure. The rooms were described as all being comfortably furnished and having either full or partial views of the sea. In fact, we were unable to see the sea at all from our room! In addition, the air conditioning broke down twice during our stay, making life very uncomfortable in the tropical heat. The local town was described as being "just a short stroll away" but in reality it proved to be more than 30 minutes' walk up a steep hill!

Our holiday plans had included playing a lot of golf and one of our reasons for choosing the Pacific Beach Hotel was the fact that there were several good golf courses in the area within easy reach by car. Our original plans were disrupted as we were unable to hire a car until the third day even though car hire for the whole week had been included in the total price of the holiday. This also made it difficult for us to visit some of the famous sights on the island.

A further problem occurred when one of us was seriously bitten by an insect and tried to seek medical assistance. The hotel would not call a doctor and simply advised us to go to the local clinic in town. This is hardly the service one would expect of a four-star hotel, especially since it is described in your brochure as a "select hotel offering its guests the highest standards of personal care and attention".

We trust you will investigate our various complaints as quickly as possible and that you will be prepared to offer us substantial compensation for all the inconvenience and disappointment we experienced. At the very least, we would hope for some refund of the considerable cost involved in the holiday.

We look forward to hearing from you at the earliest opportunity.

Yours faithfully,

Paper 3 (English in Use)

This task is taken from Section A of the English in Use Paper. For information on how to approach this section of Paper 3, see the information and the facsimile questions on pages 47–49. The answer sheet for the English in Use Paper is reproduced on pages 299–301. Allow approximately 30 minutes for this task.

Try doing these exam practice exercises under examination-like conditions (i.e. no notes, dictionary, etc. to help you)

Key

1 **Multiple choice cloze**

1	C	9	A
2	B	10	C
3	D	11	A
4	C	12	D
5	A	13	B
6	B	14	B
7	D	15	A
8	C		

2 **Open cloze**

16	*few*	24	*their*
17	*these/they*	25	*which/that*
18	*the*	26	*if/when*
19	*in*	27	*it*
20	*has*	28	*who*
21	*other*	29	*what*
22	*for*	30	*or/and*
23	*while/whereas*		

Paper 4

This task is taken from Sections A and B of the Listening Paper. For information on how to approach this section of Paper 4, see the information and the facsimile questions on pages 57–59. The answer sheet for the Listening Paper is reproduced on page 302. Allow approximately 15 minutes for this task.

Tapescript A

(fade in) Right, nice to see you. Welcome to your first circuit training class. I hope you're going to enjoy it. Have any of you ever done any circuit training before? [no well a bit, but a long time ago]. Right then, well to start I I'll just tell you a bit about what you're going to be doing. Now you'll see round the hall there's all these bits of equipment and things right. Like over there there's some weights and over there are some other kinds of weights. There you've got a step at the back there. There's a weighted ball and in the corner there is just a pole. There's fifteen different activities in all. Some make use of equipment and others don't, and you'll see a notice by each one telling you what each one is OK? Now the idea is that you go round each of the activities and do them one at a time. Ten of each first time, 15 second time and 20 third time [oh, you must be joking!, ah] Don't worry, I haven't told you the worst yet! You'll be working against the clock and in between each activity you'll all come together in the middle here to do some exercises together.

OK? Hope that doesn't sound too terrible. Has anybody got any questions? [no, no] OK right now all of these exercises are designed to develop different muscles in your body to sort of well improve your muscle tone and of course your breathing. When you do the exercise the exercises in the middle, you may find yourselves puffing and panting a lot. You'll be doing stuff like skipping and running on the spot, star jumps, lunges – that's meant to help your breathing and your heart rate. Well you probably won't know what half these exercise are. You've got bicep curls for example, pressups, situps, stomach twists, back extensions. Anyone got any idea what they are? [no, don't tell me no] Oh well well don't worry. I'll give you a demonstration of each before we get going. And I'll be coming round to see if you're on the right tracks.

Now before you start, I'll just have to give you a bit of warning. It's a bit off putting maybe but it's meant at least to be for your own good. We just have to check that you really think you're fit enough to do all this you see. 'Cos exercise is good for you but, if you do the wrong kind, or at the wrong rate, or at the wrong moment, it can actually damage you. It ends up doing you more harm than good. So I'm just going to read a list of things out to you. If any of them is true for you, then you really shouldn't be doing any of this without seeing your doctor or having a word with me, right? So what you've got to watch for is if you've ever had any heart trouble, or any pains in your heart or chest. OK now what about blood pressure and things well? If you've often felt faint or dizzy or you've been told that you had high blood pressure, come and have a word. And watch it if you've ever had an injury, you know broken bones or any kind of joint problem that kind of stuff. If your doctor's told you that exercise can make these worse, then come and have a word with me before we get started.

Right, is that everything? No, hold on. Is anyone here over sixty five? [I feel it] It certainly [feel it] it certainly doesn't look like it! And last of all I just need to ask you if you've been doing any vigorous exercise recently? [no] Vigorous exercise? Right, well that doesn't mean haring around like a maniac or playing squash three times a day. No more like exercise for at least 20 minutes a time on a regular basis. So two or three times a week for two months or more? Even walking to college or work every day at a good pace? Right that means we need to take it slowly at the beginning and build up gradually [that's it]. Right. So you're all fit and healthy? [well, I think so, ah, mm] Good, then let's get started. I'll just show you how to (fade)

Tapescript B

Pat: And now for our regular health spot – the Doctor's Surgery. Doctor Ellie Field is back with us in the studio to help you out with anything you want to know about your health. Any problems you have or your friends or family, just give us a ring if you want to have a word. Remember, the number is 071 336 5730, that's right 071 336 5730. Ellie, it's nice to see you again.

Ellie: Thanks Pat. It's nice to be here and hello to all your listeners, it's good to be back with you too! As usual, I'll be here answering your letters and your calls. There's a pile of letters here waiting for me, so we'll start with them. Now, the first one is from Brian Quinn. That's Brian Quinn from Nottingham. Now Brian, you write that you have been feeling really low of late, low and listless. You say you've got no energy and you seem to be catching all the bugs around: 'flu, coughs and colds, stomach bugs … You say you've always been very healthy and never had anything wrong with you. You play lots of sport – or at least you used to – and just can't understand what's going on. You say that you've felt like this for about 3 months now, but you haven't been to the doctor because you didn't want to make a fuss or waste his time. And last of all you give your age. You're 24.

Well, Brian. Um you're low and listless whereas you used to be full of go, and you're picking up bugs that have passed you by before. It's well it's hard to judge what might be up with you just from what you've said. What you need to look at first of all, I'd say, is if there have been any changes in your life over the last 3 months or longer even. Have you ever had any changes in diet, for instance? Or has your work been particularly stressful? Have you moved house? Moving house has been shown to be one of the most stressful things you could do, you know. It means pulling up roots and starting all over again and that can be hard and lonely. I don't know if that's the case but, if it is, your health could have suffered for it.

And what about other parts of your emotional life? Er, relationships for example. Have you had to break up with a partner or has anyone else left your life in any way? Lots of people, especially men, tend to think they should be able to cope with anything on the emotional front and even that it's a sign of weakness not to be able to do so. Well, that is definitely not the case. I mean, we're not machines, thank goodness. And and if and if anything goes wrong in our emotional lives, it can have an effect on our health. It's a blow to the whole system. So don't be afraid to admit it if something of that kind is wrong. Now, if there has been some kind of change in your life that has left you feeling low, you could maybe try talking to someone about it. A friend maybe, a counsellor or even me. I'd be pleased to talk about things with you. If you can't think of anything that has changed in your life, it might be worth going to the doctor for a checkup, you know, to get your blood pressure checked, for instance, or to have a few routine tests. Doctors aren't only there to repair broken bones or to get rid of excruciating pains you know. Lots of people go to the doctor when they're simply feeling under the weather as you seem to be. And a doctor will gladly see you with the kinds of symptoms you describe.

Well Brian I I I hope I've been able to give you some help. Do write again, or even ring if you want to talk things over a bit more, or give a few more details. It was good to hear from you and I hope things will soon start to pick up for you. And now Pat I believe we've got a caller on the line(fade).

Key

Section A

1	B	4	D	7	B
2	D	5	B	8	A
3	B	6	D	9	B

Section B

10 *listless*
11 *catching lots of bugs*
12 *he didn't want to make a fuss/waste doctor's time*
13 *good*
14 *work*
15 *relationships*
16 *admit*
17 *discuss (them)*
18 *a check up*
19 *ring Ellie*

Paper 5 (Speaking)

This task is taken from Phase A of the Speaking Paper. For information on how to approach this section of Paper 5, see the information and the facsimile questions on pages 68–70.

Try to find two English-speaking friends to work with you in a group of three: one person to be the 'examiner', one person to take the part of Candidate A, and one person to take the part of Candidate B.

In Task 1 the assumption is that the two students already know one other, so they are asked by the examiner to introduce each other. Task 1 includes some of the questions the examiner is likely to ask. Decide in advance whether it is more appropriate for you to use the first or second set of questions, depending on whether you are likely to take the examination in Britain or in your own country.

In Task 2 the assumption is that the two students do not know each other, so the examiner asks them to introduce themselves. The continuation will be the same as for Task 1 above.

You should try practising both the Task 1 and Task 2 approaches.

For the actual examination you may or may not be paired with someone you know already.

Six: Everyday objects

A

Inventions

Starter activities

✱ 2   This activity practises a Paper 5 (Speaking) task (Phase C).

Key
1

Invention	Name of inventor?	Where?	Which century?
telephone	Alexander Graham Bell	USA	19th
parachute	François Blanchard	France	18th
printing press	Johannes Gutenberg	Germany	15th
jet engine	Frank Whittle	GB	20th
microscope	Zacharias Janssen	Netherlands	16th
pendulum clock	Christiaan Huygens	Netherlands	17th

✱ Listening

One of the tasks in CAE Paper 4 (Listening) is a once-only listening. This is an example. Take time to read the notes in the box so that you know what you are listening for. Write just a few words for each answer.

After the task, you may like to replay the tape and note those occasions when information was actually repeated within the conversation. Remember that even in a once-only listening task, you may actually hear the information you need <u>more</u> than once because it is 'recycled' naturally by the speakers.

If you put 1875 for item (8), then remember in future that sometimes it's important not to focus immediately on a possible answer but to listen for relationships between different points that are mentioned.

Tapescript
V1: (male):   835 7740 – Kevin speaking.
V2: (female): Kevin…hi…it's Penny here! Listen, [Oh, hi Penny] I've managed to do that background research we talked about for our class project. Shall I give you the information so you can add it to what we've already got?

V1: OK…fine…let me just get a pen…right, go ahead…
V2: OK well, I found out quite a lot about Alexander Graham Bell…you know we thought he was American…well he was actually born in Scotland and only moved to North America in 1870 [oh]…his family went first to Canada and later to the States…I guess he must've been in his mid–twenties by then…
V1: Have you got his dates there?
V2: Sorry, oh yes, eighteen forty-seven to nineteen twenty-two.
V1: (Writing) Eighteen forty-seven to…nineteen…
V2: …twenty-two.
V1: OK…go on.
V2: Well, apparently his father'd been a teacher for the deaf, and when Bell arrived in Boston in the States that's what he did too – he taught deaf children by day and did experiments with electricity at night.
V1: Right.
V2: He had this idea for a new type of telegraph instrument…you know…for sending messages. Anyway, he drew up some plans…took them to an electrical shop in Boston to get the instrument made…and that's where he met Thomas Watson [oh, right]. They became friends and decided to work together on the new telegraph project.
V1: Hang on, hang on…(writing)…Thomas Watson.
V2: That's right; it took them several months but eventually they worked out a way of sending speech sounds along an electric wire; and after that they built what I suppose you could say was the first model of a telephone.
V1: So when exactly was this…we'd better make sure we've got a date when the telephone was invented?
V2: Well by this time it was 1875, but [right] they had a lot of problems with the early version…so it wasn't really until the following year that the first sentence was actually heard over the telephone – so that's the officially recorded date. Actually, there's an interesting story attached to this…apparently the two men were working on the instrument…one in one room and one in another room…when Bell suddenly knocked over a bottle of acid and spilt some on himself. He called for Watson to come and help him and Watson only heard him because of the telephone…at least that's how the story goes…anyway, that was it…they immediately patented the invention and the first telephone line ever was opened between New York and San Francisco in 1915. So will that be OK for the historical bit of the project?
V1: Yeah, I'm sure it will…thanks for doing the work on that section. I've typed up the part on how a telephone works…and I found some really good pictures of telephone designs through the 20th century which we can use…so I'll add this to the introduction and bring in a draft for you to look at tomorrow…OK? We can make any changes then.
V2: Fine. I'll see you tomorrow then…bye (fade out)…

Key

1	1922	2	Scotland
3	USA/America	4	teacher for deaf children
5	electricity		
6	telegraph instrument	7	Thomas Watson
8	1876	9	San Francisco

Reading

1   Don't worry about unfamiliar vocabulary. Just look for the type of phone being referred to. (NB 'whopper' is sometimes used informally to mean a big lie as in 'he told me a whopper')

3   This section focuses attention on the formation of compound nouns and adjectives by looking at examples taken from the texts.

Tapescript

V1:

satellite links	lie-detector	wrong number
read-out	front door	household appliance
close-up	peephole	videophone
civil rights	ear-pieces	best-sellers

Key

1   truth phone and videophone

2   *Truth phone* – advantages (A) and disadvantages (D)
- tells the user when someone on the other end of the line is lying (A)
- could be useful for surveillance/counter-surveillance in spying (A)
- could be useful for checking employees' honesty (A)
- could be useful for checking validity of insurance claims (A)
- is very expensive to buy (D)
- could be an invasion of personal privacy (D)
- could be misused in the wrong hands (D)
- depends on very careful procedures for use and on correct analysis (D)

Videophone – advantages (A) and disadvantages (D)
- you can see who you're speaking to (A)
- could be a more personal and informative means of communication (A)
- could reveal more than you wish (D)
- could cause you to become preoccupied with how you look before answering (D)
- could result in embarrassing breakdowns of communication (D)
- conference calls could be hard to handle (D)
- secretaries may find it harder to disguise the fact that their boss doesn't want to take the call (D)
- not clear what will happen to picture quality on a bad line (D)

3   2   a   *satellite links, lie-detector, household appliance, peephole, videophone, ear-pieces*
      b   *best-sellers, civil rights, front door, wrong number*
      c   *close-up, read-out*
    3   ˈsatellite ˈlinks, ˈlie-deˈtector, ˈwrong ˈnumber, ˈread-out, ˈfront ˈdoor, ˈhousehold apˈpliance, ˈclose-up, ˈpeephole, ˈvideophone, ˈcivil ˈrights, ˈear-pieces, ˈbest-ˈsellers
    4   a   ˈtelephone-ˈusers, ˈtelephone ˈconsole, ˈbenchmarks, ˈmodesty ˈblind, ˈconference ˈcall,
      b   ˈdigital ˈreading, ˈcrossed ˈline, ˈretail ˈoutlet, ˈanswering maˈchine, ˈbottom ˈline
    5   a   *pin-sharp*
      b   *voice-only*
      c   *pull-down*
    6   *long-awaited, widescreen, tell-tale, real-life, long-distance, well-known, would-be, much-vaunted, voice-stress, stress-free*
    7   adjective + verb
      adjective + noun
      verb + noun
      adverb + verb
      verbal auxiliary + verb
      noun + noun
      noun + adjective

Ways of learning: deducing meaning from context

1–3   Activity 1 offers you a step-by-step approach to working out the meaning of an unfamiliar word using: (1) clues from the text; (2) your knowledge of the way English works; and (3) your knowledge of the world.

Key

1   a   *noun*
    b   *red*
    c   *shirt collar*
    d   *married*
    e   *apologising/saying sorry, inquisitive/curious*
    f   *mark/stain*
    g   *lipstick*
    h   *ink*

Grammar reminder: order of adjectives

Key

2   1   *a beautiful seventeenth century French castle*
    2   *exquisite traditional black lacquer plates*
    3   *important recent sociological studies*
    4   *clever new technological approach*
    5   *expensive new red Italian sports car*

✱ Writing

This task gives you practice in completing a Paper 2 (Writing) Section B task.

B

The art of persuasion

🔲 Listening

✳ Read the table carefully and think about the likely content and form of the missing words.

Tapescript
Extract 1
V1: Have you ever actually done a commercial?
V2: I've done, yes I have, um, I've only done one, but it was, it was memorable in as much as, um, it was for um, a sort of yoghurty-custard um snack [right], and er, which was called "Heart", and um, it was um, it was a particularly disgusting product actually; um, but the, the catch for it was that they wanted, I had to dress up in this, in this sort of lion suit and er, I had to sing a song from, er, "The Wizard of Oz", um, the song that the cowardly lion sings [oh, yes, yes] "If I only had a heart" [Bert Lahr sing it]; yeah, that's right, and um, and not only did I have to er, you know, dance as a lion, sometimes on all fours and sometimes on two legs, but I also had to sing this song; and um, and at the end I had to eat a spoon of this, um, this yoghurty-custardy product; and er, because there was so much um, you know, I had, I had to do so much coordination, very rarely did I actually get it right, um, but each time I had to eat a spoonful of this stuff; and as the day wore on, I was getting sicker and sicker, and more and more tired, and er, finally, when on the final take I actually managed to get the steps, the dance, the song and the spoon in my mouth all together, and I was so relieved, that, um, I just threw up…all over…
V1: What, in front of the camera!
V2: Well, thankfully, you know, the camera had actually stopped running at that point [oh, right], but you know, it was, it was a, it was an embarrassing moment…
V1: I bet it was yes.

Extract 2
V3: So what was it you were advertising again?
V4: Um, it was a, a skin preparation; um, it was in fact, it was before I was ever an actor or anything and er, my mother knew somebody that was er, worked for this advertising agency and they were looking for somebody with, er, with um, spots which I had at the time; and um, so I was sent up for this interview and er, it's sort of one of those before and after commercials and you know, "oh my confidence has grown since I used this product", I can't remember the name of it; and um, so I got the job because I was, as I say, I was covered in spots, you know the kind of thing, and um, almost sort of the day that they, they rang to say that I'd got it, it seemed that from that moment on they started disappearing; and er, come the day for the filming, I'd got a clear complexion; it was awful, you know, I thought I was going to walk in there and they'd um, they'd just tell me to get out, but um, they sort of they'd done a few of these commercials with other people and apparently it's not uncommon for this sort of thing to happen, and they had somebody standing by with make-up, so in fact they made up a lot of spots on me and um, it suddenly struck me that,

you know, they could've used anybody in that case; you don't actually need anyone with, with spots if you've got somebody in the make-up but they made this horrific sort of acne rash on my face and then we did the first bit and then they washed them all off and um, so it was all faked really, when you think about it, it's actually sort of against the advertising code because I didn't actually have a skin condition that was improved by the product…
V3: But I suppose it would have been even worse for them if you had kept the spots and you'd used the product and then they couldn't have done the after if they hadn't cleared up
V4: Well, yes, mm, yeah, that's a, that's another point, isn't it? but I…

Key

	Actor 1	Actor 2
What was the product?	• a snack called Heart	• a skin product/ preparation for spots
Why was the actor chosen?	• acting/ singing/dancing experience	• suffered from spots
What did he/she have to do?	• dress up as a lion • sing and dance • eat a spoonful of the product	• be filmed before and after using the product
Were there any problems in making the advert?	• was very sick at the end of the filming	• spots disappeared before filming so needed to use make-up

✳ Reading

1 This is similar to a CAE Paper 3 (English in Use) Question 5 task. The task is to insert the correct sentence into each gap. There are more sentences to choose from than there are gaps.

Read the whole text first and think not just about the meaning of individual words and sentences, but also about the way that the meaning of the text as a whole is constructed. Look out for regular references backwards and forwards throughout the text which make it cohere. Then select the correct sentence to fill each gap.

Think about the clues you used to select each sentence. Notice the specific clues that are in the text.

You may like to consider why the distracting sentences would not fit into the gaps.

2–3 Take plenty of time to read the text carefully and identify the writer's opinions, as well as to consider your own views in the light of what you have read.

4 This is designed to extend your knowledge of words and phrases relating to advertising, and help your awareness of the connotation that a word or phrase may carry. Remember that although some words may carry a fixed positive or negative connotation, the connotation of a word often depends on its context and on the perspective of the speaker or writer.

Key

1 (1) B   (2) F   (3) A   (4) D

3

		Writer's view
1	**Advertising often promotes a particular lifestyle.**	✓
2	**Advertising usually distorts the truth.**	✗
3	**Advertising is incompatible with an environmentally sensitive lifestyle.**	✓
4	**Advertisements often project an imaginary world.**	✓
5	**Advertising can't sell anything to anyone unless they really want to buy it.**	
6	**Advertisements can create dissatisfaction with life as it really is.**	✓
7	**Advertisements often portray a product as a solution to your problem.**	✓
8	**Advertising changes people's behaviour.**	

4   positive: *reliable, imaginative, green, rural, environmentally/socially sensitive, carer-sharers, status, style, success*
neutral: *powerful, lifestyle, public, mythical*
negative: *urban, thrusting, self-satisfied, high-consuming, yuppie, escapist, contradictory, money grabbing, fairy tale*

✳ Speaking

1 Speaker A will describe a picture of a family car with all the luggage unpacked. Speaker B has a picture of the same family car but with all the luggage packed inside.

2 Speaker B will see a picture of a young mother on the telephone. Speaker A has a picture of an old lady on the telephone.

Grammar analysis: cleft sentences

1 Using a cleft sentence structure enables the writer to focus on a particular part of a sentence and the information in it. For example, if you want to emphasise one noun group and make the whole clause say something about it, you can use the "It…" structure or the "What…" structure: e.g. It's *people's value systems* that advertising affects not their buying habits or, What advertising affects is *people's value systems*.

2 Work through the example so that you are clear about how the two parts fit together structurally and in terms of meaning.

3 This activity gives you more practice in manipulating cleft sentence structures. Note that there may be more than one cleft sentence structure which can be used to focus on the underlined information (see Key).

You may like to extend the activity by playing around with the five sentences to see how many different cleft sentences you can produce from each one.

4 This activity offers practice in selecting a suitable cleft sentence to complete a text. Notice that although both sentences would fit within the text, one is more appropriate than the other in terms of emphasis.

Key

2   1   *What telephone engineers are working on now is a compact version of the videophone for the home.*
  2   *What is clearly going to be needed as a matter of urgency is a videophone equivalent of the answering machine.*
  3   *It's in the business world that the implications of the truth phone could be devastating.*
  4   *It's personal privacy which is an issue as much as anything.*
  5   *What people could be measuring is your emotional response without you knowing.*

3   Possible approaches to changing structures: Advertisements offer their products as solutions to problems.
  a) What advertisements do is *offer their products as solutions to problems.*
  b) What advertisements offer is *their products as solutions to problems.*
  c) *Offering their products as solutions to problems* is what advertisements do.
  d) *It's solutions to problems* that advertisements offer through their products.
  e) *It's their products* that advertisements offer as solutions to problems.
  f) *It's advertisements* that offer their products as solutions to problems.

1 *It's as solutions to problems that advertisements offer their products.*
   What advertisements offer their products as is solutions to problems.
2 *What market research does is uncover new social trends.*
   Uncovering new social trends is what market research does.
3 *It's new social trends that market research uncovers.*
   What market research uncovers is new social trends.
4 *What advertisers do is feed back to us versions of ourselves.*
   Feeding back to us versions of ourselves is what advertisers do.
5 *It's versions of ourselves that advertisers feed back to us.*
   What advertisers feed back to us is versions of ourselves.
   Versions of ourselves is what advertisers feed back to us.

4 *1 (b) what 'advertisements for cars speak of' is being contrasted with what 'advertisements for (most other) products tell you'.*
   2 (a) 'images of successful, high-consuming young executives' are being contrasted with 'socially and environmentally sensitive images'.

C

Paper 1 (Reading): Multiple matching

Introduction

Remember that there are 3 main formats for the reading tasks in the CAE Reading Paper: multiple choice, multiple matching, and gap filling. Here the focus is on the multiple matching format.

What does a multiple matching exercise look like?

1 Multiple matching involves correctly matching one set of items to another. Whatever the type of matching involved, the correct answer must be selected from a number of possible options available. Activity 1 illustrates this. Read the definitions and then select the correct term for each one. Notice that although there are only five definitions, there are eight possible options given to choose from.

2 This activity illustrates another multiple matching format – matching headings to paragraphs. Read the introductory paragraph of the text on contact lenses. Then look at how **D** is the best option to select for paragraph (1) because of the

connections between the heading and the text. When you are confident about the sorts of clues to look for, complete the task.

Key

1 1 A   2 C   3 E   4 D   5 G
2 2 H   3 I   4 A   5 K   6 G   7 F   8 E   9 J

Exam practice

There are three slightly different multiple matching activities within this exam practice: matching problem to source; opinion to speaker; and appropriate advice to the general situation.

Key

1	B, D	
2	A, B, C, D	
3	G	
4	E	
5	D	
6	B	
7	A	
8	C	
9	E	

What techniques help you to complete multiple matching reading exercises?

This section explains the different sorts of layout for multiple matching exercises which are commonly found in Paper 1. Look at the suggested examples and consider how the layout might affect the order in which you read or process the questions, options, and text. The arrows suggest possible approaches:

- For **a** start from the answer options, then move to the text and refer back to the options.
- For **b** start from the questions or statements, then move to the text and refer back to the questions/statements.
- For **c** start from the questions, then move to the text and then refer to the separate answer options, finally checking back against the questions.

Reflections

It may be useful to look at examples of multiple matching tasks from past papers or practice tests.

Key

1

- matching person to opinion/comment/attitude ✓
- matching paragraph to heading ✓
- matching paragraph/short text to name/content description ✓
- matching specific details to a set
- matching a person/object/event to a factual detail
- matching a cause to effect ✓
- matching a problem to a solution ✓
- matching a person/object to an attribute
- matching a text/caption to a picture

Seven: Jobs

A

What about getting a job?

Starter activities

3 Words with more than two syllables usually carry secondary as well as main stress, particularly when the words are said in isolation. Weak vowel sounds often reduce to /ə/, schwa.

Key

1 Possible answers:
1 solicitor, secretary, draughtsman
2 librarian, author, translator, interpreter
3 optician, chemist, speech therapist, pharmacist
4 engineer
5 (none)
6 economist, systems analyst
7 (none)
8 architect, advertiser, actor
9 policeman, dustman, customs officer, shop assistant
10 barman

3

op`tician	`systems `analyst	`draughtsman
lib`rarian	`pharmacist	`chemist
trans`lator	`architect	shop a`ssistant
`builder	e`conomist	`sales
`customs `officer	`dustman	repre`sentative
engi`neer	`speech `therapist	`barman
`author	po`liceman	so`licitor
`secretary	in`terpreter	
`advertiser	`actor	

Reading

NB Fictional texts are not used in the CAE exam. However, wide ranging reading can help you to perform better in Papers 1, 2 and 3. It is important for preparation to read as much as possible.

1 This text is the beginning of a science fiction story.

3 Use the text to find clues to the word meanings.

✱ 5 This text is the last part of the Dorcas story. Before you read it try to predict the ending. This activity is a 'cloze' test like those in Paper 3, English in Use. Don't just guess the missing words but use clues in the text, before and after each blank, to get an idea of the meaning and part of speech of the missing words.

Key
2 Employment record form

Species:	chimp
Name:	Dorcas
Type of work undertaken:	domestic work
Qualifications:	Class A Domestic, plus Nursery duties reasonable vocabulary
Training:	trainable, amenable
Personality:	good-natured, conscientious
Competence for job:	strengths: good training, good at all domestic chores
	weaknesses: some annoying habits, a bit slow to learn certain things

3 Possible answers
1 *snorted* – said abruptly and indignantly
2 *flipped* – turned over a series of pages quickly and for no particular purpose
3 *slurred* – not precise, indistinct
4 *squawked* – spoke in a loud, piercing way (like the noise a parrot makes)
5 *butt* – cigarette end
6 *wear off* – diminish, become less
7 *took her in his stride* – accepted her without fuss
8 *was taken off my hands* – taken away from my responsibilities/no longer my responsibility

4 Possible answers:
servants
trained
domestic work
routine manual labour
uniform
maid
jobs

5 (1) *no*
(2) *door*
(3) *from*
(4) *own*
(5) *so*
(6) *done*
(7) *intended/meant/ involved*
(8) *throw/cast*
(9) *being/race*
(10) *only*
(11) *time/effort*
(12) *ever*
(13) *very*
(14) *obvious/clear/evident*
(15) *both*

✱ Writing

Decide what information to include, what order the information should go in and what style/register to write in. The letter should be relatively formal in style as it is a reference to an unknown agency. Here are some useful expressions to include in your letter.

Thank you for your letter of (date) or With reference to your letter of (date)…I have known (Dorcas) for (X) years … As far as her qualifications are concerned…I have no hesitation in recommending Dorcas for…

Grammar reminder: words for linking sentences/clauses

Key

1   contrast: *despite, although, even though, in spite of*
    exception: *apart from, except for*
    comparison: *in relation to, in comparison with*
    addition: *along with, besides, furthermore, apart from*

2   1   *In comparison with/In relation to*
    2   *apart from/except for*
    3   *Along with/Besides*
    4   *Along with/Besides*
    5   *in comparison with/in relation to*
    6   *Besides/Along with/Apart from*
    7   *Despite/In spite of*
    8   *Apart from/Except for*

✳ Listening

Tapescript

Lisa Green

Presenter: Six months ago she was just another 17 year old hopeful modelling for teenage magazines. Today Lisa Green can earn £12,000 a day for her skills on the international catwalk, making her one of Britain's highest paid teenagers. But despite being the envy of thousands of schoolgirls, Lisa still longs for quiet days at home with her family in Tooting, South London.

Lisa: Yes, it can be quite lonely. Sometimes I would give up everything to be at home. Don't get me wrong, it's a good job, but what's fashion? It's just clothes. It's not about people dying and people getting Aids.

Presenter: While she enjoys the parties and the champagne lifestyle that come with the job, Lisa deliberately avoids the obsession with image that she sees in some of her rivals.

Lisa: You see, reality for supermodels is not the reality that normal people are used to. They're rich, they're young and they're totally beautiful. For some people it can become an obsession. I know a few models who take pills for their skin – in fact a lot of models; but then it is your job. What I don't understand is how they can keep going so long. It sounds easy money being a catwalk model, but there are fittings and rehearsals as well as the show itself. I feel so tired. I've never been aware of the girls taking drugs to keep them going – but some probably do to keep up with the day.

Presenter: Lisa had this to say about the pressures on her following her meteoric rise to fame:

Lisa: I don't know about being an up and coming 18 year old. Sometimes this job makes you feel 50. You have to grow up fast doing modelling – it makes you older. You have to book flights, sort out your finances and get wise to people.

Presenter: Another concern of Lisa's is the bitchiness that inevitably accompanies a career on the catwalk. She admits she is still capable of being hurt by it (fade…)

Keith Walker

There were two reasons why I applied for my first job – money and parental threats. Looking back to those first few days after leaving school my strongest memory is one of sheer joy of being able to do absolutely nothing every day. I knew it couldn't go on, though, and after a while I started applying for jobs. My first interview was at the BBC where a fearsome personnel officer asked me questions that, to my surprise, I found I was able to answer. Anyway, I was given a six, yes six month contract to work on the night shift at BBC running copy to the presenters, photocopying and delivering cups of tea to those in need.

The two things I learnt were to rely on others' experience when you've got none of your own, and to do what you're told. The vast majority of the time I followed the routine, doing the tasks I'd been set, gradually getting to know the people I worked with and enjoying what I was doing.

Everyone was older than me, and it surprised me at first that it was possible to build up relationships with these people that were totally different from those I'd had with parents or teachers. Outside the BBC building in North London the world was quiet and dark, but inside, there we were, all working for the same end, giggling behind the presenters' backs, arguing and supporting each other like, well like a large extended family.

I really enjoyed those six months, oh er apart from the times late in the evening when I had to leave my girlfriend and friends with the immortal words 'sorry, I've got to go to work'.

And I still remember BBC for – of all things, the breakfast. At the end of the night's work I would head for the canteen with my work mates, buy a big breakfast and then we'd sit outside next to the river. We'd just chat and sit in the sun and know that when we left for home and a bit of sleep, everyone else would be just starting their working day. It was a wonderful feeling.

Key

1   (a) Modelling and working on a night shift (delivering copy and drinks).
    (b) They both enjoy(ed) their jobs.

2

	Lisa	Keith
a good salary		
interesting work		✓
good promotion prospects		
a good pension scheme		
acceptable working hours	✓	
good people to work with		✓
a good physical environment		
job security		
status and prestige		
freedom		

✱ Speaking: ways of comparing

2   The discussion work follows the exam format of Paper 5 Phases C and D.

Key

2   1   It's more important… It's not so important…
   2   It's much more important…
   3   It's so much more important … It's nothing like so important … There's no comparison … It's not half so important… You just can't compare them…

B

Will I get a job?

Reading

1–3   This article looks long and serious. Don't be tempted to read it word for word.

1   Set yourself a time limit (e.g. three minutes). Read only for specific information.

2   You can do this activity by yourself. If you don't know the words look in the text for clues rather than going straight to the dictionary.

Tapescript

2   1. haphazard
   2. a correlation
   3. to inherit
   4. affluent
   5. to capitalise
   6. plain
   7. a peer
   8. to rise through the ranks
   9. awkward
   10. a high-flier
   11. to cope
   12. a self-help manual
   13. to forge your way to the top

✱ **3**   This is a multiple matching task of simple design. This type of task (with one level of matching) tends to occur in the first part of Paper 1. Gist read in 2 minutes.

✱ **4**   This is a Paper 3 exam practice task, gapped sentences. To complete it successfully use the same techniques as for cloze texts. Also read for gist to identify the general topic of each paragraph to see which sentence is likely to go where.

Key

1   having wealthy parents
   good looks
   being tall
   being good organisers
   getting on with people
   having a difficult childhood
   going on courses
   reading self-help manuals
   trying different things when what you've tried hasn't worked
   the right attitude and motivation
   coping with disaster
   leaving school early

2   Possible answers:
   haphazard – chance
   a correlation – a relationship
   to inherit – to receive as an heir
   affluent – well–off
   to *capitalise* – to make the most of
   plain – ordinary, unremarkable
   a peer – someone of the same age
   to rise through the ranks – to go up the ladder of promotion until you reach the top
   awkward – difficult, hard to get on with
   a high-flier – an ambitious person who has made it to the top
   to cope – to manage in difficult circumstances
   a self–help manual – an instruction book that is designed for those learning on their own
   to forge your way to the top – to fight your way steadily to success

3   A 6   B 15   C 17   D 4, 10   E 10   F 5   G 9   H 11, 12

4   1 F   2 E   3 C   4 A

Listening

Tapescript

Presenter: Richard Price knows from bitter <u>experience</u> how fickle fortune can be. Last June he became the proud owner of a <u>degree</u> which he thought would be the key to a glowing future in broadcasting. Eight months on, he is unemployed and penniless;

his only offer of a job in the past few weeks is to sweep the floor of an abattoir.

Richard's story is just one example of the downward spiral that has struck thousands of college leavers. Unemployment among them is suspected to be running at the highest level for nearly a decade; at anything up to 12%.

Jo Morris is another unemployed graduate. She graduated as a landscape architect. Here's her story:

Jo: Like most students I really worked hard for my final university exams, and then I got very drunk. And that was it. It felt as if I'd fallen off a cliff. Suddenly there was nobody to talk to. I was lonely and very isolated. It started to affect my opinion of myself. I could feel my self-esteem and confidence draining out of me.

Presenter: Gary Roberts is also a graduate, this time in international marketing. He's found the alienation of unemployment compounded by relatives and friends who can't understand why anyone with a degree should land on the dole.

Gary: Yeh, it's like having a physically disabled brother or something. People just don't realise how widespread graduate unemployment's become, so as far as they're concerned, I'm a failure.

Presenter: But these college leavers are still nourished by hope: Jo Morris is expecting to start a job soon in her chosen profession of landscaping, and Gary Roberts has kept on filling in application forms even though two of the jobs he was shortlisted for fell through before he got to interview. As for Richard Price, he's been bruised by the whole experience.

Richard: That's right. I just never thought it could backfire. I knew it'd be difficult to land my dream job, but it never occurred to me that I wouldn't be able to find any job at all. Well I was stunned, to be honest. I've got no regrets though. I'd do it again. Those three years in college really developed my personality. I know I can do it now. I know I can achieve my ambition to be a director. I know I will get there… eventually.

Key

1 1 B, C, D, E   2 B, C, D, E   3 B, C, D, E

Grammar reminder: more words for linking sentences/clauses

Key

1

REASON	PURPOSE	RESULT
since	in order to	owing to
seeing as	so that	due to
because	so as to	
because of	so	
as	in order that	

2 b1   c3   d7   e6   f4   g2

Vocabulary summary

1 Revise the vocabulary of the unit before you begin.

Tapescript

Answer these questions as quickly as you can. We will give you a clue – just a letter – and you must say the word, for example: What 'l' works in a library? The answer is 'librarian'. Another example: what 't' means you've learnt how to do what you're doing? The answer is 'training'. Now for the real quiz; let's begin:

Number 1.	What 'e' designs or makes engines or machines?
Number 2.	What 'd' makes drawings or plans for buildings?
And number 3.	What 's' gives legal advice to customers and barristers?
Followed by number 4.	This 'p' means you're on your way up.
And number 5.	These 'q's' help you get jobs.
And number 6.	This 'p' is a power to impress and influence.
Here comes number 7.	Pigs do this 's' and so do some humans when they laugh.
And number 8.	This 's' means you're really not pronouncing clearly.
Followed by number 9.	What 'b.m.o.' means the way you did something?
Here's number 10.	What 'u.t.' means it all depends on you?
How about number 11?	When you are this 'a' you have a lot of money.
Try number 12.	This 'p' is the same age as you.
And number 13.	This 'c' means you can manage.
Followed by number 14.	What 'h.f.' means you're rising and near the top.
Number 15.	This 'c' means there's a relation between things.
Followed closely by number 16.	This 'i' comes from your parents usually.
And number 17.	This 's.d.' certainly doesn't help you.
Number 18.	This 'b' means you have no money at all.
Next to last number 19.	You fill in this 'a.f.' to put in for something.
And finally number 20.	You get this 'd' when you complete a university course.

2 Remember that collocations are words that frequently occur together e.g. to study hard, to pass an exam, industrial revolution.

3 In this activity just write down the names of people these collocations remind you of. It doesn't matter who you are reminded of. If a word reminds you of nobody leave it blank. The idea behind this activity is that a colourful association for the collocations may help you to remember them better.

Key

1
1 *engineer*
2 *draughtsman*
3 *solicitor*
4 *promotion*
5 *qualifications*
6 *prestige*
7 *to snort*
8 *to slur*
9 *by means of*
10 *up to*

11 *affluent*
12 *a peer*
13 *to cope*
14 *a high-flier*
15 *a correlation*
16 *inheritance*
17 *self-destructive*
18 *broke*
19 *application form*
20 *degree*

C

Paper 2 (Writing): Section A

Introduction

This section of the paper is designed to imitate real-life writing situations e.g. writing a letter to a language school after you have read brochures from different schools, writing a letter of application after you have read the job ad. and job details.

The examiners assess the writing not just in terms of its language accuracy but very much in terms of its communicative power. For this part of the exam:

- Read the source documents carefully and extract from them the relevant information.
- Don't lift text inappropriately from the source documents.
- Plan your answer carefully, paying attention to the order in which you present information.
- Read the instructions very carefully and make sure you carry all of them out.
- Use appropriate language (i.e. formal, informal or neutral language) and appropriate layouts for the types of texts and target audience concerned.
- Write accurately using the full range of language that is appropriate to the task.
- Always check your work for inaccuracies after you have finished it.
- Pay equal attention to information content, appropriacy and accuracy.

NB The marks awarded for Section A are out of the same total as for Section B, so don't spend all your time on Section A just because it looks longer.

Key

2   Possible answer:
In this task you have to read one or more introductory texts before you write your answer because the texts contain information about why you are writing, who to, what about, why, and in what style.

How to approach Section A tasks

Memorise the steps **identify, select, connect**.

3 and 4   The features of formal and informal language are tendencies rather than hard and fast rules; formal language is generally used in formal situations and vice versa, but much language use is neutral and also people can and do use informal language in formal situations and vice versa.

Key

1   Some possible joining words:
for sequencing: *first, first of all, firstly, then, next, finally, last of all*
for contrasts: *but, however, on the one hand…on the other, in spite of…*
for adding information: *and, what's more, in addition, moreover*

3   1   You normally write informally to friends because you know them well. You write formally to people you don't know or to people in some kind of authority.

2   Informal writing gives the impression of friendliness, sometimes of lack of planning and improvisation; formal writing gives an impression of anonymity

3   David's letter
4   David's letter
5   David's letter
6   David's letter
7   P. Simmons' letter
8   P. Simmons' letter
9   David's letter

The letter from David is informal and the one from P. Simmons is formal.

4

Features of formal language	Features of informal language
longer sentences	shorter sentences
few contracted forms	more contracted forms
precise punctuation	loose punctuation
precise vocabulary	less precise vocabulary
more use of words derived from Latin	more use of Anglo-Saxon based words
more complex grammar in sentences	simple sentence grammar
more anonymous style	more personalised style

Eight: Crime and punishment

A

Crime and society

Starter activities

1–2 Make sure you cover the pictures after looking at them. The key allows for some flexibility of interpretation about what is happening during the robbery.

Key

1
1   an off-licence (i.e. a shop where you can buy – but not drink – alcohol)
2   2 (+1 in the car?)
3   30s–40s?
4   dark trousers, anoraks/jackets, hats
5   woolly hat, baseball cap, earring, stubble
6   shotgun and bag
7   8.00 p.m.
8   car
9   towards the city

Reading

1 Think about the headline and what clues it gives to the likely content of the text. Remember that by looking at the title, headline etc., before you read a text, you can activate a lot of useful information.

2–✱3 The first activity introduces some of the more specialised vocabulary in the text, while the second requires you to read the text in more detail.

4 These activities are designed to help you understand how referring expressions are used in the text.

Key

1   firing an air pistol; the judge

2
1 G	8 E
2 H	9 C
3 F	10 M
4 L	11 B
5 D	12 N
6 I	13 J
7 K	14 A

3   1 B 2 D 3 B 4 A 5 C

4
1   *a Colwood–area teenager, the accused teenager, the 17–year–old boy, he, her client, the boy*

2   *a Colwood–area teenager – a*
the accused teenager – d
the 17-year-old boy – c
he – b or e
her client – d
the boy – b or e

3   *pellet pistol – a pellet gun, a handgun, a gun, a weapon, an air pistol, the pistol*
an 11-year-old boy – his victim, the young cyclist, he, the boy, the young victim, the younger boy, him, the victim
three young males – the group, the boys, the teenagers, them
defence counsel – Dianne McDonald, she, McDonald
a car – the vehicle, the car

🔈 Listening

✱ **1–2** Before playing the tape, check your understanding of each of the crimes and punishments listed. Think about the sort of vocabulary associated with each one.

Tapescript

V1: At Liverpool Crown Court yesterday, two fifteen-year-old boys were found guilty of deliberately starting a fire. The fire last summer completely destroyed a children's playground in a city park and caused over 100,000 pounds' worth of damage. The boys were each sentenced to 100 hours of community service and the judge ordered them to help in the reconstruction of the play area.

V2: In Saudi Arabia this week, four Pakistanis were beheaded for smuggling drugs into the country. The severity of the sentence shows how seriously the Saudi Arabian authorities regard the crime of drug-trafficking and is intended to act as a strong warning to foreigners visiting the country.

V3: In the Philippines, a woman who killed a man with a single punch has been jailed for ten years. Jessica Arenasa punched Verdandino Redilosa after he teased her about her dress as he drank with friends.

V4: The Crown Court yesterday heard how a mother became angry when her son's school sent her a form to update. The woman, aged 32, attacked a secretary and bit a teacher's leg after being told that the headmistress could not see her immediately. She was given a two-year probation order.

V5: Michael Bassani was convicted at the Suffolk County Court this week of being at the wheel of a car while under the influence of alcohol and of causing criminal damage after he crashed into a telephone box in the centre of town. The judge stated that it was a miracle no-one had been hurt. Bassani was given a £200 fine and his licence was suspended for 3 months.

Key

1   1 C 2 D 3 A 4 F 5 G
2   6 H 7 B 8 C 9 D 10 E

* Speaking

1–2 There are no 'correct answers' for 1 or 2 (Speaking). The results will depend very much on your own background and your views.

Grammar reminder: reporting orders/requests/advice

Remember, these reporting verbs do not always have to take the person or people addressed as their object, e.g. *he requested silence, she advised caution.*

Key

1 a *ordered/the bank clerks –* 'Put your hands above your heads!'
   b *warned/them –* 'Don't touch the alarm!'
   c *told/the youth –* 'Your behaviour was/has been stupid and dangerous.'

2 2 The judge instructed the jury to disregard the evidence of that witness.
   3 The bank clerk begged the gunman not to shoot.
   4 The thieves commanded the shopkeeper to open the safe and put the money in the bag.
   5 The policeman advised the students to lock their bicycles whenever they left them anywhere.
   6 A/My friend urged me to report the theft to the police.
   7 The court forbade the young man to possess guns, ammunition or explosives for five years.
   8 The detective warned his men not to touch anything until they'd dusted for fingerprints.

B

Crime and the writer

Starter activities

2 Ruth Rendell is one of Britain's most famous and popular crime novelists. She has won many awards and several of her novels have been successfully dramatised for British television.

3 The term "blurb" is commonly used to describe the summary of contents which you find on the back or inside cover of a book.

Reading

1 The article you are going to read is Ruth Rendell's own account of how 'A Fatal Inversion' was dramatised for television. Read the article quickly, ignoring details.

2 Read the article again more carefully, and make notes in answer to the questions.

3 These activities focus on some of the vocabulary in the text which relates to novels, TV/film production etc. They also deal with aspects of word-building.

Key

1 She was very satisfied because the TV adaptation was faithful to the book.

2 1 the young man who came to design her conservatory
   2 her own garden
   3 Ecalpemos – 'someplace' spelled backwards
   4 its contemporary setting, the high level of suspense in the plot, the youth and vitality of the characters
   5 the choice of the house, the furnishings (carpets, curtains, pictures, ornaments), the design of the garden

3 1 a *setting, publication, adapted, plot, story*
     b *the small screen, shooting, cast, acting, performances, actors, video, viewers*

   2 *adaptation – to adapt, adaptable, adaptability, an adaptor*
     production – to produce, a producer, a product, productive, productivity
     setting – to set, a set
     film – to film, filming
     performance – to perform, a performer, performing (arts)
     actor – to act, an act, actress, acting, action, active, activity

Grammar analysis: relative clauses

These activities help you to understand and practise using relative clauses. In activities 4 and 5 notice the difference between a defining relative clause and a non-defining relative clause. The information contained in a defining relative clause is essential in order to distinguish clearly the main clause.

A non-defining relative clause provides supplementary rather than essential information about a main clause and is normally enclosed in commas.

In sentence (a) the relative clause is a defining relative clause. In sentence (b) the relative clause is a non-defining relative clause.

Key

1	first part	relative pronoun	second part
	a terrace	*on which*	*there were statues*
	the country house	*that*	*had been picked as the setting*

2 *who, whom, which, where, when, that, whose*

3 1d *whose*
   2c *where*
   3e *where*
   4b *when*
   5a *who*

4 1b, 2a and 3a contain defining relative clauses.
   1a, 2b and 3b contain non-defining relative clauses.

Listening

1–7 This short story was originally published in a popular weekly magazine and has been recorded in the style of a short story broadcast for radio.

Tapescript

There it lay – small, black, business-like – on the centre of the table, the red cloth forming a backdrop like some exclusive window display. Light reflected off its shiny smooth contours. The man's fingers caressed the surface, tracing its outline, marvelling at its functional lines and economy of design. He picked it up and balanced it in the palm of his hand, enjoying the feel of it, and the way it adapted comfortably to his grip. The compact object was lighter than he'd expected. He pressed the catch that emptied it and then reloaded once again. This was the first time he'd used one but, now he'd got the hang of it, it seemed relatively simple. He was certainly getting better at each attempt. Satisfied, he finally slipped it into his jacket pocket. It was a snug fit. He patted his coat, confident that it would not be noticeable to anyone unaware of its presence.

(tone) He began to get cold feet, wondering whether he would actually have the nerve to go through with it. He'd lost count of the times he had gone over it, visualising the possible snags. He recalled the feeling of inspiration when the idea had first occurred to him, although its audacity had filled him with apprehension. Set in his ways, he was perhaps a little old fashioned – he certainly wasn't cut out for this sort of thing. He would draw attention to himself. Naturally reticent, he'd always shunned the limelight – going out of his way to avoid any kind of fuss or confrontation. But it was rather late in the day to harbour second thoughts now. One thought outweighed the rest, helping him overcome his hesitation. It's now or never, Jim – you won't get another chance. If he didn't grasp the opportunity, he would would always regret it. He must think positive. It was quite feasible that he would achieve his objective. And if he didn't? If truth were told, he was past the point of caring. He would at least have the consolation of knowing that he had tried. He fought the bitterness that threatened to overwhelm him. Why on earth should he be placed in this position? Things should never have been allowed to get so out of hand. It didn't seem fair. Life wasn't fair.

(tone) "Jim, could you pop into the library for me?" Dorothy was slowly coming down the stairs. Quickly, he checked the living room for any telltale evidence. He thought it was better that Dorothy didn't know. Her health was failing rapidly and, on top of everything else, their son David's breakdown had been the final blow. She'd already suffered too much. If he pulled it off, she'd know soon enough. He put on his spectacles and studied his face in the mirror above the fireplace. The last eye test he'd had resulted in a prescription change and the thick-rimmed frames had certainly helped to change his appearance a little. As extra insurance, he picked up his cap and pulled it well down over his face. He mentally ticked off his checklist. A growing anger helped to strengthen his resolve – he would do it for Dorothy. It was purely by accident that he had found out what was going on.

(tone) He arrived early, but quite a large crowd had gathered outside. She was already there. Fortunately, he saw her first and was able to dodge out of sight before she spotted him. The crush of people afforded him plenty of cover. It was essential that she remain ignorant of his presence and what he planned to do, otherwise his careful plan would be jeopardised. He found a

seat towards the back, on the end of a row. The interior of the hall was warm and there was a noisy buzz of conversation. His new glasses misted over and he removed them to wipe the lenses. It was essential that he could see as clearly as possible. He patted his pocket, reassured by the shape tucked away inside. A display of colourful pictures on the nearest wall caught his attention and, for a moment, his thoughts started to drift. How he wished things had been different. They could never have foreseen the outcome. She had become totally vindictive, seeming to delight in all the heartache and unhappiness she'd caused. He sighed. It was too late now for regrets…the damage was done. The lights dimmed. Once the interior was dark, he'd feel safe enough to remove his cap. There was a strong smell of peppermint. A fat woman sat next to him chewing, an open bag of sweets on her huge lap. She glanced at him and looked about to start a conversation. It was no good, that was the last thing he needed. He'd have to move. Turning round, he could see a small group of people standing at the back – they'd obviously arrived too late to get seats. He decided that perhaps it would be better to join them. Standing up would also give him a much better vantage point. Anxious to draw as little attention to himself as possible, he rose quietly and edged his way towards the back. She was clearly visible, seated several rows back from the stage, her dark, wavy hair contrasting with the pale cream collar of her coat. Was she conscious of his gaze? He used to joke that she had eyes in the back of her head. Carefully, he removed the expensive purchase from his jacket pocket. It had cost a lot of money, more than he could really afford, but he considered it worth all the expense. It seemed an ideal solution to the problem. He then checked his line of vision to ensure that nothing was blocking his line of fire and tried to keep his hands as steady as possible. He aimed towards the stage area, his finger tensed.

(tone) The hall lights went out and the red stage curtains began to open. The moment he was waiting for had arrived. Just for a second he thought he had fluffed it. His hands felt clumsy and wooden, and he nearly dropped it. But then he regained his composure. A feeling of elation swept over him. He could do it. He *would* do it. She was completely off her guard. And now it was too late – there was absolutely nothing she could do to stop him. He pressed the zoom switch on the tiny camcorder and directed it at the brightly lit stage. Pressing the record button on the miniature camera, he focused on his objective. It was a struggle to contain his emotion. The bitterness and frustration were forgotten as the elderly man concentrated on the actions of the children and, in particular, one small boy. The old man's heart swelled with pride. It was Jamie, their beloved grandchild. Their only grandchild. Their estranged grandchild. Dorothy would be thrilled when he showed her the recording. She would be able to see how much Jamie had grown. She'd be so proud, watching his role in the end of term school play…

Key

2 Possible answers: apprehensive, hesitant, bitter

3 Dorothy – in poor health, has a son, upset by her son's nervous breakdown
Jim – wears spectacles, has a son, keeps a secret from Dorothy
1 elderly
2 husband and wife

6   Jim and Dorothy are an elderly couple whose son has suffered a nervous breakdown probably due to the failure of his marriage. Their estranged daughter-in-law has made it difficult for Jim and Dorothy to stay in contact with their grandson.

✱ Writing

As preparation, think about the elements usually included in a review of a book/film/TV programme/etc.

Vocabulary summary

1   This paragraph describes the court system of Britain and many other countries.

Key

1	1 crime	6 defence
	2 trial	7 Witnesses
	3 jury	8 evidence
	4 prosecution	9 judge
	5 defendant	10 sentence

C

Paper 3 (English in Use): Section B

Introduction

Remember that being able to recognise and correct errors and inappropriacies in written work is a valuable skill.

Identifying and correcting errors in a text

1–5   These activities focus your attention on different types of error which can be found in written text and on the importance of correct spelling, punctuation and sentence structure.

Key

1–3

aged 32	→	aged 32,	missing comma
bite	→	bit	wrong form of verb
sons	→	son's	missing possessive apostrophe
bournemouth	→	Bournemouth	capital letter missing in name
yesteday	→	yesterday	missing letter in a word
two year	→	two-year	missing hyphen

4   Most lines contain an extra word.

5   Unnecessary words: *he, the, did, all, be, when*

Exam practice 1

1–2   These two tasks give you the chance to work through CAE–type exercises. Try to use the approaches identified and discussed in previous activities.

Key

1	1 *their*	4 *chaos. People*	7 *delivered*
	2 *thousands*	5 *hit",*	8 *additional*
	3 *✓*	6 *Hatch*	9 *$150,000*

2	1 the	6 was
	2 when	7 of
	3 from	8 at
	4 which	9 that
	5 ✓	10 more

Choosing appropriate words and phrases to use in a text

1–5   These activities show how vocabulary and structure can be used to reflect a degree of greater or lesser formality in what we write.

Key

1   C and A, B and D

2   A a personal letter to a friend – informal
B a car park notice – formal
C an official letter – formal
D a short note to a friend informal

3
Formal	Informal
immediate settlement	clear straight away
account	bill
legal proceedings initiated	take to court
loss or damage	pinched or bashed
cannot accept liability	college won't want to know

4   *broken into – burgled*
got home – arrived home
found – discovered
'd smashed – had forced
got in – gained access to
cheque book and credit cards – valuables
£25 in – £25 worth of
worth – valued at
couple of rings and a brooch – items of jewellery
gone – stolen
a terrible mess – considerable damage
put out – issued
had something to do with – been involved
a couple of characters – two young males

5
(1) burgled	(8) £25 worth of
(2) arrived home	(9) items of jewellery
(3) discovered	(10) stolen
(4) had forced	(11) considerable damage
(5) gained access to	(12) issued
(6) valued at	(13) two young males
(7) valuables	(14) been involved

Exam practice 2

This task gives you the chance to work through a CAE-type exercise. Remember that all the gaps should be completed using no more than 2 words.

Key

(1) *quarrels/arguments/ disagreements*
(2) *started/begun*
(3) *individuals*
(4) *organisations/agencies*
(5) *answer*
(6) *sides*
(7) *fix (up)*
(8) *talk about/talk through*
(9) *job/task*
(10) *keep things/everything*
(11) *an answer/a solution*
(12) *suits*
(13) *keen/eager*
(14) *more information*
(15) *a ring/a call*

Nine: Feelings

A

Recognising feelings

Starter activities

✳ Tapescript

2 1. It makes no difference to me, whatever you say.
2. That's fabulous, the best news I've heard in years.
3. I'm not very sure, I really can't decide, you know.
4. It was my favourite pen – I'd had it for years – my grandfather gave it to me when I was a child – where on earth can I have put it?
5. This wretched computer – why can I never get it to work properly?
6. I don't know, I don't really – I've tried and tried and it hasn't got me anywhere, has it?
7. I'll do it, I've absolutely made up my mind – I don't care how long it takes me.
8. Mm, I like your suit. I'd give an arm and a leg for a suit like that.

Key

2 1 *indifference*
2 *delight*
3 *uncertainty*
4 *sadness*
5 *frustration*
6 *weariness*
7 *determination*
8 *jealousy*

3 *fright, downheartedness, elation, boredom, loneliness, reluctance, aggression/aggressiveness, confusion, fury, fascination, frustrated, angry, desperate, uncertain, delighted, sad, irritated, determined, depressed, jealous, weary, indifferent.*

✳ Speaking

This activity follows the format of phases C and D of the Paper 5 (Speaking) paper.

📼 ✳ Listening

Tapescript
1–2

Daughter: It's not fair. Why can't I go?
Mother: We're not saying you can't go; we just want you to make sure that you're going to go in a safe way.
Daughter: Oh well, it is safe. I know loads of people who've done it and had a really good time. You're just…you're just being…you're just being spoilsports. You never let me do what I want to do.
Father: Charlotte, you're not serious anyway.
Daughter: I am serious. I've saved up all the money to go. I'm not asking you for any money. It's not like I'm trying to sponge off you or something.
Father: It's going to cost you a fortune. Anyway, why would you want to go to the States?
Daughter: It's not going to cost me a fortune, that's the whole point; the flights are cheap, and then this bus trip's really, really cheap. That's why young people go on it.
Father: [What bus trip?]
Mother: All sorts of people will be travelling on that bus, you know, any…any number of undesirable people…
Father: [Just a minute, I didn't know anything about a bus trip.]
Daughter: [You're such a snob, mum.]
Father: You're not seriously thinking about going on a bus around the States!
Mother: It's got nothing to do with being a snob [yes]! I just would much rather you stayed in one place, and just had a holiday in one spot, and didn't keep travelling around all over the place.
Daughter: …we do that every year, like when we went before and I had to do exactly what you said, and it was…I just…I just want to do something on my own. I'm 16, it's about time I was allowed a bit of my…you know a bit of my own freedom.
Father: Who are you thinking of going with?
Daughter: Clare. And her mother and father are fine about it, not like you.
Mother: Yes, but Clare…
Father: Clare…
Mother: Yes, but Clare's that bit older than you.
Daughter: No, she's not; she's only six months older than me.
Father: Wasn't it Clare that you went to Brighton with only three months ago, and took a lift off some stranger when you'd when you'd missed the last bus home?
Daughter: Yes, but
Father: This is the sort of thing you get involved in.
Mother: Now look, don't [it's ridiculous] try and stay calm, shall we?
Father: She's useless in this country; I can't imagine her going all that way.
Daughter: Well, I'm going anyway, I don't care what you say.
Mother: Now, Charlotte, Charlotte, if you just…
Father: You're not, my girl.
Daughter: I am.

Mother: Charlotte, will you listen to me now. Now look, if you want…if you're prepared to just go to Los Angeles and stay with Bob and Carol, then that's absolutely fine with both of us, isn't it?

Father: Exactly [no].

Daughter: There's no way I'm going to stay with them; there's no way…

Father: Well, you get on with their children…Ted and Alice, they're lovely. [they're awful]

Mother: Look, Los Angeles, there's so much to see and do there, you know, you can stay in the one place and just move around from there. Then you can go to Disneyland and you can…you know you can lie on the beach.

Daughter: But you can't see nearly as

Father: And Bob taxies you round everywhere; he's so good to you.

Daughter: You can't see nearly as many places as cheaply as you can on this bus trip.

Father: And you can't get into trouble, that's the thing, isn't it?

Daughter: It's not. Look, it's advertised in all the student magazines. It's advertised in the newspapers;…it's you know…the green tortoise, you know, it's famous, loads of people…

Mother: Well, I've never heard of it.

Daughter: Well, that's not surprising, is it?

Father: My daughter's turning into a teenage mutant ninja turtle before my very eyes. [it's ridiculous]

Daughter: No dad, it's a play on words; you know…Greyhound bus; it's the opposite of that…green tortoise. Oooh, get real!

Mother: Well, obviously it doesn't go very fast, does it?

Father: Let's talk about this some other time when we've all calmed down. Alright, Charlotte.

Daughter: That's the whole point…[fade]

2 This is an exam format task, typical of Section C of Paper 4. You may need to hear the cassette twice to complete this task.

3 Before you begin this activity check that you know the meaning of all the words.

4 Try to repeat the extracts as expressively as possible.

Tapescript

1. It's not fair. Why can't I go?
2. Oh well, it is safe.
3. You're just being spoilsports.
4. It's not like I'm trying to sponge off you or something
5. What bus trip?
6. You're not seriously thinking about going on a bus?
7. I just want to do something on my own.
8. This is the sort of thing you get involved in.
9. Well, I'm going anyway, I don't care what you say.
10. You're not my girl.
11. There's no way I'm going to stay with them; there's no way.
12. Oooh, get real!

Key

Possible answers

1 (a) a daughter, a father, a mother
 (b) It's about the daughter's wish to go with a friend on holiday to the States and to travel round while there.
 (c) The daughter wants to go on holiday with her friend and travel round the USA. The mother doesn't mind her daughter going but doesn't want her to travel around. The father seems unhappy about her going at all, especially with her friend Clare; he also doesn't want her to travel around.

2 1 F 2 M 3 D 4 D 5 F 6 M,F 7 M 8 D 9 F

3 Possible answers:

rude - D, F	furious - F
firm - D, F	appalled - F
frustrated - D	reasonable - M
angry - D, F	worried - M
resentful - D	

Reading

✱ 1 As this task requires reading for gist, set yourself a time limit (e.g. three minutes).

2 Make sure you use all the clues in the text to try and decide the meaning of these words.

Key

1 e

2 Possible answers
 1 affecting the functions of the body
 2 a hormone that induces fear, anger etc.
 3 red
 4 covered in sweat
 5 a neutral substance given as medicine that is intended to work because the patient believes it is effective medicine
 6 salt solution
 7 a 'pretend' participant
 8 very happy/ecstatic
 9 initiate/cause/set in motion
 10 to consider

3 1 D 2 B 3 B 4 D

Grammar analysis: phrasal and prepositional verbs

The purpose of this section is to help you distinguish between the sometimes different grammatical patterns of phrasal and prepositional verbs.

Key

1 a T
 b T
 c T
 d F – they generally occur in informal language;
 e F – it is normally unstressed in prepositional verbs and stressed in phrasal verbs;
 f T

2 1 phrasal
   2 prepositional
   3 phrasal
   4 phrasal
   5 prepositional
   6 phrasal
   7 prepositional

3 There are no fixed answers to this activity.

Vocabulary summary

Key

2

Noun	Adjective	Negative Adjective	Adverb	Verb
happiness	happy	unhappy	happily	
delight	delighted	–	delightedly	to delight
determination	determined	undetermined	determinedly	to determine
irritation	irritated	–	irritatedly	to irritate
desperation	desperate	–	desperately	to despair
boredom	bored	–		to bore
guilt	guilty	not guilty	guiltily	
frustration	frustrated	–	frustratedly	to frustrate
contentment	content	discontented	contentedly	to content
fright	frightened	–		to frighten
depression	depressed	–		to depress

B

Expressing your feelings

✳ Listening

Tapescript

Amy stood at the school gates under the shelter of her umbrella. She looked at her watch. Rosie was very late. Wherever could she be?

All the other children had spilled out, laughing and talking several minutes ago. Now the playground was deserted and it had started to rain. But there was no sign of Rosie.

Amy peered anxiously up and down the road. Rain drummed on her umbrella and splashed to the pavement. Her feet felt uncomfortably damp. She checked the time again, frowning in puzzlement. A small boy ran down the street to where his mother stood waving beside a car, his school bag jolting rhythmically at his side.

'Excuse me!' cried Amy. 'Have you seen my daughter anywhere? Rosie Lister, she's called.'

The boy stopped, panting for breath. 'Ah, sorry,' he said, 'she's not in my class.'

Amy drew her coat more closely around her and went through the gates, across the empty playground and into the main entrance.

Could it be that Rosie had stayed behind for some reason? It would soon be Easter. Perhaps she'd wanted to finish drawing her a card or a picture.

Maybe Miss Edmondson had stayed behind too, to help her. She was such a conscientious teacher. And Rosie liked to make a proper job of things. That must be the answer. Why hadn't she thought of it before? Rosie would be quite safe with Miss Edmondson.

Amy fondly imagined her daughter's Easter offering – eggs and chicks and rabbits, all in crayon with big, uneven writing. She would pin it on the kitchen wall with the other drawings when they got home.

But the school was empty except for the cleaners and a teacher Amy didn't know. They hadn't seen Rosie and seemed anxious for Amy to leave so they could go home.

Fighting her rising panic, Amy sat on a desk and tried to think clearly. Rosie had never before left school alone, but supposing, just supposing that today as a surprise, she'd gone to the newsagent's on the corner to buy her mother an Easter egg? Sometimes they called there on the way home, so she'd know the way.

Mr. Phillips, the young owner of the shop, was as jovial as ever. 'Hello there, Mrs. Lister, and how are you this wet and weary day?' 'Has Rosie been in just now?' asked Amy, scanning the empty shop, checking behind the tall stand of cards.

He shook his head, his smile fading. 'I'm sorry, I haven't seen her, I'm afraid.' 'I don't know what to do, she's missing!'

Amy's hands were icy cold and trembling. She found it almost impossible to think straight. Where could Rosie be?

Deep in her mind something was stirring, like a foreboding, a certainty that this wasn't going to be alright, a mother's instinct crying out to be heard and urging her to do something quickly before it was too late.

'Now calm down,' said Mr. Phillips. 'Don't get all worked up. It won't do you any good. It's bound to be alright, you know, kiddies being what they are.'

But Amy wasn't reassured. 'I'm going,' she said, trying desperately to keep her voice steady. 'Perhaps we've missed each other and she's there waiting for me. Yes, that's what I'll do.'

Outside it was raining harder than before. Amy splashed heedlessly through the puddles, her heart racing. And then she saw Rosie! She was standing on the corner of the High Street holding Miss Edmondson's hand. She was skipping on the spot in excitement and waving. Her hood was down and raindrops glistened on her chestnut hair. 'Mummy,' she called, 'Mummy, I'm here.' Thank heavens she was alright! Tears of relief filled Amy's eyes and spilled down her cheeks. Oh, what a fuss, a silly, silly fuss she'd been making. She started forward desperate to reach Rosie and hold her safely in her arms again.

But something was wrong. Her feet wouldn't move properly. She felt breathless and dizzy. Rosie was running towards her now, getting closer and closer, but swirling and shimmering before her eyes. And then, as the little girl reached her, the world slid gently away into the blackness.

Mr. Phillips stood, white with shock, mumbling replies to the policeman's questions. He couldn't take his eyes from the slim bundle lying on the pavement, over which someone had mercifully draped a coat. 'It's Mrs.…er…Mrs. Lister. She'd just been into the shop. I can't believe it. I was talking to her a few minutes ago, that's all. Are you quite sure we can't do anything for her, officer?'

The policeman shook his head. 'I'm sorry,' he said. 'There's no response at all. I think it must have been a heart attack. That's what it looks like anyway. We'll know for sure when the ambulance gets here.' 'She was in a bit of a state in the shop,' said Mr. Phillips, 'Quite upset. I suppose that could have brought it on.'

The policeman frowned. 'What was she upset about?' Mr. Phillips pulled out a large handkerchief and blew his nose self–consciously. 'Er Rosie, her daughter,' he said at last. 'The little girl died, you see, in a tragedy at that school around the corner. Rosie and a teacher, both killed outright.' He shook his head. 'Mrs. Lister's got a bit confused recently,' he said, 'wandering around the streets looking lost, hunting for her little girl. She used to wait outside the school for her sometimes. It was pathetic to see her.'

Rain dripped on to the policeman's notebook, making round, swollen blotches on the paper. 'Poor lady,' he said quietly. 'Yes,' said Mr. Phillips. 'It's awful. All these years…I wasn't even born when it happened, you know. Rosie and her teacher had stayed behind after school for some reason and a gas boiler exploded, right next to their classroom.'

For one last time, and to reassure himself that nothing more could be done, he lifted the rain-splashed coat and gazed down at the pale, wrinkled face with its frame of soft white hair. It was then he noticed the old lady was holding something in her hand…a child's drawing, it looked like, in bright crayon and with big uneven words. He could just make out the letters – 'HAPPY…EASTER…'
And Mrs. Lister, at peace at last, was smiling.

2 This is an exam format task. Please note, however, that listening texts in the exam are not as long as this one, nor do they include stories.

Key
2 F D A I B H C E G

3 Possible answers
spill out – to come out in an unorderly way; as the children left school
peer – to look closely or intently; Amy looking up and down the road
drum – to thump; the rain on Amy's umbrella
jolt – to bump; the boy's bag against his side
scan – to glance briefly; Amy looking round Mr. Phillips' shop
stir – to begin to move; Amy's feelings
glisten – to sparkle; the raindrops on Rosie's hair
swirl – to whirl about; Rosie running towards her mum
shimmer – to glisten and shine; Rosie running towards her mum
mumble – to speak indistinctly; Mr. Phillips talking to the policeman
frown – to look puzzled or discontented; the policeman talking to Mr. Phillips

gaze down – to look in a non–focused way; Mr. Phillips looking down at Amy

Grammar reminder: *as* and *like*

Key
a	*as*	f	*like*
b	*as*	g	*like*
c	*as*	h	*like*
d	*like*	i	*as*
e	*like*	j	*as*

Reading

3 Use both grammatical and vocabulary clues to work out the answers. It's also useful to gist read the paragraphs to see what might fit where before reading more carefully.

Key
2 • women found to have greater verbal fluency, prefer amicable solutions, be non-competitive, be better at arithmetic, be capable of storing more random information and better at identifying matching objects in a hurry
• men found to be more decisive, aggressive and driven by money, more mechanically-minded, better at activities which require spatial reasoning
• different levels of testosterone in men and women
• babies thought to be born with mental gender differences
• evidence suggesting that three-year-old boys are better than girls at targeting objects

3 1 E   2 A   3 D   4 B

4 Possible answers:
1 a clue that can't be missed
2 the slightest hint of a breaking of the voice
3 a wrinkled brow
4 not to hide your feelings, be up front with your feelings
5 be slightly better than
6 make you consider a problem from a new perspective
7 people who take part in experiments
8 add seriousness to
9 aim at and hit
10 from the complete beginning
11 straightening out an imbalance

Writing

There is a tradition in English language newspapers of readers' letters to the editor. Before you start writing this letter, plan it by thinking about the style you are going to use, what effect you want to have on the reader, the level of formality of language, and the useful letter conventions you may want to employ, such as:

Dear Sir/Madam/Editor, With reference to your article of (date) *on* (subject)

Dear Sir/Madam/Editor, I am writing to…

Your letter should follow these guidelines:

Target audience:	Newspaper editor
Style:	Probably formal or neutral, though informal would be possible
Format:	A letter with appropriate layout and paragraphing
Effect on reader:	This will be up to you, the strength of your opinions and your style
Content:	Paragraph 1 will make reference to the article and where you read it
Paragraphs 2/3:	These will outline your position and your reasons for adopting that position. They will probably contain references to arguments used in the article
Paragraph 4:	Is likely to contain your conclusion
Paragraph 5:	Is likely to contain a request for a reaction from the editor
Language:	Check the accuracy of the grammar and vocabulary you've used.

C

Paper 4 (Listening): Section C

An example of CAE Paper 4, Section C

Tapescript

Presenter: At 9 a.m. on the 24th of July Yvonne Lawrence was going to the post office to buy a pint of milk. A woman rushed up and stopped her as she reached the door.

Yvonne: She told me she'd seen an armed man inside.

Presenter: Seconds later, Yvonne spotted a man, wearing an anorak with a hood hiding his face, dash inside.

Yvonne: It suddenly dawned on me that I was witnessing an armed robbery.

Presenter: Peering through the windows of the post office and general store, Yvonne recognised a friend trapped inside with the two raiders. As the seconds ticked by, she became more frightened. Then the raider wearing the anorak backed out of the door with a shotgun. Yvonne watched him dash across the road. Moments later she heard a car starting up. Then a second man raced out of the post office.

Yvonne: Without stopping to think what I was doing, I swung at him with my shopping bag, then I thought to myself 'You're not getting away with this,' and I went for him!

Presenter: Startled shoppers looked on as plucky Yvonne grabbed the robber. Collapsing to the ground, he was pinned down by her 200 pound frame.

Yvonne: I held him by his pullover and an elderly man trapped him by his legs.

Presenter: Then they were joined by another woman who helped to hold on to him until the police arrived. Mother of three, Yvonne, was determined to keep hold of the robber.

Yvonne: I knew his accomplice had a gun and there was a good chance he was armed, too. But it didn't cross my mind at the time. At first he struggled, but after a while he seemed to realise it was hopeless and just lay on the road.

Presenter: The full impact of it all hit Yvonne when she heard sirens and saw the police van pull up.

Yvonne: I started shaking then. I thought about what I'd done and I was really frightened!

Presenter: As the police bundled the robber into their van, they found a gun lying beside him and the post office cash box which he had dropped as he tried to flee. Yvonne was even able to give the police the number of the getaway car. When she arrived home later, her children were shaken by their mum's brush with danger – and very proud.

Yvonne: My eldest son, Kevin 23, who's a bus driver, kept asking 'Are you really a hero mum?' – he'd heard about it from his work mates. For once my 200 pound build was an asset! I'm always thinking about dieting, but this time I think my weight actually helped!

Presenter: The Metropolitan police praised Yvonne's bravery, but a senior officer warned the public to be wary of trying to apprehend an armed criminal because it could end in disaster. He added that she did really well, though, and was quite a hero. The post office owner, James Concagh, is also full of praise.

James Concagh: I was still inside the post office when Yvonne helped catch the robber. She was so brave. I just can't thank her enough.

Key

1 C 2 D 3 D 4 A 5 C 6 D

Exam practice

Tapescript

Interviewer: So Jason, I understand from erm, you know, various newspaper clippings that I have read that you're a bit of a parachute freak on the quiet [oh yeah]. Do you want…can you tell me a bit…how did you get into that?

Jason: Well, I first parachuted when I was in the aircadets; I mean, you know, long before starting up the singing; erm so, I did a jump, and we did like about 4 days' preparation; it was just brilliant, and erm…I tried to then every six months or so go back to the same place, because if you stayed with the cadets you could keep doing two jumps a year; and then eventually I had to leave the cadets, erm, but then, once I started getting a bit of money from the singing, it's something I started looking into again; and I joined this club which is down at Bigginhill [yes]; and that's where, that's where I go sort of every weekend now.

Interviewer: Every weekend you do it [absolutely, yeah]; my goodness, that must be quite…I mean it's not a cheap thing to do, is it, parachuting?

Jason: No, but er, well, with the two records in the charts at the moment [well obviously, mm, mm], money's no object at the moment; we don't just jump from there, I mean we go out to…we've been…We've jumped in France and we're going out to America next year [yes]; we're going to jump off the canyon. [My goodness]… you know, down into the Grand Canyon.

Interviewer: It must be terrifying, though?

Jason: Well, it's, sort of, it's…I think that's the appeal of it; it's like…I can't imagine being quite as frightened as you are before you jump, but then once you've jumped then, it's just the most amazing feeling, 'cause…the fear sort of transcends into something else [yes]…which is, which is the greatest excitement I think you could ever have really.

Interviewer: I've always, I've always wondered… is it very, when you first jump out, is it very noisy or is it very quiet?

Jason: Yes, no, it's very well, that again is a funny thing, if you, well there's a book written, I can't remember the guy, but he wrote this book about parachuting last year, and he said; it is incredibly noisy in a literal sense, but at the same time it's a feeling of great calm as well; especially when you jump out the plane, and obviously there's the noise of the wind in your ears, but…you know, there's just you and the elements [yes] and the ground underneath you, and if you're like at ten thousand feet or something, I mean you can't even see it moving, and it's like you're suspended above the earth; it's marvellous.

Interviewer: And when your parachute opens, is there…is there an enormous change?

Jason: Oh yeh, yeh, it's a big, big jerk.

Interviewer: And it actually, does it pull you up?

Jason: It feels as if…because you're not aware by that time that you're actually falling, so it suddenly feels that you've been hoiked upwards; whereas in fact, of course, it's just deceleration; you're slowing down quickly [I see, yes] and it feels as if somebody's just pulled you up on a piece of string; but a it's a very violent sensation, but at the same time it's a good sensation because you know well the parachute's opened, so [which must be a relief] yes, yes, yes.

Interviewer: And have you ever had any, any bad falls?

Jason: Yes, there was a time when I was jumping with Mark who's also in the group, and erm, we were…we were quite close together in this jump, and er his parachute opened early, and er, some of it sort of got attached to me, or was wrapping around me in the wind; and I thought I've got to

get away from this; and erm, and then mine went off; I don't know what happened, I must have been struggling to try and get the… his cord away from me and pulled my ripcord; and so the two chutes were sort of then tangled up, and er, you know, I could see him looking at me, wondering what to do, and erm, we just followed really what is the basic procedure, which is to get rid of your main chute and then rely on your reserve [yes]; and we were at a good height; there was no danger of hitting the ground or anything, so we, we…I released mine and he released his more or less at the same time; and then we separated and then er opened the reserve chutes and that was fine; down we went; and you know it was a bit of a shaker at the time; [I bet] a change of clothes when we got down (laughter) but that's the most dodgy thing that's happened, yes.

Interviewer: And, er…have you erm, have you got any you know, any future plans? Is there anything that you…as far as the parachuting goes?

Jason: Well, we're doing the Canyon thing next year, we hope [yes, yes, lovely]. Yeh, but me mother wants me to give it up. She…but I'm going to keep doing it.

Interviewer: It must be quite hair-raising for those nearest and dearest to you…

Key

(1) *was a member of/belonged to* (2) *a parachuting club* (3) *he makes money from his records/gets money from singing* (4) *before you jump* (5) *excited* (6) *hoiked up/jerked up* (7) *a friend's/Mark's* (8) *the Grand Canyon*

Ten: Assertiveness

A

What is assertiveness?

Starter activities

2 Be sure to distinguish between the weakly and strongly stressed syllables.

Key

1 **Some possible answers:**
   for the person under the umbrella: *victimised, rejected, defensive, uptight*
   for the person behind the counter: *threatening, humiliating, angry*

2 `threatening, res`pectful, re`jected, re`bellious,
`victi`mised, clear, `equal, de`fensive, `self-`confident,
hu`mili`ating, `angry, `up`tight, di`rect, `fed-`up

3 The person under the umbrella is passive and the
person behind the counter is aggressive.

Reading

1 Read for detail.

Key

1 c

2 powerful – wimpish
strong – small
effective – ineffectual
communicative – uncommunicative
calm – angry
easy – stroppy
good – tempered - grumpy
appropriate – maladroit
at ease – anxious
passive – aggressive
aggressive – passive
respectful – manipulative

3

1C	7A
2F	8C
3D	9C
4B	10D
5A	11D
6E	

Grammar analysis: modal verbs for speculation and deduction

3 Try to imagine as many explanations and predictions as you can.

Key

1 1, 2, 3, 6, 7, 8, 10, 11

2 (a) can, may, might, must
(b) `have`
(c) certainty in the speaker's mind
(d) a degree of doubt in the speaker's mind

▣ Listening

✱ 2 Write short answers only, as required in the exam for this kind of task (Paper 4 Section A). NB You are marked for accuracy of your spelling in the exam (except in proper nouns).

Tapescript

Lecturer: Most 'unassertive' people take no for an answer much too easily. There is a growing awareness in our society that this tendency is jeopardising the rights of large numbers of people. For example, in recent years there has been an upsurge in consumer protection organisations and pressure groups. This is a welcome development as there will always be a need for such organisations to protect the interests of individuals and minorities in a competitive society. The danger is that we become over-dependent on professional workers for our rights and lose the art of asserting ourselves. It is better for your self-esteem and relationships with other people if you can learn the art of persistence for yourself.

Now, we have to learn to ignore some of the not-so-pleasant messages that may be ringing in our unconscious minds, such as:

'If you ask once more, I'll flatten you'
'You're a nagger – just like your mother'
'Don't make a scene'
'Anything to keep the peace'

The main technique that we use in assertiveness training to practise the art of persistence is called Broken Record. When a record is scratched we hear one sentence over and over again until we reach screaming pitch and jump up to turn it off.

Broken Record is the skill of being able to repeat over and over again, in an assertive and relaxed manner, what it is you want or need, until the other person gives in or agrees to negotiate with you.

Now this technique is extremely useful for:
- dealing with situations where your rights are clearly in danger of being abused.
- coping with situations where you are likely to be diverted by clever, articulate but irrelevant arguments.
- situations where you are likely to lose your self-confidence because you know you could be affected by 'digs' and 'put-downs' to your self-esteem.

The beauty of using Broken Record is that once you have prepared your lines you can relax. You have nothing to worry about because you know exactly what you are going to say, however abusive or manipulative the other person tries to be.
As with most assertive techniques, it must be used appropriately. It is a self–protective skill and is not designed to foster deep, interesting conversations and friendships with people! It is primarily of use in situations where your time and energy is precious.

For example:
- when a persuasive colleague rings you up at tea time and you don't want to spend hours explaining why you cannot help with doing some shopping for him.
- and when it's your only free shopping day in the month and you want your money back on unsatisfactory goods so that you can quickly replace them elsewhere.

When you've mastered the first Broken Record exercise, you can then move on to practising a more sophisticated variant. You can practise conveying the same message but using slightly different words each time.

Key

1 **Some possible answers:**
Broken Record; An Assertiveness Technique; A Step towards Assertiveness etc.

2 (1) *consumer protection organisations*
  (2) *dangerous*
  (3) *messages*
  (4) *repeating*
  (5) *gives in*
  (6) *agrees to negotiate with*
  (7) *don't change/stay the same*
  (8) *time and energy*
  (9) *slightly different/similar*

2

	Formal	Informal	Assertive	Passive	Aggressive
2. description	✓				✓
3. complaint	✓		✓		
4. complaint	✓			✓	
5. refusal	✓	✓		✓	
6. refusal		✓			✓
7. criticism	✓		✓		
8. request	✓			✓	
9. request	✓		✓		

B

Being assertive

🔲 Listening

1 This is a gist listening activity. Your answers should only be brief notes. Replay the cassette to see how much intonation can vary.

Tapescript

1. Get out of my way, will you?
2. Brown…made of leather…wheels on it…it's got a big scratch on top of it and my name, of course, on the name tag.
3. I bought these shoes here last week and I'm afraid they've split already. Could you change them for me, please?
4. Erm, excuse me, erm, sorry to bother you, it's these shoes, you see, well, erm, I'm afraid…
5. Oh…erm…well…erm…well…not really…I
6. No way, definitely not.
7. I'd just like to talk for a bit about your work. I know you've been getting a bit behind of late.
8. Erm…sorry…excuse me…er…could you pass me the sugar please?
9. Excuse me, could you pass me the sugar, please?

Key

1 1 **asking someone to get out of the way**
  2 **describing a lost suitcase**
  3 **complaining about split shoes**
  4 **complaining about shoes**
  5 **refusing**
  6 **refusing**
  7 **discussing someone's performance at work**
  8 **asking someone to pass the sugar**
  9 **asking someone to pass the sugar**

Speaking

You could carry out this activity by taking on both parts in the role play.

Reading

Key
Correctness and context

The following go with one another:
really fantastic/had a ball/smashing/great/a lucky so and so/look us up/quite a riot/See ya!

very enjoyable/had a good time/lovely/nice/very lucky/come and see us/a lot of fun/All the best

most entertaining/was quite enchanted/ particularly agreeable/charming/most fortunate/allow us to return your hospitality/a pleasant little occasion/Warmest regards

Being consistent

Possible answers:
1 *inflicted on my property – you've done to my place*
2 *a fag – a cigarette*
3 *Furthermore, I require – and*
4 *OK – acceptable*
5 *were possessed by a feeling of intense consternation – suddenly became very anxious*

✳ Writing

This is an exam format task found in Paper 3, English in Use.

Key
Possible answers
(1) *complaint*
(2) *several*
(3) *receipt*
(4) *managed/was able*
(5) *However/ Unfortunately*
(6) *broke down*
(7) *highly/clearly/quite*
(8) *considerable*
(9) *refund*
(10) *inconvenience*

Grammar reminder: adjectives + prepositions

Key

1   (Possible answers)

[with]:   *indignant, rude, sensitive, angry, discontented, fed up, pleased, hostile, kind, capable, bad*

[at]:   *indignant, astonished, angry, discontented, pleased, capable, bad, deficient, fed up*

[for]:   *responsible, pleased, thankful, bad*

[to]:   *reluctant, rude, sensitive, kind*

[about]:   *hostile, kind, ashamed, bad, right, doubtful*

[of]:   *capable, ashamed*

[in]:   *interested, bad, deficient*

'At' has a meaning of 'in relation to', 'about' has a meaning of 'on the subject of'.

C

Paper 5 (Speaking): Phase B

Phase B of Paper 5 is designed to give each participant a chance to talk uninterruptedly. The tasks are usually some kind of 'describe and identify/match/draw/order' activity. You are <u>not</u> marked down for giving the 'wrong' answer i.e. identifying/ordering/drawing etc. incorrectly. The assessors mark the quality of the communication.

How should candidates behave?

Passive or aggressive behaviour will not help you but assertive behaviour certainly will, particularly as you are assessed for your interactive abilities.

Key

1   passive
2   assertive
3   aggressive (probably)
4   assertive
5   assertive
6   passive (possibly)
7   assertive
8   aggressive

What are the examiners looking for?

These assessment criteria are used by the examiners to assess the whole of the Paper 5.

You might try to carry out the Phase B task by taking on the roles of both participants. Record yourself speaking and then try to assess your performance using the exam's assessment criteria.

Ways of learning: situations in which we use different styles of language

Think about when appropriate uses of language occur in your own language. See Unit 7, Section C page 100 for the characteristics of formal and informal language.

Key

2   topic of conversation, setting of conversation, status of participants in relation to one another, how well the participants know one another.

Revision Exam Practice 2

Paper 1 (Reading)

This task is taken from the multiple matching section of the Reading Paper. For information on how to approach this section of Paper 1, see the information and the facsimile questions on pages 86–90. The answer sheet for the Reading Paper is reproduced on page 298.

Allow approximately 20 minutes for this task.

Key

1	A, B, C	8	B, C
2	D, E	9	B
3	A, B, C	10	E
4	A	11	A, B, C, D
5	F	12	D, E
6	B, C	13	D, F
7	C	14	A

Paper 2 (Writing)

This task is taken from section A of the Writing Paper. For information on how to approach this section of Paper 2, see the information and the facsimile questions on pages 99–100.

Allow approximately one hour for this task.

Key

Possible answer:

1. Letter

Dear Sir or Madam,

I've just read your ad for camp helpers, and I'm really interested in applying for one of these jobs. In your ad you ask for details of my experience, qualifications and personality. Let me give them to you.

I'm 20 years old and I come from Spain. I finished school two years ago, and since then I've been working as an assistant in a sports shop selling all kinds of sports goods and advising customers on the kinds of things that would be best for them. So as you see, I have constant contact with the world of sport. I also play a lot of sport – I've belonged to a tennis club for the last 8 years, I play basketball, and in the summer I go to the sea and do all the usual sea sports: swimming, water skiing, canoeing etc. In fact, last year I helped out at a beach sports club.

As for my personality, well, I suppose I'm quite extrovert. I love being with other people. Generally I'm quite patient and I like to think I'm understanding.

Could you give me some further details about the job? I'd like to know about what kind of accommodation there would be, whether I'd receive any pay, and also what kind of working hours I'd be expected to do each day and for how many days a week. Many thanks.

I look forward to hearing from you and hope that you will be able to offer me a job.

Yours faithfully,

2. Postcard

Thanks a lot for the card and the ad – that was a great idea. I've written off already and hope to hear soon. So we should be working alongside one another in a couple of months' time. Keep your fingers crossed.

Cheers,

Paper 3 (English in Use): Section B

This task is taken from Section B of the English in Use Paper. For information on how to approach this section of Paper 3, see the information and the facsimile questions on pages 109–112. The answer sheet for the English in Use Paper is reproduced on page 299–301.

Allow approximately 30 minutes for this task.

Key

1	1	accepted	8	✓
	2	✓	9	shops
	3	paid	10	worth
	4	reduce	11	✓
	5	crime	12	help
	6	presence	13	arranging
	7	security	14	vision/visibility

2 Possible answers
(15) resident/residing
(16) not accept
(17) to establish/to determine
(18) essential
(19) unoccupied
(20) valuables
(21) unattended/unsupervised
(22) a personal/an individual
(23) admission/entry
(24) be reported
(25) regulations
(26) be obtained
(27) advisable
(28) to purchase

Key

1P	6M
2M	7P
3F	8P
4F	9F
5M	

Paper 4 (Listening)

This task is taken from Section C of the Listening Paper. For information on how to approach this section of Paper 4, see the information and the facsimile questions on pages 122–124. The answer sheet for the Listening Paper is reproduced on page 302.

Allow approximately 10 minutes for this task.

Tapescript

Mr Buckhurst: Now Flora erm sit yourself down. I've been talking to Mrs Petts er and as as you already know she has a few problems with you.

Flora: Just a few. Well er I've got a few problems with her as well.

B: Well that's what I wanted to hear.

F: Well I don't really want to go first because then I feel I have to put my neck on the line. Er, it's just er I don't feel I'm being given enough responsibility at the moment.

Mrs Petts: I think part of the problem is is is that you haven't really shown yourself really capable of taking any more responsibility.

F: Er but that's because you're not giving me the chance.

P: Ah well there are plenty of opportunities for you. Let me give you an example Mr er Buckhurst. [hm hm] Erm we we we recently have as you know been having training sessions with the new computer software. Now as far as I know according to Miss Beatty anyway, Flora didn't actually show up for the main for most of [yes, why is that?] she wasn't actually there.

F: Because I had to got to the Doctor's. I phoned you and it was all okayed.

B: Well Miss Beatty er

P: Fair enough on one occasion but I think I think as far as far as I can see there were four different occasions where you didn't actually show up for these sessions.

F: Yes but I had to make appointments because I had a series of tests being run and I had to go back for the results. I can't help that.

B: Yes but Flora does it sound to you as though someone that's doing this sort of thing is that interested in promotion?

F: Ha, well quite honestly I'd just given up the idea of promotion because every time I gave suggestions then they were just knocked on the head. I I mean I've got qualifications. I've got skills in Wordperfect, I've got all the right you know things for this job and I'm not being given the opportunity to use them and these training things they're just lip service as far as I can see. I've been asking and asking and by that time I've just had enough, because for me to go along to the training sessions would just mean that I would had had the training and then be left in the same place because that's what's happened before. That's what happened when I went away on that course last year.

P: The thing is though you see at the moment your job description says that you are a secretary therefore your skills are those of a secretary. Now it seems to me [yeah] that what you are saying is [want to] you actually want to be doing a different sort of job, which is not the job [I want] that is not the job which you are being employed to do.

F: No, I do not do not want to be doing a different sort of job. What I don't want is to be called into the office and asked to take memos all day and just type letters because quite frankly [Miss Mac] you could employ a pet dog to do that.

B: Miss MacDonald please please …

P: But that's what you're employed to do.

B: Exactly that is part of your job description.

F: I I I

B: You surely understood that when you took the job.

F: Yes I do understand that, but what was specified at that interview was that there would be a chance to move onwards and upwards possibly for promotion in the …

B: By impressing Mrs Petts and Miss Beatty …

F: Why

P: She

F: But

P: How long have you actually been here?

F: Three months.

P: Well exactly – three months – and what are you expecting you're expecting now to be to be doing to having the sort of responsibility that somebody who'd been here a year wouldn't have, and the other thing is that your whole attitude is that of somebody reluctant, surly, bad tempered. You never come to er er brer er group meetings you know and you …

F: I do come to group meetings.

F: I don't come to group meetings as often as I should because all I do is get shouted down by you and I don't think that it's fair just because you're in a position of authority over me that all that you do is crush my ideas and it comes to a point when any employee is in a position where they get tired of giving ideas and giving of themselves and just come in and do the job and leave and and hence you end up with employees bored and fed up and they've had no challenges and no responsibilities which is how I feel and I've been made to feel like that (fade)

Key

1	P		6	B
2	B		7	B
3	F		8	P
4	F		9	F
5	B			

Paper 5 (Speaking)

This task is taken from Phase B of the Speaking Paper. For information on how to approach this section of Paper 5, see the information and facsimile questions on pages 133–134.

Eleven: Learning

A
Learning at school

Reading

1 Set a time limit, e.g. four minutes, for this gist reading.

Key

1 The schooling in the United States is unusual because it is undertaken by Brazilian students who come to the States for a short time to live and study. St. Christopher School, Letchworth is unusual because it is a boarding school and also has a particularly relaxed and supportive atmosphere.

✱ 2 A 1,2   B 1,2   C 1   D 1   E 1,2   F 2   G 1   H 1,2   I 1,2   J 2

3 1 budget, cramming, host family, curfew, tough, lug, economize, the target, reimbursed
   2 a soap, gossip, wave machines, strict, the loo, roller skates, clay trainers, snooker, a chore

✱ Writing

This is an exam practice task similar to those in Section 2 of Paper 2. Before you write your letter decide who the target reader of the letter is, what style would be best for the letter, the effect of the letter on the reader and the organisation of information in your letter.

Key

Content:	This should cover all the points mentioned in the rubric.
Register:	This will probably be neutral to informal as it is a letter home.
Effect on target reader:	This is likely to be positive in as much as the letter will be friendly. It could also worry those at home if the content showed that the writer wasn't settling in very well.
Language:	This should be accurate and show as much range as is demanded by the letter (possibly not much in this case). Wording should not be lifted inappropriately from the rubric.

Grammar reminder: indirect questions

Try to remember and write down the rules about how to make indirect questions before you read them. You could then check your answers against what it says on page 145.

Key

1 (1) *if I was/am enjoying my stay*
   (2) *how long I've/I had been here*
   (3) *if I like/liked American food*
   (4) *why I came/had come to the United States*
   (5) *what I will/would remember most and best about the United States*

📼 Listening

Tapescript

Woman: Well I always thought I wanted to be a hairdresser, you know, because I thought, I thought I wanted to do that from the age of about 5 and then I did it for my work experience.

Man: Oh, I did work experience as well.

Woman: Did you?

Man: Yeh, I…I did it in a lift factory of all places [Oh, Cor]. I don't…I do know why…because it was really really close to my house, so I thought [Oh, right]…well, I might as well [yeh] kind of thing and it was O.K.

Woman: Did you go on and work in the factory?

Man: No, I didn't really. Well, the only reason I did it was because it was so close to my house [yeh] that I could kind of get home early [yeh] and it would be better than going to school.

Woman: So, what sort of things did you have to do for that then?

Man: Well. I don't know, you just kind of join in on lots and lots of tea-making really. Erm, but you join in, just to see how it works, walk around and become a part of it. What…did you actually cut people's hair?

Woman: Oh no, I mean it was really boring. I worked at this place called Raimondo's, and I thought I'd be like washing hair and stuff like that [yes], and all I ended up doing was sticking the towels in the tumble drier, erm mopping up a bit of hair [yeh] and putting the…filling up the conditioner bottles. It was really boring [yeh], so that put me off for life. So I'm going to do physiotherapy now.

Man: Oh, that's good, but I mean, was it worth doing do you think I mean…?

Woman: Well, it was a good laugh and I…I met my boyfriend there [oh], and we're getting engaged [that's alright]. That's that's the only good thing I'd say about the work experience really.

Man: Hm, I haven't got many good things to say about it really, but then it did introduce me to the workings of a factory [right] erm, so I've got a bit of insider knowledge now. [right, yeh]

Key

1 The woman worked in a hairdresser's doing things such as cleaning and filling up bottles. The man worked in a lift factory making cups of tea.

2 A–W
B–M
C–W and M
D–W
E–W
F–M
G–W

B

What makes us learn

Starter activity

NB Hothousing is a way of bringing up children. It involves intensively teaching very young children to do all kinds of things e.g. language, reading, writing, maths, that are usually taught much later to children.

Listening

This extract is taken from a true story.

Tapescript

Presenter: There was little that was conservative about Aaron Stern when, thirty-five years ago, he gathered the media at a Brooklyn hospital for a remarkable event. Stern was about to launch perhaps the most flamboyant and brazen hothousing experiment of all time. 'Gentlemen of the press,' he announced as he was photographed by the cot of his infant daughter, I'd like you to meet my daughter, Edith. I am going to make her a genius and a perfect person.'

Edith was to be a human experiment. Her father, who now lives in Miami, had developed a theory that the world's evil was nothing more than the result of barbaric stupidity. If men and women could be made more intelligent, he reasoned, they would henceforth be less likely to follow another Hitler. Edith was to be the incarnation of his ideas, and in our cynical world, of course, something of a hostage to fortune.

Aaron Stern could not work as he was disabled, so he began to devote his time to teaching and developing his child. He spoke to her constantly, holding forth on philosophy and explaining the theories of Darwin and Freud as he fed her from a bottle. His wife Bella was not permitted to nurse the baby. That, said Stern, was valuable learning time; Edith could read by the time she was two. He purchased second-hand volumes of the

Encyclopaedia Britannica and placed them in her cot. By the time she was four she'd read them. Aaron Stern took Edith to museums and operas. In fact, he took her everywhere he might want to go, reading, training, explaining, even when he could not tell if she understood.

She was able to speak in full sentences by the time she was a year old. From that moment onwards, while living in conditions of some deprivation (one room without a window) he conducted a running dialogue with her; she could read at two, play music at three, chess at four.

School was not a happy time for Edith. One teacher called her arrogant; another said she knew a lot of stuff, but had a mediocre mind. Her father withdrew Edith from state school at the age of nine to educate her full time at home. She had made no long-term friends, and entered college at twelve. At fifteen, Edith became an assistant professor of mathematics – the youngest in American history – at Michigan State University, while she studied for a doctorate.

Edith was not, Stern now stresses, a natural Einstein, but today she has an IQ of 203 and works for IBM in secret computer software research and development.

In most respects it would seem that as an adult, Edith Stern comes near to her father's ideal, though he sometimes complains now that she does not really love him. 'She doesn't have the love she should have for a father with a pacemaker,' he says. ('Do you love him?' we asked. 'Sometimes, yes,' Edith replied.)

Now thirty five with shoulder length brown hair and glasses that constantly slip down her nose, Edith is softly spoken but blunt and impatient, and does not suffer fools – or journalists – gladly.

Edith and her husband, a computer programmer, live in a house full of books, with one entire room full of science fiction. Her father thinks her preoccupation with science fiction is a waste of time; she regards it as a wonderful mental exercise and both she and her husband are active in the local sci-fi society. Edith is the mother of a six-year-old son, whom she teaches and hothouses much as her father taught her.

Key

* 2

> **A portrait of Edith Stern**
> 1 Father's name: Aaron Stern
> 2 Father's occupation: none; unemployed because of disablement/full-time hothouser
> 3 Mother's name: Bella
> 4 Methods employed by father to 'develop' his child: Constantly talking to her on advanced subjects, taking her to museums, operas etc., always giving her challenges, always exploiting any situation for its learning potential, full-time education at home
> 5 Age at which accomplished the following:
> read: 2
> read the *Encyclopedia Britannica*: 4
> spoke in full sentences: 1
> played music: 3
> played chess: 4
> went to college: 12
> became an assistant professor of mathematics: 15
> 6 IQ: 203
> 7 Current job: researcher in secret computer software
> 8 Physical description: brown shoulder-length hair, wears glasses
> 9 Character description: impatient, direct
> 10 Age: 35
> 11 Marital status: married (with one child)
> 12 Interests: science fiction

Reading

1 Set yourself a time limit e.g. two minutes for this gist reading.

2 Try to work out the meaning of the vocabulary items from the context if you don't know the meaning.

Key

1 It seems to suggest that both are strong.

2 *talent will out* – special abilities will reveal themselves
startling – amazing
to discern – to notice
to track down – to hunt
determining – deciding
a mapping technique – a way of showing where things are
a riddle – a puzzle
innate – inborn
a brain scanner – a machine that reads cerebral activity
distinctive – special
lateralisation – a process involving the development of one side of the brain
all–round – general
to give ammunition – to strengthen

3 a T
b F (she believes talent will out)
c F (he hopes he may have)
d T
e T
f F (she hasn't proved it; her studies seem to indicate that this is true in the States at least)
g F (lateralisation seems to occur more strongly in boys than girls; when it is extreme it seems to aid the ability to do mathematics)
h F (proportionally, Chinese boys seem to be better at maths than Chinese girls; however there seem to be more Chinese girls than American girls who are good at maths)
i T

4 (1) E (2) A (3) D (4) F (5) B

5 (1) spend   (5) style/way
(2) parental   (6) However
(3) cause   (7) sure
(4) both   (8) guarantee

Grammar analysis: the present perfect and present perfect continuous tenses

Key

1 (1) *present*
(2) *past*
(3) *influence/effects/results*
(4) *duration*
(5) *finished/terminated*

2 1 *have been studying*
2 *have never read*
3 *have really enjoyed/have really been enjoying*
4 *has marked*
5 *has always had*
6 *have been sending*
7 *has always believed*
8 *have been studying*

Vocabulary summary

Key

Possible answers:
ambitious – unambitious
tough – lenient
temporary – permanent
cosy – cold
strict – lenient or *tolerant*
ahead – behind
tolerant – intolerant or *strict*
dull – bright
fresh – stale
protest – acceptance
ban – allow
gifted – ungifted
exaggerated – normal
distinctive – ordinary
innate – cultivated

stimulating – boring
alert – dull
clear – unclear or *confused*
shoot ahead – lag or *trail behind*
fascinate – bore
narrow–minded – open–minded

Ways of learning

This section points out once again that it is not necessary to read in the same way for all tasks, and indeed that to do so can be counter-productive. How you read depends on why you are reading.

Key

2   understand the general meaning of the text: Section A, page 143, activity 1; Section B, page 148, activity 1
understand each word in the text: none
understand the details of particular parts of the text: Section A, pages 143-44, activities 2 and 3; Section B, page 148, activity 3
understand the general meaning of particular sentences: Section B, page 148, activity 4.

C

Paper 1 (Reading): Gapped paragraphs

Understanding lexical and grammatical clues

1   Note down the steps you go through to reach your decisions. This will help you do activity 2.

2   It is not always easy or obvious how to complete a gapped paragraph task. You should try to develop as systematic a way of approaching this task as you would for multiple choice, for example. Some gaps are usually easier to fill than others and you could begin with these and then tentatively try to complete the others by a process of elimination. What you need to do is get a feel for the argument/chronology/development of the text, so you can almost predict what will come next. See the key below for discussion of the various strategies.

3   Not all the clues in this text are circled!

Key

1   1A   2E   3C   4D   5B   6G

3   1   *my first week at university*
    2   *a first*
    3   *he slept late in the mornings*
    4   *adult life*
    5   *the sketchiest of weekly timetables...defining time*
    6   *a book/a few pages*

7   *lecture notes*
8   *strategy*

4   a   is not a good idea. Detailed understanding of the whole text is rarely required for this kind of task.
    b   is not a good idea. It will be quite possible to carry out the task without understanding every word. Reading on this level is also very slow and would eat up valuable time.
    c   is a good idea. Probably the best thing to do first with these texts is to read them for gist.
    d   may be a good idea but not necessarily. If some answers seem obvious from the beginning, it will be useful to note these down to act as clues for the rest of the answers. Be careful though, these answers may be wrong. They will need to be confirmed by further reading of the text and the completion of the other blanks.
    e   No, don't make final decisions as you go through. Just make tentative decisions which will need to be confirmed or otherwise once you have finished. All the text is so interdependent that if one answer is wrong at least one other answer will also be wrong.
    f   This can be a good idea, and some people certainly like to work in this way. Don't end up underlining everything though, as this could be quite confusing.
    g   There will probably be more than one clue for each gap. These may be before and/or after the gap.
    h   Yes, definitely.
    i   This can be a good idea, as it is quite easy to forget what you have decided should go where. It also helps you to read through the text in order when looking for further clues.
    j   This can be useful, especially if you aren't very sure of your answers, as it will help you get into the development of the text.

Exam Practice

Key
1 D   2 C   3 E   4 A

Twelve: Leisure activities

A

Time off

Starter activities

1–2 Use a dictionary if you need to and remember to check the correct pronunciation of any new vocabulary.

Key

1 surfing, watching a football match, going to the theatre, hill-walking.

2 Possible answers: reading, eating out, playing chess, attending a pop concert, taking a coach tour, drinking with friends.

Listening

1–✷ 2 There is inevitably some degree of overlap between the time-periods listed, but in general they are seen as being fairly distinct in English. ('The small hours' is the term often used to describe the early hours of the morning, anytime between about one and three o'clock in the morning.) Do not expect the speakers always to use the words in the answer options; they may paraphrase them or provide clues by which it's possible to infer the time of day being referred to and the reasons for a speaker's preference. This is often a feature of the Section D listening extracts and you need to be actively listening for relevant clues.

Tapescript

V1: I think my favourite time of day is probably first thing after breakfast…I like the feeling of the day still stretching out in front of you…and it's probably because I like to feel I have everything ahead of me properly organised, sort of neatly planned out…er you see, I'm not too good at coping with the unexpected!

V2: Yeah, funnily enough the best time of day for me is the middle of the night…um, I'm often awake for two or three hours in the very early morning, but I don't really mind because, that's the time when I do a lot of my thinking or reading, things I rarely have time to do during the rest of the day. I'm the sort of person who needs plenty of time and space to myself so, you know, perhaps it's just as well!

V3: I find it takes me a while to get going…and I'm terrible first thing in the morning so that's not my best time at all…but after lunch I'm usually raring to go and really keen to pack as much as I can into what's left of the day…and from then on it takes a lot to wear me out!

V4: I suppose I'm what you'd call a night-owl…by the time everyone else is ready for bed, I'm ready to get up and

go…which doesn't always go down too well with my friends and family. I've always been a bit unconventional in the hours I keep but then I've always been confident enough to do my own thing and not be forced into a so-called 'normal' routine.

V5: I think the end of the day is probably my favourite time…you know, when the working day is over and everyone's at home enjoying a meal together or just relaxing. Summer evenings at home in the garden…just as the sun's going down…that's the time when I get a real sense of contentment and well-being…I wouldn't want to be anywhere else!

Key

2	1	B		6	B
	2	H		7	F
	3	D		8	D
	4	G		9	C
	5	E		10	A

Reading

1 As usual, you do not need to read and understand every word in the text to answer the initial questions. Set yourself a time limit if necessary.

2 Try organising any new vocabulary from these two fields so that it becomes easier to learn and remember. For example, you could draw a pair of cartoons: one – a miserable man at work surrounded by think bubbles containing illustrations and vocabulary for the different leisure activities he wishes he was doing; the other – the same man, but much happier now because he's shown enjoying one of the leisure activities and surrounded by think bubbles illustrating aspects of the working life that he's temporarily left behind.

✷ 3 You will need to read the text more carefully to answer the multiple choice questions. Refer back to the guidance given in Section C of Unit 1 (page 26) if necessary.

Key

1 senior business executives; to take the services of a 'leisure adviser'

2 a *corporations, captain of industry, workers, tycoon, board of directors, schedule of appointments, senior executive, burnout, the office, faxes, overseas subsidiaries, deal, bankers, lucrative client*

  b *ease up, luxurious yacht, beach house, play golf, climb mountains, ride river rapids, go scuba diving, play tennis, holiday home, leisurely walk*

3 1 C   2 C   3 C   4 A   5 B

Grammar reminder: *would* and *used to*

Key

1	1	*used to*	2	*used to/would*	3	*used to*
	4	*used to/would*	5	*used to/would*	6	*used to*

B

Moving images

I often bring work home and finish it off while watching TV

Reading

1–2   Remember that this type of popular quiz is designed for fun and shouldn't be taken too seriously. You might like to consider the value or otherwise of such a quiz.

3   These activities focus on some commonly-used phrasal verbs in English.

After compiling a list of all the phrasal verbs from the two texts, focus attention on those particular phrasal verbs which you are less familiar with. To help yourself learn new phrasal verbs you could make up a display with examples or illustrations. Alternatively, keep two boxes/envelopes – one containing cards with the new phrasal verbs and the other containing cards with explanations and illustrations for the verbs. From time to time, pick out a card from one of the boxes and then challenge yourself to find the matching phrasal verb/explanation.

Key

3

turn on	*work out*
tune in	*send off*
find out	*finish off*
settle down	*fall into*
get to	*get out (and about)*
glaze over	*lie back*
put together	*guard against*
get off (to sleep)	*flake out*
jot down	*nod off*
look forward to	*miss out on*
flick between	*rush off*
jump at	

Grammar analysis: time clauses

Key

1   2 *until*   3 *when*   4 *before*   5 *after*

2   1b 2e 3d 4a 5c

3   a   *before, prior to*
     b   *while, whilst, during, at the same time, as, whenever*
     c   *after, subsequently*
     d   *when, the moment, once, as soon as, immediately*
     e   *since, until, till, by the time*

5   *...I dislike being interrupted while watching my favourite programmes...*
     ...when watching a debate...I often work out what I'd say...
     I am annoyed when my favourite programmes are being shown at the same time...
     ...when I watch a travel or holiday programme I'm transported into another world...
     I usually have the TV on in the background while I do jobs around the house

📼 Listening

1   Make sure you take time to think about the eight statements thoroughly before listening to the extract. This will help you to activate relevant vocabulary and aid your comprehension while listening.

✳2   The discussion on tape is quite long. On the first listening don't worry about understanding every word but focus on identifying the topic.

3   On the second listening try and concentrate on the various opinions expressed; you may still not understand everything but that needn't stop you from picking out the different speakers' opinions.

4   This time focus your attention during listening on the way in which speakers' comments are often punctuated with hesitation expressions. Notice that hesitating is a very natural feature of native-speaker English. Play the first quarter of the conversation to illustrate this (*in fact, um, you know*). Then go on and listen to the rest of the conversation and tick the other phrases used. Hesitating allows the speaker valuable time to organise their thoughts, restructure what they are saying, maintain their turn in the conversation etc. Learning to hesitate properly in English may help to make a non-native speaker sound more fluent.

Tapescript

V1:   ...(fade in) I remember actually seeing previews and trailers when I'd gone to see other films at the cinema, and I was completely put off because I don't especially like going to sit through a violent film, if I'm forewarned then I won't go and I, and I really didn't want to go and see that; what I think really upsets me more, if I go to see a film – and I've not been prepared in any way for the violence that actually happens (yes) within the film, that upsets me more; in fact I went to see, I think it was a Clint Eastwood film and it was it was a cowboy, and I just, I left, I actually walked out because I thought, had I 've been given the choice, had I have gone in with the knowledge that this was going to be a violent film – fine, but I wasn't, and I felt really subjected to something that I hadn't chosen and *that* upset me more...

V2:   Didn't, weren't you a bit naive to see (No!) to go into a Clint Eastwood cowboy film and not imagine you're going to see violence?

V1:   No I think not because I think with those sort of cowb- cowboy films they, you *do* expect a certain level of, um, high action (mm) and I'm prepared for that and they are action films and you know, the nature of sort of one character going through the entire film you come into these sort of violent sequences but a lot of people were meeting very very nasty ends and...

V2:   But, but I mean, I think I know the film that you're talking about and the thing is what you'd call high action is when you see, when guns go pop pop pop and people just get killed and the, and you're objecting to a film where you actually see the consequences of of of a gun being shot at close range (No...), and surely that makes the violence more real and more horrible, yes, but it makes you realise that it isn't just cowboys and indians; I mean people talk about cowboys and indians films and they're about killing (yeah, I…), but they're, but they're just bland entertainment, and a, and a film that makes you realise what real violence is (mm, I know, I know this…) how offensive you find it I think it's genuine…

V1: Yeah, I know this Nick, and I, and I appreciate what you're saying there but what, what I feel in this instance is actually I was drawn in to see a film that had been portrayed as being a sort of a wholesome action film – and, and I went in and to me what I saw was a completely different type of film.

V3: Don't you think the directors could do so much more by just leaving things to the imagination?

V1: I think, I mean, I think, I think the power of, of a good film is when you see something happening on the screen and then maybe there is a cut away and you realise something has happened and they don't actually have to spell it out and show all the blood (but I…)…

V3: Do you think the censors could do more? I've…

V2: I think the censors are a waste of time, really because it's like any form of prohibition, once the cat's out of the bag, so to speak, once there're violent films or whatever you're talking about you're trying to prohibit, once it's there people are going to get to it whatever (mm) and prohibition really just blurs the issue (yes, I…)

V3: But it, but it certainly stops a lot of outlets, if you, if you had a, if you had um censorship for videos for, you know as, as we do which are largely the same as censorship for films in the cinema, um, surely that would stop certain younger people getting hold of the wrong (no, not at all…)

V1: Well I actually saw the news only the other night and what's happening now, um, apart from the censorship that's already seemingly implied on video, you know, video nasties so-called shouldn't be available to, um, people below a certain age, but I mean older children or whichever video outlet is making it accessible for young children to actually see these things, but now there is a telephone line as well, so you can even just over your telephone tap in a certain number and pick up computerised images (mm), um, of all manner of porn and violent films, and the big worry in fact, it was, it was on the news only about a week ago, the big worry is that children are going to have easy access to this.

V3: Mm, so isn't that then the case for banning them all together?

V2: Well I don't, I just think, talking of banning and censorship is going down a blind alley because all it does is glamorise the things that you're trying to prohibit and people will get their hands on them whatever, and they'll be more inclined to try and see them when you, when you censor them than if you, you know, it's very difficult because you're in a position where you've gone this far, you've made the films, the films exist, and therefore people'll want to see them (fade)…

Key

2 c

3

	Opinion	Speaker's view
1	It's better to know if a film contains scenes of violence before you go and see it.	✓
2	Cowboy films don't usually show the real effects of violence.	✓
3	Violence on screen encourages violent behaviour in society.	
4	A good film is one where the audience is encouraged to use their imagination.	✓
5	Young people need to be protected from seeing certain films and videos.	✓
6	Censorship is unfair on both film-makers and the viewing public.	
7	There is a case for banning all pornographic and violent films.	✓
8	Censorship can simply make things appear even more attractive.	✓

4 *um, er, well, in fact, you see, you know, sort of, I mean, I think, so to speak*

✱ Speaking

If you can find an English-speaking friend, this activity gives you a chance to discuss further the issue of censorship. Try and make use in your discussion of the hesitating expressions from listening activity 4.

✱ Writing

Make use in your writing of some of the ideas and language previously encountered during this unit. Before you write, consider how to write an appropriate beginning and ending for a formal letter of complaint.

✱ Vocabulary summary

Key

2 1 C 2 B 3 A 4 C 5 B 6 D 7 B 8 D 9 A 10 C

C

Paper 2 (Writing): Section B

Introduction

During the course so far you have already carried out a number of writing tasks similar to those included in Section B of Paper 2. This section reinforces much of the work on writing done in earlier units and highlights important features relating specifically to the preparation and execution of Paper 2 Section B tasks. The three steps, identify, select and connect, reinforce and build upon approaches studied in Section C of Unit 7.

Key

(1) *4/four*   (4) *purpose*
(2) *1/one*   (5) *intended audience*
(3) *content*   (6) *250*

Identifying the task

1–3 These activities give you a chance to revise and practise identifying the important elements in any writing task: audience, purpose, content, organisation, style. There are no correct answers for activity 3 but you should be able to justify your suggestions.

Key

Possible answers:

1
- **Who am I writing for?**
- **Why am I writing?**
- **What am I going to include?**
- **How am I going to organise it?**
- **What sort of style am I going to adopt?**

2
1 **an English friend**
2 **to respond to his letter and offer some useful advice**
3 **thanks for the letter and enthusiastic response to the idea, ideas on places to visit, means of travel, places to stay, possible work, invitation to visit**
4 **order as in 3**
5 **friendly, positive, encouraging, helpful**

Selecting the format

1–5 These activities are designed to improve your awareness of issues relating to format and layout in writing tasks, and give you relevant practice. There are no correct answers for activities 3, 4 and 5, but again you should be able to justify the suggestions you make.

If possible, supplement these activities by looking at examples of English language newspapers, magazines, travel brochures, entertainment guides, information leaflets etc. This will help you develop a sense of the variety of formats and layout features which are possible, and the different effects which they create.

Key

1   1 B   2 C   3 A

2

Layout feature	Text A	Text B	Text C
section headings		✓	
numbering	✓		
shorter paragraphs		✓	
longer paragraphs			✓
instructions	✓		
letter layout			
note form (rather than full sentences)			
short, simple sentences	✓		✓
longer, more complex sentences		✓	
illustrations/diagrams			✓

Connecting the ideas

1–4 As you write, check that the style is consistent, appropriate referring expressions (e.g. pronouns) are used where possible, appropriate link words are used to help paragraphs proceed smoothly, and information is consistent from one paragraph to another, etc.

Ways of learning: understanding the instructions for a task

1–4 These activities are designed to raise your awareness of the importance of carefully reading and understanding the instructions for a writing task. The annual CAE Examination Report regularly states that students need to be encouraged to read the questions carefully and consider what type of writing is being asked for. The task instructions are skilfully designed to supply you with sufficient information about the context of a task to enable you to select an appropriate style and register. They also give precise guidelines on the necessary content. In the examination you should always choose sensibly from the selection of tasks on offer in Section B. For example, it might be unwise to choose a work-related writing task if you have little or no experience of work.

Key

1   1 **choose one task only**
     2 **follow the instructions given**
     3 **write about 250 words**

2   **the reader is a friend (informal style)**

     the format should be notes (not a report or an essay)

     the purpose is to provide useful/helpful information (and avoid anything irrelevant)

     the content should include how, where, who etc.

3 there is no correct answer for this activity but suggestions could include: *place in your own country, good holiday destination, account of how to travel, where to stay, what to see, anything else of interest*

4 they highlight essential information for the writer concerning the context and content of the task

h *moving her head*
i *move her head*
j *the situation*

The main function of these words is to avoid repetition and to make the text stick together.

2 a *it*
b *it*
c *do*
d *did too/so did other people/did so too*
e *did (it/so)*
f *do*
g *does*
h *it*

Pronouns and auxiliary verbs.

Thirteen: The world around us

A

It's a weird world

Reading

1 This text is a factual account, i.e. it isn't fiction. NB. in Christian tradition the Virgin Mary is said to be the mother of Jesus Christ. In many Christian countries it is common to find shrines to her on roadsides.

Key

1 The weird phenomenon is the different movements made by the statue.

2 a *wayside*   k *dissipated*
  b *tilted*   l *a gasp*
  c *shivering*
  d *intrigued*
  e *grotto*
  f *to witness*
  g *a shrine*
  h *swaying*
  i *shrugging*
  j *untoward*

✱ 3 1 A   2 D   3 D   4 A   5 A

Grammar reminder: cohesion through substitution

Key

1 a *the shrine*
  b *Virgin Mary*
  c *passers-by*
  d *to worship*
  e *worship*
  f *the statue*
  g *witness a miracle*

📼 Listening

1 Fictional texts such as this are not used in the CAE exam. This one is included here to give you an opportunity to listen to English for pleasure.

2 The answers to this question will vary from person to person.

4 Take notes on the story then try to piece it together with a partner if possible.

Tapescript

Story teller: The night was clear and fine above us. The stars shone cold and bright, while a half-moon bathed the whole scene in a soft, uncertain light. Before us lay the dark bulk of the house, its serrated roof and bristling chimneys hard outlined against the silver spangled sky. Broad bars of golden light from the lower windows stretched across the orchard and the moor. One of them was suddenly shut off. The servants had left the kitchen. There only remained the lamp in the dining-room where the two men, the murderous host and the unconscious guest, still chatted over their cigars.

Every minute that white, wool plain which covered one half of the moor was drifting closer and closer to the house. Already the first thin wisps of it were curling across the golden square of the lighted window. The farther wall of the orchard was already invisible, and the trees were standing out of a swirl of white vapour. As we watched it the fog-wreaths came crawling round both corners of the house and rolled slowly into one dense bank, on which the upper floor and the roof floated like a strange ship on a shadowy sea. Holmes struck his hand passionately on the rock in front of us and stamped his feet in his impatience.

'If he isn't out in a quarter of an hour the path will be covered. In half an hour we won't be able to see our hands in front of us.'

'Shall we move further back upon higher ground?'

'Yes, I think it would be as well.'

So as the fog bank flowed onwards we fell back before it until we were half a mile from the house, and still that dense white sea, with the moon silvering its upper edge, swept slowly and inexorably on.

'We are going too far,' said Holmes. 'We dare not take the chance of his being overtaken before he can reach us. At all costs we must hold our ground where we are.' He dropped on his knees and clapped his ear to the ground. 'Thank Heaven. I think I hear him coming.'

A sound of quick steps broke the silence of the moor. Crouching among the stones we stared intently at the silver-tipped bank in front of us. The steps grew louder, and through the fog, as through a curtain, there stepped the man whom we were awaiting. He looked round in surprise as he emerged into the clear, star-lit night. Then he came swiftly along the path, passed close to where we lay, and went on up the long slope behind us. As he walked he glanced continually over either shoulder, like a man who is ill at ease.

'Hist!' cried Holmes, and I heard the sharp click of a cocking pistol. 'Look out! It's coming!' There was a thin, crisp, continuous patter from somewhere in the heart of that crawling bank. The cloud was within fifty yards of where we lay, and we glared at it, all three, uncertain what horror was about to break from the heart of it. I was at Holmes' elbow and I glanced for an instant at his face. It was pale and exultant, his eyes shining brightly in the moonlight, but suddenly they started forward in a rigid fixed stare and his lips parted in amazement. Lestrade gave a yell of terror and threw himself downwards upon the ground. I sprang to my feet, my inert hand grasping my pistol, my mind paralysed by the dreadful shape which had sprung out upon us from the shadows of the fog. A hound it was, an enormous coal-black hound, but not such a hound as mortal eyes have ever seen. Fire burst from its open mouth, its eyes glowed with a smouldering glare, its muzzle and hackles and dewlap in flickering flame. Never in the delirious dream of a disordered brain could anything more savage, more appalling be conceived than that dark form and savage face which broke upon us out of the wall of fog.

With long bounds the huge creature was leaping down the track, following hard upon the footsteps of our friend. So paralysed were we by the apparition that we allowed him to pass before we had recovered our nerve. Then Holmes and I both fired together, and the creature gave a hideous howl, which showed that one at least had hit him. He did not pause, however, but bounded onwards. Far away on the path we saw Sir Henry looking back, his face white in the moonlight, his hands raised in horror, glaring helplessly at the frightful thing which was hunting him down.

But that cry of pain from the hound had blown all our fears to the wind. If he was vulnerable, he was mortal, and if we could wound him, we could kill him. Never have I seen a man run as Holmes ran

that night. I am reckoned fleet of foot, but he outpaced me as much as I outpaced the little professional. In front of us as we flew up the track we heard scream after scream from Sir Henry and the deep roar of the hound. I was in time to see the beast spring upon its victim, hurl him to the ground and worry at his throat, but the next instant Holmes had emptied five barrels of his revolver into the creature's flank. With a last howl of agony and a vicious snap in the air, it rolled upon its back, four feet pawing furiously, and then fell limp upon its side. I stooped, panting, and pressed my pistol to the dreadful, shimmering head, but it was useless to pull the trigger. The giant hound was dead.

Sir Henry lay insensible where he had fallen. We tore away his collar, and Holmes breathed a prayer of gratitude when he saw that there was no sign of a wound and that the rescue had been in time. Already our friend's eyelids shivered and he made a feeble effort to move. Lestrade thrust his brandy-flask between the baronet's teeth, and two frightened eyes were looking up at us.

'My God!' he whispered. 'What was it? What, in Heaven's name, was it?'

'It's dead, whatever it is,' said Holmes. 'We've laid the family ghost once and for ever.'

In mere size and strength it was a terrible creature which was lying stretched before us. It was not a pure bloodhound and it was not pure mastiff; but it appeared to be a combination of the two – gaunt, savage and as large as a small lioness. Even now, in the stillness of death, the huge jaws seemed to be dripping with a bluish flame, and the small, deep-set cruel eyes were ringed with fire.

Key

1   Yes it is successful, as they get rid of the Hound of the Baskervilles for ever and also solve the mystery of what the monster is.

✳ Writing

Before you do this task, think about its contents and layout. Reports don't have a fixed layout but they do often make use of headings. The headings in Lestrade's notes are useful ones. Think too about how formal the report should be, how detailed, the effect it should create and what sequence it should follow.

Key

Content: to cover all points outlined in instructions

Register: neutral or formal

Target audience: a chief inspector in the police

Effect on target reader: precision and efficiency

Range of language: as appropriate to task – in this case, quite detailed

B

It's a damaged world

Starter activities

3 The word stress in some of these words may be difficult to pronounce. Try to get it as accurate as you can.

Tapescript

2 fossil fuels, plastics, chemicals, domestic waste, industrial waste, gases, car exhausts, air pollution, water pollution, soil pollution, chemical pollution, acid rain, transport pollution, water contamination, energy production, noise pollution.

3 plastics, chemicals, domestic waste, industrial waste, gases, car exhausts, soil pollution, chemical pollution, acid rain, transport pollution, water contamination, energy production, noise pollution.

Key

2   Pollutants: fossil fuels, plastics, chemicals, domestic waste, industrial waste, gases, car exhausts

Pollution: air pollution, water pollution, soil pollution, chemical pollution, acid rain, transport pollution, water contamination, energy production, noise pollution

3   ˈplastics   chemical poˈllution
    ˈchemical   ˈacid ˈrain
    doˈmestic ˈwaste   transport poˈllution
    inˈdustrial ˈwaste   water contamiˈnation
    ˈgases   energy proˈduction
    ˈcar exˈhausts   noise poˈllution
    ˈsoil poˈllution

🔖 ✳ Listening

This text is taken from Rachel Carson's book *Silent Spring,* a book about how people are destroying the world through polluting it. This book came out in the 1950s and was very influential in developing the environmental movement.

Tapescript

1 There was once a town in the heart of America where all life seemed to live in harmony with its surroundings. The town lay in the midst of a chequerboard of prosperous farms, with fields of grain and hillsides of orchards where, in spring, white clouds of bloom drifted above the green fields. In autumn oak and maple and birch trees set up a blaze of colour that flamed and flickered against a backdrop of pines. Then foxes barked in the hills and deer silently crossed the fields, half hidden in the mists of the autumn mornings.

Along the roadsides flowering bushes and wild flowers delighted the traveller's eye through much of the year. Even in winter the roadsides were places of beauty, where countless birds came to feed on the berries and on the seed heads of the dried weeds rising above the snow. The countryside was, in fact, famous for the abundance and variety of its bird life, and when the flood of migrant birds was pouring through in spring and autumn, people travelled from great distances to observe them. Others came to fish the streams, which flowed clear and cold out of the hills and contained shady pools where trout lay. So it had been from the days many years ago when the first settlers raised their houses, sank their wells, and built their barns.

2 Then a strange blight crept over the area and everything began to change. Some evil spell had settled on the community: mysterious maladies swept the flocks of chickens; the cattle and sheep sickened and died. Everywhere was a shadow of death. The farmers spoke of much illness among their families. In the town the doctors had become more and more puzzled by new kinds of sickness appearing among their patients. There had been several sudden and unexplained deaths, not only among adults but even among children, who would be stricken suddenly while at play and die within a few hours.

There was a strange stillness. The birds, for example – where had they gone? Many people spoke of them, puzzled and disturbed. The feeding stations in the backyards were deserted. The few birds seen anywhere were moribund; they trembled violently and could not fly. It was a spring without voices. On the mornings which had once throbbed with the dawn chorus of scores of bird voices there was now no sound; only silence lay over the fields and wood and marsh.

On the farms the hens brooded but no chicks hatched. The farmers complained that they were unable to raise any pigs – the litters were small and the young survived only a few days. The apple trees were coming into bloom but no bees droned among the blossoms, so there was no pollination and there would be no fruit.

The roadsides, once so attractive, were now lined with browned and withered vegetables as though swept by fire. These, too, were silent, deserted by all living things. Even the streams were now lifeless. Anglers no longer visited them, for all the fish had died.

In the gutters and on the roofs, a white granular powder still showed a few patches; some weeks before it had fallen like snow upon the roofs and the lawns, the fields and streams.

No witchcraft, no enemy action had silenced the rebirth of new life in this stricken world. The people had done it themselves.

Key

2   1   *sickness and death*   4   *apple trees*
    2   *illness and death*   5   *roadsides*
    3   *disappearing*   6   *lifeless*

Grammar analysis: the future

Key

1   **going to a**   **present continuous c**
    will/shall d, e, f   **present simple b**

2   1   *will come in/is coming in/comes in*
    2   *I will recycle/am going to recycle*
    3   *is going to get bigger*
    4   *won't be*
    5   *am going to take part in/am taking part in/will be taking part in*

6 *will go on*
7 *will become*
8 *will stop/are going to stop*
9 *will ban*
10 *change/will change*

3 (letters refer to views of future given in 1)
   1 f/c/b 2 e/a 3 a 4 d 5 a/c 6 d 7 d 8 f/a
   9 d 10 b/f

✳ Reading

2 You may know the answers to some of these items from your general knowledge. Read the diagram to check your answers. NB Answers that can call on general knowledge do not appear in the exam.

Key
1 1E 2B 3F 4C 5A 6G 7H 8I
2 1F 2D 3C 4A 5E 6B

◼ Vocabulary summary

After you have finished the quiz, try saying the answers out loud to practise pronunciation.

Tapescript

Number 1.	What 'm' is a wild stretch of open country?
Number 2.	What 's' is a man-made figure often made of stone?
Number 3.	What 'w' is an injury?
And number 4.	What 's' means shaking with cold?
Number 5.	What 'a.r.' is caused by atmospheric contamination?
Here's number 6.	What 't' is a spotted, fresh-water and edible fish?
Number 7.	What 'l' is a long and sudden jump?
Here's number 8.	What 'g' shines softly in the dark?
Number 9.	What 'i' means you're puzzled?
Number 10.	What 'h.w.' is stuff we throw out from our homes.
Followed by number 11.	What 'f.f.' are made from ancient organisms?
Number 12.	What 's' moves your shoulders?
Try number 13.	What 'd' is an animal that usually lives in forests?
Number 14.	What 'r' is found at the edge of roads?
And number 15.	What 'c.e.' are the harmful thing that car engines produce?
Number 16.	What 'h' do chicks do at birth?
Number 17.	What 't' fires a gun?
Here's number 18.	What 'l' often made of glass helps you see better?
Number 19.	What 's' means you've got the strength to continue to live?
And finally number 20.	What 'w' means very, very strange?

Key

1	*moor*	11	*fossil fuels*
2	*statue*	12	*shrug*
3	*wound*	13	*deer*
4	*shivering*	14	*roadsides*
5	*acid rain*	15	*car exhausts*
6	*trout*	16	*hatch*
7	*leap*	17	*trigger*
8	*glow*	18	*lens*
9	*intrigued*	19	*survive*
10	*household waste*	20	*weird*

C

Paper 3 (English in Use): Section C

Gap-filling at phrase or sentence level

Gap-filling at phrase or sentence level is similar to cloze in that finding the right answers depends on looking for lexical and grammatical clues both before and after the gap. Items which provide cohesion within a text (e.g. conjunctions, punctuation, relative pronouns, pronouns, words within a lexical field, substituted words etc.) are particularly important clues in this type of task. Notice that there are always more removed sentences/phrases than gaps and the removed sentences/phrases will all start with a lower case letter or a capital letter but not a mix of these.

1 As you do this activity, think about how you approach it and even note your strategies down. This will give you a basis for your work in activity 2.

Key
1 (1) D (2) C (3) F (4) H (5) I (6) A
3 D *they* = Eskimos; *less* = short; *surface areas* = arms and legs
   C *enabling* = larger blood volume (i.e. grammatical clue); *them* = people living in the tropics; *more* = than other people (implied)
   F *sweat* = sweat
   H *they* = Nigerians; *start* = start; *sweating* = sweat glands; *more* = than British men (implied)
   I *for* = tendency (grammatical clue); *salt* = salt; *sweat* = sweating
   A *salt* = salt

Exam practice 1

Key
(1) G   (2) H   (3) I   (4) B   (5) E   (6) A   (7) J   (8) F

Notes expansion

This task is marked in the exam at item level not at text level i.e. each numbered item is marked by itself. How the sentences join up to the sentences in the next item is not taken into consideration when marking.

Key

1   no

2   articles, auxiliary verbs, prepositions, conjunctions, relative pronouns

3   there can only be one

4   no, they change if necessary

5   no

6   neutral in this case, as is fitting for the poster presentation

7   not always

Exam practice 2

Key
Possible answers:
(1) At home we're going to always turn out the lights and we're going to avoid using spray cans.
(2) Seven people in our class smoke, which is harmful to them and to others, so they're going to give up.
(3) Instead of asking for or accepting any more lifts from our parents, we're going to start walking, cycling or using public transport, which is better for our health too.
(4) As for litter such as sweet papers, drinks cans, burger wrappings etc. etc., well, they'll be going in the bin.
(5) We want to tell other people about environmental dangers as well by using posters, debates, articles in the press and campaigns.
(6) And finally, we're going to be collecting lots of money that we'll be sending to environmental projects.

Reflections

Do the second part of this activity.

Fourteen: Relationships

A
Personal relationships

Starter activities

Key
1
Possible answers:
bride, bridegroom, bridesmaids, best man, church, bouquet, wedding ring(s), marriage service, wedding reception, wedding cake, toasts, wedding presents

2   1 e
    2 f
    3 g
    4 h
    5 a
    6 b
    7 c
    8 d

Reading

1   Check that you understand the meaning of *increasing, decreasing* and *remains stable* before you use them.

✱ **2–3**   You are *not* supposed to read this text word by word. Read it superficially at first to find those sections which are relevant to the task and from which you can extract the information to answer certain questions.

 4   Dates, large numbers and fractions often present difficulties even to quite advanced students. Focus on stress and rhythm to improve fluency.

✱ **5**   This activity is in the form of an open cloze task and is similar to the second task in Paper 3 Section A. Remember that only one word must fit each gap.

Tapescript
in the early nineteen seventies
since eighteen ninety one
eighty-five percent of men
ninety-one percent of women
eleven point six per thousand
fourteen point nine per thousand
one hundred and forty-three thousand six hundred and sixty-seven
three hundred and forty-eight thousand four hundred and ninety-two
between nineteen seventy-nine and nineteen eighty-eight
from two point seven per cent to seven point seven percent

fifty fifty
two and a half times
two thirds of marriages

Key

2 1 B 2 A 3 A 4 A 5 A

3 1 H 2 I 3 D 4 I 5 E 6 C

5 (1) *with*   (6) *is*
   (2) *the*   (7) *as*
   (3) *that*   (8) *in*
   (4) *what*   (9) *their*
   (5) *if*   (10) *such/these*

Grammar analysis: 'empty' *it*

Having a subordinate clause as the subject or object in a sentence can be unwieldy. By substituting *it*, this clumsiness can be avoided to produce a much neater sentence structure.

Key

1 1 c
   2 b
   3 a

2 1 **It is much easier now to get a divorce than it was fifty years ago.**
   2 **It has become much more common in recent years for children to be born outside marriage.**
   3 **The Family Policy Studies Centre finds it worrying to see so many marriages ending in divorce.**
   4 **It is widely accepted by the experts that on average married people tend to live longer than unmarried people.**

Listening

1 Remember that you will not need to understand everything said to answer the question.

✱ 2 Take some time to read the notes about Claire and Philip, and to identify the sorts of information and opinions you are listening for.

Tapescript

Speaker 1: When I was a little girl, um, my best friend was was called Beverley, and er her father was um a guy called Simon Hardcastle, and er he was he was actually a war correspondent for the for the Times, and um he was a very glamorous figure to er to both of us, I mean he was absent a lot of the time, and er, often you know in exotic places – he was sort of in Beirut during that particular conflict, and er Uganda and places like that, and um, and my dream as a child was to become a war correspondent like him and he had a profound influence on many decisions that I made. When I went to university I studied er history and languages, um with the intention of becoming a journalist, and er in fact I did, I started working um for a local paper in East Sussex where I lived, and um and then I went on to er work for the Independent which is what I'm doing now; um and er funnily enough Simon er is er has become a friend of mine. He now works for the ITN news, um but er we're still in touch and um he's really become a very close friend as well as being an influence on my life…

Speaker 2: Um I think one person who had a particularly strong influence on me was um a master where I was at school. Where I went to school there was a lot of er discipline and I was brought up in quite a strict family too; um but this master, he was very young, to us he looked old – he was actually only about 22 but um I was 15 at the time and he appeared a much older person. He came into the school to take over the Music Department, but he then opened up all sorts of other areas and he he challenged us to challenge the authority that the school and possibly our upbringings had er imposed on us; um and up until that point I'd I'd never questioned anything like that, um, I'd accepted what I was er told to do; and um he made me ask why um I behaved like that and whether the instructions I were given were valid; um it completely broke broke all um barriers for me really; it was a new area, and um he also opened up a musical area in my life and I found that I wasn't particularly academically very strong but suddenly there's another area in which you can um move forward and it gives you a confidence of a different kind; um and we used to go several of us used to go for long walks um with this master and we'd start these um very animated and philosophical discussions which we often used to get lost on but he'd keep us all up and um make us question everything that came our way and it was a very refreshing way to think; and um I still think back to him when people tell me to do things and er I feel it's my right to question them.

Key

1 b and d

2 (1) *a little girl/a small child/still very young* (etc.)
   (2) *war correspondent/journalist*
   (3) *exotic/exciting/dangerous places* (etc.)
   (4) *glamorous/exciting/exotic figure/person* (etc.)
   (5) *history and languages*
   (6) *journalism*
   (7) *(still) at school/a teenager/only 15* (etc.)
   (8) *challenge/question*
   (9) *accepting/doing*
   (10) *thinking about/looking at things/life*
   (11) *musical*
   (12) *sense of confidence/self-confidence*

B

Working relationships

Starter activities

Key

Listening

1   As usual on first listening, you don't need to understand
everything the speakers say.

2   Take time to read and understand the ten opinions listed.
This time you will have to listen more carefully. Note that a
speaker does not always state an opinion explicitly, but may
express it by implication, by agreeing with or endorsing the
opinion expressed by the previous speaker.

Tapescript

Interviewer: I think er a sense of achievement is something
that we all like to feel, um but I think probably
coming first in a race or winning a competition
[mm] isn't always the most important [mm]
thing, I think the taking part seems to be the chief
the chief element, that actually "being part of a
team" factor, I mean, would you would you say
that being part of a team is something that you
particularly enjoy, Pam?

Pam: Um, yes, I think so, I think um the the experience
that um that I most remember is about ten years
ago, I travelled to New Zealand, [mm] and I was
there for about a 9-month period and I, I decided
to do a survival course which was [yeah] [oh] um
quite out of character really, but er, um and it was
extraordinary, I mean meeting you know absolute
strangers, [mm] um who'd all got together for
one reason or another and we were together for a
week and we were split into two teams we had to
get from A to B in the best way we could [yes]
and obviously we had all various pieces of
equipment, you know ropes and stuff like that,
um and we also did some white water rafting
which was pretty exhilarating [oh yeah] I have to
say it was just quite it was the most exhilarating
thing I think I've ever done in my whole life more
or less, um but the thing about it was we we um it
was extraordinary it was I think the thing I
learned from it was it was kind of an inroad into
into people's personalities really because um
people were in the teams you know who from all
different walks of life I mean you know business
people [yes], accountants, teachers, um nurses,
and [so] the more cautious ones [yes] um given a
situation where you know they really had to you
know like your life in their hands sort of thing I

mean came to the fore and their sort of
leadership qualities came out in extraordinary
ways you know some people who you'd never
think in a million years would be able to to get
something like that together…

Neil: Um, barriers come down quickly [yes] don't they
[yes, barriers do come down] yes I know what
you mean [was that your experience as well?] yes
yeah you it's a great leveller isn't it being part of a
team…

P: Absolutely, yes [yes].

N: If you have if you want to survive in it you've got
you have to kind of throw all your judgements
and um inhibitions and things out the way [yes]

Int: And of course you're thinking of the survival not
only of yourself but of people around you you
know [yes] say in a situation in which you can
help another person [exactly] that's also part of
the [exactly]…

N: That I found an interesting thing I was on a
similar sort of thing to you it was a it was a
naval um selection test to go into the navy
[mm] and we were put together and very often
there's a personal survival instinct which you
have to almost sacrifice to remain part of a
team [yes, yes] and you have to think on a
bigger scale instead of just thinking well I know
what I'm going to do I'm going to get across
that bridge and go this way [yes] [yes] you have
to think about how as a group you you're going
to work.

P: Yes [yes] and in some instances there are certain
people who are who are you know very obviously
weaker [mm] than others [yes] and it's amazing
how the ones who are caring and have got more
concern [yes] that comes out to the fore as well
[mm] because they're concerned about you know
they take care [yeah, I…] if you like play the
mother goose rather…

Int: I wonder did you ever worry about the particular
skills that you personally could bring to a team,
did you…

P: Oh absolutely, absolutely!

N: Yes, oh yes.

Int: Did you think oh is my contribution enough? [yes]
[yes, oh yes]

P: Yes but I think that er you soon began to realise
that, that that really didn't matter I mean um it
was extraordinary I mean um everybody was
very supportive of each other I mean there were
moments where you know we had a few little sort
of hysterical outbursts [yes] you know people just
sort of said I can't do this I can't do this and…

Int: …and they were coaxed on by the others in the
group who…

P: …and yes, then they were sort of reassured um
by the others and then suddenly found that they
were able to do it something you know because
you're coming up against fears as well [yes].

N: Did you did you find that taking decisions
whereas in the past you may have only taken
them for yourself the responsibility of taking a
decision for the group is really quite worrying?

Int: [Yes] Yes that's something else isn't it [yes]

because it's all right some people feel very cosy being a part of a team [yeah] but when it comes to something that only you can bring and you have to make a decision [yeah] um obviously that's you're putting a number a number of other people's well in that case lives at stake [yes absolutely yes] aren't you?.

P: Yes it's it it brings out all sorts of different elements I think um especially when you're with um it's different when you're with absolute strangers [mm] I mean if you've been in a team you know [yes] with with with people that you've known for a long time [mm] then that's quite different.

Int: I think it is so I mean so would you say then in general that actually what is important is being part of a team or being recognised as being a champion being a winner of a race would you say that both of you very quickly, being a part of a team is the most important thing?

P: I think taking part…

N: Taking part – learning to listen but not being afraid to speak out too…

P: …yes flexibility, [yeah] flexibility and adjusting.

Int: Thank you both very much.

N: Thank you.

Key

1 a …a survival course (in New Zealand).
   b …a naval selection test (to get into the navy).

2 1 P
   2 P N
   3 P N
   4 N
   5 P
   6 P N
   7 P
   8 P N
   9 P
   10 N

Reading

1 If you have little personal experience of problems in the workplace, try drawing on your general knowledge.

2 Give yourself only one minute to glance through the text and decide the best title.

3 Take more time to read the text in detail and complete the multiple matching task.

4 Part 1 focuses on positive and negative connotation in a selection of nouns, verbs and adjectives.

Key

1 Possible answers: jealousy, sense of superiority/inferiority, resentment, competition, misunderstanding, mutual attraction/dislike, sexual harassment etc.

2 B

3 1 A, C, D, E, G   2 A, D, F, H   3 A, B, C, D, E, G, I

4 1 Positive: *willing, compliment, cooperation, satisfaction, interesting, well-being, fair*
      Negative: *hypocritical, ignorance, conflict, denigrate, suspicion, problem, superficial, criticise, hostility*

   2 *uninteresting*
      inessential
      impersonal
      uncomfortable
      infrequent
      anti-social/unsocial
      unfair
      dissatisfied
      informal
      unspecific/non-specific
      abnormal
      uncooperative
      unwilling
      impossible
      unimportant

Grammar reminder: conditional sentences

Key

1 a 3   b 5   c 6   d 1   e 2   f 4

2 1 If they got to know him better they *would find* he's not so bad after all.
   2 You will see an improvement in your working relationships if you *follow* some basic rules.
   3 If he *had looked* me/*looked* me in the eye when we talked, I'd have a much better idea of what he really thought.
   4 If they'd both made more of an effort, they *would get on/would have got on* much better together.
   5 You spend a lot of your time talking to people if you *work/are working* in an office.
   6 If the boss *had not criticised* his secretary in public, she never would have left the company.
   7 If I lost interest in what she was saying, I *would transfer/transferred* my attention to the photograph on the wall behind her.
   8 Life can be very difficult if you *share/are sharing* an office with someone you dislike.

✳ Writing

1–2 This activity is similar to the error correction task found in Section B of Paper 3. Refer back to the advice given in Section C of Unit 8 (page 109) either before or after doing the task.

Key

1 1 *it's*   6 (*not*
   2 *John*   7 *suspicious*
   3 *self-esteem'.*   8 *usually*
   4 *affirm*   9 ✓
   5 ✓

Vocabulary summary

Key

social skills
working conditions
close friends
divorce rate
vital element
life expectancy

single parent
serious illness
dramatic rise
popular culture
significant proportion
family life

C

Paper 4 (Listening): Section D

Introduction

1–2 These activities are designed to introduce you to the content and format of Section D Paper 4 (Listening). This task is normally built around a series of short listening extracts.

Tapescript
1 For Section D of CAE Paper 4 you will hear a series of short extracts, each of which will be between 10 and 30 seconds in length. All the extracts will be linked in some way and there will be a brief pause between each one. You will hear the whole series twice. The questions may test how well you can identify what topic is being talked about in each extract, the purpose of each one, who the speaker is in each extract, and what their attitude may be.

Key
(1) *short*
(2) *10–30 seconds*
(3) *brief*
(4) *linked*
(5) *twice*
(6) *topic*
(7) *purpose*
(8) *speaker*
(9) *attitude*

Identifying the topic

1–2 Think about the sorts of clues you might use, e.g the vocabulary (especially any keywords relating to a topic), aspects of the speaker's approach/style/tone, number of speakers involved etc.

3 Notice the importance of the keywords related to a single idea: *showers, dry, cloud, rain, cooler, wind, temperatures*. Other keywords relate to geographical references. Notice too the speaker's approach – friendly and informative. Think about the pattern of tenses used – beginning with present perfect to describe the recent situation, and moving on to future tenses to describe what is to come. You probably also used your world knowledge.

4 The next extract is a short sports report but you must identify the particular sport concerned using similar clues to those in activity 3.

Tapescript
2 (fade in)…so let's put in the details for today then; let's start with the whole of southern England and the South Midlands. Well, there've been one or two showers around on the south coast, but basically it's been mainly dry; and for the first part of the afternoon there'll be further isolated showers, but then we're going to see cloud tumbling its way into south-west England bringing with it some more persistent rain; this cloud and rain will continue to move east during the afternoon; it'll feel cooler today with a breezy south-westerly wind and temperatures only reaching 21 degrees at best, perhaps nearer 17 to 18 in the south west of England…(fade)

4 After so much English success in the pool over recent days, Northern Ireland and Scotland can both look forward to a share of the spotlight in the finals. Marian Maguire is third fastest for the 200 metres butterfly giving rise to hope of a first ever Irish medal. Helen Otter from Scotland goes in the 200 metres backstroke, while fellow-countrymen Graham Wilson and Peter Frith challenge the mighty Australians in the 1500 metre freestyle; and England, Wales and Scotland all contest the last event, the men's medley relay.

Key
2 the weather
4 swimming (key words: *pool, butterfly, backstroke, freestyle, medley relay*; also references to the distances)

Identifying the speaker

1 This time the focus is not on the topic but on the speaker.

2 Think about the clues you were aware of using: probably the choice of words and relationship to the topic, perhaps also the style of speaking.

3 Play the second extract using a similar approach.

Tapescript
1 Well my coach always said I was in with a chance of getting a medal…but even though I knew I was running well I still don't think I really believed it…so to get gold…well that was quite something…it probably won't sink in until tomorrow!

3 The trouble is, Chris, if you don't start taking things more seriously, you're going to find yourself in real trouble before too long. Your other teachers tell me your marks leave a lot to be desired and you still haven't handed in that history essay I set for the class over 2 weeks ago – it's just not good enough – I want to see some improvement (fade)

Key
1 c
3 b (clues = *your other teachers, your marks, you still haven't handed in, history essay I set for the class*)

Identifying a speaker's attitude or opinion

1 Note that, in addition to paying attention to the words a speaker chooses to use, we can often infer a speaker's attitude or opinion by taking account of different features of the person's speech.

The pitch of a speaker's voice will move up and down in normal conversation, but movement and tempo may reflect, according to the variation, strong emotion.

2 Replay the two extracts. This time try and suggest the attitude of the speaker.

Tapescript

2 Well my coach always said I was in with a chance of getting a medal…but even though I knew I was running well I still don't think I really believed it…so to get gold…well that was quite something…it probably won't sink in until tomorrow!

The trouble is, Chris, if you don't start taking things more seriously, you're going to find yourself in real trouble before too long. Your other teachers tell me your marks leave a lot to be desired and you still haven't handed in that history essay I set for the class over 2 weeks ago – it's just not good enough – I want to see some improvement (fade)…

Key

2 Extract 1: a (fast tempo, raised voice, high pitch)
  Extract 2: b (slower tempo, lowered voice, low pitch)

Identifying purpose or intention

1 Remember that when we speak we are usually using language to achieve a particular purpose or function, e.g. to ask for something. Play the short extract to identify the topic first and then try and explain what the speaker is actually doing in the extract. Play the extract a second time if necessary.

2 Read the various phrases which are appropriate for (1) 'describing a new car'. Then think about the phrases you might expect to hear if you overheard someone arranging to borrow a car from a friend (2), e.g. *I wonder if I could possibly…, I need to…, I'll make sure…, I promise I'll…, naturally I'll pay…,* etc. Do something similar for (3) to (5).

3 Play the two extracts on cars to gain practice in identifying the speaker's purpose/intention.

4 Think about which of the words and phrases you thought of in activity 2 were actually used in the listening extracts for activity 3. It is quite possible that some of your suggestions were paraphrased, so look out for any examples of this.

Tapescript

1 Oh, I'm really pleased with it – it's a dark blue Toyota, a couple of years old, only one owner, erm, loads of room in the boot – I only picked it up from the garage yesterday and it feels like I've been driving it for ages already…

3 I feel awful about it – I must've just caught the the concrete pillar as I was coming out of the car park and it's scraped a bit of paint off the wing – I'm terribly sorry, I should've been more careful. I just, I do hope the garage will be able to match the colour and of course, you must let me know how much it costs…

It's in excellent condition as you can see – it's had regular services since it was new, but even so it's very reasonably priced, and of course we may well be able to arrange a part exchange deal on your existing car. Would you like to take it out on the roads for a test drive to help you decide?

Key

1 a a car
  b to describe a new car which has been bought
3 Extract 1: 3
  Extract 2: 5

Exam practice

Here you listen to a set of five short listening extracts and complete a task from Section D of Paper 4 (Listening). Try to use the techniques discussed and practised in previous activities. You should write your answers, while you are listening, into the spaces in your book. Play the recording twice.

Tapescript

1 **(museum assistant to school group)**
Now if you come over here children, you can see several different instruments that were used by people in the past for telling the time, before mechanical clocks as we know them were even invented. Perhaps some of you have seen a smaller one of these in your kitchen at home – see how the glass can be turned upside down so that the sand runs through the narrow opening in the middle…when all the sand had gone from the top half to the bottom half, people knew that an hour had passed…

2 **(elderly lady to antiques expert)**
Now this has been in my family for as long as I can remember – I think it was originally bought by my great grandfather…
Ah, now this is a very nice piece of work, probably made sometime during the nineteenth century by Thomas Goldsmith and Son in London – yes, look, you can see the maker's name on the clockface there. You know, it was quite common at that time for the door of the case to be made with a glass panel in it so you could actually see the pendulum swinging. In this condition I could imagine it fetching ooh erm, oh several hundred pounds at auction…

3 **(grandparent giving a present to daughter-in-law for her grand-daughter)**
I got this for Sara's birthday – I know she's a bit young to be able to tell the time yet but I thought she might enjoy watching the figures move…
Oh – how kind of you, it's lovely – it's ideal for her bedroom and it'll fit perfectly on the wall above her bed. Actually she's just beginning to recognise numbers so it's ideal…oh, what a lovely idea – thank you so much, Mum!

4 **(shop assistant to customer)**
This one's got a second hand – and it's waterproof – is that the sort of thing you're looking for?
Well, I'm not really sure that's going to be big enough – the face is a bit small and I don't really want something with a strap. What I really need is something I can easily carry around in my pocket and use to time the children's performances in the pool – [what about this then?] yes, that's the sort of thing I had in mind…

5 **(customer to shop assistant)**
Excuse me, I bought this from you recently and I've brought it back because the alarm isn't working properly. Actually I'm rather annoyed because I specifically bought it to take with me on a business trip abroad and in the end I

had to rely on the hotel giving me an alarm call every morning…

Oh I'm sorry to hear that madam – would you like me to replace it or would you prefer a refund?

Key

1	E	6	G
2	C	7	H
3	H	8	F
4	A	9	B
5	G	10	C

Ways of learning: focusing attention in Section D Listening tasks

This final activity highlights the different approaches which can be adopted when answering the questions in the Section D task, given that the tape is heard twice.

Fifteen: People watching

A

Let's peoplewatch

Starter activities

Key

1 observing other people

Speaking

Key

2

Generalisations: *Generally speaking…In general…By and large…As a rule…*

Exceptions: *The exception is…There are exceptions… Apart from…You can't really say that about…*

Reading

1 You may well recognise this face – it is Leonardo da Vinci's *Mona Lisa*.

2 You will need to understand these words to get the most out of the next activity.

3, 4 There are no fixed answers to these activities.

Key

2

positive: *witty, an unflinching gaze*

negative: *sinister, lose her temper, bawdy, callousness, flab, greedy, a spendthrift, fickle*

it depends: *plump, enigmatic, a glint in her eyes, a mole*

✳ Writing

Think about these points before you do the writing task: the target reader, style, appropriate language, the effect on the reader, layout, sequencing of information, accuracy of language.

Key

	First task	Second task
content	to cover all points mentioned in instructions	to cover all points mentioned in instructions
register	any	formal probably or neutral
target reader	general audience	author of *Mona Lisa* passage
effect on target reader	interesting	persuasive
range of language	good range of descriptive language, especially adjectives and nouns	good range of structures to match formality of tone

Grammar analysis: verbs taking two objects

Key

1 Correct sentences: 2, 3, 4, 6, 7, 8, 9, 10

2   1 *I lent her a record/I lent a record to her.*

    5 *They offered them a drink/They offered a drink to them.*

   11 *I asked him a question.*

   12 *We owe them some money/We owe some money to them.*

    [If the indirect object pronoun comes before the direct object, *to* is omitted. If it comes after it must be included.]

3   *write, play, take, teach, send, grant*

4   a 4 b 3 c 5 d 5 e 4 f 1 g 2 h 1 i 3 j 2

    6 Our friend was promised some help/Some help was promised to our friend

    7 He was read a story/A story was read to him

    8 I was saved some chocolate/Some chocolate was saved for me

9 The ticket was handed to him/He was handed the ticket

10 A job was found for me/I was found a job

11 He was asked a question/A question was asked of him

12 Some money is owed to them/They are owed some money

Listening

Tapescript

Speaker 1: Watching people's faces fascinates me. I always wish I had a little miniature polaroid camera that I could carry round with me when I'm walking through the street or on a bus or whatever, and I could just whip round and take a picture of that wonderful expression on somebody's face, whether it's somebody being told off, somebody telling somebody off, somebody having an argument, somebody having a good laugh, and finding something very funny. The face can tell a very interesting story, I think.

Speaker 2: I like watching people watching other people. Er, I like to see people reacting to situations going on around them, because erm, it's something…there's something very honest and erm unthinking about it. It's erm…when it's erm an extreme situation, like er, I don't know…somebody who's drunk getting on the er…the tube train, and er it's just very interesting watching people react to that. Er, you often get people with some deep…behaving in an extraordinary way right next to them, and they're desperately trying to pretend it's not happening, and I find that very amusing. Erm, so I…I watch people watching other people.

Speaker 3: Well, er, yes, I have to admit, I do like peoplewatching; partly because I'm terribly short-sighted, and I'm always squinting, so I kind of think they probably don't think I'm looking at them anyway. Erm, but erm, it's normally mannerisms, 'cos I think I've got quite a few, so erm, and shoes, feet; if they're sort of kicking their legs out and things on trains, or erm facial expressions, flinches and erm, little ticks perhaps, what they do with their hands, erm I find that quite interesting; erm, and it's always good to see, see people on trains, because you're in such close prox…proximity to people that erm erm they obviously don't like, normally like you to catch their eye, so I quite like the way people avert their gaze; that's always an interesting one.

Speaker 4: I don't really like watching people. Erm, I don't like eating outside, I don't like travelling on public transport. The trouble is, if you…if you look at people you see them doing all sorts of disgusting things like picking their noses, and I…I just think that's really disgusting and I…don't like it at all. And er…I don't like watching people scratching themselves and things, because they always do that, and they're all passing, and you're trying to

have a meal, and someone's scratching themselves in your face. I think it's just…I prefer to stay indoors really.

Key
1

	Speaker 1	Speaker 2	Speaker 3	Speaker 4
feet			✓	
faces	✓		✓	
arguments				
hands			✓	
scratching				✓
people watching other people		✓		
people getting drunk				
mannerisms			✓	

2

Which speaker likes or dislikes watching …?	Speaker 1	Speaker 2	Speaker 3	Speaker 4
people's disgusting habits				✓
people pretending not to notice something embarrassing		✓		
people watching other people		✓		
people on trains			✓	
people avoiding your glance			✓	
faces that tell stories	✓			
people's mannerisms			✓	

B

Reasons for peoplewatching

Starter activities

There is no fixed answer to either of these tasks as they are a matter of opinion.

✴ 📼 Listening

Tapescript

Speaker 1: I love the cool dude in the waistcoat. He has a very mad look about him. But I find him slightly intimidating. I'd probably be frightened to approach him. I wouldn't mind him approaching me, though! Clothes really affect how I feel about people. I can't stand shoes that are too shiny or falling apart. I'd be happy to take him to an office party, though!

Speaker 2: She's really pretty – but in the pink she looks like a bimbo. The most attractive is the office outfit. I like women who dress smartly and you can tell she's high-powered and classy. She's probably got a nice car and she's certainly got a good brain. I wouldn't mind the number of her mobile phone!

Speaker 3: The one in the flowery dress. She's got all the qualities I find attractive in a woman – intelligence, smart appearance. The dress really stands out from the rest. It isn't too short, it isn't too revealing and her heels aren't too high. I can't say any more because my girlfriend will be here in a minute…!

Speaker 4: I wouldn't want to meet him in the waistcoat. All he'd have to say is 'Look at me.' But he looks much nicer in those jeans – neat, casual and trendy. I'd be quite happy to go out with him.

Speaker 5: The one in the jeans looks like a real human being. I'd definitely talk to her. She looks very natural, approachable, comfortable and confident. She isn't trying to be anything other than who she is. Even her make-up isn't over the top. She looks as though she dresses for herself.

Key
1 1 h   2 c   3 b   4 e   5 a

2 1 C   2 B, D   3 B, D   4 A, F   5 A, F, G

Grammar reminder: indirect statement

2 You could do further practice by playing other parts of the recordings.

Key
2 *She said she loves/loved the cool dude in the waistcoat.*

She said she can't/couldn't stand shoes that are too shiny.

He said he wouldn't mind/wouldn't have minded the number of her mobile phone.

He said his girlfriend would be there soon.

She said she'd be/she'd have been quite happy to go out with him.

He said she wasn't/isn't trying to be anything other than who she is/was.

Reading

Key
1 The original title for this passage was D.

2 1 D   2 F   3 E   4 A   5 C   6 B

3 1 D   2 D   3 A   4 D   5 D

Vocabulary summary

Choose ten words and write out the clues, then return to the clues a few days later to see if you can work out which words they refer to.

C

Paper 5 (Speaking): Phases C and D

Introduction

Phase C is a concrete communicative task and Phase D a more abstract discussion based on the theme of the Phase C task. Candidates are not always asked to report back on their decisions in Phase D. The examiners may use this phase to encourage less forthcoming students to talk or to get more language from candidates to whom they are unsure what mark to give. However, if candidates are asked to contribute during this phase they should not interpret this as meaning anything special; it may simply be a wish on the part of the examiner to continue the discussion.

NB Dominant candidates must be careful not to be too forceful. They will lose marks for interactive communication if they are. Less forthcoming candidates must do their best to hold forth in these phases – examiners can only judge what they've heard; they cannot judge a candidate's potential. Remember the quality of your ideas is not assessed.

Useful language for Phases C and D: Interacting with other speakers

Key
A 1, 2, 3, 5, 8   B 4, 7, 11   C 6, 9, 11, 12   D 1, 10

Useful language for Phase D: Reporting your decisions

Key
A 2, 9, 10, 14, 15, 16, 17   B 3, 11   C 1, 8, 12, 15
D 4, 5, 6, 7, 12, 13

Exam practice

Do these tasks by taking on the roles of both candidates or by discussing with yourself. Record yourself, then use the assessment criteria to assess your performance.

Reflections

Base your answers to these questions on your findings from assessing the recording.

Revision Exam Practice 3

Paper 1 (Reading)

This task is taken from the Gapped Paragraphs Section of the Reading Paper. For information on how to approach this section of Paper 1, see the information and the facsimile questions on pages 151–155. The answer sheet for the Reading Paper is reproduced on page 298.

Allow approximately 20 minutes for this task.

Key
1 B	4 E
2 G	5 D
3 C	6 F

Paper 2 (Writing)

This task is taken from Section B of the Writing Paper. For information on how to approach this section of Paper 2, see the information and the facsimile questions on pages 165–168.

Allow approximately 1 hour for this task.

Remember to choose the task sensibly and to read the instructions carefully. When you have finished the writing task, you could ask an English-speaking friend to assess your written work using the Marking guidelines for teachers shown below.

Marking guidelines

In assessing written work, try to take account of the official assessment criteria used by CAE examiners. These relate to content (points covered), organisation/cohesion, range of vocabulary and structures, register (formality/information), accuracy, and the effect on the target reader. On a rising scale of 1 to 5, give an impression mark based upon a combination of accuracy of language and task achievement. You may also want to mark up errors and add specific comments relating to accuracy, content, style, etc.

The following questions may help focus your attention during the marking process:

Has the student thought about the purpose and the audience in terms of choice of appropriate language, style and layout?

The vocabulary and structure used should be relevant to the topic; the style should be appropriate to the target audience and purpose in writing; and the layout should be matched to the instructions.

Has the student succeeded in planning and organising their writing?

Well-planned and organised work leads the reader clearly through from start to finish and achieves its intended objective. Poorly planned and organised written work is usually confusing, exhausting to read and distracts from its purpose.

Has the student done everything the question asks within the specified word limit?

An underlength answer probably means that the task is incomplete in some way and that important elements have been omitted. An overlength answer could mean that irrelevant material has been included which may in turn have a negative effect on the target reader.

Has the student checked for accuracy of grammar, punctuation and spelling?

While occasional errors need not be heavily penalised, persistently poor spelling, grammar or punctuation can have a negative effect on the target reader and may adversely affect the achievement of the task.

Would the writing achieve the required objective?

Give an impression mark based upon a combination of accuracy of language and task achievement. Remember that clarity of handwriting can have an important effect on a target reader, so poor handwriting should be penalised.

Paper 3 (English in Use)

This task is taken from the Gap-filling and Note-expansion Section of the English in Use Paper. For information on how to approach this section of Paper 3, see the information and the facsimile questions on pages 176–179. The answer sheet for the English in Use Paper is reproduced on pages 299–301.

Allow approximately 30 minutes for this task.

Key
1   1C   2G   3D   4B   5I   6A   7F

2   Possible answers:
   (1) The description which is given of them is the same the world over and describes them as being about 2 metres tall and weighing about 300 kilograms.
   (2) They tend to have different names in different places; for example the Abominable Snowman, the Yeti, the Wild Man and the Sasquatch.
   (3) The proof of their existence comes from their footprints, which have been found in snow and mud, and sightings of them that have been reported in different places.
   (4) The best evidence of their existence has been provided by a Russian scientific expedition which took place near Lake Balkhash and reported two sightings as well as footprints and smashing sounds.
   (5) The problem is that as yet no one has managed to take any photos or movies of them.
   (6) Another expedition to prove the existence of the Ape Man is leaving soon, but it needs money, so please give generously.

Paper 4 (Listening)

This task is taken from Section D of the Listening Paper. For information on how to approach this section of Paper 4, see the information and the facsimile questions on pages 188–190. The answer sheet for the Listening Paper is reproduced on page 302.

Allow approximately 10 minutes for this task.

This exam practice task should be done under conditions similar to those that you will encounter in the CAE examination itself. You should write your answers, while you are listening, into the boxes provided in your book. Play the recording twice and at the end of the task, give yourself two or three minutes to transfer your answers from the book onto the answer sheet facsimile provided.

Tapescript
V1: Sports teacher (complimentary)
…well, all in all, we're really very pleased with his progress over the past year – especially his ball skills…and as captain of the swimming team I think he was instrumental in their success at the schools championships a couple of months ago. They did tremendously well so I do hope he'll stay with the team and perhaps even get involved in coaching some of the younger boys, you know he's a born teacher…

V2: French teacher (disappointed)
…I have to say I find it rather a shame that James has shown so little interest in the subject recently – especially since he was doing so well in both his oral and written work last year – and it was a great pity he decided not to go on the school trip because he would have got such a lot out of it, it would have helped his pronunciation enormously…

V3: Music teacher (cautious)
Well…it's difficult to know quite what to say…although James is making quite good progress with the theoretical part of the course, I'm not really so sure about his practical work…perhaps if he were to practise on a more regular

basis, maybe even join the orchestra, then I might feel a bit more confident that he'll do himself justice in the long term…

V4: Chemistry teacher (critical)
I really think he's going to have to revise his attitude over the next few months if he wants to get a satisfactory grade – there's nothing wrong with either his understanding of the theory or his practical experimental work but his written projects are virtually always late and often incomplete…and to be perfectly honest, his behaviour in the laboratories sometimes verges on the dangerous…!

V5: History teacher (supportive)
I do realise that James has missed rather a lot of the course because of illness this year and that has had an effect on his performance…it's made it rather more difficult for him to keep up-to-date with all the reading and so on, but we've had some extra classes together and, as a result, his essay on causes of the American Civil War was a good effort and showed real understanding of the political and social conditions of the time…

Key
1 E   2 F   3 A   4 D   5 H   6 D   7 B   8 C   9 H   10 G

Paper 5 (Speaking): Phases C and D

This task is taken from Phases C and D of the Speaking Paper. For information on how to approach this section of Paper 5, see the information and the facsimile questions on pages 199–202.

298

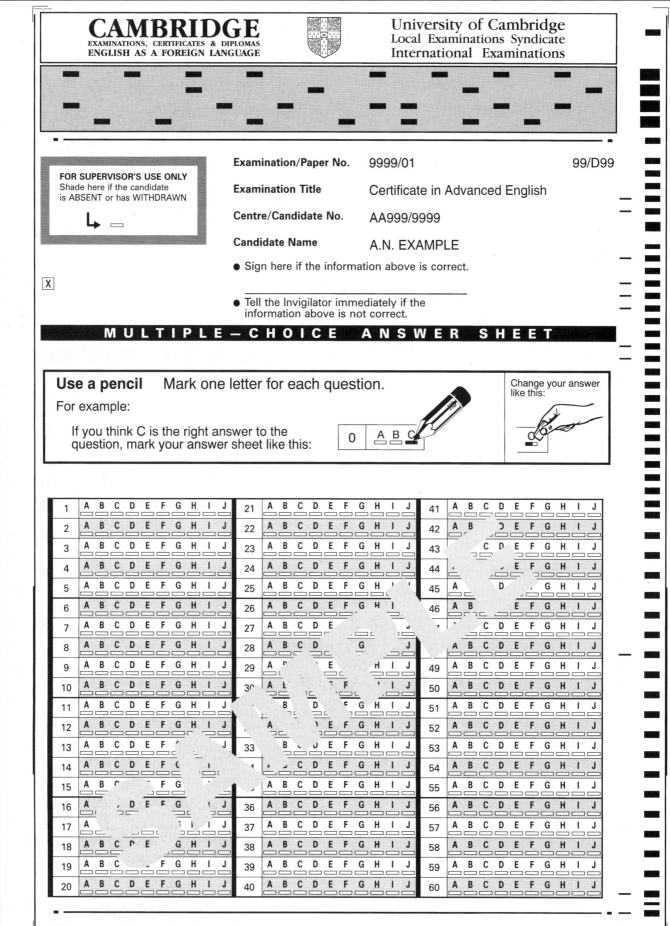

CAMBRIDGE
EXAMINATIONS, CERTIFICATES & DIPLOMAS
ENGLISH AS A FOREIGN LANGUAGE

University of Cambridge
Local Examinations Syndicate
International Examinations

Examination/Paper No.	9999/01	99/D99
Examination Title	Certificate in Advanced English	
Centre/Candidate No.	AA999/9999	
Candidate Name	A.N. EXAMPLE	

FOR SUPERVISOR'S USE ONLY
Shade here if the candidate
is ABSENT or has WITHDRAWN

X

● Sign here if the information above is correct.

● Tell the Invigilator immediately if the
information above is not correct.

MULTIPLE — CHOICE ANSWER SHEET

Use a pencil   Mark one letter for each question.

For example:

If you think C is the right answer to the
question, mark your answer sheet like this:

0   A B C

Change your answer
like this:

CAMBRIDGE
EXAMINATIONS, CERTIFICATES & DIPLOMAS
ENGLISH AS A FOREIGN LANGUAGE

University of Cambridge
Local Examinations Syndicate
International Examinations

FOR SUPERVISOR'S USE ONLY
Shade here if the candidate
is ABSENT or has WITHDRAWN

Examination/Paper No.	9999/03	99/D99
Examination Title	Certificate in Advance English	
Centre/Candidate No.	AA999/9999	
Candidate Name	A.N. EXAMPLE	

● Sign here if the information above is correct.

● Tell the Invigilator immediately if the
information above is not correct.

CAE - PAPER 3 - ANSWER SHEET ONE

1	1	19	19
2	2	20	20
3	3	21	21
4	4	22	22
5	5	23	23
6	6	24	24
7	7	25	25
8	8	26	26
9	9	27	27
10	10	28	28
11	11	29	29
12	12	30	30
13	13	31	31
14	14	32	32
15	15	33	33
16	16	34	34
17	17	35	35
18	18	36	36

Continue on ANSWER SHEET TWO →

FOR OFFICE USE ONLY

	0 1 2		0 1 2		0 1 2
81		84		87	
82		85		88	
83		86		89	

CAE-3 (1)   KENRICK JEFFERSON   Printers to the Computer Industry   DP116/34

CAMBRIDGE
EXAMINATIONS, CERTIFICATES & DIPLOMAS
ENGLISH AS A FOREIGN LANGUAGE

University of Cambridge
Local Examinations Syndicate
International Examinations

FOR SUPERVISOR'S USE ONLY
Shade here if the candidate
is ABSENT or has WITHDRAWN

Examination/Paper No.	9999/03 99/D99
Examination Title	Certificate in Advance English
Centre/Candidate No.	AA999/9999
Candidate Name	A.N. EXAMPLE

- Sign here if the information above is correct.

....

- Tell the Invigilator immediately if the
information above is not correct.

CAE - PAPER 3 - ANSWER SHEET TWO

37		37	59		59
38		38	60		60
39		39	61		61
40		40	62		62
41		41	63		63
42		42	64		64
43		43	65		65
44		44	66		66
45		45	67		67
46		46	68		68
47		47	69		69
48		48	70		70
49		49	71		71
50		50	72		72
51		51	73		73
52		52	74		74
53		53	75		75
54		54	76		76
55		55	77		77
56		56	78		78
57		57	79		79
58		58	80		80

Continue on the OTHER SIDE of this sheet →

CAE-3 (2)   KENRICK ■ JEFFERSON   Printers to the Computer Industry   DP118/36

81

82

83

84

85

86

87

88

89

UCAM59 GLYN 22-JUL-91 REVERSE DP118 & DP119
SEE INK REFERENCES

CAMBRIDGE
EXAMINATIONS, CERTIFICATES & DIPLOMAS
ENGLISH AS A FOREIGN LANGUAGE

University of Cambridge
Local Examinations Syndicate
International Examinations

FOR SUPERVISOR'S USE ONLY
Shade here if the candidate
is ABSENT or has WITHDRAWN

X

Examination/Paper No. 9999/04   99/D99

Examination Title   ANY CAMBRIDGE EXAM

Centre/Candidate No.   AA999/9999

Candidate Name   A.N. EXAMPLE

● Sign here if the information above is correct.

● Tell the Invigilator immediately if the
information above is not correct.

LISTENING COMPREHENSION ANSWER SHEET

ENTER TEST
NUMBER HERE →

FOR OFFICE
USE ONLY →

FCE	CAE	CPE
[1]	[5]	[3]

[00][10][20][30][40][50][60][70][80][90]
[0][1][2][3][4][5][6][7][8][9]

1		1	21		21
2		2	22		22
3		3	23		23
4		4	24		24
5		5	25		25
6		6	26		26
7		7	27		27
8		8	28		28
9		9	29		29
10		10	30		30
11		11	31		31
12		12	32		32
13		13	33		33
14		14	34		34
15		15	35		35
16		16	36		36
17		17	37		37
18		18	38		38
19		19	39		39
20		20	40		40

Acknowledgements

The authors would like to thank staff at Cambridge University Press, Geraldine Mark and Liz Sharman in particular, for the guidance and care with which they have supported this project.

The authors and publishers are grateful to the following for permission to reproduce copyright material. In a few cases, it has not been possible to identify the sources of the material used and in such cases the publishers would welcome information from copyright owners.

For permission to reproduce texts:

p16 from *A communicative competence: theory and practice* by Sandra Savignon. Copyright © 1983 by Addison Wesley Publishing Company. Reprinted with permission; pp20, 26, 27, 139, 147, 149, 152, 155, 185 *The Independent/The Independent on Sunday*; p23 Maeve Binchy; pp30, 80, 159 First printed in *British Airways High Life*; p33 (D) Gold Medal Travel Group; p36 British Airways; pp41, 79 © Times Newspapers Ltd; p53, 97 *Foresight Magazine* Summer 1992/Sun Alliance/BLA Group; pp55, 154-5, 206-7 © *The Guardian*; pp24 (entry from Collins COBUILD English dictionary copyright HarperCollins Publishers 1995), 61 (from *The articulate mammal* by Jean Aitchison - Unwin Hyman Ltd), 125-6 (from *Assert yourself* by Gael Lindenfield - Thorsons) all reproduced by permission of HarperCollins Publishers; p24 entry from the Concise Oxford Dictionary by permission of Oxford University Press; p33-4 from *Paradise News* by David Lodge (Reed Consumer Books Ltd); p64 Reprinted with permission of Simon & Schuster from *How to start a conversation and make friends* by Don Gabor. Copyright © 1983 by Don Gabor; p67 Extract reproduced from *Inside information* by Jacquetta Megarry with the permission of BBC Enterprises Limited; p84 from *Understanding the media* by Andrew Hart (Routledge); p87 from a patient information leaflet 'Made to fit beautifully, an introduction to contact lenses', reproduced by the kind permission of Hydron UK Ltd; p89 © *The Telegraph* plc, London, 1993; pp92-3 from *Of time and stars* by Arthur C. Clark (Victor Gollancz Ltd). Reprinted by permission of the author and the author's agents Scovil, Chichak, Galen Literary Agency, Inc, New York/ David Higham Associates Limited; p97, 177, 206 *Focus Magazine*; pp117-18 (from *Know yourself* by Vernon Coleman 1988 © Vernon Coleman 1988), reproduced by permission of Penguin Books Ltd; pp112, 138 Crown copyright is reproduced with the permission of the Controller of HMSO; p115 from *A first course in psychology* by Nicky Hayes (Thomas Nelson); p131 from *Write better English* by Jon Ward (Cambridge University Press) Watson, Little Ltd (Licensing Agents); pp160-1 reproduced by kind permission of *TVTimes*; p166 (B) from *The cookery year* (Reader's Digest Association Ltd), (C) from *Weather and climate* by Keith Lye (Heinemann Educational Books); p169 *Fortean Times*; pp171, 177 from *The nature of things* by Lyall Watson. Reproduced by permission of Hodder and Stoughton Limited; p175 from *Blueprint for a green planet* by John Seymour and Herbert Giradet (Dorling Kindersley); pp185, 187 from *All this and work too* by Maryon Tysoe (Fontana Paperbacks); p197 from *Manwatching* by Desmond Morris (Jonathan Cape), CAE specifications, question formats and answer sheets reproduced by permission of the University of Cambridge Local Examinations Syndicate.

For permission to use listening texts:

Unit 4 (Section C) from 'Why the stars of rock who sing of their pain...' by Annabel Ferriman © *The Observer* 7.6.92; Unit 5 (Section A) from *The articulate mammal* by Jean Aitchison - Unwin Hyman Ltd; Unit 7 (Section A) from *Foresight Magazine* Winter 1993/Sun Alliance/BLA Group (Section B) from *The Guardian* 16.2.93; Unit 8 (Section B) from 'Good shot' by Sally Wildman (*Best* 24.3.94); Unit 9 (Section B) from 'Looking lost' by Hazel Shaw (Section C) from 'I was determined to stop the thief' by Jill Chadwick (both *Bella* 7.4.93); Unit 10 (Section A) from *Assert yourself* by Gael Lindenfield - Thorsons) reproduced by permission of HarperCollins Publishers; Unit 11 (Section B) from *Hothouse people* by Jane Walmsley and Jonathan Margolis (Pan 1987); Unit 12 (Section A) from 'Are you an owl or a lark?' (*Best* 24.3.94); Unit 13 (Section B) from *The silent spring* by Rachel Carson (Hamish Hamilton 1963) reproduced by permission of Hamish Hamilton Ltd and Houghton Mifflin Company.

For permission to reproduce photographs:

We are grateful to the following for their permission to reproduce copyright material and photographs:

Accelerated Learning Systems Ltd, Aylesbury, UK for page 13 (bottom left, middle, right); Adidas (UK) Ltd for pages 215 (bottom), 220 (bottom); American Airlines/BMP DDB Needham for page 82 (middle); Amsterdam Airport Schiphol for page 38; Associated Press for page 146; Caroline Bird for page 22 (except top left); Maeve Binchy/Christine Green for page 23 (bottom); The Anthony Blake Photo Library for pages 214 (top and middle), 219 (top and middle); Britvic Soft Drinks Ltd for page 82 (top right); The Bridgeman Art Library/Giraudon for page 192; Bruce Coleman Ltd/Leonard Lee Rue for page 60 (middle right), /Kim Taylor for page 60 (top right); Comstock for page 50 (bottom), 184 (top right); Lupe Cunha for page 15 (lower middle middle, lower middle right); James Davis for pages 216 (middle), 221 (right); Illustration based on item from 'Blueprint for a Green Planet', by Seymour & Giradet. Dorling Kindersley Adult 1987 for page 175; Elida Faberge Limited for page 82 (top left); En Famille Agency (Britain) for page 13 (top right); Greg Evans International Photo Library for pages 15 (upper middle right), 32 (top left, upper middle, bottom right), 156 (bottom right), 180 (upper middle left), 184 (bottom middle), 216 (left, middle right, right), 221 (left, middle left); Eye Ubiquitous/Roger Chester for page 184 (bottom left); Fiat Auto (UK) Ltd for pages 213 (top), 218; Geoff Franklin for page 144; Photographie Giraudon for pages 214 (bottom), 219 (bottom); Robert Harding Picture Library for pages 32 (top right), 35 (bottom), 53, 97 (left), 180 (top left), 209 (bottom left), /Robert Cundy for pages 216 (middle left), 221 (middle right); Icaro-Varig Inflight Magazine for page 143; The Image Bank/1993 Per-Erik Berglund for page 184 (bottom right), /Werner Bokelberg for page 120, /Jay Brousseau for page 15 (top left), /Wendy Chan for page 15 (top middle right), /David De Lossy for page 15 (bottom right), /L.D.Gordon for page 15 (top right), /Marc Grimberg for page 15 (top middle left), /Janeart for page 209 (bottom right), /John P.Kelly for page 209 (top middle left), /Elyse Lewin for page 180 (bottom right), /Marc Romanelli for page 15 (bottom middle), /Simon Wilkinson for page 15 (lower middle left); Impact/Piers Cavendish for page 201 (bottom left), /James Fraser for page 209 (top middle right); Independent On Sunday for page 136; MOGGY for page 136; Network/Mike Goldwater for page 180 (bottom left), /Jonathan Olley for page 184 (top left), /Homer Sykes for page 201 (top left); NHPA /Walter Murray for page 60 (bottom right), /Tsuneo Nakamura for page 60 (bottom left), /Robert Thompson for page 60 (top left); ©Oxford University Press. Reprinted by permission of Oxford University Press for pages 212 (left), 217 (top); Penguin Books/Comstock for page 105 (right); Nick Pearson for pages 125 (left), 126; Premier Magazine/British Airways, 'Highlife' for page 80, /Lawrence Edwards for page 159; Radio Times/Mark Thomas for page 101; Reflections Photolibrary for page 180 (lower middle right); Rex Features for page 105 (left), /SIPA Press for page 72; Science Photo Library /Peter Skinner for page 51 (top left, bottom left); Cartoons redrawn with permission of Simon & Schuster from 'How to start a conversation and make friends', by Don Gabor. Copyright ©1983 by Don Gabor/ SPCK/Sheldon, 1985 for pages 63 (bottom), 64; Mary Spratt for page 22 (top left); Stay Still /Sven Arnstein for page 106; Tony Stone Images for pages 32 (lower middle), 33, /Dave Cannon for page 156 (top right), /Joe Cornish for page 201 (right), /Dale Durfee for pages 180 (top right), 209 (top right), /Wayne Eastep for page 156 (bottom left), /Peter Langone for page 201 (middle), /Jo McBride for page 156 (top left), /Dennis O'Clair for page 51 (bottom right), /David Stewart for page 180 (upper middle right), /Jess Stock for page 50 (middle), /Rosemary Weller for page 180 (lower middle left); Telegraph Colour Library 35 (top), 209 (bottom middle), /B&M Productions for page 15 (bottom left), /F.P.G. ©T.Anderson for page 15 (top middle), /F.P.G. ©M.Hart for page 58, /L.Lefkowitz for page 50 (top), /Masterfile for page 209 (top left); Times Newspapers Limited/Tim Bishop for page 41, /Jim Mawtus for page 79; Volkswagen/BMP DDB Needham for page 82 (bottom); John Walmsley for page 145; Liam White Photography for page 23 (top); Wordsworth Editions for page 172; Zefa Pictures/DAMM for page 166, /Minden for page 60 (middle left).

All other photography was taken on commission for Cambridge University Press by Trevor Clifford.

We have been unable to trace the copyright holder for the items on pages 97 (right), 132 and would be grateful for any information to enable us to do so.

Picture Research by Hilary Fletcher.

For permission to reproduce illustrations:

Gerry Ball, Rachel Busch, Allan Drummond, Alex Green, Kira Josey, Jill Newton, Andrew Roberts, Martin Waite, Kath Walker, Sara Walker, Emma Whiting.